DATABASE AND DATA COMMUNICATION NETWORK SYSTEMS

Techniques and Applications

VOLUME 2

DATABASE AND DATA COMMUNICATION NETWORK SYSTEMS

Techniques and Applications

VOLUME 2

Edited by

Cornelius T. Leondes

Professor Emeritus
University of California
Los Angeles, California

ACADEMIC PRESS
An imprint of Elsevier Science

Amsterdam   Boston   London   New York   Oxford   Paris
San Diego   San Francisco   Singapore   Sydney   Tokyo

Front cover: Digital Image © 2002 PhotoDisc.

This book is printed on acid-free paper. ∞

Copyright © 2002, Elsevier Science (USA).

All Rights Reserved.
No part of this publication may be reproduced or transmitted in any form or by any means, electronic or mechanical, including photocopy, recording, or any information storage and retrieval system, without permission in writing from the publisher.

Requests for permission to make copies of any part of the work should be mailed to: Permissions Department, Harcourt Inc., 6277 Sea Harbor Drive, Orlando, Florida 32887-6777

Academic Press
An imprint of Elsevier Science
525 B Street, Suite 1900, San Diego, California 92101-4495, USA
http://www.academicpress.com

Academic Press
84 Theobalds Road, London WC1X 8RR, UK
http://www.academicpress.com

Library of Congress Catalog Card Number: 20016576

International Standard Book Number: 0-12-443895-4 (set)
International Standard Book Number: 0-12-443896-2 (volume 1)
International Standard Book Number: 0-12-443897-0 (volume 2)
International Standard Book Number: 0-12-443898-9 (volume 3)

PRINTED IN THE UNITED STATES OF AMERICA
02 03 04 05 06 07 MM 9 8 7 6 5 4 3 2 1

CONTENTS

CONTRIBUTORS xiii

CONTENTS OF VOLUME 2

10 Multimedia Database Systems in Education, Training, and Product Demonstration
TIMOTHY K. SHIH

    I. Introduction   328
   II. Database Applications in Training—The IMMPS Project   333
  III. Database Applications in Education—A Web Document Database   341
  IV. Future Directions   350
      Appendix A: The Design and Implementing of IMMPS   350
      Appendix B: The Design and Implementation of MMU   353
      References   364

11 Data Structure in Rapid Prototyping and Manufacturing
CHUA CHEE KAI, JACOB GAN, TONG MEI, AND DU ZHAOHUI

    I. Introduction 368
   II. Interfaces between CAD and RP&M 376
  III. Slicing 395
  IV. Layer Data Interfaces 400
   V. Solid Interchange Format (SIF): The Future Interface 409
  VI. Virtual Reality and RP&M 410
 VII. Volumetric Modeling for RP&M 412
      References 414

12 Database Systems in Manufacturing Resource Planning
M. AHSAN AKHTAR HASIN AND P. C. PANDEY

    I. Introduction 417
   II. MRPII Concepts and Planning Procedure 418
  III. Data Element Requirements in the MRPII System 433
  IV. Application of Relational Database Management Technique in MRPII 452
   V. Applications of Object-Oriented Techniques in MRPII 457
      References 494

13 Developing Applications in Corporate Finance: An Object-Oriented Database Management Approach
IRENE M. Y. WOON AND MONG LI LEE

    I. Introduction 498
   II. Financial Information and Its Uses 499
  III. Database Management Systems 505
  IV. Financial Object-Oriented Databases 508
   V. Discussion 515
      References 516

14 Scientific Data Visualization: A Hypervolume Approach for Modeling and Rendering of Volumetric Data Sets
SANGKUN PARK AND KUNWOO LEE

    I. Introduction 518
   II. Representation of Volumetric Data 520
  III. Manipulation of Volumetric Data 525
  IV. Rendering Methods of Volumetric Data 538
   V. Application to Flow Visualization 540

VI. Summary and Conclusions   546
References   547

15 The Development of Database Systems for the Construction of Virtual Environments with Force Feedback
HIROO IWATA

I. Introduction   550
II. LHX   554
III. Applications of LHX: Data Haptization   557
IV. Applications of LHX: 3D Shape Design Using Autonomous Virtual Object   563
V. Other Applications of LHX   570
VI. Conclusion   571
References   571

16 Data Compression in Information Retrieval Systems
SHMUEL TOMI KLEIN

I. Introduction   573
II. Text Compression   579
III. Dictionaries   607
IV. Concordances   609
V. Bitmaps   622
VI. Final Remarks   631
References   631

CONTENTS OF VOLUME 1

CONTRIBUTORS   xiii
FOREWORD   xvii
PREFACE   xxi

1 Emerging Database System Architectures
TIMON C. DU

I. Introduction   2
II. History   6
III. Relational Data Model   8
IV. Next Generation Data Model   10
V. Hybrid Database Technologies   22
VI. Future Study Related to Database Technologies   26
VII. Future Database Applications   31

VIII. Summary 38
    References 38

2 Data Mining
DOHEON LEE AND MYOUNG HO KIM

I. Introduction 41
II. Overview of Data Mining Techniques 46
III. Data Characterization 47
IV. Classification Techniques 67
V. Association Rule Discovery 72
VI. Concluding Remarks 74
    References 75

3 Object-Oriented Database Systems
HIROSHI ISHIKAWA

I. Introduction 77
II. Functionality 78
III. Implementation 87
IV. Applications 103
V. Conclusion 119
    References 120

4 Query Optimization Concepts and Methodologies in Multidatabase Systems
CHIANG LEE

I. Introduction 124
II. Semantic Discrepancy and Schema Conflicts 126
III. Optimization at the Algebra Level 130
IV. Optimization at the Execution Strategy Level 151
V. Conclusions 170
    References 171

5 Development of Multilevel Secure Database Systems
ELISA BERTINO AND ELENA FERRARI

I. Introduction 175
II. Access Control: Basic Concepts 178
III. Mandatory Access Control 180
IV. Multilevel Security in Relational DBMSs 183
V. Multilevel Security in Object DBMSs 188
VI. Secure Concurrency Control 194
VII. Conclusions 199
    References 200

6 Fuzzy Query Processing in the Distributed Relational Databases Environment
SHYI-MING CHEN AND HSIN-HORNG CHEN

    I. Introduction   203
   II. Fuzzy Set Theory   205
  III. Fuzzy Query Translation Based on the α-Cuts Operations of Fuzzy Numbers   207
  IV. Fuzzy Query Translation in the Distributed Relational Databases Environment   214
   V. Data Estimation in the Distributed Relational Databases Environment   217
  VI. Conclusions   231
     References   231

7 Data Compression: Theory and Techniques
GÁBOR GALAMBOS AND JÓZSEF BÉKÉSI

    I. Introduction   233
   II. Fundamentals of Data Compression   235
  III. Statistical Coding   243
  IV. Dictionary Coding   255
   V. Universal Coding   269
  VI. Special Methods   271
 VII. Conclusions   273
     References   273

8 Geometric Hashing and Its Applications
GILL BAREQUET

    I. Introduction   277
   II. Model-Based Object Recognition   278
  III. Principles of Geometric Hashing   279
  IV. Examples   281
   V. Implementation Issues   284
  VI. Applications   284
     References   286

9 Intelligent and Heuristic Approaches and Tools for the Topological Design of Data Communication Networks
SAMUEL PIERRE

    I. Introduction   289
   II. Basic Concepts and Background   291
  III. Characterization and Representation of Data Communication Networks   294

IV. Intelligent and Hybrid Approaches   305
V. Heuristic Approaches   312
   References   325

CONTENTS OF VOLUME 3

17 Information Data Acquisition on the World Wide Web during Heavy Client/Server Traffic Periods
STATHES HADJIEFTHYMIADES AND DRAKOULIS MARTAKOS

I. Introduction   635
II. Gateway Specifications   637
III. Architectures of RDBMS Gateways   643
IV. Web Server Architectures   655
V. Performance Evaluation Tools   656
VI. Epilogue   659
   References   660

18 Information Exploration on the World Wide Web
XINDONG WU, SAMEER PRADHAN, JIAN CHEN, TROY MILNER, AND JASON LOWDER

I. Introduction   664
II. Getting Started with Netscape Communicator and Internet Explorer   664
III. How Search Engines Work   670
IV. Typical Search Engines   679
V. Advanced Information Exploration with Data Mining   686
VI. Conclusions   689
   References   690

19 Asynchronous Transfer Mode (ATM) Congestion Control in Communication and Data Network Systems
SAVERIO MASCOLO AND MARIO GERLA

I. Introduction   694
II. The Data Network Model   697
III. A Classical Control Approach to Model a Flow-Controlled Data Network   701
IV. Designing the Control Law Using the Smith Principle   703
V. Mathematical Analysis of Steady-State and Transient Dynamics   707

VI. Congestion Control for ATM Networks   709
VII. Performance Evaluation of the Control Law   711
VIII. Conclusions   715
  References   716

20 Optimization Techniques in Connectionless (Wireless) Data Systems on ATM-Based ISDN Networks and Their Applications

RONG-HONG JAN AND I-FEI TSAI

I. Introduction   719
II. Connectionless Data Services in ATM-Based B-ISDN   724
III. Connectionless Data System Optimization   727
IV. Solution Methods for the Unconstrained Optimization Problem   733
V. Solution Methods for the Constrained Optimization Problem   739
VI. Construction of Virtual Overlayed Network   745
VII. Conclusions and Discussions   748
  References   749

21 Integrating Databases, Data Communication, and Artificial Intelligence for Applications in Systems Monitoring and Safety Problems

PAOLO SALVANESCHI AND MARCO LAZZARI

I. Setting the Scene   751
II. Data Acquisition and Communication   757
III. Adding Intelligence to Monitoring   758
IV. A Database for Off-Line Management of Safety   770
V. Integrating Databases and AI   771
VI. Conclusions   781
  References   782

22 Reliable Data Flow in Network Systems in the Event of Failures

WATARU KISHIMOTO

I. Introduction   784
II. Flows in a Network   789
III. Edge-δ-Reliable Flow   800
IV. Vertex-δ-Reliable Flow   804
V. m-Route Flow   810
VI. Summary   821
  References   823

23 Techniques in Medical Systems Intensive Care Units
BERNARDINO ARCAY, CARLOS DAFONTE, AND JOSÉ A. TABOADA

    I. General Vision on ICUs and Information   825
   II. Intelligent Data Management in ICU   827
  III. Knowledge Base and Database Integration   838
  IV. A Real Implementation   844
      References   856

24 Wireless Asynchronous Transfer Mode (ATM) in Data Networks for Mobile Systems
C. APOSTOLAS, G. SFIKAS, AND R. TAFAZOLLI

     I. Introduction   860
    II. Services in ATM WLAN   861
   III. Fixed ATM LAN Concept   863
   IV. Migration from ATM LAN to ATM WLAN   869
    V. HIPERLAN, a Candidate Solution for an ATM WLAN   872
   VI. Optimum Design for ATM WLAN   881
  VII. Support of TCP over ATM WLAN   891
 VIII. Mobility Management in ATM WLAN   896
   IX. Conclusion   898
      References   899

25 Supporting High-Speed Applications on SingAREN ATM Network
NGOH LEK-HENG AND LI HONG-YI

     I. Background   902
    II. Advanced Applications on SingAREN   903
   III. Advanced Backbone Network Services   905
   IV. SingAREN "Premium" Network Service   908
    V. Key Research Contributions   911
   VI. Proposed Design   913
  VII. Multicast Service Agent (MSA)   915
 VIII. Scaling Up to Large Networks with Multiple MSAs   921
   IX. Host Mobility Support   928
    X. Conclusions and Future Directions   931
      References   932

INDEX   935

CONTRIBUTORS

Numbers in parentheses indicate the pages on which the authors' contributions begin.

C. Apostolas (859) Network Communications Laboratory, Department of Informatics, University of Athens, Panepistimioupolis, Athens 15784, Greece

Bernardino Arcay (825) Department of Information and Communications Technologies, Universidade Da Coruña, Campus de Elviña, 15071 A Coruña, Spain

Gill Barequet (277) The Technion—Israel Institute of Technology, Haifa 32000, Israel

József Békési (233) Department of Informatics, Teacher's Training College, University of Szeged, Szeged H-6701, Hungary

Elisa Bertino (175) Dipartimento di Scienze dell'Informazione, Università di Milano, 20135 Milano, Italy

Hsin-Horng Chen (203) Department of Computer and Information Science, National Chiao Tung University, Hsinchu, Taiwan, Republic of China

Shyi-Ming Chen (203) Department of Computer Science and Information Engineering, National Taiwan University of Science and Technology, Taipei 106, Taiwan, Republic of China

Jian Chen (663) Department of Mathematical and Computer Sciences, Colorado School of Mines, Golden, Colorado 80401

Carlos Dafonte (825) Department of Information and Communications Technologies, Universidade Da Coruña, Campus de Elviña, 15071 A Coruña, Spain

Timon C. Du (1) Department of Industrial Engineering, Chung Yuan Christian University, Chung Li, Taiwan 32023; and Department of Decision Sciences and Managerial Economics, The Chinese University of Hong Kong, Shatin, NT Hong Kong

Elena Ferrari (175) Dipartimento di Chimica, Fisica e Matematica, Università dell'Insubria – Como, Italy

Gábor Galambos (233) Department of Informatics, Teacher's Training College, University of Szeged, Szeged H-6701, Hungary

Jacob Gan (367) School of Mechanical and Production Engineering, Nanyang Technological University, Singapore 639798

Mario Gerla (693) Computer Science Department, University of California—Los Angeles, Los Angeles, California 90095

Stathes Hadjiefthymiades (635) Department of Informatics and Telecommunications, University of Athens, Panepistimioupolis, Ilisia, Athens 15784, Greece

M. Ahsan Akhtar Hasin[1] (417) Industrial Systems Engineering, Asian Institute of Technology, Klong Luang, Pathumthani 12120, Thailand

Li Hong-Yi (901) Advanced Wireless Networks, Nortel Research, Nepean, Ontario, Canada K2G 6J8

Hiroshi Ishikawa (77) Department of Electronics and Information Engineering, Tokyo Metropolitan University, Tokyo 192-0397, Japan

Hiroo Iwata (549) Institute of Engineering Mechanics and Systems, University of Tsukuba, Tsukuba 305-8573, Japan

Rong-Hong Jan (719) Department of Computer and Information Science, National Chiao Tung University, Hsinchu 300, Taiwan

Chua Chee Kai (367) School of Mechanical and Production Engineering, Nanyang Technological University, Singapore 639798

Myoung Ho Kim (41) Department of Computer Science, Korea Advanced Institute of Science and Technology, Taejon 305-701, Korea

Wataru Kishimoto (783) Department of Information and Image Sciences, Chiba University, Chiba 263-8522, Japan

Shmuel Tomi Klein (573) Department of Computer Science, Bar-Ilan University, Ramat Gan 52900, Israel

Marco Lazzari[2] (751) ISMES, Via Pastrengo 9, 24068 Seriate BG, Italy

Doheon Lee (41) Department of BioSystems, Korea Advanced Institute of Science and Technology, Daejon, Republic of Korea

---

[1] Current address: Industrial and Production Engineering, Bangladesh University of Engineering and Technology (BUET), Dhaka-1000, Bangladesh

[2] Current address: Dipartimento de Scienze della Formazione, Università di Bergamo, Bergamo 24029, Italy

Chiang Lee (123) Institute of Information Engineering, National Cheng-Kung University, Tainan, Taiwan, Republic of China

Mong Li Lee (497) School of Computing, National University of Singapore, Singapore 117543

Kunwoo Lee (517) School of Mechanical and Aerospace Engineering, Seoul National University, Seoul 151-742, Korea

Ngoh Lek-Heng (901) SingAREN, Kent Ridge Digital Labs, Singapore 119613

Jason Lowder (663) School of Computer Science and Software Engineering, Monash University, Melbourne, Victoria 3145, Australia

Drakoulis Martakos (635) Department of Informatics and Telecommunications, University of Athens, Panepistimioupolis, Ilisia, Athens 15784, Greece

Saverio Mascolo (693) Dipartimento di Elettrotecnica ed Elettronica, Politecnico di Bari, 70125 Bari, Italy

Tong Mei (367) Gintic Institute of Manufacturing Technology, Singapore 638075

Troy Milner (663) School of Computer Science and Software Engineering, Monash University, Melbourne, Victoria 3145, Australia

P. C. Pandey (417) Asian Institute of Technology, Klong Luang, Pathumthani 12120, Thailand

Sangkun Park (517) Institute of Advanced Machinery and Design, Seoul National University, Seoul 151-742, Korea

Samuel Pierre (289) Mobile Computing and Networking Research Laboratory (LARIM); and Department of Computer Engineering, École Polytechnique de Montréal, Montréal, Quebec, Canada H3C 3A7

Sameer Pradhan (663) Department of Mathematical and Computer Sciences, Colorado School of Mines, Golden, Colorado 80401

Paolo Salvaneschi (751) ISMES, Via Pastrengo 9, 24068 Seriate BG, Italy

G. Sfikas[3] (859) Mobile Communications Research Group, Center for Communication Systems Research, University of Surrey, Guildford, Surrey GU2 5XH, England

Timothy K. Shih (327) Department of Computer Science and Information Engineering, Tamkang University, Tamsui, Taipei Hsien, Taiwan 25137, Republic of China

José A. Taboada (825) Department of Electronics and Computer Science, Universidade de Santiago de Compostela, 15782, Santiago de Compostela (A Coruña), Spain

R Tafazolli (859) Mobile Communications Research Group, Center for Communication Systems Research, University of Surrey, Guildford, Surrey GU2 5XH, England

I-Fei Tsai (719) Wistron Corporation, Taipei 221, Taiwan

[3]Current address: Lucent Technologies, Optimus, Windmill Hill Business Park, Swindon, Wiltshire SN5 6PP, England

Irene M. Y. Woon (497) School of Computing, National University of Singapore, Singapore 117543

Xindong Wu (663) Department of Computer Science, University of Vermont, Burlington, Vermont 05405

Du Zhaohui (367) School of Mechanical and Production Engineering, Nanyang Technological University, Singapore 639798 s# 10

MULTIMEDIA DATABASE SYSTEMS IN EDUCATION, TRAINING, AND PRODUCT DEMONSTRATION

TIMOTHY K. SHIH

Department of Computer Science and Information Engineering, Tamkang University, Tamsui, Taipei Hsien, Taiwan 25137, Republic of China

I. INTRODUCTION 328
    A. Multimedia Presentation 328
    B. Multimedia Database Management System 329
    C. Multimedia Synchronization 330
    D. Multimedia Networking 331
    E. Reusability 331
    F. Other Considerations 333
II. DATABASE APPLICATIONS IN TRAINING—THE IMMPS PROJECT 333
III. DATABASE APPLICATIONS IN EDUCATION—A WEB DOCUMENT DATABASE 341
IV. FUTURE DIRECTIONS 350
APPENDIX A: THE DESIGN AND IMPLEMENTATION OF IMMPS 350
APPENDIX B: THE DESIGN AND IMPLEMENTATION OF MMU 353
    REFERENCES 364

Multimedia computing and networking changes the style of interaction between computer and human. With the growth of the Internet, multimedia applications such as educational software, electronic commerce applications, and video games have brought a great impact to the way humans think of, use, and rely on computers/networks. One of the most important technologies to support these applications is the distributed multimedia database management system (MDBMS). This chapter summarizes research issues and state-of-the-art technologies of MDBMSs from the perspective of multimedia presentations. Multimedia presentations are used widely in different forms from instruction delivery to advertisement and electronic commerce, and in different software architectures from a stand alone computer, to local area networked computers and World Wide Web servers. These different varieties of architectures result in different organization of MDBMSs. The chapter discusses MDBMS architectures and examples that were developed at our university.

I. INTRODUCTION

Multimedia computing and networking changes the way people interact with computers. In line with the new multimedia hardware technologies, as well as well-engineered multimedia software, multimedia computers with the assistance of the Internet have changed our society to a distanceless and colorful global community. Yet, despite the fantasy gradually being realized, there still exist many technique problems to be solved. This chapter summarizes state-of-the-art research topics in multimedia computing and networking, with emphasis on database technologies for multimedia presentations. The chapter addresses many problems from the perspective of multimedia applications. Theoretical details are dropped from the discussion not because of the lack of their importance but due to the avoiding of tediousness. A list of carefully selected references serves as suggested readings for those who are participating in this research area.

In this section, the discussion starts with the preliminary concepts of multimedia presentations widely used in education, training, and demonstrations. The supporting multimedia database management systems (MDBMSs) and related techniques in terms of reusability, distribution, and real-time considerations are then presented. In Section II and Section III, two MDBMSs are discussed. The first is an intelligent multimedia presentation design system for training and product demonstration. The second is a World Wide Web documentation database used in a distance learning environment. These systems are also illustrated in the Appendices. Finally, some suggestions for future extensions of MDBMSs are presented in Section IV.

A. Multimedia Presentation

One of the key reasons for making multimedia computers become attractive and successful is the availability of many varieties of multimedia presentation software, including many CD-ROM titles carrying educational software, entertainment, product demonstrations, training programs, and tutoring packages. Most presentations are hypertext like multimedia documentation [1,8,26]. These documents, while retrieved, involve a navigation topology, which consists of hyperlinks jumping from hot spots to other presentation windows. The underlying implementation mechanism of this type of documentation traversal may rely on a message passing system and an event-based synchronization scheme. Discussions of these mechanisms are found in [6,16,18,19,37,39,40].

Other new areas related to multimedia are intelligent tutoring [32] and intelligent interface [4,5,11,12,36]. The incorporation of Expert System technology has caused multimedia presentations to diversify. An intelligent multimedia presentation can learn from its audiences through interactions. The feedback is asserted into the knowledge base of the presentation. Therefore, after different audiences of different backgrounds interact with a tutorial or a training program, the multimedia workstation may act according to the individuals and give different appropriate guidance.

B. Multimedia Database Management System

In order to support the production of multimedia presentations, the management of multimedia resources (e.g., video clips, pictures, sound files) is important. Also, presentations can be designed as building blocks to be reused. To facilitate presentation design, many articles indicate the need for a multimedia database [27,29,30,33,40,41]. A multimedia database is different from a traditional relational database in that the former is object-oriented while the latter uses an entity relation diagram. Moreover, a multimedia database needs to support binary resource types of large and variable sizes. Due to the amount of binary information that needs to be processed, the performance requirement of a multimedia database is high. Clustering and indexing mechanisms supporting multimedia databases are found in [28,43]. In general, there are four ways to maintain multimedia resources:

- use a primitive file system,
- use a relational database to store multimedia resources,
- use an object-oriented database to organize multimedia documents, and
- build a multimedia database from scratch.

The first approach is too limited in that it is relatively hard to share resources among multimedia documents. Also it is hard for a presentation designer to keep track of various versions of a resource. Using a relation database will partially solve this problem. However, since multimedia documentation is object-oriented, using a relational database will introduce some overhead. Therefore, many researchers suggest using an existing object-oriented database system for building multimedia databases [9,12,13,29,41]. However, there are still some problems yet to be solved:

- *Quality of service*. Multimedia resources require a guarantee of the presentation quality. It is possible to use a specific file structure and program to control and guarantee the quality of service (QoS). A traditional OODBMS does not support QoS multimedia objects.
- *Synchronization*. Synchronization of multiple resource streams plays an important role in a multimedia presentation, especially when the presentation is running across a network. In our projects, we are not currently dealing with this interstream synchronization problem. We use an event-based synchronization mechanism in the current systems. Interstream and other synchronization issues are left for future development. However, in the future we plan to break multimedia resources into small pieces in order to implement interstream synchronization, which is especially important in a distributed environment.
- *Networking*. A distributed database requires a locking mechanism for concurrent access controls. Using our own architecture design, it is easy for us to control some implementation issues, such as a two-phase locking mechanism of the database, database administration, and control of traffic on the network.

In order to ensure the synchronization of a multimedia document, a multimedia system needs to have full control of data access activity and its timing. It is sometimes difficult to have a total control of the performance of an object-oriented database, especially when the multimedia database is distributed. Therefore, if needed, a multimedia database must be built using only primitive multimedia programming facilities.

Building a multimedia database requires three layers of architecture to be considered.

- the interface layer,
- the object composition layer, and
- the storage management layer.

The tasks that we must deal with in the interface level include object browsing, query processing, and the interaction of object composition/decomposition. Object browsing [8] allows the user to find multimedia resource entities to be reused. Through queries, either text-based or visualized, the user specifies a number of conditions to the properties of resource and retrieves a list of candidate objects. Suitable objects are then reused. Multimedia resources, unlike text or numerical information, cannot be effectively located using a text-based query language. Even natural language presented in a text form is hard to precisely retrieve a picture or a video with certain content. Content-based information retrieval research [21,49] focuses on the mechanism that allows the user to effectively find reusable multimedia objects, including pictures, sound, video, and the combined forms. After a successful retrieval, the database interface should help the user to compose/decompose multimedia documents. The second layer works in conjunction with the interface layer to manage objects. Typically, object composition requires a number of links, such as association links, similarity links, and inheritance links to specify different relations among objects. These links are specified either via the database graphical user interface, or via a number of application program interface (API) functions. The last layer, the storage management layer, needs to consider two performance issues: clustering and indexing. Clustering means to organize multimedia information physically on a hard disk (or an optical storage) such that, when retrieved, the system is able to access the large binary data efficiently. Usually, the performance of retrieval needs to guarantee some sort of QoS [44]. Indexing means that a fast-locating mechanism is essential for finding the physical address of a multimedia object [28]. Sometimes, the scheme involves a complex data or file structure. Media synchronization should be considered in both issues.

There are other issues in multimedia database research, including transaction processing, object locking mechanisms and concurrent access, persistency, versioning, security, and referential integrity. Most of these are also issues of traditional database research. The research of multimedia databases has become an important issue in the community of multimedia computing.

C. Multimedia Synchronization

Multimedia information is processed in real-time. Therefore, the temporal aspect of multimedia information coherence–synchronization is one of the most interesting research topics in multimedia computing [3,7,14,15,17,19,22, 23,25,31,42,45,47,48]. Synchronization mechanisms are, in general, divided into the intra- and the interstream-based schemes. The former focuses on the simultaneous demonstration of one or more sources of information in one multimedia resource stream (e.g., a video file contains both motion pictures and sound data). The later discusses the simultaneous process of multiple streams holding different resources (e.g., an animation video is synchronized with a MIDI music file and a sound record).

Among a number of synchronization computation models, timed Petri net [20,31] seems to be a powerful model for describing the behavior of real-time systems. A Petri net is a bipartite directed graph with two types of nodes: places and transitions. A place node holds tokens, which are passed to transitions. A place can also represent a multimedia resource, which is demonstrated for a period of time before its token is passed to a transition. A transition controls the synchronization of those places adjacent to the transition. Timed Petri net is found to be one of the most suitable models for multimedia synchronization controls. Another theoretical computation of synchronization is based on temporal interval relations [2]. There are 13 types of relations between a pair of temporal intervals. Temporal interval relations can be used to calculate the schedule of a multimedia presentation [38]. Synchronization information can also be embedded into multimedia resources. Synchronization can also be controlled by event and message passing. The research of multimedia synchronization becomes a challenge if the mechanism is to be implemented on a distributed environment.

D. Multimedia Networking

In line with the success of the Internet, the needs of multimedia communication has brought the attention of many software developers and researchers [10,24,34,35,46]. Two important issues are network transmission protocols and network infrastructure. The former includes mechanisms enabling transmissions of a guaranteed quality and security. The later focuses on the structure of communication system so that reliability and traffic management is feasible. At the top of multimedia network systems (either intra- or inter-networking), many applications are available. Multimedia client-server based applications include the World Wide Web (WWW), multimedia documentation on demand (e.g., video-on-demand and news-on-demand), electronic catalog ordering, computer-supported cooperative work (CSCW), video conferencing and distance learning, and multimedia electronic mail. The combination of multimedia and networking technologies changes the way people think of, use, and rely on computers.

E. Reusability

Multimedia presentations are software, which need a specification to describe their functions. Nevertheless, the well-defined specification does not realize an improved functionality of a system. From the perspective of software development, reusability is one of the most important factors in improving the efficacy of multimedia presentation designs and multimedia database access. Many articles discuss reusability—one of them [50] analyzes nine commonly believed software reuse myths, and points out why reusability has not played a major role in improving software productivity. One article [51] points out that there are three common approaches to achieve software reuse: subroutine libraries, software generators, and object-oriented languages. However, each individual approach raises problems. Therefore, the author takes the best features from each of these and develops an object-oriented language, called Meld. Another reuse mechanism via building blocks is proposed in [52]. The authors apply the concept to systems programming and achieve a great success. The authors also indicate that there are three important aspects of reusability: the abstraction level, customization methods, and reusability conditions. In [53], reusability criteria are proposed for the Ada language. The author suggests that, to be reusable, a program must be transportable, be context independent, and be independent of the runtime environment. According to the discussion given in [54], there are two levels of reuse: the reuse of knowledge and the reuse of software components. In order to support the fast retrieval of reusable objects, a classification scheme for grouping together objects sharing a common characteristic is required. A classification scheme organizing a software reuse library is proposed in [55]. Instead of using a centralized repository, the author proposes a generic design that can be applied to different environments. Another article [56] proposes two concepts, domain and theme, to allow software component classification by the services that they offer and by application domain.

The value of object reuse needs to be evaluated. A quantitative study of reuse through inheritance is found in [57]. The author studies several software systems containing a large number of classes. The results show reuse through inheritance is far less frequent than expected. Another article [58] measures cohesion versus reuse through inheritance, and determines that reuse through inheritance results in a lower cohesion. Fortunately, many articles propose solutions to software reuse. The RSL (Reusable Software Library) prototype [59] is a software system incorporating interactive design tools and a passive database of reusable software components. Each component is associated with some attributes to be used in their automatic retrieval. Another author [60] claims that reusable components are not enough. Software engineers need an intelligent support system to help them learn and understand how to reuse components in a software environment. A set of tool kits is implemented to support object reuse. NUT [61,62] is an object-oriented programming language/environment that supports class and object reuse. In NUT, classes are prototypes; when they are reused, initial values (could be nil values) are assigned according to the class specification. Objects can also be implicitly generated. For instance, program objects can be generated when equations are processed. Knowledge in the NUT environment can be reused in the following ways:

- As a super-class,
- When a new object is created via the "new" operator,
- As a prototype for specifying components of another class,
- As the specification of a predicate, and
- As a specification of problem conditions in problem statements.

Only the first two are typical at conventional object-oriented systems.

The above discussions consider reusability from the perspective of software development. A multimedia presentation contains a collection of presentation components as does a software system. To achieve object reuse in a multimedia database, we consider four tasks:

- *Declare building blocks.* Presentation sections are the building blocks of a multimedia presentation. These sections are objects to be reused.
- *Retrieve building blocks.* A presentation system should provide a tool for assisting the user in retrieving appropriate building blocks.
- *Modify building blocks.* The building blocks to be reused may be modified to fit the need of a new presentation.
- *Reorganize database storage.* Database storage should be reorganized so that information sharing is feasible and disk space is used efficiently.

Building block declaration is achieved by means of an object grouping mechanism at different levels of our database. These reusable objects can be retrieved using a browser. After finding the reusable presentation components, the presentation designer establishes links and possibly modifies the component. Finally, we have a storage management mechanism to allow information sharing on the disk.

F. Other Considerations

There are other challenges in developing a multimedia DBMS. For instance, the design of a visual query language for content-based retrieval of multimedia information is a difficult problem yet to be solved. Since multimedia information is not stored as text or numbers, traditional database query commands are no longer suitable. Quick retrieval of information based on the semantics of a multimedia resource is an important research topic. In our system, we did not address content-based retrieval. However, we developed a visual database browser that facilitates selection of resources. Another important issue relates to the quality of service [44]. Within the limits of hardware and operating system performance, we must organize multimedia information on the disk and across the network in such a way that we can guarantee to exceed a minimum level of presentation quality. In our system, we have a sophisticated storage management and indexing mechanism for the efficient retrieval of large multimedia resources. These concepts are further discussed with the two MDBMSs in the following sections.

II. DATABASE APPLICATIONS IN TRAINING—THE IMMPS PROJECT

As multimedia personal computers become widely available with reasonable prices, multimedia PCs built with sound card, CD-ROM, and high-resolution graphics display unit are used broadly by business persons, engineers, and others. Due to the impressive sound effects, graphics animation, and video play, the importance and business opportunity of multimedia presentation systems are realized by researchers and commercial software developers. Presentation design software packages are also available at affordable prices. However, most presentations generated by these systems communicate with the addressee in a single direction manner. That is, the presentation software does not listen to the listeners' response. For this reason, we have developed an Intelligent Multimedia Presentation System (IMMPS) [36,39] to overcome the shortage.

IMMPS is one of the database applications that we have created. In the development of this project, our research focuses on the following issues:

- Canonical representation of knowledge,
- Intelligent presentation of specification language,
- Specification and learning of addressee characteristics, and
- Multimedia DBMS with reuse controls.

Presentation intelligence is represented by a canonical rule-based format. The knowledge not only includes the addressee's background (i.e., common sense of the person who watches the presentation) but allows human reactions to be learned by the presentation program. A database management system is also designed for the CD ROM title designers for organizing and storing multimedia resources and presentations. This database is associated with a presentation reuse control model. An intelligent specification language is designed. The language provides facilities for hypermedia access and rule-based statements for knowledge representation. Our system supports personalization. Not only can the graphical user interface of the generated presentation be fully customized, but the underlying knowledge of the addressee can be easily updated. The system also provides a learning subsystem to be included in the generated software title, which allows an addressee's interaction to be asserted into the knowledge base. This learning environment, the presentation inference engine, and other components can be included in the runtime environment of a CD-ROM title. Figure 1 illustrates the software architecture of the IMMPS system.

We suggest that a presentation can be designed from two different perspectives: the navigation view and the representation view. Figure 2 shows a presentation navigation subsystem and a knowledge inference subsystem facilitating these two views. A window I/O control subsystem collects the audience's navigation messages and performs multimedia operations. The navigation subsystem communicates with the inference subsystem via messages that assert or retract knowledge so that the audience's behaviors will be learned by the computer. The knowledge inference result can also produce a side effect that sends a message to the navigation subsystem for some actions. Similarly, via message passing, the end user's navigation information is passed from the window I/O control system to the navigation system. Also the content of a presentation, such as a video play, is presented by the media control interface (MCI) functions provided by Microsoft.

From the navigation view, a presentation is a graph with nodes as presentation windows and edges as navigation links. From the representation view, information that can be shared among windows includes background of the audiences (e.g., the addressee's name or knowledge of the presentation topic), multimedia resources (e.g., a text document file or a video file showing a mechanical operation), or other knowledge useful in the presentation. A property

MULTIMEDIA DATABASE SYSTEMS   **335**

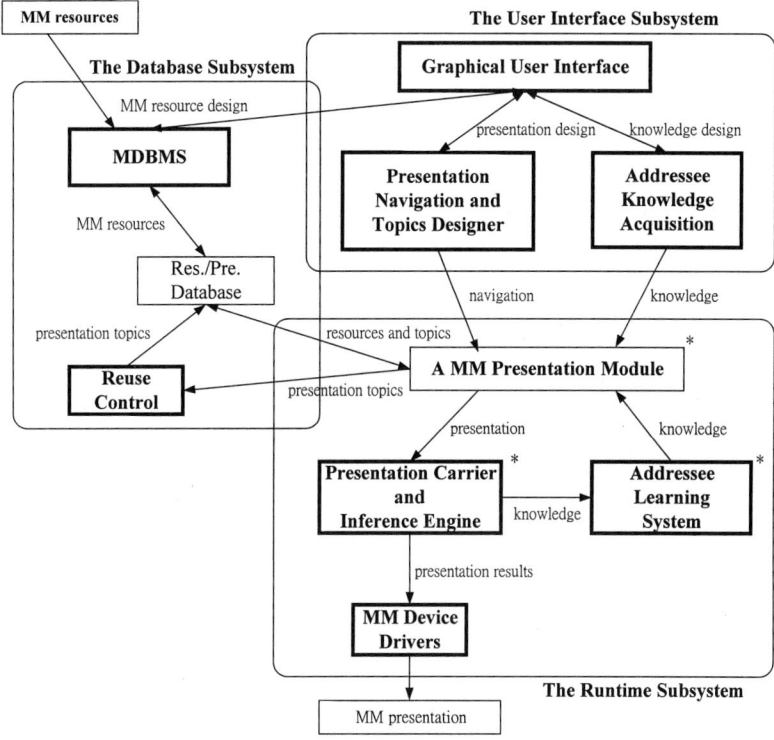

FIGURE 1 The software architecture of IMMPS.

inheritance structure such as a tree or a DAG (directed acyclic graph) is suitable for our knowledge representation architecture. Figure 3 illustrates these two structures. In the figure, a presentation window (i.e., PWin) is a composed object that represents a topic that a presenter wants to discuss. A presentation window may contain push buttons, one or more multimedia resources to be

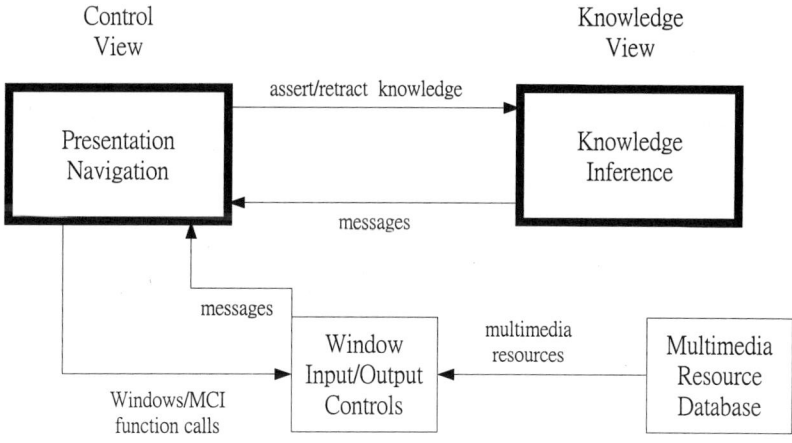

FIGURE 2 A presentation from different points of view.

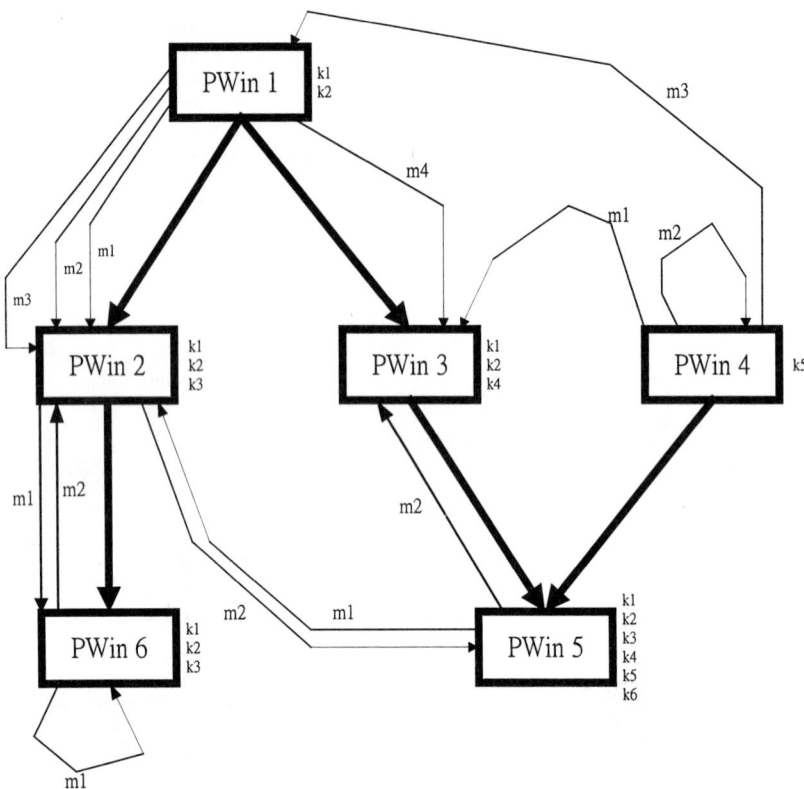

FIGURE 3 Graph and DAG representations of a multimedia presentation.

presented, and a number of knowledge rules (e.g., k1, k2, k3). A message (e.g., m1, m2) with optional parameters can be passed between two presentation windows (or passed back to the same presentation window). The graph edges representing navigation links are shown in thin lines, with message names as labels. The DAG edges representing knowledge inheritance are shown in thick lines without labels. In the figure, to the right of each presentation window, we show the knowledge rules that can be used in the presentation window. Even though knowledge rules "k1" and "k2" are shared among PWin 1, PWin 2, PWin 3, PWin 5, and PWin 6, they are stored only once in PWin 1. Note that multiple inheritance is also allowed, as PWin 5 inherits knowledge rules from both PWin 3 and PWin 4.

There are a number of restrictions applied to our message passing system and knowledge inheritance system. For instance, a message passed between two presentation windows has a unique name. Only the destination presentation window can receive the specific message sent to it. Each message has only one source and one destination. A child presentation window inherits all knowledge rules and facts from its parent presentation windows. The relation of knowledge inheritance is transitive. However, the inheritance architecture is acyclic. That is, a presentation window can not be a parent presentation window of its own. If a child presentation window contains a knowledge rule that has the same rule name as one of the rules the child presentation window inherits (directly or indirectly), the rule defined in the child presentation window

MULTIMEDIA DATABASE SYSTEMS

overrides the one from its parent presentation windows. If two rules belonging to two presentation windows have the same name, the rule should be stored in a common parent presentation window only once to avoid inconsistency.

IMMPS can be used in general purpose presentations or demonstrations in different fields such as education, training, product demonstration, and others. This system serves as a sample application showing our multimedia database research results [40,41]. The multimedia database of IMMPS has two major layers: the frame object layer and the resource object layer. Figure 4

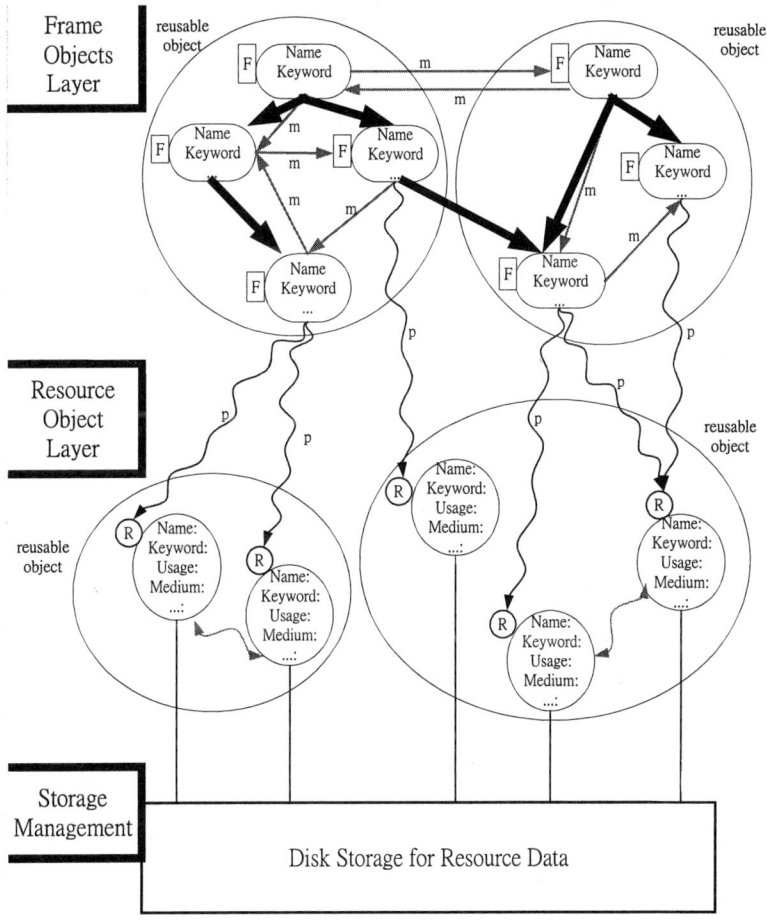

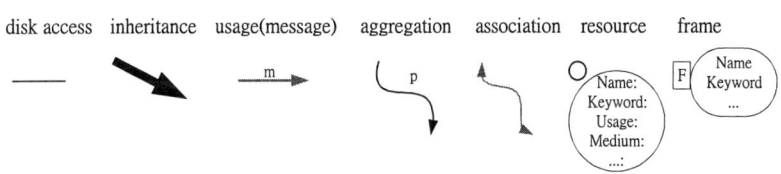

FIGURE 4 The object-oriented database hierarchy of IMMPS.

gives an overview of the database architecture. The two types of objects in our database are frames and resources. A frame is denoted by a box while a resource is represented by a circle with its associated properties given in an attached, rounded box. The actual data of a resource are stored in a commercial multimedia file format on the hard disk. This approach allows our system to be fully portable. Since the underlying multimedia file format is independent of the operating system (such as MS Windows 98), the database server program can be recompiled and used in a different environment (such as UNIX).

In the database architecture, the frame object layer contains presentation frames. A frame, similar to a presentation window, may contain a number of presentation items, such as video clips and music background. These presentation items are stored in the resource object layer. In the frame object layer, each frame is associated with a number of attributes:

- *Name:* a unique name of the frame.
- *Keyword:* one or more keywords are used to describe the frame.
- *Inheritance links:* pointers to other frames that inherit properties from the current frame.
- *Usage links:* messages from the current frame to the destination frames, including possible parameters.
- *Aggregation links:* pointers to resources that are used in the current frame.
- *Presentation knowledge:* presentation properties and knowledge represented as logic facts, rules, and a query used in the frame.
- *Frame layouts:* screen coordinates of resources.

To create a high-quality multimedia presentation, one needs good multimedia resources as well as a good presentation design environment. Multimedia resources are recorded or captured via camera, tape recorder, or video camera, converted to their digital formats, and saved on disk. Each resource can be associated with a number of attributes. We use the following attributes for multimedia resources in the resource object layer of our database:

- *Name:* a unique name of the resource.
- *Keyword:* one or more keywords are used as the description of a multimedia resource. For instance, "Paris" is a keyword of a bitmapped picture of Paris.
- *Usage:* how the resource is used (e.g., background, navigation, or focus).
- *Medium:* what multimedia device is used to carry out this resource (e.g., sound, animation, MPEG-coded video, or picture).
- *Model:* how the resource is presented (e.g., table, map, chart, or spoken language).
- *Temporal endurance:* how long the resource lasts in a presentation (e.g., 20 or permanent).
- *Synchronization tolerance:* how does a participant feel about the synchronization delay of a resource. For instance, a user typically expects an immediate response after pushing a button for the next page of text; however, one might be able to tolerate a 2-s delay for a video playback.

- *Detectability:* how strongly a resource attracts attention (e.g., high, medium, or low).
- *Startup delay:* the time between a request and the presentation of the corresponding resource starts, especially when the resource is on a remote computer connected via a network.
- *Hardware limitation:* what kind of hardware is essential to present the resource ensuring a minimal quality of service (e.g., MPC level 1, level 2, level 3, or other limitations).
- *Version:* the version of this resource file.
- *Date/time:* the date and time this resource file was created.
- *Resolution:* the resolution of this resource file, specified as $X \times Y$ screen units, or 8-bit/16-bit for sound.
- *Start/end time:* for nonpermanent resources, the starting cycle and the ending cycle of the piece of video, sound, or other kind of resources. A cycle can be a second, one-tenth of a second, or an interval between two consecutive video frames of a video clip.
- *Resource descriptor:* a logical descriptor to a physical resource data segment on the disk.
- *Association links:* pointers to other resources who have the coexistence relation with the current resource.

The attributes in the two object layers are used in database queries to retrieve suitable objects for a multimedia presentation. These attributes are specified in a database browser when a query is requested by the user. Since each resource has a number of attributes, it would be cumbersome to require each query searching for a resource to contain all of these attributes. Thus, we propose an intelligent mechanism to simplify a query. The system contains several inference rules. Each rule describes an if–then relation between two attributes. For example, the following are some of the rules used in our system:

If usage = focus then detectability = high
If model = illustration then medium = picture
If medium = picture then temporal_endurance = permanent
If medium = MPEG then hardware_limitation = MPEG_card
If model = map then medium = picture
If ... etc.

In this way, nonspecified attributes can be deduced from others. Thus, a user does not need to specify all attributes of a resource when he/she is using a query to search for the resource.

Data mining has become a hot research topic in the community of database systems. We can analyze the dependencies among the above multimedia attributes and use data mining techniques to improve our system. For instance, we found that many presentation designers use a bit-mapped picture with a low detectability for background. A MIDI resource is often used as background music. We are constructing an interactive database subsystem to collect the ways that presentation designers use our database. Based on past usage, the subsystem may suggest a suitable resource to a designer.

A presentation is a heterogeneous collection of resource groups and frame groups. A multimedia class database is a heterogeneous collection of resource object classes and frame object classes. Groups in a presentation are co-related since aggregation links and usage links are used among groups for resource access and navigation. However, in a class database, object classes are individual elements.

We are led to a two-layered approach by the nature of reusable objects. The reuse of a presentation script (i.e., in a frame group) and the reuse of multimedia resources (i.e., a resource group) are the two levels of reuse. Other reuse processes can be modeled by a combination of the two levels. For instance, the reuse of a whole presentation can be achieved by grouping the presentation as a frame group with several resource groups. The reuse of a single resource can be achieved by treating the single resource as a resource group. Therefore, the two-layered approach is a natural design. A multimedia presentation is a collection of frame groups and resource groups. Strictly speaking, a presentation is not a part of the database, at least from the database modeling perspective. Similarly, the underlying storage management layer is not a part of the database model. However, the two-layered model is to emphasize the two levels of object reuse.

There are also other models that can be used for presentations (e.g., the Petri net model). Petri nets, especially timed Petri nets, are suitable for interstream synchronization, which is not the mechanism used in our presentation system. Our system, on the other hand, relies on event-based synchronization with assistance from a message passing mechanism. Therefore, the Petri net model was not adopted.

We present an overview of the database storage management, which includes memory management and disk storage management. Memory management is used to run a presentation. A presentation contains a number of object groups (frame groups and resource groups). Each object group is a set, represented by a dynamic array that contains addresses of frames or resource descriptors. Object classes are also represented using dynamic arrays. A DAG is used to store frames and the inheritance links among them. At the resource object level, a digraph with bi-directional pointers (association links) is used to store resource descriptor addresses. Each resource descriptor contains a resource file name. The binary resource data are loaded at run time. This strategy avoids the dynamic memory from being over used by the huge amount of binary data. Pointers (aggregation links) to resource descriptors are stored in a frame for the frame to access its resources. The disk storage is rather complicated. Figure 5 pictures a simplified overview. The database server (MDBMS) allows multiple databases. Two types of databases are allowed: the presentation database (i.e., P.Database) and the object class database (i.e., C.Database). Each database has two files: a data file and an index file. A database may store a number of presentations or object classes. Each presentation contains several pointers to frame groups and resource groups. Each object group (frame or resource) contains a number of chained records. Similarly, an object class has a number of chained records. These records of resource groups (or resource object classes) are pointers to the BLOBs and attributes of multimedia resources, which can be shared. The index file has two types for presentation indices (P. Indices) and object class indices (C. Indices). Each part is a hashing table that contains data file offsets and other information, such as locking statuses.

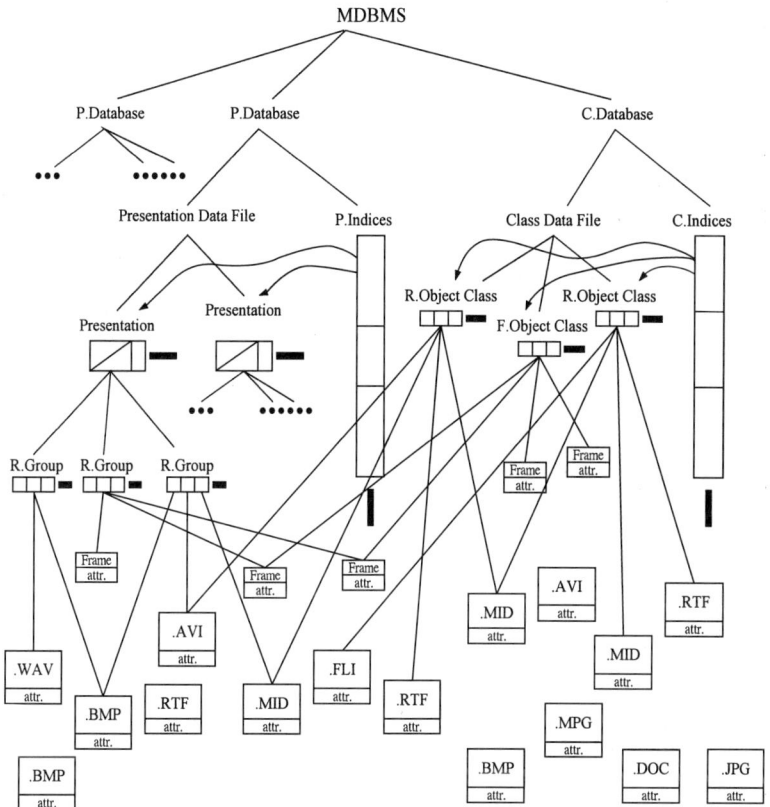

FIGURE 5 Disk storage management of the database.

III. DATABASE APPLICATIONS IN EDUCATION—A WEB DOCUMENT DATABASE

Multimedia Micro-University (MMU) is a joint research project with the participation of researchers from around the world. The primary goal of the MMU consortium is to develop technologies and systems for the use of virtual university. In this section, we propose the software architecture for a multimedia-based virtual course system. The architecture supports a multiplatform due to the availability of Web browsers and the Java virtual machine. We aim to provide a system on the Internet for instructors to design and demonstrate lectures. This system serves as a step toward our research goal—virtual university over the Internet. The primary directive of our MMU systems has four goals:

• *Adaptive to changing network conditions.* The system adapts to QoS requirements and network conditions to deliver different levels of service.

• *Adaptive to changing user needs.* Users are using the system from different perspectives. Types of users include students, instructors, and administrators. The system supports the demand of various kinds of information delivery from time to time.

• *Adaptive to Web-based environment.* The system is Web-savvy. That is, a standard Web browser is the only software required to students and

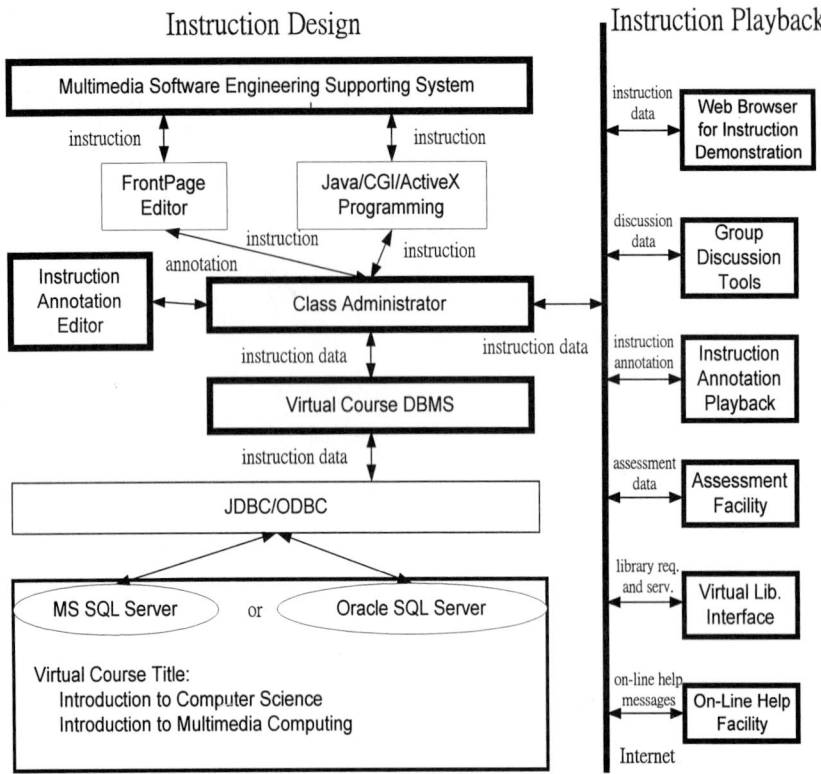

FIGURE 6 Overview of the MMU Project.

administrators. The instructors will use our system running on a Web browser in conjunction with some commercial available software.

• *Adaptive to open architecture.* A minimal compatibility is defined as the requirement for the open architecture. Compatibility requirements include presentation standard, network standard, and database standard.

Figure 6 illustrates the system architecture of our MMU system. On the instruction design side, we encourage instructors to use the Microsoft FrontPage Web Document editor, or an equivalent on a Sun workstation, to design virtual courses. Virtual courses may also be provided via some Java application programs, which are embedded into HTML documents. Since HTML and Java are portable languages, multiplatform courses are thus feasible. An instruction annotation editor, written as a Java-based daemon, is also running under the Java virtual machine (which is supported by Web browsers). This annotation daemon allows an individual instructor to draw lines, text, and simple graphic objects on top of a Web page. Different instructors can use the same virtual course but with different annotations. These annotations, as well as virtual courses, are stored as software configuration items (SCIs) in the virtual course database management system. An SCI can be a page showing a piece of lecture, an annotation to the piece of lecture, or a compound object containing the above. A class administrator performs bookkeeping of course registration and network information, which serves as the front end of the virtual course DBMS. The implementation of the virtual course DBMS uses JDBC (or ODBC) as the open database connection to some commercial available database systems, such as the MS SQL server, Sybase, Informix, or Oracle servers. Currently, our system uses the MS SQL server.

On the other side of the system architecture, a student can use an ordinary Web browser to traverse virtual lectures. However, some underlying subsystems are transmitted to a student workstation to allow group discussions, annotation playback, and virtual course assessment. We also provide an interface to the virtual course library. The interface allows object searching and browsing. These subsystems, again, are written as Java-based daemons running under the Internet Explorer or the Netscape Navigator. Help facilities are provided.

This research project, besides providing a prototype system for virtual university realization, also focuses on some research issues in multimedia computing and networking. From the perspective of software engineering, several paradigms were used in software development (e.g., water-fall model, spiral model, object-oriented model). Can these models be applied to multimedia course development? Or, can we refine these models to be used? On the other hand, how we estimate the complexity of a course and how we perform a white box or black box testing of a multimedia presentation are research issues that we have solved partially. From the perspective of CSCW, the virtual course system maintains the smooth collaboration and consistency of distributed course designs. A software configuration management system allows checking in/out of course components and maintains versions of a course. All instruction systems require assessment. The virtual course system has methodologies to support the evaluation of student progress and achievement.

To support the storage requirement of our Web document development paradigm, we have designed a Web document database. We use an off-the-rack relational database system as the underlying supporting system. In this section, we discuss the design considerations of our database system. We design the database based on three objectives: object reuse, object distribution, and resource sharing. In this subsection, a three-layered database hierarchy is proposed (see Fig. 7). In the Web document DBMS, multiple Web document databases are allowed. Each database can have a number of documents. Each document is identified by a unique script name. A script, similar to a software system specification, can describe a course material or a quiz. With respect to a script, the instructor can have different tries of implementation. Each implementation contains at lease one HTML file, and some optional program files, which may use some multimedia resources. A course document is used by several instructors. An instructor can use our annotation tool to draw lines and text to add notes to a course implementation. Thus, an implementation may have different annotations created by different instructors. To test the implementation, test records are generated for each implementation. Also bug reports are created for each test record. The database has three layers. Objects in the three layers contain the following attributes:

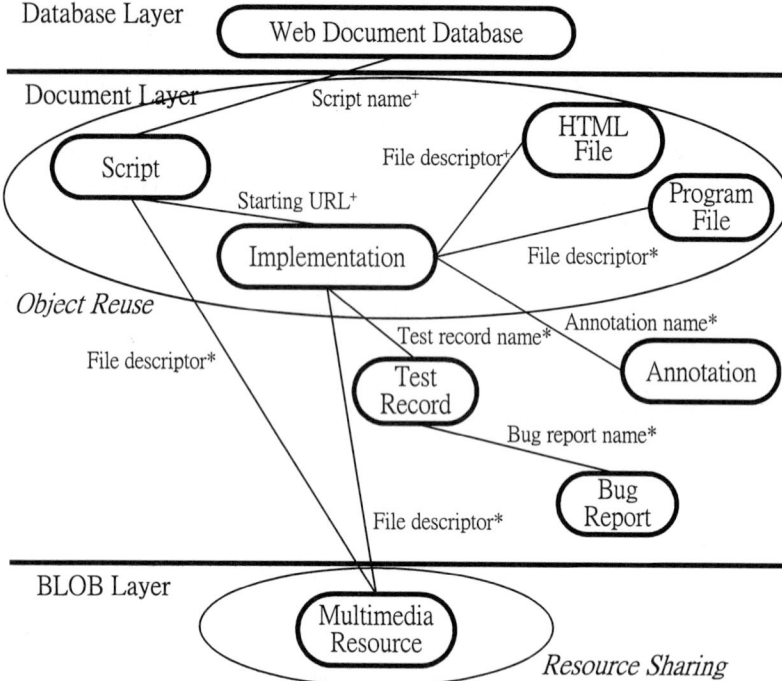

FIGURE 7 The three-layered database architecture of the MMU system.

Database Layer

- *Database name:* a unique name of the database.
- *Keywords:* one or more keywords are used to describe the database.
- *Author:* author name and copyright information of the creator.
- *Version:* the version of this database.
- *Date/time:* the date and time this database was created.
- *Script names:* pointers to script tables belong to the database.

Document Layer

- *Script table:* content of a script object.
- *Implementation table:* content of an implementation object.
- *Test record table:* content of a test record.
- *Bug report table:* content of a bug report.
- *Annotation table:* content of an annotation.
- *HTML files:* standard HTML files used in the implementation.
- *Program files:* add-on control program files used in the implementation.
- *Annotation files:* Annotation files that store document annotations.

BLOB Layer

- *Multimedia sources:* multimedia files in standard formats (i.e., video, audio, still image, animation, and MIDI files). Objects in this layer are shared by instances and classes.

In the database hierarchy, objects in each layer are represented as rounded boxes. Each object may be linked to other relative objects. A link in the hierarchy is associated with a label, which has a reference multiplicity indicated in its superscript. A "+" sign means the use of one or more objects, and a "*" sign represents the use of zero or more references. Database objects can be reused. The ellipses in the document layer indicate that a number of database objects are grouped into a reusable component. The component can be duplicated to another compound object with modifications. However, the duplication process involves objects of relatively smaller sizes, such as HTML files. The ellipses in the BLOB layer indicate that, BLOBs in large sizes are shared by different compound objects, including different scripts and implementations. However, BLOB resource sharing is limited to a workstation. Upon demand, BLOB objects may be duplicated in other workstations in order to realize real-time course demonstration.

The document layer contains the most important items of a Web document. Since we use a relational database management system to implement our object hierarchy, we summarize some content of major tables here.

Script Table

- *Script name:* a unique name of the document script.
- *Keywords:* keywords of the script.
- *Author:* the author of the document.
- *Version:* the version of the document.
- *Date/time:* the creation date and time.
- *Description:* the content of the script, which is described in text. However, the author may have a verbal description stored in a multimedia resource file.
- *Expected date/time of completion:* a tentative date of completion.
- *Percentage of completion:* the status of current work.
- *Multimedia resources:* file descriptors point to multimedia files.
- *Starting URLs:* foreign key to the implementation table.
- *Test record names:* foreign key to the test record table.
- *Bug report names:* foreign key to the bug report table.
- *Annotation names:* foreign key to the annotation table.

Implementation Table

- *Starting URL:* a unique starting URL of the Web document implementation.
- *HTML files:* implementation objects such as HTML or XML files.
- *Program files:* implementation objects such as Java applets or ASP programs.
- *Multimedia resources:* implementation objects such as audio files.
- *Script name:* foreign key to the script table.
- *Test record names:* foreign key to the test record table.
- *Bug report names:* foreign key to the bug report table.
- *Annotation names:* foreign key to the annotation table.

Test Record Table

- *Test record name:* a unique name of the test record.
- *Testing scope:* local or global.
- *Web traversal messages:* windowing message controls Web document traversal.
- *Script name:* foreign key to the script table.
- *Starting URL:* foreign key to the implementation table.
- *Bug report names:* foreign key to the bug report table.

Bug Report Table

- *Bug report name:* a unique name of the bug report.
- *Quality assurance engineer:* name of the QA person.
- *Test procedure:* a simple description of the test procedure.
- *Bug description:* the test result.
- *Bad URLs:* a number of URLs that cannot be reached.
- *Missing objects:* multimedia or HTML files missing from the implementation.
- *Inconsistency:* a text description of inconsistency.
- *Redundant objects:* a list of redundant files.
- *Test record name:* foreign key to the test record table.

Annotation Table

- *Annotation name:* a unique name of the annotation.
- *Author:* the author of the annotation.
- *Version:* the version of the annotation.
- *Date/time:* the creation date and time.
- *Annotation file:* a file descriptor to an annotation file.
- *Script name:* foreign key to the script table.
- *Starting URL:* foreign key to the implementation table.

The Web document database, when updated, should be proceeded in a consistent way. Each Web document SCI has a number of references. We use these references to maintain the referential integrity of the database. Figure 8 illustrates a referential integrity diagram. Each link in the diagram connects two objects. If the source object is updated, the system will trigger a message, which alerts the user to update the destination object. Each link in the diagram is associated with a label, with various possible alert messages:

- 1: one message
- ∗: zero or more messages
- +: one or more messages

For instance, if a script SCI is updated, the corresponding implementations should be updated, which further triggers the changes of one or more HTML programs, zero or more multimedia resources, and some control programs.

Due to the locking mechanism used in object-oriented database systems, we have defined an object-locking compatibility table. In general, if a container has a read lock by a user, its components (and itself) can have the read access by another user, but not the write access. However, the parent objects of the

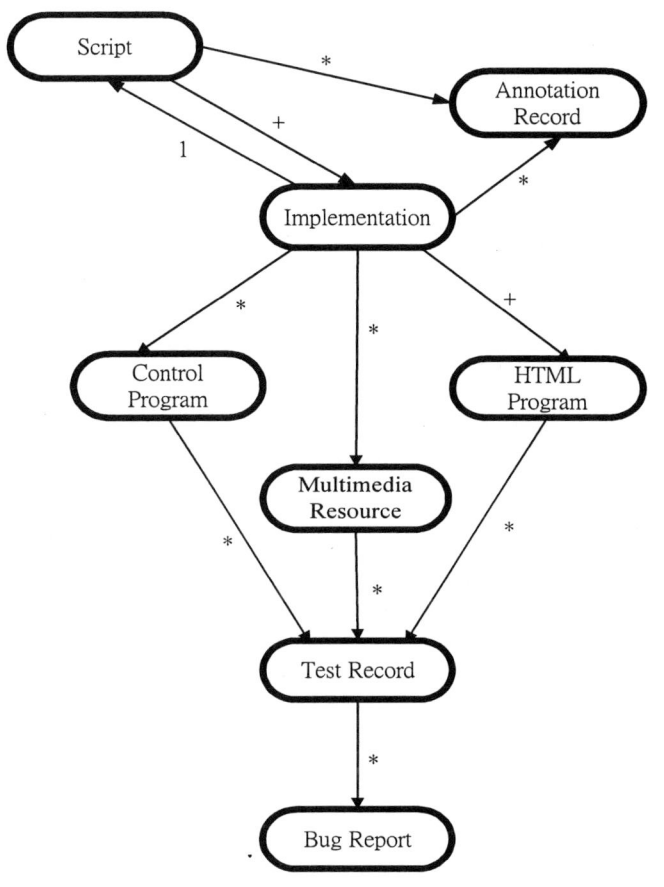

FIGURE 8 Referential integrity diagram.

container can have both read and write access by another user. Of course, the accesses are prohibited in the current container object. Locking tables are implemented in the instructor workstation. With the table, the system can control which instructor is changing a Web document. Therefore, collaborative work is feasible.

Web documents are reusable. Among many object reuse paradigms, classification and prototyping are the most common ones. Object classification allows object properties or methods at a higher position of the hierarchy to be inherited by another object at a lower position. The properties and methods are reused. Object prototyping allows reusable objects to be declared as templates (or classes), which can be instantiated to new instances. A Web document in our system contains SCIs for script, implementation, and testing. As a collection of these three phrases of objects, a Web document is a prototype-based reusable object. Object reuse is essentially important to the design of Web documents. However, the demonstration of Web documents may take a different consideration due to the size and the continuous property of BLOB.

Web documents may contain BLOB objects, which are infeasible to be demonstrated in real-time when the BLOB objects are located in a remote station due to the current Internet bandwidth. However, if some of the BLOB objects are preloaded before their presentation, even though the process involves the use of some extra disk space, the Web document can be demonstrated in real-time. However, BLOB objects in the same station should be shared as much as possible among different documents. We aim to provide a system to make distributed Web documents to be reused in a reasonable efficient manner.

The design goal is to provide a transparent access mechanism for the database users. From different perspectives, all database users look at the same database, which is stored across many networked stations. Some Web documents can be stored with duplicated copies in different machines for the ease of real-time information retrieval. A Web document may exist in the database at different physical locations in one of the following three forms:

- Web document class
- Web document instance
- Web document reference to instance

A document class is a reusable object, which is declared from a document instance. A document instance may contain the physical multimedia data, if the instance is newly created. After the declaration of the document instance, the instance creates a new document class. The newly created class contains the structure of the document instance and all multimedia data, such as BLOBs. The original document instance maintains its structure. However, pointers to multimedia data in the class is used instead of storing the original BLOBs. When a new document instance is instentiated from a document class, the structure of the document class is copied to the new document instance and pointers to multimedia data are created. This design allows the BLOBs to be stored in a class. The BLOBs are shared by different instances instantiated from the class.

A document instance is a physical element of a Web document. When a database user looks at the Web document from different network locations, the user can access the Web document in two ways. The first is to access the document directly. The second mechanism looks at the document via document reference. A document reference to instance is a mirror of the instance. When a document instance is created, it exists as a physical data element of a Web document in the creation station. References to the instance are broadcast and stored in many remote stations.

When a document instance is retrieved from a remote station more than a certain amount of iterations (or more than a watermark frequency), physical multimedia data are copied to the remote station. The duplication process may include the duplication of document classes, which contain the physical BLOBs.

The duplication process is proceeded according to a hierarchy distribution strategy. Assuming that, N networked stations join the database system in a linear order. We can arrange the N stations in a full m-ary tree according to a breadth first order. A full m-ary tree is a tree with each node containing exactly m children, except the trailing nodes. The nth station, where $1 <= n <= N$, in the linear joining sequence has its ith child, where $1 <= i <= m$ at the following position in the linear order:

$$m^*(n-1) + i + 1.$$

In a Web document system utilizing a distance learning system, an instructor can broadcast lectures to student workstations. Essentially, the broadcast process is a multicasting activity. With the appropriate selection of m, the transmission of physical data can be proceeded in an efficient manner, starting from the instructor station as the root of the m-ary tree. The implementation of this multicasting system has a broadcast vector containing a linear sequence of workstation IP addresses. The system maintains the sizes of m's, based on the number of workstations and the physical network bandwidth for different types of multimedia data. This design achieves one of our project goals: adaptive to changing network conditions.

On the other hand, a student can look at an off-line lecture presentation prepared by the instructor. In this case, the instructor station serves as a lecture server. Lecture presentations are transmitted to student workstations upon demands. The broadcast route can use an inverse function of the above expression. The kth station, where $1 <= k <= N$, in the linear joining sequence has its unique parent at the following position in the linear order:

$$(k - i - 1)/m + 1, \quad \text{where} \quad i = (k - 1) \bmod m, \text{ if } i \,|\, m;$$
$$i = m, \text{ otherwise.}$$

The duplication of lecture presentations is upon demand. A child node in the m-ary tree copies information from its parent node. However, if a workstation (and its child workstations) does not review a lecture, it is not necessary to duplicate the lecture. The station only keeps a document reference in this case. Since the duplication process may involve extra disk space, one may argue that disk spaces are wasted. However, the duplicated document instances live only within a period of time. After a lecture is presented, duplicated document instances migrate to document references. Essentially, buffer spaces are used only. However, the instructor workstation has document instances and classes as persistence objects. The above equations are proved by mathematical induction and double-induction techniques. They are also implemented in our system.

Another issue of object propagation is that objects in the BLOB layer of the database are shared by objects at a higher level in the hierarchy. That is, in both the instructor station and the student station, BLOBs are shared among different lecture presentations. Since an individual multimedia resource is used only by a presentation in a workstation with respect to a time duration, concurrent access is not a consideration. This strategy avoids the abuse of disk storage.

As discussed previously, the database has three sorts of objects: classes, instances, and references. Document classes support object reuse. Instances are physical objects of a Web document, which are referred by document references. In the proposed virtual university architecture, in order to support off-line learning, we encourage students to "check out" lecture notes from a virtual library. Web document instance are stored in the virtual library. An instructor has a privilege to add or delete document instances, which contain lecture notes as Web pages. Students can check out and check in these Web pages. However, in general, there is no limitation of the number of Web pages to be checked out. The check in/out procedure serves as an assessment criterion to the study performance of a student. We provide a browsing interface, which allows students to retrieve course materials according to matching keywords, instructor names, and course numbers/titles. This virtual library is Web-savvy. That is, the searching and retrieve processes are running under a standard Web browser. The library is updated as needed. The mechanism follows another guidance of our project goals: adaptive to changing user needs. We are developing three Web courses based on the virtual library system: introduction to computer engineering, introduction to multimedia computing, and introduction to engineering drawing.

Distance learning, virtual university, or remote classroom projects change the manner of education. With the tremendous growing amount of Internet users, virtual university is a step toward the trend of future university. However, most development of distance learning systems relies on the high bandwidth of a network infrastructure. As it is not happening everywhere on the Internet to meet such a high requirement, it is worthwhile to investigate mechanisms to cope with the real situation. Even in the recent future, with the next generation of Internet, the increasing amount of users consumes an even higher network bandwidth. The primary directive of the Multimedia Micro-University Consortium is looking for solutions to realize virtual university. Some of our research results, as pointed out in this chapter, adapt to changing network conditions. Using an off-line multicasting mechanism, we implemented a distributed virtual course database with a number of on-line communication facilities to fit the limitation of the current Internet environment. The proposed database architecture and database system serves as an important role in our virtual university environment. We are currently using the Web document development environment to design undergraduate courses including introduction to computer science and others.

IV. FUTURE DIRECTIONS

Future multimedia applications will be even more attractive. For instance, intelligent agents, based on artificial intelligence techniques, will further assist multimedia software to interact with its users. Also, intelligent searching mechanisms will add power to content-based retrieval of multimedia information. Advanced input/output devices, such as head-mounted displays, sensors, auditory displays, and haptic displays, will further improve the efficiency of human–computer communication. High-speed processors, high-performance multimedia hardware architectures and networks, and high-capacity optical storage will support the need of high-quality multimedia applications in the future.

APPENDIX A: THE DESIGN AND IMPLEMENTATION OF IMMPS

The Multimedia Information Network (MINE) Lab at Tamkang University focuses on the development of many research projects related to multimedia presentation and MDBMS. In the past few years, we have developed several multimedia presentation design systems. In this appendix, we discuss two such systems in terms of database design and the graphical user interface. The first is an intelligent presentation system used in product demonstrations. The second is a Web-based documentation development environment.

FIGURE A1 The main window of IMMPS.

We present the graphical user interface of IMMPS. The first window is the main window of IMMPS shown in Fig. A1. This window allows the user to drop various presentation topics in the design area shown in the subwindow. Presentation topics may include text, audio, etc. shown as buttons on the left side of the window. The main window is used in conjunction with the presentation knowledge inheritance window and the presentation messages passing window shown in Fig. A2. The knowledge inheritance hierarchy is constructed by using different functions shown in the menu bar of the window. Inheritance links among presentation window objects are thus created as the inheritance relations are declared.

To add a usage (or message) link, the user accesses the presentation messages passing window. A vertical bar represents a presentation window indicated by its name on the top of that bar. Messages are passed when a button in a presentation window is pushed (or, as a side effect of a knowledge inference). Push buttons are shown as boxes on vertical bars. Each message, with its name displayed as the label of a usage link (shown as a horizontal arrow), is associated with one or more parameters separated by commas. These parameters are entered in the message window shown in the lower-left corner of Fig. A2.

To add rules or facts to the knowledge set of a presentation window, the presentation intelligence window shown in Fig. A3 is used. When a message is received by a presentation window, the corresponding actions that the presentation window needs to perform will be entered in the presentation action control window in Fig. A3. The presentation button control window is used to specify actions associated with each button when it is clicked.

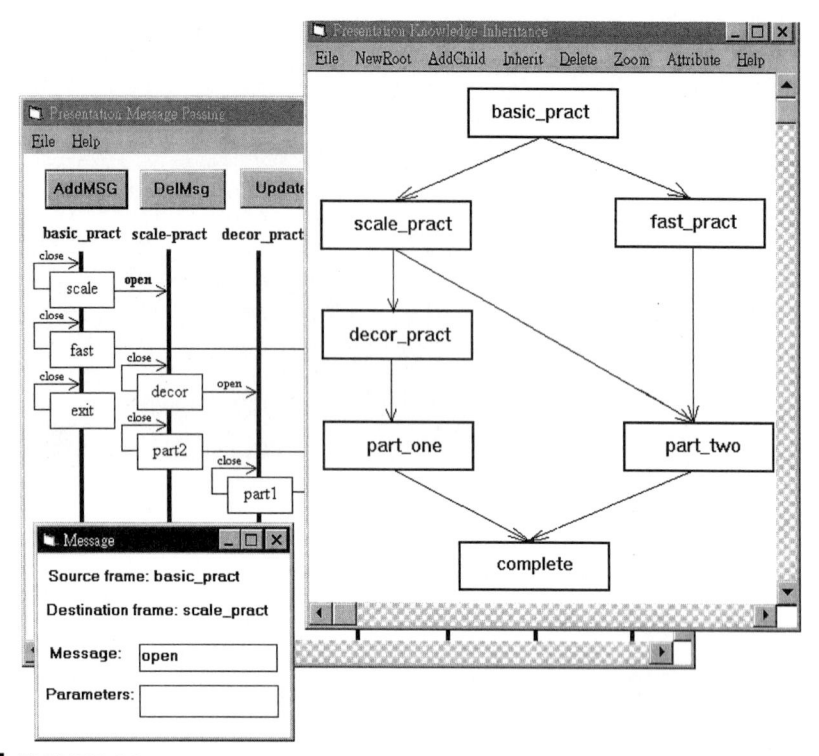

FIGURE A2 The presentation knowledge inheritance window and the presentation message passing window.

A multimedia resource browser (Fig. A4) is designed to allow a user to retrieve resources ready for inclusion in presentations. Resource attributes are selected or entered in different components of the window. When the topic button is pushed, the highlighted resource in the list box is linked to a topic of a presentation window.

Objects' reuse of presentation windows and resources is controlled by the presentation reuse control window shown in Fig. A5. Each presentation window object class or resource object class contains a number of presentation windows or resources shown in the middle list box of the individual subwindow in the presentation reuse control window. The association links are declared in the multimedia resource association control window shown in Fig. A5. Each highlighted resource (shown in the first list box from the left) is linked to a number of resources shown in the second list box. The available resources are shown in the third list box.

We use Arity Prolog as the underlying implementation language of our inference engine. However, some C^{++} functions are used to take care of presentation navigation and serve as stub functions that communicate between Prolog predicates and Basic procedures. The graphical user interface is written in Visual Basic (VB). The database management system is also implemented in Visual C^{++} (VC). No other supporting software is used, besides the underlying database management system and Windows 95/3.1. Figure A6 illustrates the implementation environment of our prototype system.

MULTIMEDIA DATABASE SYSTEMS   **353**

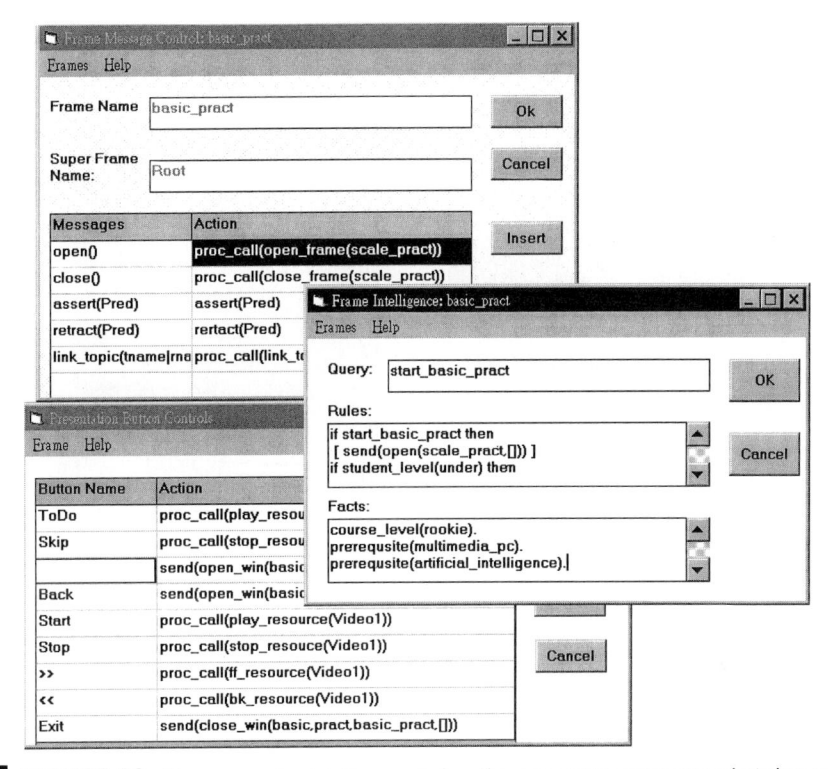

FIGURE A3 The presentation intelligence window, the presentation action control window, and the presentation button control window.

We spent about two years developing the system. In the first half of a year, we surveyed other presentation systems and researches before documenting a draft specification. The functional specification and design of IMMPS take about nine months. Two Ph.D. students and three Masters students spent about almost a year in the implementation, before the prototype was tested by a few undergraduate students for one month. About 9000 lines of VB, 4000 lines of VC, and another 4000 lines of Prolog code were used.

APPENDIX B: THE DESIGN AND IMPLEMENTATION OF MMU

We have implemented a collection of tools to support distance learning of MMU. Figure A7 illustrates a Web document development environment. The user starts from the script design phrase of the spiral model. Requirements of the document script as well as auxiliary information is given in the Web Script window (see the left of Fig. A7). According to the script, the Microsoft FrontPage editor is used to generate the Web document implementation shown in the Web browser. While the user is designing the script, he/she can look at some multimedia resources via the resource icons. In the implementation phrase, the user also needs to provide auxiliary information shown in the Web implementation window in Fig. A8.

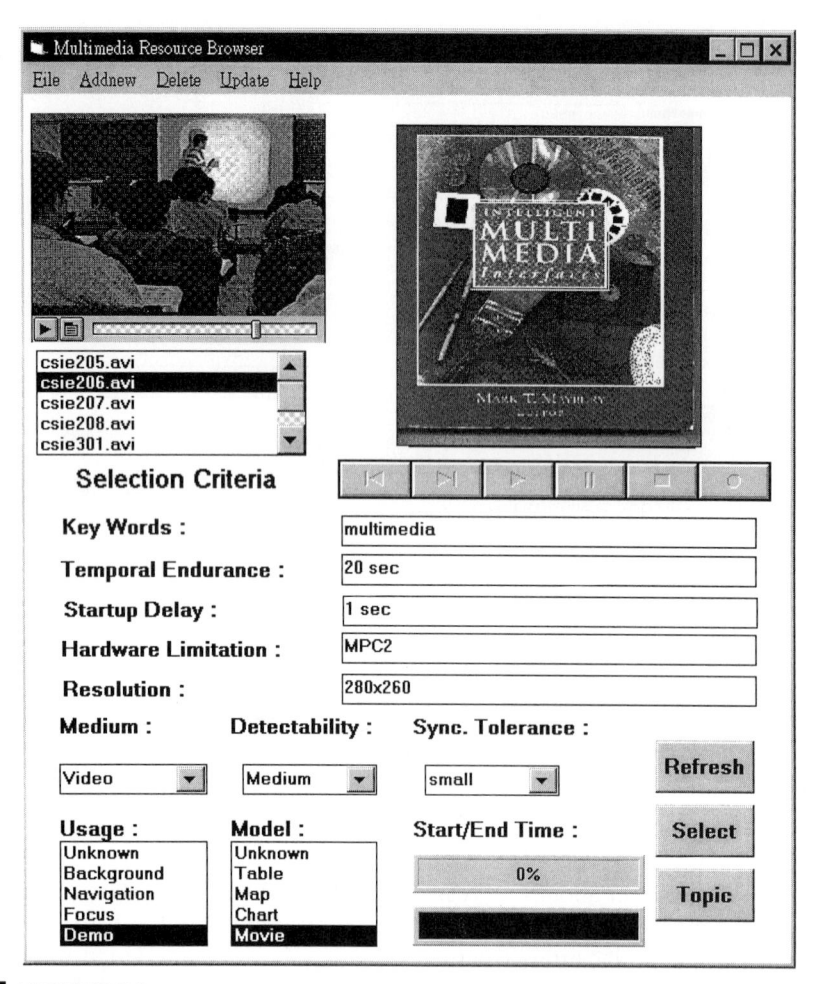

FIGURE A4 The multimedia resource browser.

The development process may proceed through several cycles in the spiral model that we have proposed. As the Web document evolves, the user may start from a Web document only containing the script portion. The implementation and test records are omitted at the beginning. In the next iteration, the user uses the FrontPage editor to design his/her Web page and add intradirectory and intrastation hyperlinks. The test record has a local testing scope in this cycle. Assessment is conducted to decide the status of the document, including checking the percentage of completeness and inconsistency, to decide whether to proceed with the next iteration. When the user starts to add interstation hyperlinks in the next cycle, the testing scope should be changed. Assessment is then performed again to decide whether to post the Web page. The evolution process of a Web document can be assessed from another perspective. A document may start from an implementation without add-on control programs. Gradually, the user adds Java applets. Regression tests should be proceeded at each cycle.

MULTIMEDIA DATABASE SYSTEMS   **355**

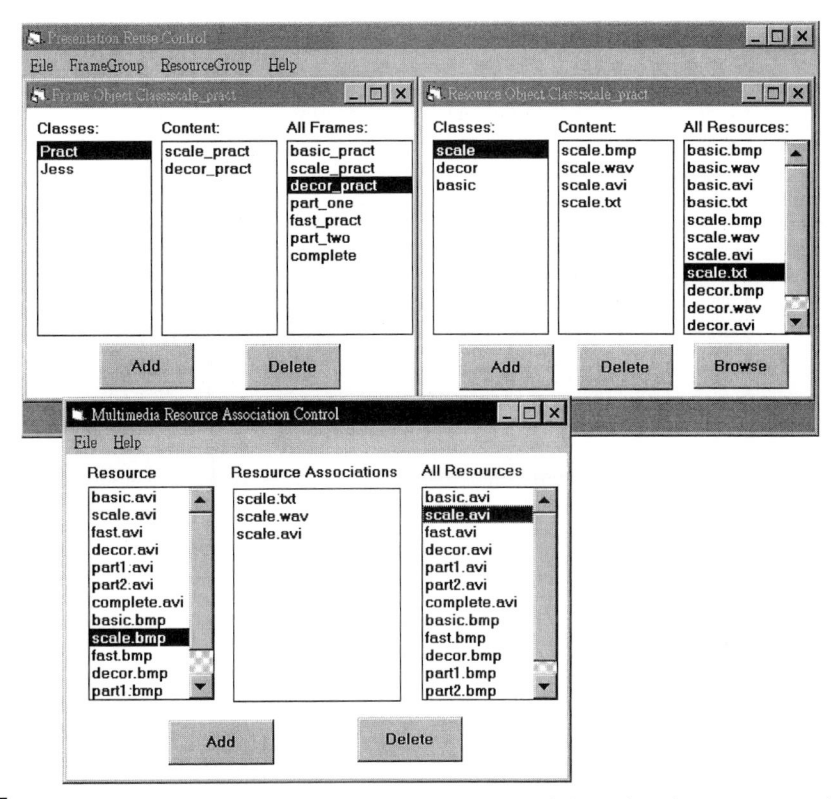

FIGURE A5 The presentation reuse control window and the multimedia resource association control window.

Another way to look at the evolution is that the user can start from a Web document without image and audio records. The user can add images in the next cycle, and audio records in the following cycle, and so on (for video clips). The spiral model can be used in different types of Web document evolutions.

After a Web document is developed, the instructor can use the document annotation editor (shown in Fig. A9) to explain his/her lecture. The annotations, as well as audio descriptions, can be recorded with time stamps encoded for real-time playback. Note that a Web document (serving as a lecture) can be used by different instructors with different annotations.

Even though the annotation system allows instructors to explain course materials, in a virtual university system, it is necessary to have on-line discussion tools for students to ask questions and conduct group discussions. Figures A10 and A11 illustrate a chat room tool, which allows multiple users to send messages to each other. The chat room tool is written in Java running on a standard Web browser. The chat room tool, as well as a white board system (see Fig. A12), has four floor control modes:

- *Free access:* All participants can listen and talk.
- *Equal control:* Only one person can talk but all participants can listen. An individual user sends a request to the speaker for the floor. The speaker

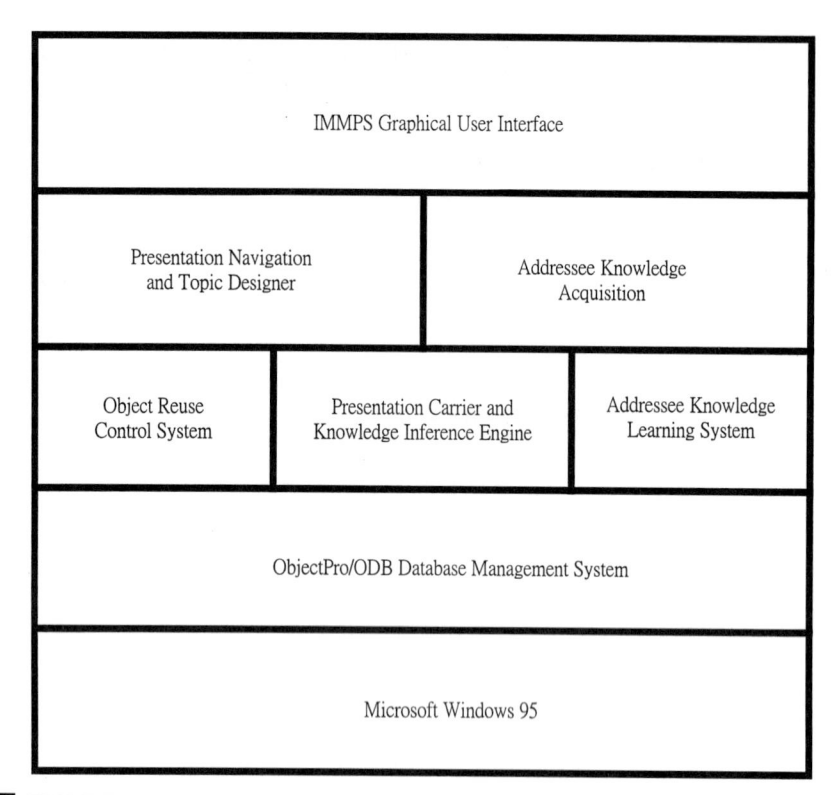

FIGURE A6 The implementation environment of IMMPS.

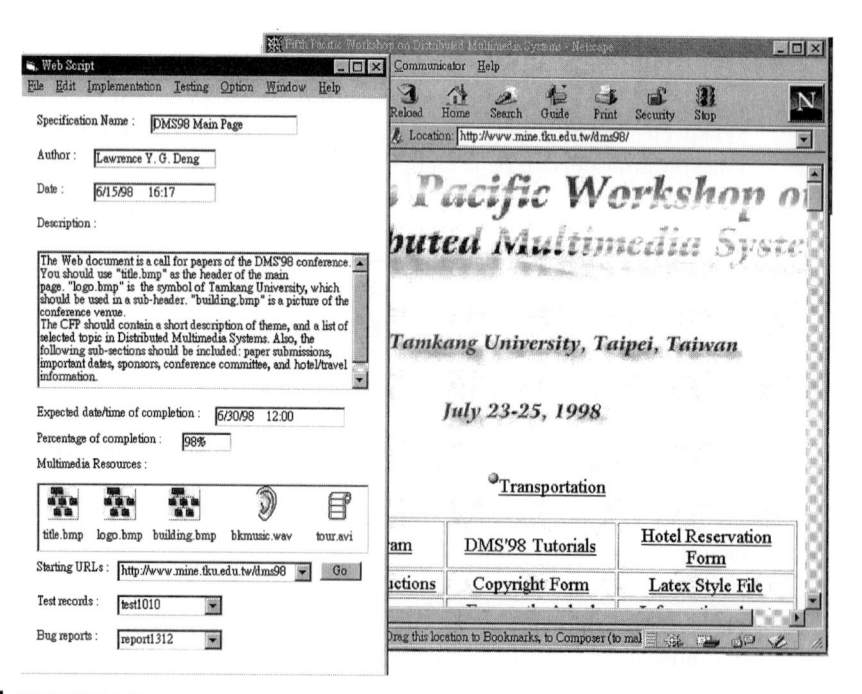

FIGURE A7 A Web document script and its implementation.

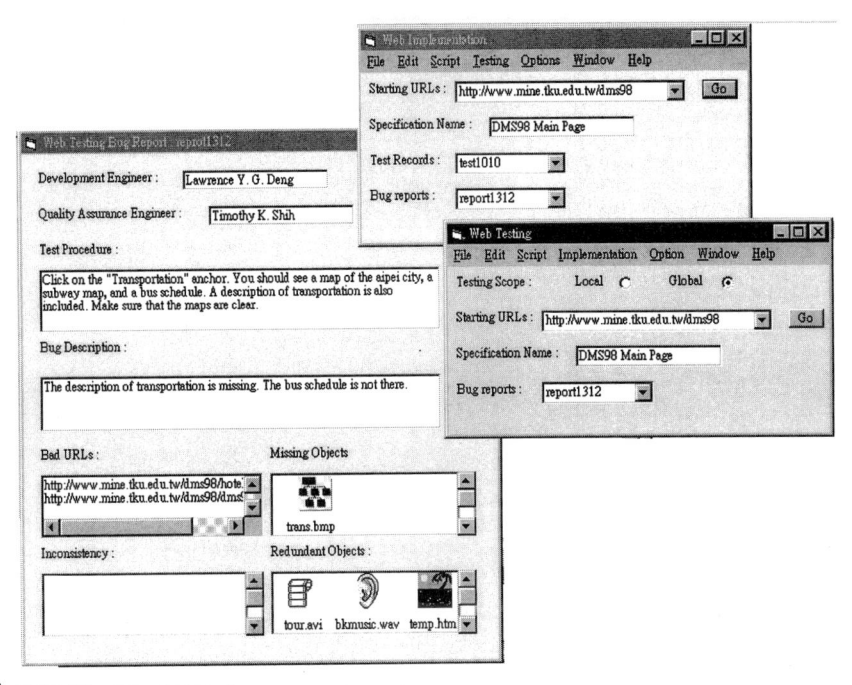

FIGURE A8 A Web document testing environment.

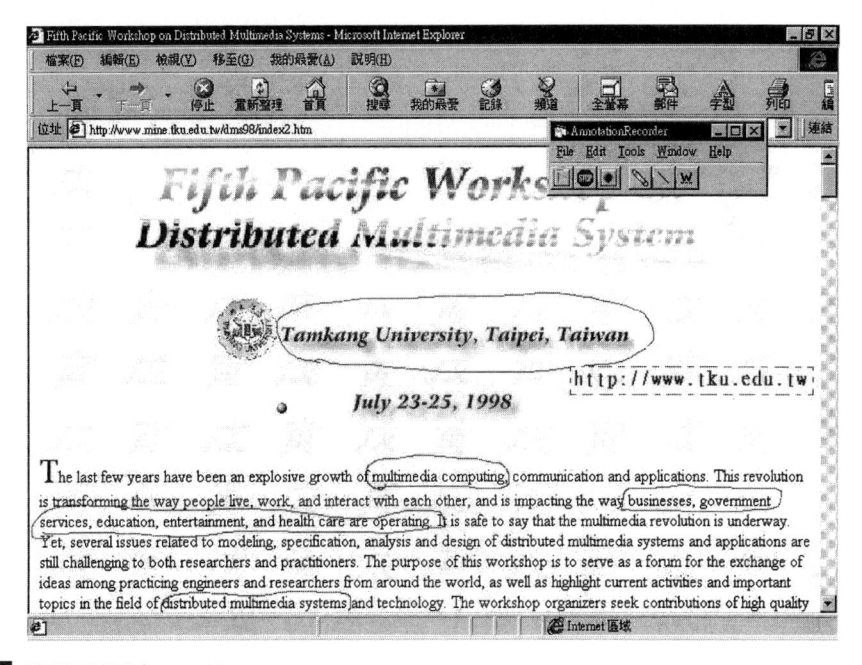

FIGURE A9 A Web course annotation system.

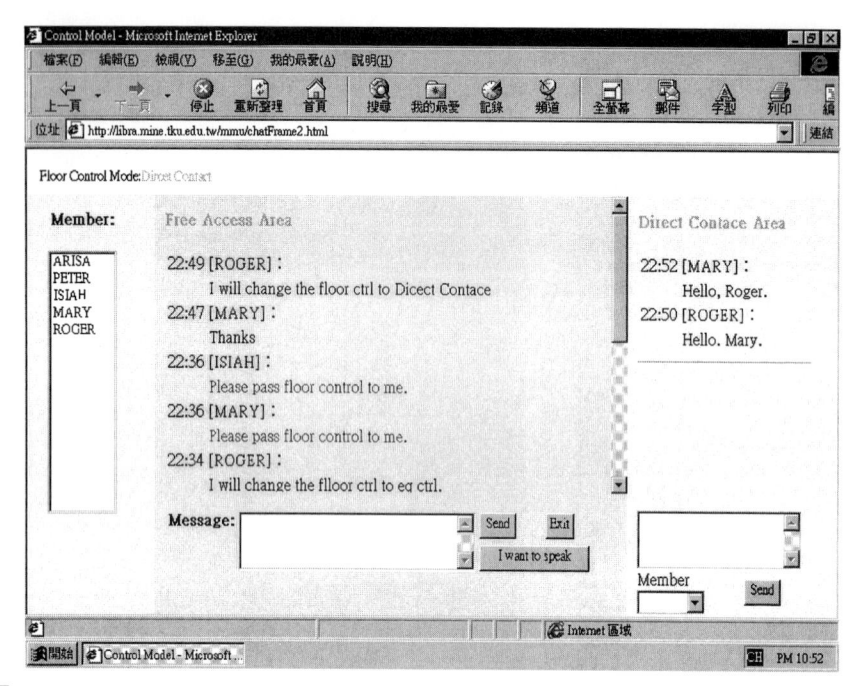

FIGURE A10 A chat room tool.

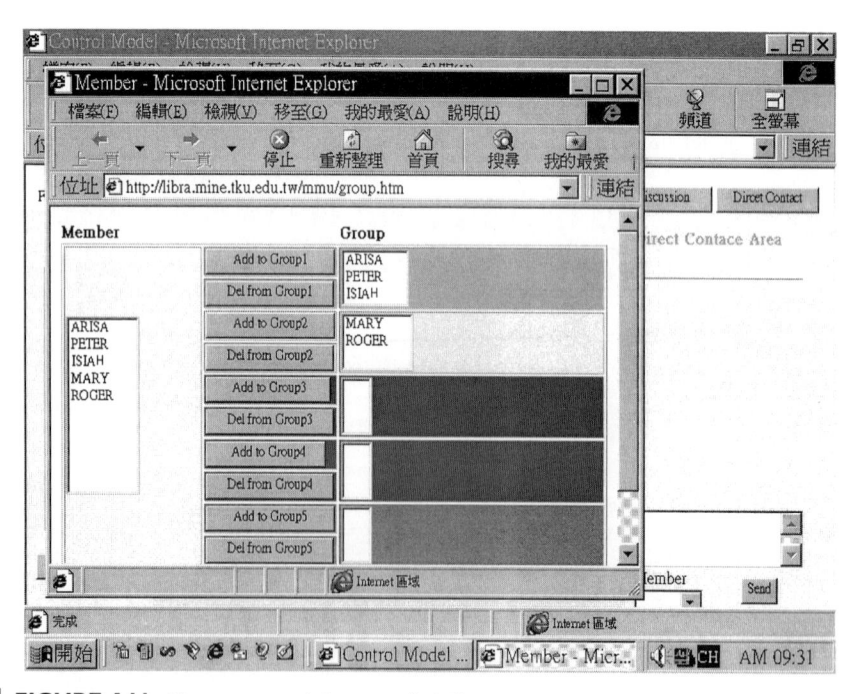

FIGURE A11 The group association control window.

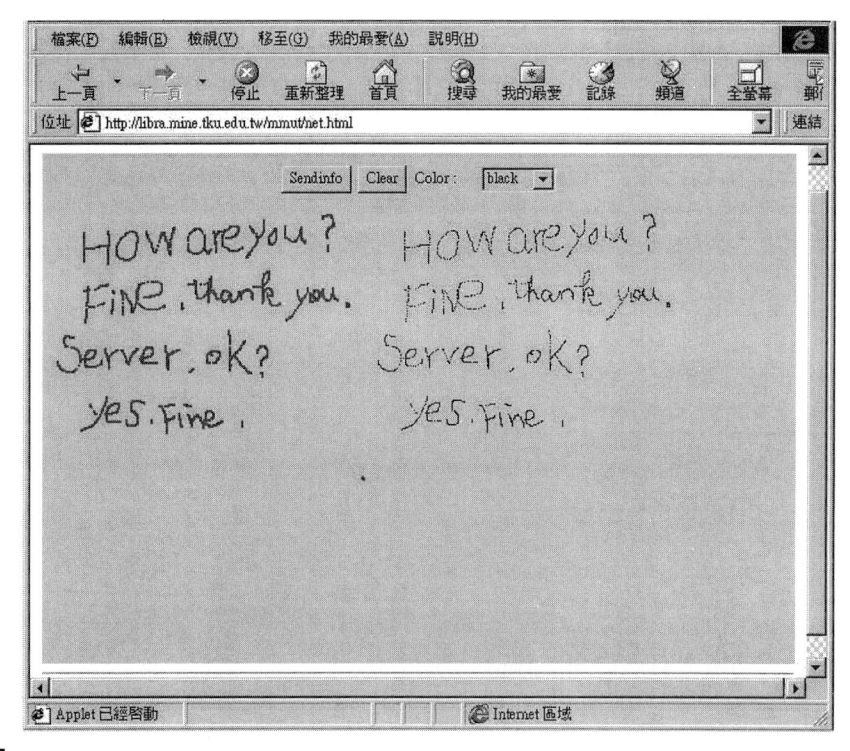

FIGURE A12 A white board system.

grants the control to the individual (first come, first serve-based). The first person logged in into the chat room has the first floor control. No chairperson is assigned. That is, everyone has the same priority.

• *Group discussion:* A participant can select a group of persons to whom he/she wants to talk and agrees to another group to whom he/she wants to listen. When an individual is asked to listen to another person, the individual can decide if he/she wants to listen. If so, the name of this individual is added to the listen group of the talking person.

• *Direct contact:* Two persons talk and listen to each other (i.e., private discussion). This is for a private conversation in the direct contact area illustrated in the GUI below. A person can have a private discussion with his/her partner while still joining the chat room.

The control mode of the discussion is decided by the course instructor. Drawing works the same as chatting in the three modes. Direct contact can be turned on/off by the instructor.

We use a relational database management system to implement our object-oriented database. The following database schema is implemented on the MS SQL server. However, a similar schema can be used in the Sybase or the Oracle database server. The schema can be used by ODBC or JDBC applications, which serve as open connections to various types of other database servers.

```sql
CREATE TABLE Database_table
(NAME              CHAR         NOT NULL,
 AUTHOR            CHAR,
 VERSION           CHAR,
 DATE/TIME         DATETIME,
 SNAME             CHAR,
 PRIMARY KEY (NAME),
 UNIQUE(NAME, AUTHOR, VERSION)
)
CREATE TABLE Script_table
(SNAME             CHAR         NOT NULL,
 AUTHOR            CHAR,
 VERSION           INT,
 DATE_TIME         DATETIME,
 DESCRIPTION       CHAR,
 E_DATE_E_TIME     DATETIME,
 P_OF_COMPLETION   INT,
 PRIMARY KEY(SNAME),
 UNIQUE(SNAME, AUTHOR, VERSION, DESCRIPTION)
)
CREATE TABLE Implementation_table
(STARTING_URL      CHAR         NOT NULL,
 SNAME             CHAR         NOT NULL,
 PRIMARY KEY(STARTING_URL),
 FOREIGN KEY(SNAME) REFERENCES Script_table(SNAME),
 UNIQUE(STARTING_URL,SNAME)
)
CREATE TABLE Test_Record_table
(TNAME             CHAR         NOT NULL,
 SNAME             CHAR         NOT NULL,
 TEST_SCOPE        CHAR,
 STARTING_URL      CHAR         NOT NULL,
 PRIMARY KEY(TNAME),
 FOREIGN KEY(SNAME) REFERENCES Script_table(SNAME),
 FOREIGN KEY(STARTING_URL) REFERENCES
    Implementation_table(STARTING_URL),
 UNIQUE(TNAME, SNAME, STARTING_URL)
)
CREATE TABLE Bug_Report_table
(BNAME             CHAR         NOT NULL,
 TEST_PROCEDURE    CHAR,
 BUG_DESCRIPTION   CHAR,
 TNAME             CHAR,
 PRIMARY KEY(BNAME),
 FOREIGN KEY(TNAME) REFERENCES
    Test_Record_table(TNAME),
 UNIQUE(BNAME, TEST_PROCEDURE, BUG_DESCRIPTION, TNAME)
)
```

```
CREATE TABLE Annotation_table
(ANAME              CHAR        NOT NULL,
 SNAME              CHAR,
 STARTING_URL       CHAR,
 AUTHOR             CHAR,
 VERSION            INT,
 DATE_TIME          DATETIME,
 ANNOTATION_FILE    CHAR,
 PRIMARY KEY(ANAME),
 FOREIGN KEY(SNAME) REFERENCES Script_table(SNAME),
 FOREIGN KEY(STARTING_URL) REFERENCES
   Implementation_table(STARTING_URL),
 UNIQUE(ANAME, SNAME, STARTING_URL, AUTHOR,
   ANNOTATION_FILE, VERSION)
)
CREATE TABLE Resource_table*
(R_ID               INT         NOT NULL,
 NAME               CHAR,
 AUTHOR             CHAR,
 DATE_TIME          DATETIME,
 SIZE               INT,
 DESCRIPTION        CHAR,
 LOCATION           CHAR        NOT NULL,
 TYPE               CHAR,
 PRIMARY KEY(R_ID),
 UNIQUE(R_ID, AUTHOR, NAME, LOCATION, TYPE)
)
CREATE TABLE Html_table*
(H_ID               INT         NOT NULL,
 NAME               CHAR,
 AUTHOR             CHAR,
 DATE_TIME          DATETIME,
 DESCRIPTION        CHAR,
 LOCATION           CHAR        NOT NULL,
 PRIMARY KEY(H_ID),
 UNIQUE(H_ID, AUTHOR, NAME, LOCATION)
)
CREATE TABLE Program_table*
(P_ID               INT         NOT NULL,
 NAME               CHAR,
 AUTHOR             CHAR,
 SIZE               INT,
 DATE_TIME          DATETIME,
 DESCRIPTION        CHAR,
 TYPE               CHAR,
 LOCATION           CHAR        NOT NULL,
 PRIMARY KEY(P_ID),
 UNIQUE(P_ID, AUTHOR, LOCATION, TYPE)
)
```

```
CREATE TABLE Keyword_table
(K_ID                   INT      NOT NULL,
 KNAME                  CHAR,
 PRIMARY KEY(K_ID),
 UNIQUE(K_ID, KNAME)
)
CREATE TABLE Script_Resource_table
(SNAME                  CHAR     NOT NULL,
 R_ID                   INT      NOT NULL,
 PRIMARY KEY(SNAME, R_ID),
 FOREIGN KEY(SNAME)        REFERENCES Script_table(SNAME),
 FOREIGN KEY(R_ID) REFERENCES Resource_table(R_id)
)
CREATE TABLE Implementation_Resource_table
(STARTING_URL           CHAR     NOT NULL,
 R_ID                   INT      NOT NULL,
 PRIMARY KEY(STARTING_URL, R_ID),
 FOREIGN KEY(STARTING_URL) REFERENCES
    Implementation_table(STARTING_URL),
 FOREIGN KEY(R_ID) REFERENCES Resource_table(R_ID)
)
CREATE TABLE Implementation_Program_table
(STARTING_URL           CHAR     NOT NULL,
 P_ID                   INT      NOT NULL,
 PRIMARY KEY(STARTING_URL,P_ID),
 FOREIGN KEY(STARTING_URL) REFERENCES
    Implementation_table(STARTING_URL),
 FOREIGN KEY(P_ID)REFERENCES Program_table(P_ID)
)
CREATE TABLE Implementation_Html_table
(STARTING_URL           CHAR     NOT NULL,
 H_ID                   INT      NOT NULL,
 PRIMARY KEY(STARTING_URL,H_ID),
 FOREIGN KEY(STARTING_URL) REFERENCES
    Implementation_table(STARTING_URL),
 FOREIGN KEY(H_ID) REFERENCES Html_table(H_ID)
)
CREATE TABLE Web_Traversal_Message_table
(WEB_ID                 INT      NOT NULL,
 TNAME                  CHAR,
 PRIMARY KEY(WEB_ID),
 FOREIGN KEY(TNAME) REFERENCES
    Test_Record_table(TNAME),
 UNIQUE(WEB_ID)
)
```

```sql
CREATE TABLE QA_Engineer_table
(Q_ID            INT      NOT NULL,
 NAME            CHAR,
 TITLE           CHAR,
 UNIT            CHAR,
 PRIMARY KEY(Q_ID),
 UNIQUE(Q_ID,NAME)
)
CREATE TABLE B_Q_table
(BNAME           CHAR     NOT NULL,
 Q_ID            INT      NOT NULL,
 PRIMARY KEY(BNAME, Q_ID),
 FOREIGN KEY(BNAME) REFERENCES Bug_Report_table(BNAME),
 FOREIGN KEY(Q_ID) REFERENCES QA_Engineer_table(Q_ID)
)
CREATE TABLE B_Bad_table
(BNAME           CHAR     NOT NULL,
 H_ID            INT      NOT NULL,
 PRIMARY KEY(BNAME, H_ID),
 FOREIGN KEY(BNAME) REFERENCES Bug_Report_table(BNAME),
 FOREIGN KEY(H_ID) REFERENCES Html_table(H_ID)
)
CREATE TABLE B_Missing_table
(BNAME           CHAR     NOT NULL,
 R_ID            INT      NOT NULL,
 PRIMARY KEY(BNAME, R_ID),
 FOREIGN KEY(BNAME) REFERENCES Bug_Report_table(BNAME),
 FOREIGN KEY(R_ID) REFERENCES Resource_table(R_ID)
)
CREATE TABLE B_Redundant_table
(BNAME           CHAR     NOT NULL,
 R_ID            INT      NOT NULL,
 PRIMARY KEY(BNAME,R_ID),
 FOREIGN KEY(BNAME)  REFERENCES Bug_Report_table(BNAME),
 FOREIGN KEY(R_ID)   REFERENCES Resource_table(R_ID)
)
CREATE TABLE B_Inconsistence_table
(BNAME           CHAR     NOT NULL,
 PRIMARY KEY (BNAME)
)
CREATE TABLE D_K_TABLE
(NAME            CHAR     NOT NULL,
 K_ID            INT,
 PRIMARY KEY(NAME, K_ID),
 FOREIGN KEY(K_ID)   REFERENCES Keyword_table(K_ID)
)
```

```
CREATE TABLE Script_Keyword_table
(SNAME                CHAR    NOT NULL,
 K_ID                 INT     NOT NULL,
 PRIMARY KEY(SNAME, K_ID),
 FOREIGN KEY(SNAME) REFERENCES Script_table(SNAME),
 FOREIGN KEY(K_ID) REFERENCES Keyword_table(K_ID)
)
```

REFERENCES

1. Agosti, M., Melucci, M., and Crestani, F. Automatic authoring and construction of hypermedia for information retrieval. *Multimedia System* 3(3):15–24, 1995.
2. Allen, J. F. Maintaining knowledge about temporal intervals. *Commun. ACM* 26(11), 1983.
3. Anderson, D. P., and Homsy, G. A continuous media I/O server and its synchronization mechanism. *IEEE Computer* 51–57, 1991.
4. Arens, Y. Presentation design using an integrated knowledge base. In *Intelligent User Interfaces* (J. W. Sullivan and S. W. Tyler, Eds.), pp. 241–258. Assoc. Comput. Mach., New York, 1991.
5. Arens, Y. On the knowledge underlying multimedia presentations. In *Intelligent Multimedia Interfaces* (M. T. Maybury, Ed.), pp. 280–306. AAAI Press, Menlo Park, CA, 1993.
6. Backer, D. S. Multimedia presentation and authoring. In *Multimedia Systems* (J. F. K. Buford, Ed.), pp. 285–303. Assoc. Comput. Mach. New York, 1994.
7. Blakowski, G., Hubel, J., and Langrehr, U. Tools for specifying and executing synchronized multimedia presentations. In *Network and Operating System Support for Digital Audio and Video* (R. G. Herrtwich, Ed.), Second International Workshop Heidelberg, Germany, pp. 271–282, 1991.
8. Botafogo, R., and Mosse, D. The MORENA model for hypermedia authoring and browsing. In *Proceedings of the International Conference on Multimedia Computing and Systems*, Washington, DC, May 15–18, pp. 42–49, 1995.
9. Chen, C. R., Meliksetian, D. S., Chang, M. C.-S., and Liu, L. J. Design of a multimedia object-oriented DBMS. *Multimedia Systems.* 3:217–227, 1995.
10. Chih-Wen Cheng, *et al.* Networked hypermedia systems. In *Proceeding of the 1994 HD-MEDIA Technical and Applications Workshop,* October 6–8, Taipei, Taiwan, 1994.
11. Chin, D. N. Intelligent interfaces as agents. In *Intelligent User Interfaces* (J. W. Sullivan and S. W. Tyler, Eds.), pp. 177–206. Assoc. Comput. Mach., New York. 1991.
12. Chung, C. M., Shih, T. K., Huang, J.-Y., Wang, Y.-H., and Kuo, T.-F. An object-oriented approach and system for intelligent multimedia presentation designs. In *Proceedings of the ICMCS'95 Conference,* pp. 278–281, 1995.
13. Gibbs, S., Dami, L., and Tsichritzis, D. An object-oriented framework for multimedia composition and synchronization. In *Eurographic Seminars, Tutorials and Perspectives in Computer Graphics Multimedia Systems, Interaction and Applications,* (L. Kjelldahl Ed.), Chap. 8, 1991.
14. Halang, W. A., and Wannemacher, M. High-precision temporal synchronization in distributed multimedia systems. In *Proceedings of the Second ISATED/ISMM International Conference on Distributed Multimedia Systems and Applications,* Stanford, CA, August 7–9, pp. 221–223, 1995.
15. Chen, H.-Y. *et al.* A novel audio/video synchronization model and its application in multimedia authoring system. In *Proceedings of the 1994 HD-MEDIA Technical and Applications Workshop,* 1994.
16. Hoepner, P. Presentation scheduling of multimedia objects and its impact. In *Network and Operating System Support for Digital Audio and Video Second International Workshop Heidelberg,* Germany (R. G. Herrtwich Ed.), pp. 132–143, 1991.
17. Hoepner, P. Synchronizing the presentation of multimedia objects—ODA extensions. In *ACM SIGOIS,* pp. 19–31, 1991.
18. Hoepner, P. Synchronizing the presentation of multimedia objects. *Comput. Commun.* 15(9): 557–564, 1992.

19. Schnepf, J. et al. Doing FLIPS: Flexible interactive presentation synchronization. In *Proceedings of the International Conference on Multimedia Computing and Systems*, pp. 213–222, 1995.
20. J. E. C. JR. and Roussopoulos, N. Timing requirements for time-driven systems using augmented Petri nets. *IEEE Trans. Software Engrg.* 9(5):603–616, 1983.
21. Kunii, T., Shinagawa, Y., Paul, R., Khan, M., and Khokhar, A. A. Issues in storage and retrieval of multimedia data. *Multimedia Systems* 3:298–304, 1995.
22. Leydekkers, P., and Teunissen, B. Synchronization of multimedia data streams in open distributed environments. In *Network and Operating System Support for Digital Audio and Video, Second International Workshop Heidelberg, Germany,* (R. G. Herrtwich, Ed.), pp. 94–104, 1991.
23. Little, T. D., and Ghafoor, A. Multimedia synchronization protocols for broadband integrated services. *IEEE J. Selected Areas Commun.* 9(9):1368–1382, 1991.
24. Little, T. D. C., and Ghafoor, A. G. Spatio-temporal composition of distributed multimedia objects for value-added networks. *IEEE Computer.* 42–50, 1991.
25. Little, T. D. C., and Ghafoor, A. Synchronization and storage models for multimedia objects. *IEEE J. Selected Areas Commun.* 8(3):413–427, 1990.
26. Lundeberg, A., Yamamoto, T., and Usuki, T. SAL, A hypermedia prototype system. In *Eurographic Seminars, Tutorials and Perspectives in Computer Graphics, Multimedia Systems, Interaction and Applications* (L. Kjelldahl, Ed.), Chapter 10, 1991.
27. Oomoto, E., and Tanaka, K. OVID: Desibn and implementation of a video-object database system. *IEEE Trans. Knowledge Data Engrg.* 5(4):629–643, 1993.
28. Ouyang, Y. C., and Lin, H.-P. A multimedia information indexing and retrieval method. In *Proceedings of the Second ISATED/ISMM International Conference on Distributed Multimedia Systems and Applications,* Stanford, CA, August 7–9, pp. 55–57, 1995.
29. Ozsu, M. T., Szafron, D., El-Medani, G., and Vittal, C. An object-oriented multimedia database system for a news-on-demand application. *Multimedia Systems,* 3:182–203, 1995.
30. Paul, R., Khan, M. F., Khokhar, A., and Ghafoor, A. Issues in database management of multimedia information. In *Proceedings of the 18th IEEE Annual International Computer Software and Application Conference (COMPSAC'94),* Taipei, Taiwan, pp. 209–214, 1994.
31. Prabhakaran, B., and Raghavan, S. V. *Synchronization Models for Multimedia Presentation with User Participation,* Vol. 2 of Multimedia Systems. Springer-Verlag, Berlin, 1994.
32. Dannenberg, R. B. *et al.* A computer based multimedia tutor for beginning piano students. *Interface* 19(2–3):155–173, 1990.
33. Rhiner, M., and Stucki, P. Database requirements for multimedia applications. In *Multimedia System, Interaction and Applications* (L. Kjelldahl Ed.), pp. 269–281, 1991.
34. Rosenberg, J., Cruz, G., and Judd, T. Presenting multimedia documents over a digital network. In *Network and Operating System Support for Digital Audio and Video, Second International Workshop Heidelberg, Germany,* (R. G. Herrtwich Ed.), pp. 346–356, 1991.
35. Schurmann, G., and Holzmann-Kaiser, U. Distributed multimedia information handling and processing. *IEEE Network,* November: 23–31, 1990.
36. Shih, T. K. An Artificial intelligent approach to multimedia authoring. In *Proceedings of the Second IASTED/ISMM International Conference on Distributed Multimedia Systems and Applications,* pp. 71–74, 1995.
37. Shih, T. K. On making a better interactive multimedia presentation. In *Proceedings of the International Conference on Multimedia Modeling,* 1995.
38. Shih, T. K., and Chang, A. Y. Toward a generic spatial/temporal computation model for multimedia presentations. In *Proceedings of the IEEE ICMCS Conference,* 1997.
39. Shih, T. K., and Davis, R. E. IMMPS: A multimedia presentation design system. *IEEE Multimedia* Fall, 1997.
40. Shih, T. K., Kuo, C.-H., and An, K.-S. Multimedia presentation designs with database support. In *Proceedings of the NCS'95 Conference,* 1995.
41. Shih, T. K., Kuo, C.-H., and An, K.-S. An object-oriented database for intelligent multimedia presentations. In *Proceedings of the IEEE International Conference on System, Man, and Cybernetics Information, Intelligence and Systems Conference,* 1996.
42. Shivakumar, N., and Sreenan, C. J. The concord algorithm for synchronization of networked multimedia streams. In *Proceedings of the International Conference on Multimedia Computing and Systems,* Washington, DC, May 15–18, pp. 31–40, 1995.

43. Smoliar, S. W., and Zhang, H. J. Content-based video indexing and retrieval. *IEEE MultiMedia,* 62–72, 1994.
44. Staehli, R., Walpole, J., and Maier, D. A quality-of-service specification for multimedia presentations. *Multimedia Systems,* **3**: 251–263, 1995.
45. Steinmetz, R. Synchronization properties in multimedia systems. *IEEE J. Selected Areas Commun.* 8(3):401–412, 1990.
46. Woodruff, G. M., and Kositpaiboon, R. Multimedia traffic management principles for guaranteed ATM network performance. *IEEE J. Selected Areas Commun.* 8(3):437–446, 1990.
47. Al-Salqan, Y. Y. *et al. MediaWare: On Multimedia Synchronization,* pp. 150–157, 1995.
48. Yavatkar, R. MCP: A protocol for coordination and temporal synchronization in multimedia collaborative applications. In *IEEE 52th Intl Conference on Distributed Computing Systems,* June 9–12, pp. 606–613, 1992.
49. Yoshitaka, A., Kishida, S., Hirakawa, M., and Ichikawa, T. Knowledge-assisted content-based retrieval for multimedia database. *IEEE Multimedia Magazine* 12–21, 1994.
50. Tracz, W. Software reuse myths. *ACM SIGSOFT Software Engineering Notes* 13(1):17–21, 1988.
51. Kaiser, G. E. *et al.* Melding software systems for reusable building Blocks. *IEEE Software* 17–24, 1987.
52. Lenz, M. *et al.* Software reuse through building blocks. *IEEE Software* 34–42, 1987.
53. Gargaro, A. *et al.* Reusability issues and Ada. *IEEE Software* 43–51, 1987.
54. Prieto-Diaz, R. *et al.* Classifying software for reusability. *IEEE Software* 6–16, 1987.
55. Prieto-Diaz, R. Implementing faceted classification for software reuse. *Commun. ACM* **34**(5): 88–97, 1991.
56. Ghezala, H. H. B. *et al.* A reuse approach based on object orientation: Its contributions in the development of CASE tools. In *Proceedings of the SSR'95 Conference,* Seattle, WA, pp. 53–62.
57. Bieman, J. M. *et al.* Reuse through inheritance: A quantitative study of C^{++} software. In *Proceedings of the SSR'95 Conference,* Seattle, WA, pp. 47–52.
58. Bieman, J. M. *et al.* Cohesion and reuse in an object-oriented system. In *Proceedings of the SSR'95 Conference,* Seattle, WA, pp. 259–262.
59. Burton, B. A. *et al.* The reusable software library. *IEEE Software* 25–33, 1987.
60. Fischer, G. Cognitive view of reuse and redesign. *IEEE Software* 60–72, 1987.
61. Tyugu, E. Three new-generation software environments. *Commun. ACM* 34(6):46–59, 1991.
62. Tyugu, E. et al. NUT—An object-oriented language. *Comput. Artif. Intell.* 5(6):521–542, 1986.

11
DATA STRUCTURE IN RAPID PROTOTYPING AND MANUFACTURING

CHUA CHEE KAI, JACOB GAN, AND DU ZHAOHUI

School of Mechanical and Production Engineering, Nanyang Technological University, Singapore 639798

TONG MEI

Gintic Institute of Manufacturing Technology, Singapore 638075

I. INTRODUCTION   368
   A. Data Structure Technique   368
   B. Rapid Prototyping and Manufacturing Technology   369
II. INTERFACES BETWEEN CAD AND RP&M   376
   A. CAD Modeling   376
   B. Interfaces between CAD Systems   379
   C. Interface between CAD and RP&M: STL Format   382
   D. Proposed Standard: Layer Manufacturing Interface (LMI)   386
III. SLICING   395
   A. Direct Slicing of a CAD File   396
   B. Slicing an STL File   397
   C. Slicing an LMI File   398
   D. Adaptive Slicing   399
IV. LAYER DATA INTERFACES   400
   A. Scanning and Hatching Pattern   401
   B. Two-Dimensional Contour Format   403
   C. Common Layer Interface (CLI)   405
   D. Rapid Prototyping Interface (RPI)   406
   E. Layer Exchange ASCII Format (LEAF)   407
   F. SLC Format   409
V. SOLID INTERCHANGE FORMAT (SIF): THE FUTURE INTERFACE   409
VI. VIRTUAL REALITY AND RP&M   410
   A. Virtual Prototype and Rapid Prototype   410
   B. Virtual Reality Modeling Language (VRML)   411
VII. VOLUMETRIC MODELING FOR RP&M   412
   REFERENCES   414

I. INTRODUCTION

A. Data Structure Technique

The efficient management of geometric information, such as points, curves, or polyhedrons is of significant importance in many engineering applications, such as computer-aided design (CAD), computer-aided manufacturing (CAM), robotics, and rapid prototyping and manufacturing (RP&M). In addition to representing the objects correctly and sufficiently, a good representation scheme maps the original data objects into a set of objects that facilitate efficient storage and computation.

In geometric computing encountered in engineering applications, it is often necessary to store multiple representations of the same data in order to facilitate efficient computation of a great variety of operators. Moreover, the same data may be utilized by categories of users and across heterogeneous systems during different phases of the product design and manufacturing process; thus more than one representation may be necessary. Multiple representations incur a significant overhead to ensure availability and consistency of the data.

A data structure is the form of organization imposed on the collection of those data elements. It is defined by specifying what kind of elements it contains and stating the rules of how to store the elements and how to retrieve them when needed. Also, data structures are the materials from which computer programs are built, just as physical materials are built from molecules of their component substances. In engineering computing, they reduce to only a few simple entities, mainly numbers and characters. Correspondingly, any kind of representation should be realized with numbers and characters.

Data structures may be classified into linear and nonlinear types [1]. Linear structures are those elements that have a sequential relationship. For example, a list of houses along a street, is a linear structure: collections of likewise elements with a clearly defined ordering. Such structures are often represented in diagrams by collections of boxes with lines to show their relationship. Linear structures occupy a special place in the study of data structures because the addressing of storage locations in a computer is nearly always linear, so the set of memory storage locations in the machine itself constitutes a linear structure. Linear structures may be further classified as addressable or sequential. Arrays are important types of addressable structure: a specific element can be retrieved knowing only its address, without reference to the others. In a sequential data structure an element can only be reached by first accessing its predecessor in sequential order. Because much engineering software is devoted to mathematically oriented tasks that involve solving simultaneous equations, arrays and metrics play a large role in its design. Nonlinear data structures are of varied sorts. One category important to the software designer is that of hierarchical structures, in which each element is itself a data structure. One key feature distinguishes a hierarchy: there is only a single unique path connecting any one element to another. Given that computer memory devices are arranged as linear strings of storage locations, there is no "natural" way of placing nonlinear structures in memory.

That more than one data structure type exist means there is no single data structure type that can be suitable for all applications. Data structure is often selectively designed for the efficiency of storing, retrieving, and computing operators. A good data structure is vital to the reliability and efficiency of a program or software.

RP&M is a set of manufacturing processes that can fabricate complex freeform solid objects with various materials directly from a CAD file of an object without part-specific tooling. Despite the fast development and worldwide installation of 3289 systems in 1998 [2], there is no suitable single information standard. The RP&M information processing involves transforming the CAD file into a special 3D facet representation, slicing the geometric form of the part into layers, generating the contours of the part for each layer, and hatching the contours of each layer.

B. Rapid Prototyping and Manufacturing Technology

For better appreciation for the need of good data structure techniques to be used in RP&M, a discussion on the various RP&M processes is in order. RP&M entails the fabrication of an object from its CAD by selectively solidifying or bonding one or more raw materials into a layer, representing a slice of the desired part, and then fusing the successive layers into a 3D solid object. The starting material may be liquid, powder, or solid sheets, while the solidification process may be polymerization, sintering, chemical reaction, plasma spraying, or gluing.

RP&M technology has the potential of ensuring that quality-assured prototypes or parts are developed quickly for two major reasons. There are almost no restrictions on geometrical shapes, and the layered manufacturing allows a direct interface with CAD to CAM, which almost eliminates the need for process planning. These advantages of RP&M technology bring the results with enhancing and improving the product development process and, at the same time, reducing the costs and time required for taking the product from conception to market. The technology has already shown potential and valuable in ever-increasing application fields, including the manufacturing/tooling industry, automobile industry, architecture, and biomedical engineering.

1. RP&M Principle and Processes

Over the past few years, a variety of RP&M techniques has been developed. RP&M processes are classified into variable energy processes and variable mass processes [3]. Variable energy processes are those where a uniform mass is selectively activated, removed, or bonded by a variable energy controlled by the layer description. These processes include molecule bonding, particle bonding, and sheet lamination. Variable mass processes are those where a constant source of energy is used to fuse or solidify a variable mass controlled by the layer description. These processes are the droplet deposition process, the particle deposition process, and the melt deposition process.

Liquid Solidification Processes

The photopolymerization processes are those where the optical energy like laser or UV light driven by layer information solidifies the scanned areas of thin photopolymer resin layers.

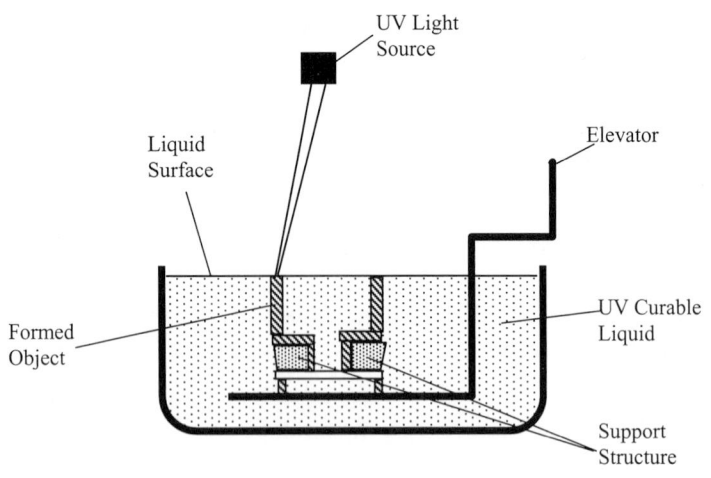

FIGURE 1 SLA process.

1. SLA—Stereolithography Apparatus. The SLA process was developed and commercialized by 3D Systems [4,5]. Its product models include SLA-190, SLA-250, and SLA-500. The process of the SLA system is a kind of liquid solidification process as shown in Fig. 1 [6].

First, a three-dimensional CAD solid model file is loaded into the system. If needed, supports are designed to stabilize the part during building and post-curing. Then the control unit slices the model and support into a series of cross sections from 0.004 to 0.020 in. thick.

After that, the cross-sectional information is passed onto SLA machines. The process of SLA begins with the vat being filled with the photopolymer liquid and the elevator table set just below the surface of the liquid. Then a computer-controlled UV light source scans the photopolymer liquid that is partially cured to form one layer. After a layer is formed, the elevator is lowered to allow uncured liquid to flow over the top of the part, in preparation for scanning the next layer's features. This process continues building the part from bottom to top, until the system completes the product. Finally, UV post-curing following scanning of the entire part in an oven completes the production cycle.

2. SGC—Solid Ground Curing. The SGC process was developed by the Cubital Ltd [7]. Cubital's products are the Solider 4600 and Solider 5600. SGC is the other example of photopolymerization but is different from SLA in that it uses a lamp instead of a point-by-point laser. The Cubital's Solid Ground Curing process includes three main steps: data preparing, mask generating, and model making.

In the data preparing step, the job for production is prepared and the cross sections in imaging format are transferred to a mask generator. After data are received, a mask plate is charged through an "image-wise" ionographic process. Then the charged image is developed with electrostatic toner. Then model building begins with spreading a thin layer of photopolymer of any viscosity. Secondly, the photomask from the mask generator is placed above the workpiece, in close proximity, and both are aligned under a collimated UV lamp.

Thirdly, the UV light is turned on for a few seconds. Part of the resin layer is hardened according to the photomask. Then the unsolidified resin is collectedly sunk out from the workpiece. After that, melted wax is spread into the cavities created after collecting the uncured liquid resin. Consequently, the wax in the cavities is cooled to produce a wholly solid layer. Finally, the layer is milled to its exact thickness, producing a flat solid surface ready to receive the next layer.

Particle Bonding Processes

Particle bonding process uses the modulated energy to selectively bond particles in a thin layer of powder material. Those two-dimensional layers are stacked together to form a complex three-dimensional solid object. The commercial machines use particle-bonding technology in very different designs. The typical systems using particle-bonding technology are introduced as follows.

1. 3DP—Three-Dimensional Printing. Three-dimensional printing creates parts by a layered printing process, based on the sliced cross-sectional information [8,9]. One layer is created by deposition of a layer of powder. The powder layer is then selectively joined where the part is to be formed by "ink-jet" printing of a binder material. This process is repeated layer by layer until the part is created.

Three-dimensional printing works by building parts in layers (see Fig. 2). First, a thin distribution of powder is spread over the surface of a powder bed. From a computer model of the desired part, a slicing algorithm computes information for the layer. Using a technology similar to ink-jet printing, a binder material joins particles where the object is to be formed. A piston then lowers so that the next powder layer can be spread and selectively joined. This layer-by-layer process repeats until the part is completed. Following a heat treatment, unbound powder is removed, leaving the fabricated part.

2. SLS—Selective Laser Sintering. The SLS process creates three-dimensional objects, layer by layer, from powdered materials with heat generated by a CO_2 laser [10]. This process was developed by DTM Corporation, USA. DTM's products are the Sinterstation 2000, which is capable of producing objects measuring 12 in. in diameter by 15 in. in height, and Sinterstation 2500 whose build chamber is rectangular, 15 in. in width, 13 in. in depth, and 18 in. in height, to accommodate larger parts.

The SLS process is described in Fig. 3. The three-dimensional CAD data must be in the de facto industry standard, the STL format. As the SLS process begins, a thin layer of the heat-fusible powder is deposited onto the part-building cylinder within a process chamber. An initial cross section of the object under fabrication is selectively "drawn" on the layer of powder by a heat-generating CO_2 laser. The interaction of the laser beam with the powder elevates the temperature to the point of melting, fusing the powder particles and forming a solid mass. The intensity of the laser beam is modulated to melt the powder only in the areas defined by the object's design geometry.

An additional layer of powder is deposited via a roller mechanism on the top of the previously scanned layer. The process is repeated, with each layer fusing to the layer below it. Successive layers of powder are deposited and the

Spread Powder

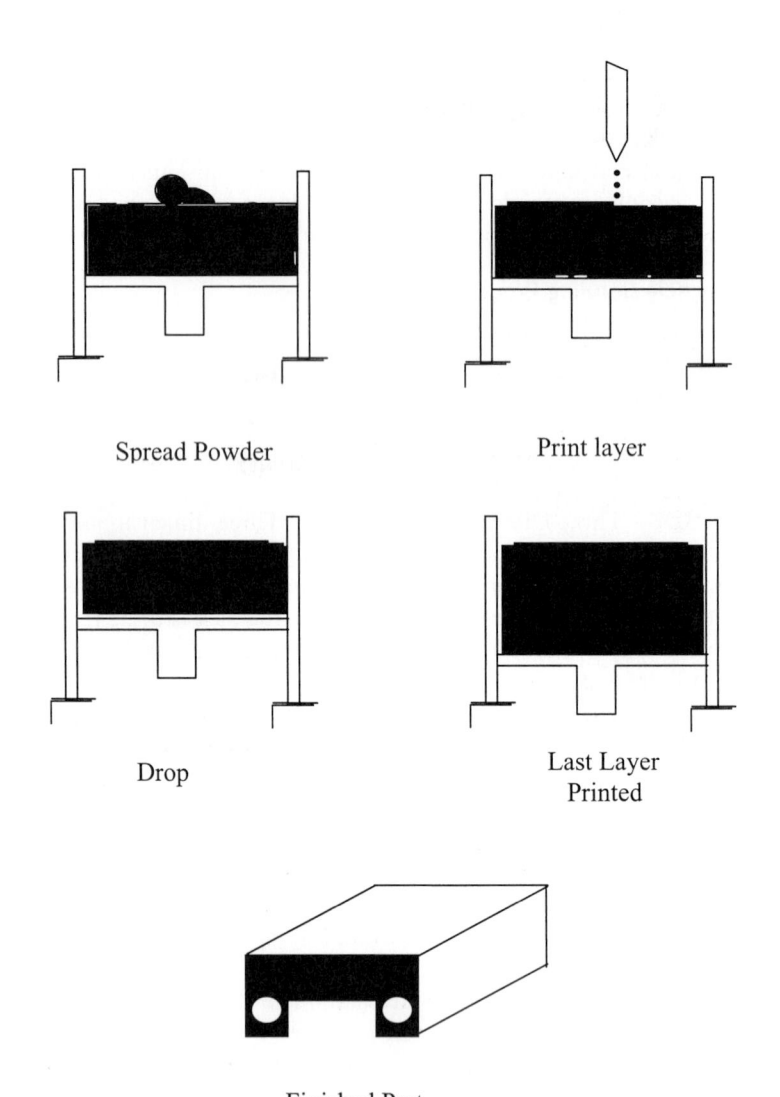

Print layer

Drop

Last Layer Printed

Finished Part

FIGURE 2 Three-dimensional printing process.

process is repeated until the part is completed. Finally, the part is removed from the build chamber, and the loose powder falls away. SLS parts may then require some post-processing, such as sanding, depending upon the application.

Sheet Lamination Processes

Sheet lamination processes are those by which layer information in the form of electronic signals is used to cut thin layers of sheet material to individual two-dimensional cross-sectional shapes. Those two-dimensional layers are bonded one upon another to form a complete three-dimensional object.

A representative sheet lamination process is the laminated object manufacturing (LOM) process, which was first developed by Helisys Inc, USA. The LOM process is an automated fabrication method in which a three-dimensional object is constructed from a solid CAD representation by sequentially

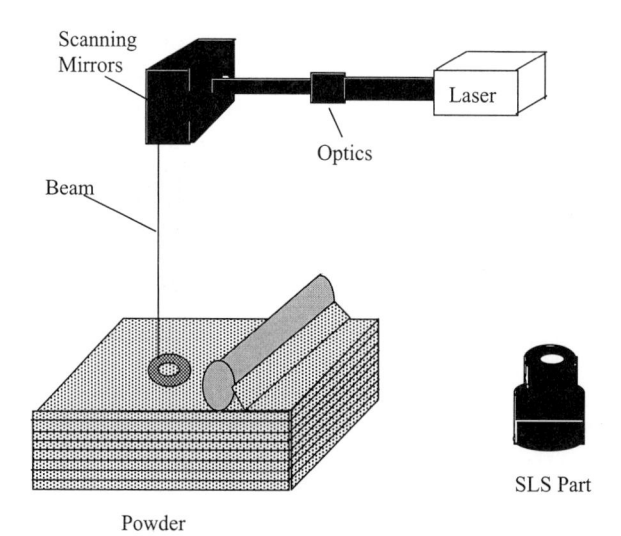

FIGURE 3 Selective laser sintering (SLS) process (with permission from Springer-Verlag).

laminating the constituent cross sections [11]. The process consists of three essential phases: preprocessing, building, and postprocessing.

The preprocessing phase encompasses several operations. The initial steps include generating an image from a CAD-derived .STL file format of the part to be manufactured, sorting input, and creating secondary data structures.

During the building phase, thin layers of adhesive-coated material are sequentially bonded to each other and individually cut by a CO_2 laser beam (see Fig. 4). The building cycle includes the following steps. Firstly, a cross section

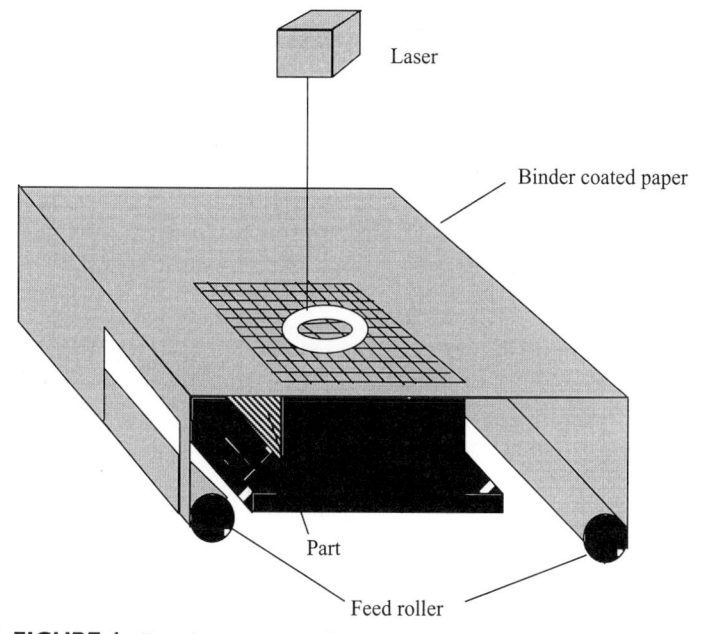

FIGURE 4 Sheet lamination manufacturing system (with permission from Springer-Verlag).

of the 3D model is created through measuring the exact height of the model and slicing the horizontal plane accordingly. Secondly, the computer generates precise calculations that guide the focused laser beam to cut the cross-sectional outline, the crosshatches, and the model's perimeter. The laser beam power is designed to cut exactly the thickness of one layer of material at a time. After that, the platform with the stack of previously formed layers descends and a new section of the material is advanced. The platform ascends and the heated roller laminates the material to the stack with a single reciprocal motion, thereby bonding it to the previous layer. Finally, the vertical encoder measures the height of the stack and replays the new height to the slicing software, which calculates the cross section for the next layer as the laser cuts the model's current layer. These procedures repeat until all layers are built.

In the final phase of the LOM process, postprocessing, the part is separated from support material. After that, if necessary, the finishing process may be performed.

Droplet Deposition Processes

Droplet deposition is a variable mass process where layer information in the form of electronic signals is used to modulate the deposition of liquid droplets in a thin layer. Successive layer formation, one atop another, forms a complex three-dimensional solid object as illustrated in Fig. 5.

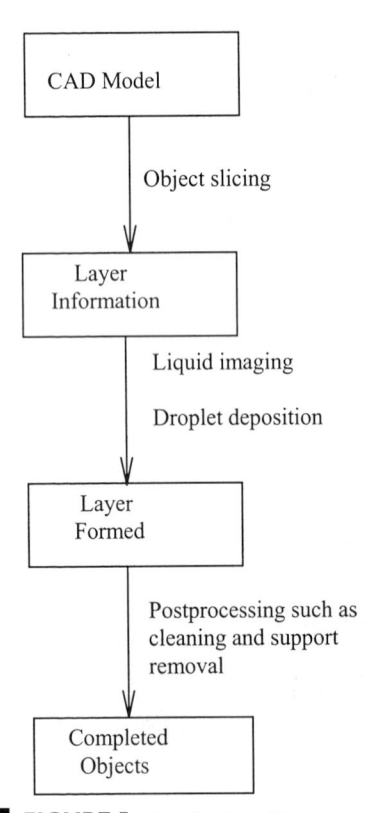

FIGURE 5 Droplet deposition process (with permission from Springer-Verlag).

The ballistic particle manufacturing (BPM) process is a typical droplet deposition process [12]. The BPM process uses three-dimensional solid model data to direct streams of material at a target. The three-dimensional objects are generated in a manner similar to that of an ink-jet printer producing two-dimensional images.

Melt Deposition Processes

Melt deposition is a variable mass process where layer information in the form of electronic signals is used to modulate the deposition of molten material in a thin layer. Successive layer formation, one atop another, forms a three-dimensional solid object.

The fused deposition modeling (FDM) process is a melted deposition fabrication process that uses the Stratasys so-called 3-D Moduler in conjunction with a CAD workstation [13,14]. The 3-D Moduler operates on the principle of a three-axis NC-machine tool. A nozzle is controlled by a computer along three axes. The nozzle guides the specific material, which is melted by heating. So the material leaves the nozzle in a liquid form, which hardens immediately at the temperature of the environment. This is realized through precise control of the temperature in the building cabinet. FDM builds the model upwards from a fixtureless base.

2. RP&M Information Processing

Rapid prototyping techniques, whether using lasers on photopolymers, particle bonding, or sheet lamination, share the common ground of quickly constructing accurate models or prototypes directly from a CAD description, under computer control. From the process principle of various RP&M techniques introduced above, it is obvious that producing parts with them requires a transformation from the geometrical description of parts into a form that can be receivable and manipulated by the particular RP&M technique.

The procedure, sometimes called information processing for RP&M, can be regarded as a generation of the computer numerical control (CNC) scanning vector from CAD models. It shows the information processing to be somewhat a reversal of the physical procedure of building the model by means of stacking a series of 2D layers together. It has been proved that the interface transferring data from the CAD to RP&M system is a very important factor because it affects the quality of the finished part and the cycle time.

The whole information processing (shown in Fig. 6) includes various manipulations with multiple types of input. One particular manipulation brings the requirements of specialized data representation, data storage, and data structure for the purpose of enhancing the reliability, improving the efficiency of algorithms, and reducing the times to access the data. Thus, various interfaces and data formats are introduced among the different phases in the procedure. However, some of the formats proposed are imperfect due to the lack of sufficient information supplied, the inclusion of errors due to the lack of data validation, the increase of the file size due to redundant information, or the difficulty of the manipulations followed. Even though these formats and data structures include internal flaws, they have been adopted so popularly since their creation that they have become de facto standards in industry. Some of those proposed

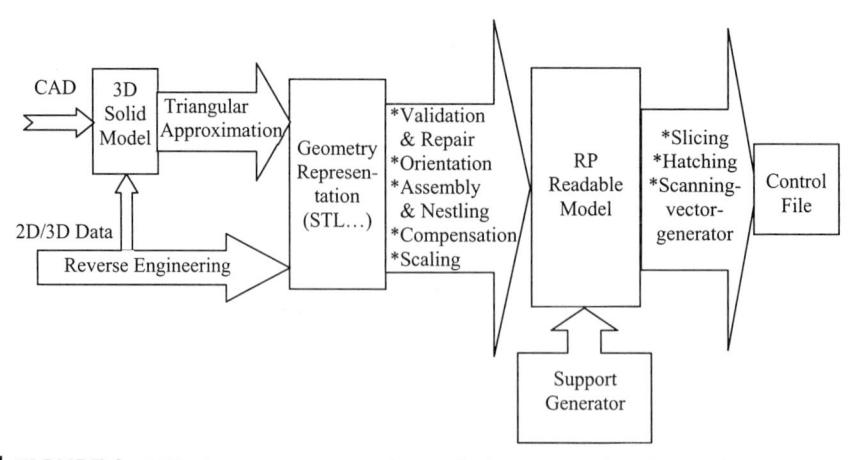

FIGURE 6 P&M information processing diagram (with permission from Springer-Verlag).

lately or to be created in the future will prove their potential as long as they overcome the existing shortcomings. In this chapter, the involved manipulations and related data structures and formats will be reviewed and discussed.

II. INTERFACES BETWEEN CAD AND RP&M

Fabrication of a physical model by RP&M requires a mathematical description of the part's geometry, which must be a solid or surface model stored in the computer. Many methods for the generation of geometric models have been developed. This kind of model can be designed and drafted by means of surface or solid modeling via commercial CAD systems which provide the application tools and commands. In other cases, although the parts already exist like human organs, limbs, or architectures, it seems impossible for designers to make a correct and detailed description in a simple way. However, nowadays various metrologies, such as CMM (Coordinate Measurement Machine), Laser Scanner, or other optical scanners, can capture the surface of the part with a cloud point set. Each point is represented by a three-dimensional coordinate (X, Y, Z). Most of the scanners like these have difficulties in measuring the inner surface of parts if the probe of the CMM or light, even including a laser, cannot touch the inside cavity because of the obstacles of the outer section of parts. In the medical imaging area, technologies including CT, MRI, PET/SPETC, X-ray, and Ultrasound are candidates for scanning three-dimensional shape data of internal and external human body structures with a series of 2-D image section planes. In order for the imaging data to be used in RP&M, they need to be converted to a 3-D geometric representation of the structures.

A. CAD Modeling

The prime purpose of a CAD system is that it should enable a designer to use the computer in his design work. While drafting-centered CAD systems could satisfy the limited requirements involved in producing engineering drawings in their first generation, it is clear that a system that allows the design to be generated in three dimensions would be more advantagious in many cases. With two-dimensional display and input devices, many attempts have been made to provide 3-D images. Since the true three-dimensional modeling first appeared in the form of a wire frame, several steps and modeling methods have been put forward. Many industrial users are now beginning to encourage the direct use of full 3-D modeling in design to replace 2-D drawings, and major benefits from complete 3-D modeling have been achieved already in many cases. However, RP&M technology requires a 3-D model of the part before building it, which makes it significant to discuss the modeling methods in CAD technology.

1. Wire-Frame Modeling

As the first tryout, the wire-frame modeling method uses lines and curves in space to represent the edges of surfaces and planes for providing a 3-D illusion of the object. When the object is displayed on a computer monitor, it appears as if wires had been strung along the edges of the object, and they are those edges being seen. So in a wire-frame modeler, entities such as lines and curves (mostly arcs) are used to connect the nodes. It is obvious that the data structure and database are relatively simple with a small amount of basic elements.

However, a wire-frame model does not have all the information about a designed object. The most obvious drawback is that such a representation includes all the "wires" necessary to construct the edge lines of every surface and feature, even if those are normally hidden from view. As a result the image is often confusing and difficult to interpret. Although it works in a limited extent, the removal of the hidden-lines involves making some assumptions regarding the nature of the nonexistent surfaces between the frames. If a wire-frame model is used to build a part by RP&M, the systems would be confused as to which side of the part should be solidified, sintered, or deposited because the frame shows no direction. Furthermore, slicing manipulation in RP&M, which cuts the 3-D model into a series of 2-D contours, would meet a large difficulty when neither plane nor surface exists in wire-frame model to intersect with the cross sections. What would be received would only a set of points instead of contours.

Partly due to the difficulties of interpreting wire-frame images and partly due to the lack of a full description of an object's information, this method has not been well utilized by industry. Therefore, a wire-frame modeler is declared not to be suitable for any commercialized RP&M systems. This brings us to the concept of surface modeling and to the next module.

2. Surface Modeling

The addition of surface patches to form the faces between the edges of a wire-frame model is an attempt to put more information about the designed object into the computer model. CAD systems that can include surfaces within the description of an object in this way are called surface modelers. Most of the surface modeling systems support surface patches generated from standard shapes such as planar facets, spheres, and circular cylinders, which is not enough to represent arbitrary shapes and thus often the case with typical parameteric surface forms such as Bezier surfaces, B-spline surfaces, and nonuniform B-spline (NURBS) surfaces.

In order to store information about the inserted surfaces, some CAD systems make use of a face list in addition to the node and entity lists. Each face list might consist of the sequence of the numbers of the entities that bound the face. The data structure is such that entities are defined as sets of nodes and faces are defined as sets of entities. For many applications, such as the aircraft industry and the design of car body shells, the ability to handle complex surface geometry, which is often called a sculptured surface for function or aesthetic reasons, is demanded. Surface modelers have sufficient sophistication in their surface types to allow these requirements to be satisfied while solid modelers are often restrictive and not needed.

Although surface modeling is simple in data organization and highly efficient, it still holds partial information about the designed object. The biggest question concerns the lack of explicit topological information, which makes certain validity checks with surface models difficult. The drawback frequently happens while using STL format as an interface between CAD and RP&M, in which the STL file can be regarded as a surface model with triangular facets to represent an object. Topological information is not provided in surface modeling to indicate how the connection is among the primitives that make up the object. Topological information may also be serviced to check the validation of data in objects. Normally, it is unnecessary for a surface model to be constrained as a close space. For RP&M application this will bring confusions as to which side is filled with material and which side is empty. Moreover, a model with open surfaces cannot be processed in RP&M. A solid modeling system is intended to hold complete information about the object being designed for that purpose.

3. Solid Modeling

Three-dimensional solid modeling is a relatively new concept for design and manufacturing, only developed in the early 1980s to overcome the limitations of early wire-frame and surface modeling CAD systems. As the name suggests, solid models provide the message as to which sections of the design space contain solid material and which sections are empty. An object is constructed from the combination of simple solid primitives with rigorously defined set operations such as union, difference, intersection, and so on. With more information including topology available in the system, it becomes possible to conduct more analysis on the design, like validation of data.

Emerging as dominant representations in commercial systems, solid modelers can usually be classified into two types: constructive solid geometry (CSG) and boundary representation (B-rep). In CSG systems, the object is built up from standard, predefined, and parameterized "primitives." Usually the primitives include truncated cones, rectangle blocks, spheres, toruses, and so on. With CSG the geometry of an object is constructed as a binary tree whose leaf nodes are oriented instances of primitives and whose nonterminal nodes are the set operations. With this type of data organization, a designer can find it a "natural" way of describing engineering parts because the brain tends to break down any complex object into simpler components and then combine them together. The user of a purely CSG system is naturally limited by the repertoire of standard primitives that is available. Many of the commercial systems provide the primitive set, consisting of a quadric surface (e.g., sphere, cylinder, cone), torus, and surfaces generated by revolving or sweeping 2D profiles. All the primitives are in closed form and can be computed with Boolean operations.

Even though the CSG modeling method maintains a large advantage in that it provides a very compact way of containing the complete information about a design, it is an implicit representation. For the slicing process in RP&M, the CSG model must be converted into a boundary representation of the solid. The same issues occur in many other applications such as finite element mesh generation.

The other usually identified approach to solid modeling is boundary representation. In B-rep, the component is stored as a collection of entities forming the boundaries of the faces, together with information about the surface patches defining those faces. In B-rep, all the faces, edges, and vertices of the faces are nodes that are connected together with arcs. The topology information of objects is explicit with the adjacency relationships. Additionally, the normal of each face in a B-rep model usually points outward of the object. The largest difference between B-rep and surface modeling is that the faces in B-rep are held in such a systematic way that the system can tell which side is within the object and which is without. Compared to a CSG structure, most B-rep modeling systems have the benefit that the information is always readily available, especially when the sequential computation is concerned.

B. Interfaces between CAD Systems

As CAD technology has evolved over more than 20 years, a lot of issues including modeling method, data technique, software/hardware upgrading, system development, and extended applications have become important. The attractive market has brought about ever-increasing commercialized systems. Normally the data structure and database are designed individually by the various system developers, which becomes an obstacle for communications between these systems. Even if the information has been generated in one of the CAD systems, it is not available for other applications as a result of inaccessible data. This urges a need for efficient storage, retrieval, and exchange of information. Many different interfaces have been developed for various systems. In order to be reliable and accepted by a wide community of both vendors and users, a standard should be stable but flexible enough to accommodate present as well as expected future developments.

1. Initial Graphics Exchange Specification (IGES)

Initial Graphics Exchange Specification (IGES) is a standard used to exchange graphics information between commercial CAD systems [15,16]. It was set up as the American National Standard in 1981. The IGES file can precisely represent CAD models. It includes four sections: Start Section, Global Section, Directory Entry Section, and Parameter Data Section.

The Start Section is designed to provide a human-readable prologue to the file. The Global Section of the file contains information describing the preprocessor and information needed by the postprocessor to handle the file. The

Directory Entry Section provides an index and contains attribute information and topological information about each entity. It also has one directory entry for each entity in the file. The Parameter Data Section of IGES contains geometrical parameter data associated with each entity.

In IGES, both constructive solid geometry and boundary representation are catered for representing models. Especially, the ways of representing the regularized operations for union, intersection, and difference have also been defined. IGES is a generally used data transfer medium between various CAD systems. It can precisely represent a CAD model. The advantages of using IGES, which include precise geometry representation, few data conversions, smaller data files, and simpler control strategies, over current approximation methods, may make it survive for a long term.

The advantages of the IGES standard are the following:

1. Since IGES was set up as the American National Standard, virtually every commercial CAD/CAM system has adopted IGES implementation.
2. It provides a wide range of entities of points, lines, arcs, splines, NURBS surfaces, and solid elements. Therefore, it can precisely represent a CAD model.

The disadvantages of the IGES standard are listed as follows:

1. Because IGES is the standard format to exchange data between CAD systems, it also includes much redundant information not needed for RP&M, such as electrical and electronic application information and architecture and construction information.
2. The algorithm for slicing an object in the IGES format is more complex than that in the STL format.
3. The support structures occasionally needed may not be easily created according to the IGES format.

2. Hewlett-Packard Graphics Language (HP/GL)

Hewlett-Packard Graphics Language (HP/GL) is a standard data format for graphic plotters [5,17]. Data types are all two-dimensional, including lines, circles, splines, and texts. The approach, as seen from a designer's point of view, would be to automate a slicing routine that generates a section slice, invokes the plotter routine to produce a plotter output file, and then loops back to repeat the process.

The advantages of the HP/GL format are listed as follows:

1. Many commercial CAD systems have the interfaces to output HP/GL formats.
2. It is a 2D geometric data format that can be directly passed to rapid prototyping and manufacturing systems without slicing.

The disadvantages of the HP/GL format include the following:

1. Because HP/GL is a 2D data format and the files would not be appended, hundreds of small files are needed to describe a model.

2. All the support structures required are generated in the CAD system and sliced in the same way before the CAD model is converted into HP/GL files.

3. Standard for the Exchange of Product Data Model (STEP)

The standard for the exchange of product data model, STEP, is a new engineering product data exchange standard that is documented as ISO 10303 [18]. The aim of STEP is to produce a single and better standard to cover all aspects of the product life cycle in all industries. European Action on Rapid Prototyping (EARP) is working on using STEP as a tool for data transfer from CAD to 3D layer manufacturing systems [19].

The reasons why STEP is recommended to be used as the interface between CAD and RP&M are given as follows:

1. It will be an international standard format to exchange product data and be supported by all CAD systems.
2. Since it is a complete representation of products for data exchange, the information in STEP is enough for the data exchange from CAD to 3D layer manufacturing systems.
3. It is efficient in both the file size and computer resources needed for processing.
4. It is independent of hardware and software.

However, STEP still has some disadvantages as the interface between CAD and RP&M.

1. It still carries much redundancy information that may be not necessary to RP&M.
2. New interpreters and algorithms must be developed to transfer data to rapid prototyping and manufacturing systems.

4. CT/MRI Data

One of the important application areas of RP&M is in medical, especially for complex surgery diagnosis, planning, simulation, and implantation. Computerized tomography (CT) scan data is one approach for medical imaging [20]. This is not standardized data. Formats are proprietary and somewhat unique from one CT scanning machine to another. The scanner generates data as a grid of three-dimensional points, where each point has a varying shade of gray indicating the density of the body tissue found at that particular point.

Originally, the models coming from the CT scan are produced using thin plates of aluminum cut according to contours on CT scans and stacked to obtain the model. Simultaneously, molds are used to make prostheses or implants in biocompatible materials. Later, CNC machines are introduced to make these models. However, these processes have reached the limits of the technique such as limited resolution and others. RP&M is very suitable for the layer-by-layer information from a CT scanner. It is possible to produce structures of human bodies by RP&M systems through interfacing the CT data to them. However, converting CT data to rapid prototyping and manufacturing systems is much more difficult than converting the STL format. A special interpreter is needed to process CT data. Currently, there are three approaches to make models out of CT scan information: through CAD systems, STL interfacing, and direct interfacing [20]. Besides a CT scanner, MRI (magnetic resonance imaging), ultrasound imaging, X-ray imaging, etc. may all be tools to generate the layered images that represent the human organs and also can be reconstructed into what they represent. Recently, the most successful reverse engineering cases that build human parts by RP&M with the layered image data are from a CT or MRI scanner.

C. Interface between CAD and RP&M: STL Format

1. STL File

The STL file, introduced by 3D Systems, is created from the CAD database via an interface to CAD systems [5,21,22]. It is a polyhedral model derived from a precise CAD model by a process called tessellation. This file consists of an unordered list of triangular facets representing the outside skin of an object. The STL has two file formats, ASCII format and binary format. The size of an ASCII STL file is larger than that of the same binary format file but is human readable. In a STL file, triangular facets are described by a set of X, Y, and Z coordinates for each of the three vertices and a unit normal vector to indicate the side of the facet that is inside the object as shown in Fig. 7.

The following is a facet representation as an example trimmed from an STL file that consists of a series of similar facets.

solid Untitled1
facet normal 9.86393923E-01   1.64398991E-01   0.00000000E+00
    outer loop
        vertex 9.73762280E-01   7.40301994E-01   1.35078953E+00
        vertex 1.00078931E+00   5.78139828E-01   1.35078953E+00
        vertex 1.00078931E+00   5.78139828E-01   3.50789527E-01
    endloop
endfacet
...

The accuracy level of a facet model represented by the STL format is controlled by the number of facets representing the model. Higher part accuracy

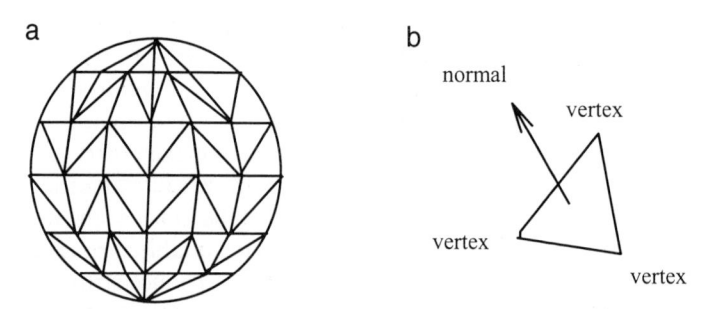

FIGURE 7 Facet model: (a) Triangular representation and (b) single facet (with permission from Springer-Verlag).

requires higher resolution on the tessellation of the CAD model. However, higher tessellating resolution means longer processing time, more and smaller triangles, and larger file size.

2. The Advantages and Problems of the STL Format

The STL format is widely used by many 3D layer manufacturing systems because of its advantages. They are the following:

   1. It is a simple solid model. The STL format provides a simple method of representing 3D CAD models. It contains only low-level vertex information and no high-level information such as splines and NURBS curves or surfaces in the boundary representation.
   2. It is independent. The STL file is a neutral file. It is independent of not only specific CAD systems but also 3D layer manufacture processes.
   3. It has been widely used. It is a *de facto* industry standard and has been implemented by most CAD systems and accepted by most 3D layer manufacturing systems.
   4. It can provide small and accurate files for data transfer of certain shapes.

However, problems still exist in the STL [23,24]. They are given as follows:

   1. It carries much redundant information. A STL file is many times larger than the original CAD data file for a given accuracy parameter. It contains redundant information such as duplicate vertices and edges as shown in Fig. 8.
   2. It is not information rich. The STL file only describes the coordinates of vertices in a triangle and the normal of the triangle. Little topological information is available. This is one reason why a long slicing time is needed.
   3. Cracks or holes exist in the facet models. The STL file format describes a CAD model solid by its surface; i.e., the solid is defined by a closed shell. The open shell means that cracks and holes exist in the model as shown in Fig. 9.
   4. Nonmanifold topology is encountered in the STL file. The tessellation of fine features is susceptible to rounding off errors, which leads to nonmanifold topology of the part where more than two facets share a single edge (Fig. 10a), or facets in different cycles meet at a single vertex (Fig. 10b).
   5. An incorrect facet normal may not be absolutely avoided. The problem of incorrect normals happens where two adjacent triangles indicate that the mass of the object is on opposite sides, as shown in Fig. 11.
   6. Facets may overlap. Overlapping may occur when one facet intersects another, or the same edge may be shared by more than two facets as illustrated in Fig. 12.

3. Verification and Validation

Except for the flaws of redundant information and incomplete representation, all the problems mentioned previously would be difficult for slicing

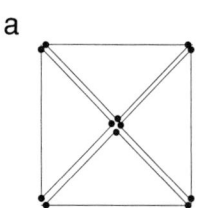

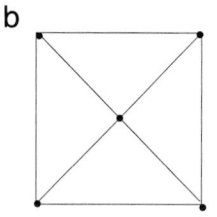

FIGURE 8 Edge and vertex redundancy in the STL file: (a) Duplicate edges and vertices in an STL file and (b) coincident edges and vertices are stored only once (with permission from Springer-Verlag).

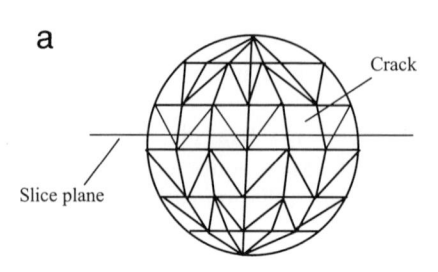

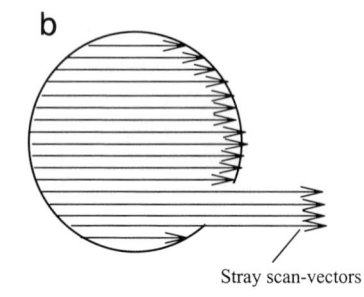

FIGURE 9 Cracks in the STL causes lasers to produce stray scan vectors: (a) Facet model with a crack and (b) cross-sectional view of a slice (with permission from Springer-Verlag).

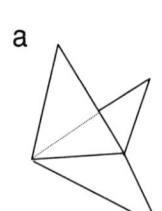

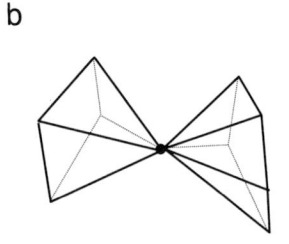

FIGURE 10 (a) Correct and (b) incorrect orientation (with permission from Springer-Verlag).

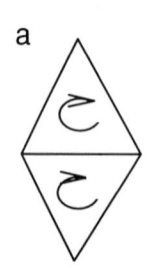

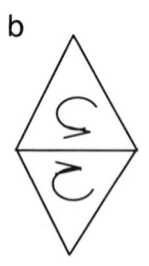

FIGURE 11 (a) Correct and (b) incorrect normal (with permission from Springer-Verlag).

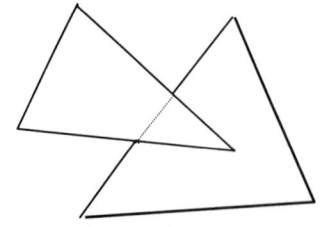

FIGURE 12 Overlapping facets in the STL file (with permission from Springer-Verlag).

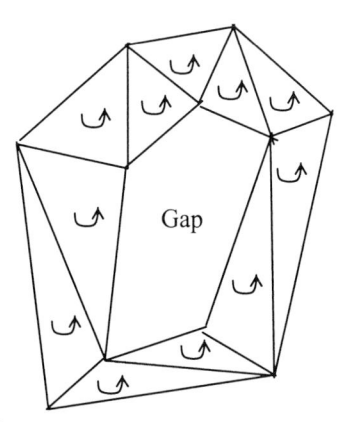

FIGURE 13 A representation of a portion of a tessellated surface with a gap present (with permission from Springer-Verlag).

algorithms to handle and would cause failure for RP&M processes which essentially require a valid tessellated solid as input. Moreover, these problems arise because tessellation is a first-order approximation of more complex geometric entities. Thus, such problems have becomes almost inevitable as long as the representation of the solid model is made using the STL format, which inherently has these limitations.

Instead of canceling the non-error-free STL format, many efforts have been made to find out the invalidation within a STL file and repair the faceted geometric model [23–26] generalizing all STL-files-related errors and proposing a generic solution to solve the problem of missing facets and wrong orientations. The basic approach of the algorithm would be to detect and identify the boundaries of all the gaps in the model. The basis for the working is due to the fact that in a valid tessellated model, there must be only two facets sharing every edge. If this condition is not fulfilled, then this indicates that there are some missing facets, which cause gaps in STL files. Figure 13 gives an example of such a case. Once the boundaries of a gap are identified, suitable facets would then be generated to repair and "patch up" the gaps. The size of the generated facets would be restricted by the gap's boundaries while the orientation of its normal would be controlled through comparing it with the rest of the shell. This is to ensure that the generated facet orientation is correct and consistent throughout the gap closure process, as shown in Fig. 14.

Some RP&M system vendors have built up the functions inside their data processing software, like SGC from Qubical, Israel. In the multifunctional Rapid prototyping system (MRPS) developed by Tsinghua University, China, topological information is generated through reading an STL file. This information is not only useful for data checking and validation, but also helpful for shortening the time on slicing with an upgraded algorithm, by which it becomes unnecessary for searching all the facets in the file when slicing one layer.

Besides RP&M vendors, several software companies supply products based on STL format. Many functions include generation, visualization, manipulation, support generation, repair, and verification of STL files. Materialise

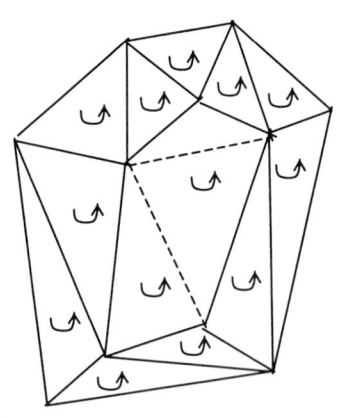

FIGURE 14 A repaired surface with facets generated to patch up the gap (with permission from Springer-Verlag).

(Belgium) provides almost all the operations in the Magic module and is popularly spread across the RP&M world. Imageware (MI, USA) offers its users several competitive advantages for the creation, modification, and verification of polygonal models. It begins every prototyping process by allowing the import and export of IGES, STL, DXF, ASCII, VRML, SLC, and 3D measurement data.

D. Proposed Standard: Layer Manufacturing Interface (LMI)

In the past, most of the RP&M systems are used to produce prototypes for visualization and verification. Now, it is expected that these technologies would be used to produce tooling, production, and functional components as well. As seen in the previous section, there is a need for improving the current *de facto* industry standard for RP&M, or STL format. This section, in which a new edge-based flexible interface, LMI, is proposed to meet the requirements of RP&M processes [27,28], will give a detailed view of how the data structure technique is applied in engineering. The LMI format supports not only faceted solids but also precise solids represented by boundary representation. Design considerations of the LMI format will be discussed first. Before the data structure of the new format is presented, the basic concepts and principles of boundary representation and the topological issues are introduced. This data structure will be mapped into the file of the LMI format, and a geometrical description of the LMI format is presented. Finally, a comparison between the STL format and the LMI format is discussed.

1. Design Considerations

The design considerations must be carefully examined to allow a smooth flow of data from CAD systems to RP&M processes. In addition, CAD solid modeling and RP&M are two expanding fields. Any attempts to specify a standard interface must take these expansions into account. The following requirements are considered in the design of LMI.

1. Facet modeling should be supported. The facet model as used in the STL format is accepted by nearly all RP&M systems. The STL file is, so far, the most common way to send a CAD model to rapid prototyping and manufacturing systems because it is a simple representation of the CAD model and is able to be generated by most CAD systems. Therefore, the newly proposed format should support the facet model. The optimization of the facet model (STL file) is necessary in the new format to avoid defects in the STL format. The improvements and intended improvements of the LMI format are given as follows:

- Add topological information. In the STL format, only unordered vertices with facet normals are provided to describe the faceted models. A vertex is the simplest geometric entity that contains little topological information. In the LMI format, the topological information is supplied by adding new geometric entities and topological data that refer to the topological relations between geometric entities.
- Remove redundant information. The STL file consists of a lot of unnecessary repeated information such as sets of coordinates and strings of text. Normals in the STL can also be omitted because they can be derived from other information.
- Repair errors existing in the STL format like cracks, nonmanifold topology, and overlaps.

2. Support precise models. With increasing experience in data transfer between CAD systems and 3D layer manufacturing systems, it is obvious that preservation of geometric accuracy and geometric intent is important. The problems occur especially with high-accuracy downstream processes such as slicing and high-accuracy machines. Therefore, the LMI format should support precise models.

3. Be flexible and extensible. Because CAD technology, especially solid modeling, and RP&M are two developing areas, flexibility and extensibility of the interface between CAD and 3D layer manufacturing systems must be considered to meet future needs.

4. Be relatively easy to be implemented and used. The format should be easy to be created robustly by CAD systems and processed in the downstream slicing process.

5. Be unambiguous. The LMI format should not contain ambiguous information.

6. Be independent of computer platforms and rapid prototyping and manufacturing processes and commercial systems. This format should be a neutral file so that it can be created by commercial CAD systems.

7. Be as compact as possible. The LMI format should not contain redundant information that would make a file unnecessarily large.

2. Boundary Representation

Geometric modeling techniques have evolved considerably over the past 20 years, embodying more and more information about the physical shape of the objects that they model. A variety of representational forms for solid models have been developed. Each form has strengths and weaknesses in the context of various applications. One approach to classifying solid modeling has been developed by Weiler [29]. Solid modeling representations can be classified based

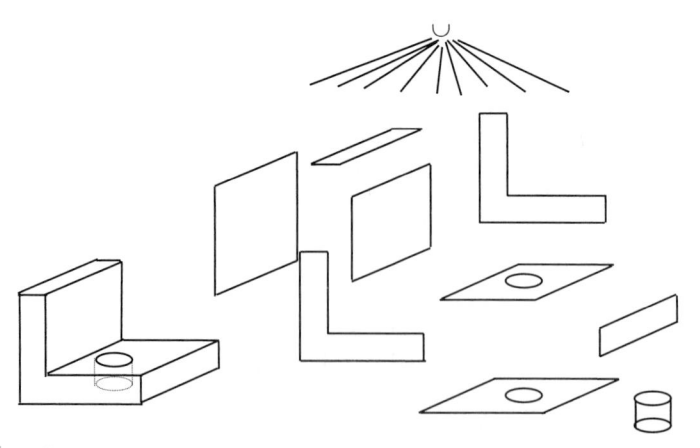

FIGURE 15 Boundary representation (with permission from Springer-Verlag).

on three independent criteria: boundary based (B-rep modeling) or volume based (CSG modeling), object based or spatially based, and evaluated or unevaluated. A representation is boundary based (B-rep, see Fig. 15) if the solid volume is specified by its surface boundary; a representation is volume based (CSG, see Fig. 16) if the solid is specified directly by its volumetric primitives. A representation is object based if it is fundamentally organized according to the characteristics of the actual solid shape; a representation is spatially based if it is organized around the characteristics of the spatial coordinate system it uses. The evaluated and unevaluated characterizations are roughly a measure of the amount of work necessary to obtain information about the objects being represented.

Boundary representation is one of the earliest and widely used geometric modeling techniques. In boundary representation, an object is defined by its boundary that contains a set of entities, such as faces, edges, and vertices embedded in 3D Euclidean space. This boundary divides the space into two distinct volumes, the inside and the outside. The information for boundary representation has two parts, topological and geometric. The geometric information is about dimensions and locations of entities in space. The topological information is the connectivity (or adjacency) information between entities on

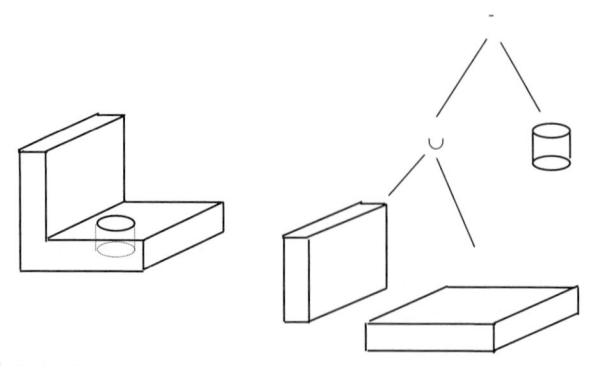

FIGURE 16 CSG representation (with permission from Springer-Verlag).

the boundary. The topological structure in a representation can simplify the application algorithms and greatly improve their efficiency.

3. Data Structure of LMI Format

Any representation requires a domain that contains the complete set of possibilities for which it is valid. It must be carefully specified because it is a key factor affecting the representation. A series of specifications on the geometric and topological domains of the data structure of the LMI format are described as follows.

- *Edge-based boundary representation.* The modified winged-edge structure, and edge-based B-rep, is applied as a representation of the solid object, where a solid is an arcwise-connected set of closed finite regions of space.
- *Compact, oriented two-manifold.* The surfaces of the solids in the data structure are of the solid compact, oriented two manifolds. This implies that the faces that self-intersect or intersect with each other are allowed, forcing the adjacency topology to carry explicitly all surface intersection information through adjacency information. The capability of orientation guarantees that the interior of a solid volume is distinguishable from its exterior.

The boundary solid representation by the data structure of the LMI format uses a graph of edges and is embedded into a compact, oriented two-manifold surface. The embedded graph divides the surface into arcwise-connected regions called faces. The edges and vertices therefore form boundaries for each face in the solid.

- *No restriction on the genus.* There is no restriction on the genus of the modeled object or on the number of interior voids it may have.
- *Pseudographs.* Pseudographs mean multigraphs and may contain self-loops, which are allowed. Self-loops are edges that have the same vertex at either end, and multigraphs are graphs where multiple edges share the same two vertices as end points.
- *Multiply connected.* Faces may be multiply connected; that is, they may have more than one boundary, such as the case of a face with a hole in it.
- *Labeled graph.* All graph elements are labeled. Therefore, each entity in the graph has a unique identity. As the result, nongeometric information to be associated with entities is allowed.

The modified winged-edge data structure, one of the B-rep data structures, is used in the LMI format to represent topological information of entities. The facet representation is a special case of the general B-rep in which polygonal planar regions are used to define the model boundary [30]. The data structure for a triangular faced model is shown in Fig. 17. When the model is a triangular faceted model, the adjacent relationships to be stored are simpler than those for general cases because of triangle characteristics. The adjacent relationship of the topological entities for the facet model is illustrated in Fig. 18.

The data structure of the facet model in the LMI format represents the edge adjacency information as a single unified structure of the modified winged-edge data structure. However, the topological information stored in this structure only consists of the adjacencies of the reference edge with other vertices and

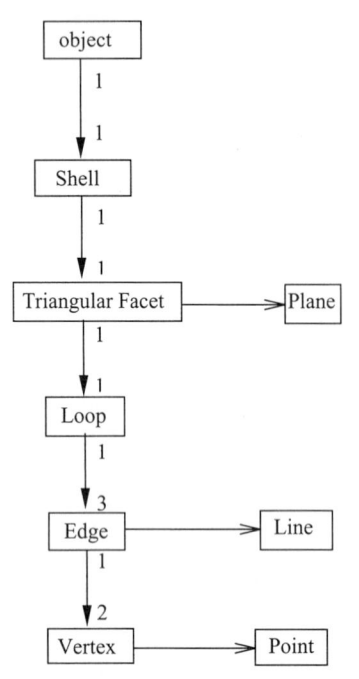

FIGURE 17 Data structure of the facet model in the LMI format (with permission from Springer-Verlag).

facets. The data structure depicted in Fig. 18 will be mapped into the LMI format file.

From the topological viewpoint, the facet modeling technique (indicating triangular facet model) models the simplest solids that have a closed oriented surface and no holes or interior voids. Each facet is bounded by a single loop of adjacent vertices and edges; that is, the facet is homeomorphic to a closed disk. Therefore the number of vertices V, edges E, and facets F of the solid satisfy

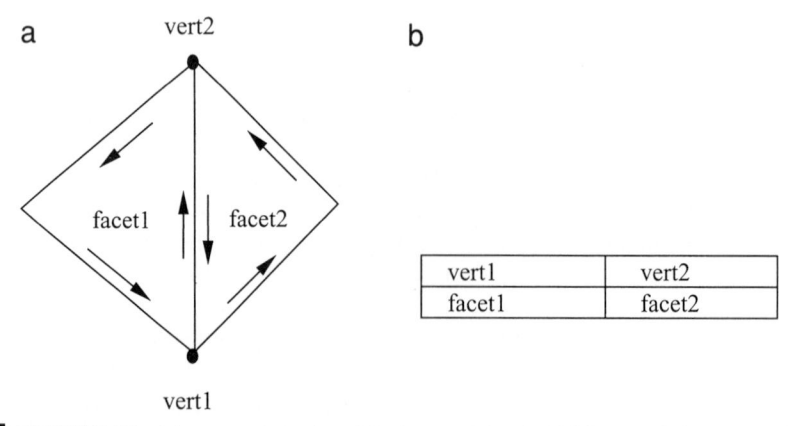

FIGURE 18 Adjacency relationship of the facet model in the LMI format: (a) diagram and (b) storage allocation description (see also Fig. 19).

the Euler formula

$$V - E + F = 2. \tag{1}$$

This fact can be used to check the correctness of the faceted model, especially for checking errors such as cracks or holes and nonmanifolds.

4. Description of LMI Format

The LMI format is a universal format for the input of geometry data to model fabrication systems based on RP&M. It is suitable for systems using the layer-wise photocuring of resin, sintering, or binding of powder, the cutting of sheet material solidification of molten material, and any other systems that build models on a layer-by-layer basis.

The LMI format can represent both the precise model and the triangular faceted model derived from the STL file. It can be divided into two parts: header and geometry.

In B-rep, the fundamental unit of data in the file is the entity. Entities are categorized as geometric or nongeometric. Geometric entities represent the physical shapes and include vertices, faces, edges, surfaces, loops, and facets. The nongeometric entity is the transformation matrix entity. All geometrical entities are defined in a three-dimensional Cartesian coordinate system called the model coordinate system. The entity is defined by a series of parameters based on a local coordinate system and a transformation matrix entity to transfer entity to the model coordinate system if needed. The parameterized expression of a general entity is given as

$$(x, y, z) = (X(u, v), Y(u, v), Z(u, v)) \begin{bmatrix} a_{11} & a_{12} & a_{13} & a_{14} \\ a_{21} & a_{22} & a_{23} & a_{24} \\ a_{31} & a_{32} & a_{33} & a_{34} \\ a_{41} & a_{42} & a_{43} & a_{44} \end{bmatrix}. \tag{2}$$

In facet modeling, vertices, edges, and facets are the three fundamental entities. Transformation matrices are unnecessary in the facet model. Therefore, the LMI format includes four sections for a facet model. Each section, except for the Header Section, starts with a keyword specifying the entity type in the section and an integer number specifying the number of the entities in the section. In the section, the data of an entity are a record. The section is ended by two words END and a keyword that is the same as the keyword at the beginning of the section. The four sections in the LMI format are Header, Vertex, Edge, and Facet.

The Header Section is a unique nongeometry section in the LMI file and designed to provide a human readable prologue to the file. The Vertex Section includes geometrical information of all vertices in the facet model. Each vertex is defined by its coordinates in 3D space. The Edge Section is a major section for an edge-based B-rep modeling. It not only gives the geometrical information about all the edges but also contains adjacency relationships between entities. In facet modeling, it contains the information of the adjacent relationship of edges and facets as well as edges and vertices. The Facet Section is a collection of all facets in the facet model. The facet is defined by the edge indices.

a

| vertex-index |
| x, y, z |

b
```
typedef struct vertex
{
  int vertex_index;
  double x, y, z;
} Vertex;
```

FIGURE 19 Vertex entity description: (a) Storage allocation and (b) C declaration.

Header Section

The Header Section is designed as a prologue for the file. It consists of a series of keywords and numbers. The keyword defines the item name and the number defines the item by the number.

VERSION: X.X specifies the LMI file format version number.
UNIT: INCH/MM indicates by which kind of units LMI data are represented.
SOLID: SOLIDNAME specifies the solid object name that is given by the user.
LIMITS: MINX, MAXX, MINY, MAXY, MINZ, MAXZ describe the X, Y and Z limitations of the CAD model respectively.

Vertex Section

The Vertex Section consists of X, Y, and Z coordinates for all vertices in the facet model. A vertex is a record. Figure 19 shows the vertex entity description. The content of the Vertex Section in a LMI format file is given as follows:

Vertices: number of the vertices
No.	X-coordinate	Y-coordinate	Z-coordinate
1	9.547921e+01	0.0000000e+00	0.000000e+00
2	7.104792e+02	4.5000000e+00	0.000000e+00

...

End Vertices

Edge Section

The Edge Section in the LMI format provides information of all the edges in a facet model. Each edge includes an edge index, two vertex indices, and two facet indices associated with it. Each edge is composed of two half-edges that have directions according to the vertices of the edges, vert1→vert2 associated with facet1 and vert2→vert1 associated with facet2 as shown in Fig. 20.

a

edge-index	
vert1	vert2
facet1	facet2

b
```
typedef struct edge
{
  int edge-index;
  int vert1, vert2;
  int facet1, facet2;
} Edge;
```

FIGURE 20 Edge entity description: (a) Storage allocation and (b) C declaration.

RAPID PROTOTYPING AND MANUFACTURING 393

a

facet-index
half_edge1
half_edge2
half_edge3

b

```
typedef struct facet
{
  int facet_index;
  int half_edge1,
      half_edge2,
      half_edge3;
}Facet;
```

FIGURE 21 Facet entity description: (a) Storage allocation and (b) C declaration.

Facet Section

The Facet Section of the LMI facet model is used to define facets in the model. Each facet is composed of three half-edges. Each half-edge is specified by the edge index and the edge side according to facet fields in the edge, facet field facet1 associated with the half-edge vert1→vert2 and facet2 with the half-edge vert2→vert1. These half-edges are arranged based on the right-hand screw rule. Figure 21 shows the facet entity description.

5. Comparison of the LMI Format with the STL format

It is necessary to make the LMI format and STL format exchangeable. A translator to convert data from STL to LMI needs to be independent of computer platforms and can be implemented on both PCs and workstations. The algorithm used by the translator is shown in Fig. 22. First, a STL file is opened but not fully read in. Otherwise, much space is needed to store a STL file. Then read the data for a facet and compare them with the existing data. After that, the topological relationship between this facet and the other facets is obtained, and the new entities like edges and facets are created and stored. These steps are repeated until the end of the file. Finally, output the LMI format.

In the algorithm, vertex, edge, and facet entities are stored in three link-lists respectively. The functions of operating link-lists, such as, comparing, searching, adding, and others, are needed.

The conversion capability has been developed, allowing the LMI format file to be generated from CAD data or the STL format. The LMI format offers a number of features that are unavailable in the STL format. The comparison between the LMI format and the STL format will be based on the following two aspects: storage and slicing algorithms.

After generating the LMI facet model from STL format data, the topology has been constructed from an unordered STL model facet. The work is done using ASCII format files. The comparison still remains valid for binary formats, because the binary and the ASCII files are identical in contents. Let the number of facets in the facet model be F, the number of edges be E, and the number of vertices be V. For the objects homeomorphic to a sphere, that is, its genus is 0, the Euler formula is

$$V - E + F = 2. \tag{3}$$

Assuming that an edge consists of two half-edges, a facet is composed of three

Routine begin

Open a STL file.

If it is not the end of the file

    Read data for a facet.

    For each of the three vertices
        Check if the vertex exists.
        If exists
            Retrieve the pointer to the vertex.
        Else
            Create and store pointer.
        end if.

    For each of the three pointers to vertices
        Check if an edge exists between each pair of the vertices.
        If exists
            Retrieve the edge pointer.
        Else
            Create and store the edge.
        end if

    Create the facet with the three edge pointers.

Else

    Output the LMI format file.

end if

End the routine.

FIGURE 22 Algorithm translating the STL format to the LMI format.

half-edges. Then

$$F = 3^*(1/2E) = 3/2E. \qquad (4)$$

For the STL format, each triangle is described by a set of X, Y, and Z coordinates for each of the three vertices. Each coordinate is a double-precision value that requires eight bytes. Therefore, the size of the storage used to describe a facet in the STL format requires 72 bytes (3 vertices × 3 doubles/vertex × 8 bytes/double). Hence, the total size of triangles in the STL file is $72F$, not including normal description and other characters for specification. Then

$$S_s = 72F. \qquad (5)$$

For the LMI format, all vertices are described by three coordinates in the Vertex Section. The edges and facets are described respectively in the Edge Section and Facet Section by index values. An index value usually requires two bytes. Therefore, referring to Fig. 19, Fig. 20, and Fig. 21, the sizes of Vertex Section, Edge Section, and Facet Section are $26V$ bytes (2 bytes + 3 vertices × 8 bytes/vertex), $10E$ (2 bytes + 2 edges × 2 bytes/edge + 2 facet × 2 bytes/edge), and $8F$ (2 bytes + 3 edges × 2 bytes/edge) respectively. Therefore, the total size of

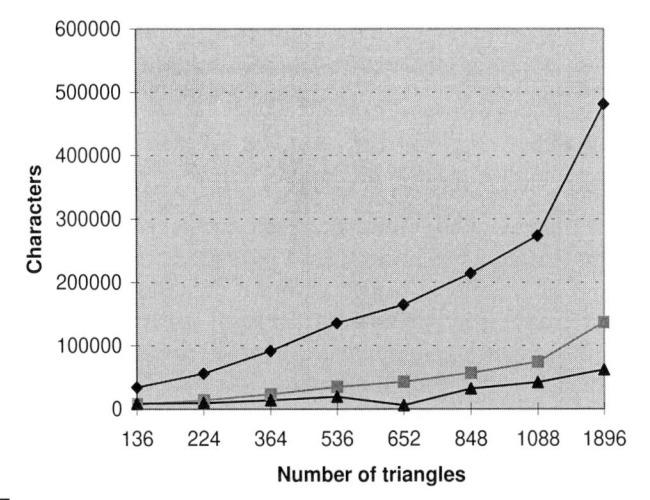

FIGURE 23 Comparison of sizes of STL (♦) and LMI (■) format files. ▲, B-rep model.

the LMI facet model is

$$S_L = 26V + 10E + 8F. \tag{6}$$

Replacing V with formula (3) and E with formula (4), then

$$S_L = 36F + 52. \tag{7}$$

Compare formula (7) with (5):

$$S_L/S_S = 36F/72F + 52/72F = 1/2 + 13/18F. \tag{8}$$

For the simplest solid object, the tetrahedron, $F = 4$. However, usually, it is much larger. Therefore, the size of the facet model in the LMI format is almost half the size of the STL format. However, the real size of the LMI format file is almost one-fourth of the size of the STL format file as shown in Fig. 23.

Figure 23 shows the comparison of the file size of STL format files with the size of corresponding LMI format files. As illustrated in the graph, the file sizes of both STL facet models and LMI facet models increase with the increase in the number of triangles. However, the size of the B-rep model only depends on the complexity of the part; it is not related to the number of triangles. In addition, not only do both the sizes of the STL and LMI facet models increase with the number of the triangles, but also the size of the LMI format is always about one-fourth of the size of the STL format when the same part has the same number of triangles. This is because there is still much other redundant information in the STL file like normal and text.

III. SLICING

Rapid prototyping relies on "slicing" a 3-dimensional computer model to get a series of cross sections that can then be made individually, typically 0.1–0.5 mm in intervals. Slicing is the process of intersecting the model with planes parallel to the platform in order to obtain the contours. There are various ways to make the slices, each of which has its own advantages and limitations.

A. Direct Slicing of a CAD File

In RP&M, direct slicing refers to slicing the original CAD model. In this way, one obtains the contours without using an intermediary faceted model such as an STL file. Direct slicing has many benefits besides avoiding an intermediary representation. One important benefit is that it makes it possible to use techniques embedded in the application program that results in parts that exhibit a better surface finish, which comes from a better precise contour sliced with the exact CAD model. The computation involves a geometry of the part designed of higher order than that of its triangular description. An approach has been proposed by Guduri *et al.* [31,32] to directly slice a model based on constructive solid geometry (CSG). In the process the primitives in the CSG assembly are sliced individually, generating a cross section for each primitive. The whole contour in the sliced layer is then calculated through combining the primitive slices based on the same Boolean operations as what connects amongst the primitives. The contour of the part in each layer is a collection of piecewise continuous curves. A similar method for manipulating CAD parts in a B-rep or surface model has been introduced. No matter which modeling method is used, the contour finding is realized through solving the degraded equations. For common quadric surfaces (sphere, cones, torus, and ellipsoids), the surface–plane intersection calculation is exact by neglecting the round-off error. For example, the description equation for the boundary of a sphere is listed as

$$X^2 + Y^2 + Z^2 = R^2, \tag{9}$$

where X, Y, Z represent the coordinates of a point on the surface of the sphere that is centered at the original point $(0,0,0)$ with a radius of R.

A given plane with height h_i that is adopted to slice the sphere could be generalized as

$$Z = h_i. \tag{10}$$

For computing the intersection of the sphere and plane, it is just needed to replace Z in (9) with Eq. (10). The result is then

$$X^2 + Y^2 = R^2 - h_i^2, \tag{11}$$

which shows the intersection is a planar circle described by a definite formulation, which is more compact and accurate than an approximate representation. For other surface catalogues, the method requires an approximation of the slice contour of the primitive. Such an approximation is still much more accurate and efficient than the linear approximations obtained from a faceted model.

It is obvious that this intersection calculation method overdepends upon the knowledge of geometric representation in individual CAD systems. Slicing, on the other hand, requires very good process knowledge and is dependent on a user's specification. It also alters the relationship between the user and the manufacturer. Therefore, slicing should be carried out by an expert normally located at the manufacturing site instead of CAD vendors or RP&M users. This

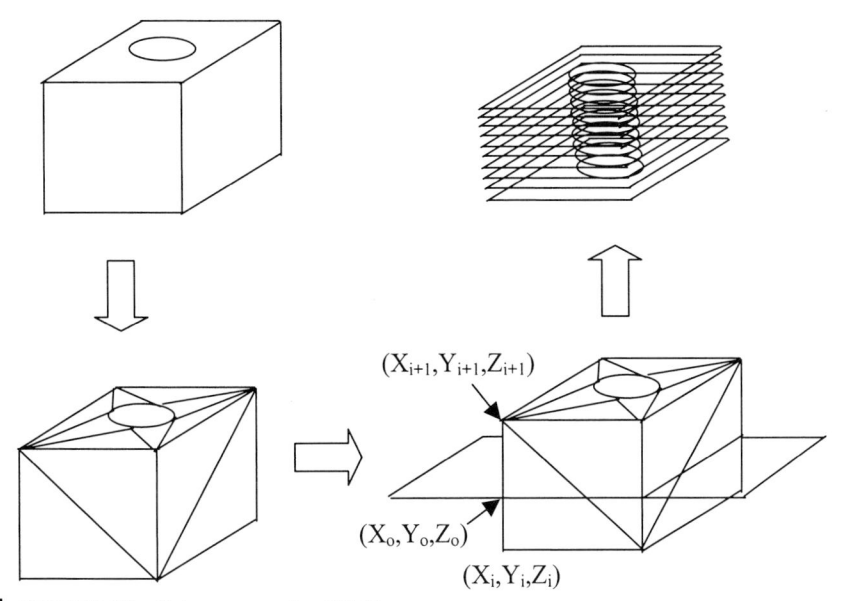

FIGURE 24 Slicing process of an STL file.

relationship will bring to RP&M many of the problems that could be avoided by using a data exchange interface between incompatible CAD and RP&M systems. However, an STL file can be generated so easily by users with little or even no knowledge of the RP&M process that many efforts have been made to slice an STL file.

B. Slicing an STL File

The operation of an STL file is classified as an indirect slice as the result of the difference from slicing with a CAD model. Figure 24 illustrates the procedure of the operation. The triangular facet used in the STL format simplifies the calculations further, since each facet is exactly convex. Mathematically, determining the intersection of a triangular facet and a slicing plane reduces to computing the intersection of the slicing plane with each of the three line segments that define the triangular facets. If the coordinates of the facet vertices are denoted $(X_i, Y_i, Z_i, i = 1, \ldots, 3)$ and the slicing plane is given by $Z = Z_o$, where Z_o is the height of the slicing plane, then the coordinates of the intersection point are obtained by solving the equation

$$\frac{Z_o - Z_i}{Z_{i+1} - Z_i} = \frac{X_o - X_i}{X_{i+1} - X_i} = \frac{Y_o - Y_i}{Y_{i+1} - Y_i}, \tag{12}$$

where (X_o, Y_o, Z_o) are the coordinates of the intersection point. Normally there will be two such intersection points for each slicing plane. These intersection points are then assembled in the proper order to produce the approximate planar contour of the part. It is obvious that the result from slicing a STL file is only polygonal contours in terms of a series of loops at each layer. Each loop is described by listing the vertices that compose the loop, and ordered according to the right-hand rule (ccw for outer loops and cw for inner loops). This approach may meet some special cases, namely degenerated facets, where a vertex, edge, or entire facet lie in the slicing plane, so that the algorithm should be robust enough to handle them.

C. Slicing an LMI File

Anyway, the random method mentioned above is not efficient since to generate each contour segment during the march is to intersect sequentially each facet with the slicing plane without considering whether the intersection may happen. The performance can be improved by utilizing topological information. Rock and Wozny [33] and Crawford et al. [34] have implemented another approach to the slicing facets model based on abstraction of the topological message from the input file and explicitly representation of adjacenct facets through a face–edge–vertex structure. The enhanced method utilizes the edge information and generates contours by marching from edge to edge. Each edge must reference its two vertices and the two facets that define the edge. Each facet must reference its neighboring faces and three edges. The method saves time on searching for the sequential facet to be sliced while other irrelevant facets are put aside untouched temporarily during current slicing. Given Rock's test case performance, it is clear that the slicing algorithm enables it as an on-line operation at the process controller during building.

The slicing of a LMI file is a topological information-based method. It is briefly described using a flow chart in Fig. 25.

Compare the slicing algorithm based on the STL format and that on the LMI format in terms of complexity:

$$\text{Complexity of the STL-based algorithm} = S^*n + S^*p, \qquad (13)$$

where S is the number of slices, n the number of facets in the model, and p the average number of points in each slice.

The algorithm in Fig. 25 shows that the searching goes from the first facet to the last facet for each slicing. Hence, the complexity of the algorithm searching for triangles that intersect the z plane is S^*n. S^*p is the complexity of the algorithm sorting intersection lines and linking them together, such that

$$\text{Complexity of the LMI based algorithm} = n + \alpha n S = n(1 + \alpha S), \qquad (14)$$

where $\alpha \ll 1$ and α is used to represent the average of the proportions over the slices. The first n occurs during the first slice in the worst case; all n facets must be checked for intersection with the slice. Subsequently, only these facets connected directly to the facets being cut need to be checked, and their number can only be a small proportion of n.

Since $\alpha \ll 1$, $n(1 + \alpha S) \ll nS$ for large n, with $S > 1$. Comparing formula (13) with (14), the cost of the slicing algorithm based on the STL format is much higher than that based on the LMI format.

The LMI format is smaller than the STL format: in the slicing algorithm based on the LMI format, the memory used to store a facet model can be easily freed step by step by freeing the space used to store facets that have been sliced. Therefore, the algorithm based on LMI uses less memory to process.

RAPID PROTOTYPING AND MANUFACTURING

```
Read a LMI file
  ↓
facet = the first facet to the last facet
    if the facet is on the bottom of the part and along the
    boundary, put it in set A.
  ↓
z=min z to max z
    facet = the first facet to the last facet in set A
        find lines of intersection
        if the facet is below the next z plane, delete it, free it from
        memory and put facets related to it at the corresponding
        place in set A.
    for each hatch direction
        Hatch contour, if required.
  ↓
Write a SLC File
  ↓
Free memory
```

FIGURE 25 Slicing algorithm based on the LMI format.

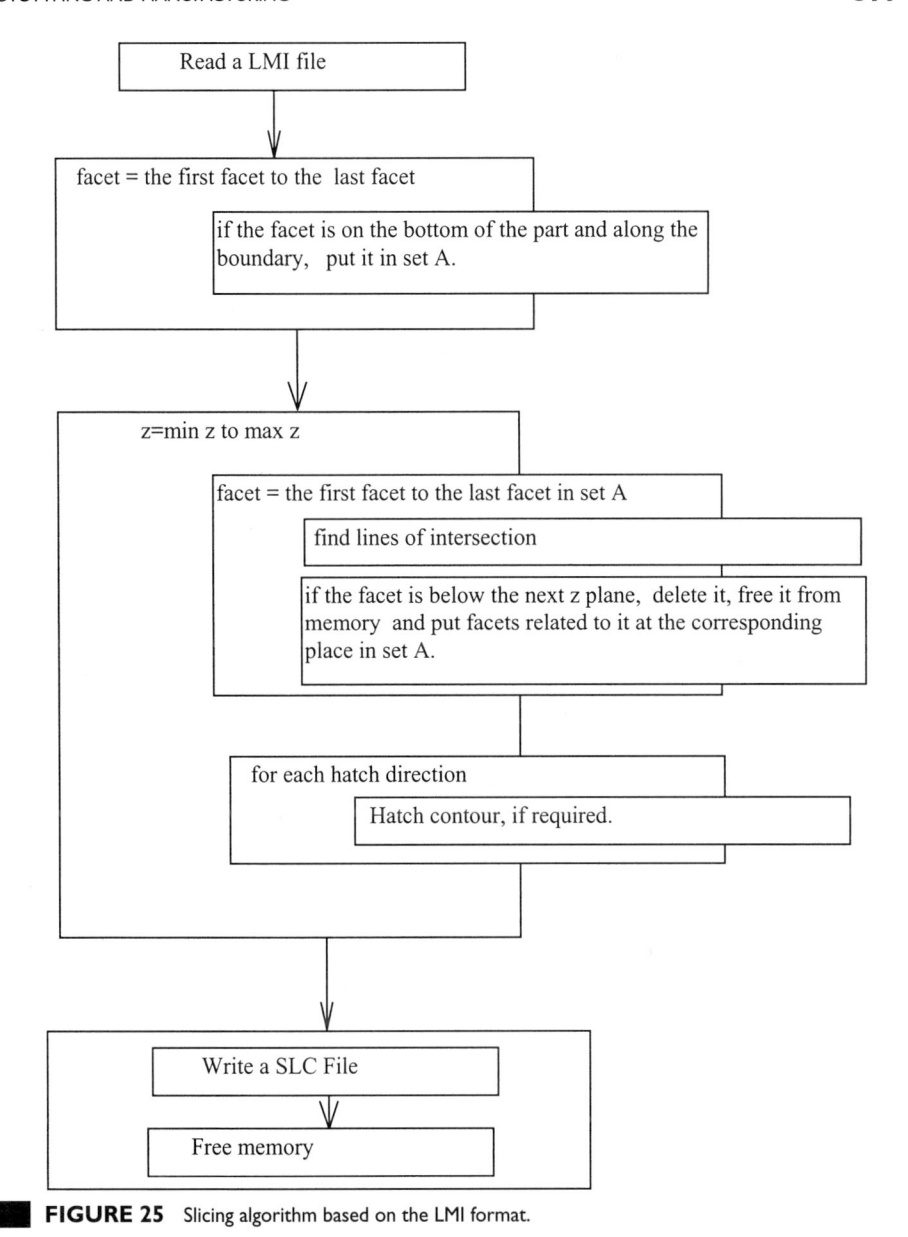

Summarily, the slicing algorithm based on the LMI format will cost less in both space and processing time than those based on the STL format.

D. Adaptive Slicing

A lot of efforts have been made continuously on improving the accuracy and efficiency of slicing. One of the results of the research is adaptive slicing [35]. The main objective is to control the staircase effect by a user-supplied tolerance. The basic principles of adaptive slicing can be generalized as that vertical and

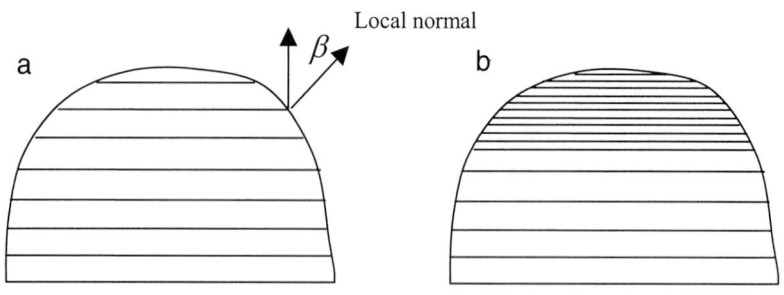

FIGURE 26 Comparison of (b) adaptive slicing and (a) slicing with constant layer thickness.

near-vertical features are built with thick layers while features with a bigger β (the angle between the local normal and building direction) are built with thin layers (as shown in Fig. 26).

Most of the adaptive slicing methods produce unnecessary layers that contribute to increasing fabrication times without improving the overall quality of the part surface; thus they are seldom commercialized. Tyberg and Bohn present an approach of fabricating each part and feature independently so that each thickness is commonly derived from the one part or feature existing at that height whose surface geometry requires the thinnest layer to meet a tolerance criterion [36].

An additional benefit is that one obtains a part with the desired surface finish using the minimal number of layers. Despite these benefits, this building technique cannot be used yet in practice. In some cases, this is due to the underlying characteristics of the RP&M processes. For example, in the FDM process, the layer thickness must be adjusted manually by the machine operator. In the LOM process developed and commercialized by Helisys, the thickness of the layer is determined by the current thickness of the sheet. In other cases, the problem is to find the optimal parameters for a given layer thickness. Let us take, for instance, the SLA. Although the SLA systems make it adjustable, both the manufacturer and the supplier of resins specify building parameters for the layer thickness within limited options.

IV. LAYER DATA INTERFACES

After the geometric model of the part has been sliced, it must be converted to scanning information that will be used to form the 2D layer. It is not clear whether the standard raster scan is the best scanning strategy for RP&M. For example, experiments have shown that tracing the boundary of a part provides a better edge definition. Additionally, the scanning pattern is much different between SLA and LOM. This section will describe the strategies that are derived from the geometric shape of a polygonal contour generated from slicing and data formats that represent the scanning vector.

RAPID PROTOTYPING AND MANUFACTURING 401

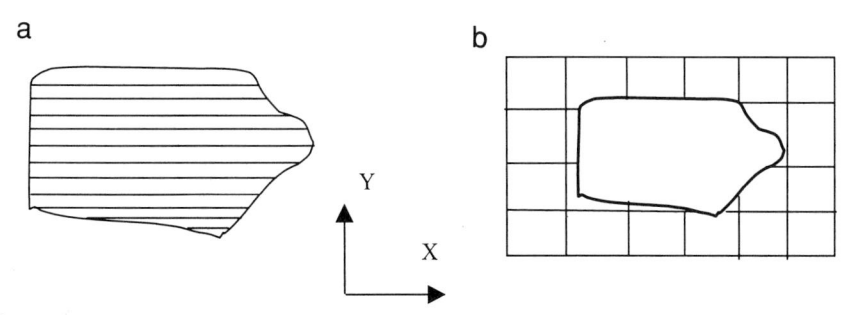

FIGURE 27 Hatching styles: (a) inside and (b) outside.

A. Scanning and Hatching Pattern

1. Raster Scanning

The scanning system from almost all of the RP&M processes consists of a set mirror mounted on a pair of X–Y linear motion or directly X–Y linear motion tables. Thus the simplest scanning pattern is raster style, in which scanning motion is always along one axis (either X or Y) only. The scanning path consists of locating points on the layer boundary at which the laser or nozzle must be on or off. The so-called "locating points" are generated through calculating the intersection points with mathematical rays directed along each scan line and each segment of the boundary contour in each layer. These intersections are then ordered one after another.

Figure 27a describes one typical scanning pattern that is along the X axis. RP&M processes like SLA and SLS solidify the liquid resin or powder and FDM depends on the nozzle extruding melted polymer to form the part with interior and boundary, which makes the scan area within the contour boundary as shown in Fig. 27a. However, LOM adopts a different concept to build one layer. In LOM, a laser is adopted to cut the paper sheet according to the contour information, which makes it unnecessary to solidify the interior of the contour. Hatch lines scanned outside of the contour boundary is for facilitating the removal of the redundant material (shown as Fig. 27b).

Of course scanning along the X or Y axis is not always parallel to the longest edge of the polygon of the contour. Thus the longest edge scan style has been considered because it results in longer uninterrupted active periods of processing material [37]. Changes in scanning direction will not only minimize the number of toggle points, but also affect the physical characteristics of the part built.

2. Boundary Scanning

Boundary scanning may improve a part's surface finish by tracing the part boundary, offset by the appropriate value-like laser beam radius or half-width of droplet of deposited material. The pattern allows the scanning to be continuous with a longer switching time. According to Wu and Beaman [37], geometric contour following for scanning control is used to refine the boundary of the parts for increasing the accuracy or to develop the capability to arrange various scanning directions and paths for improving the part strength. This benefit is

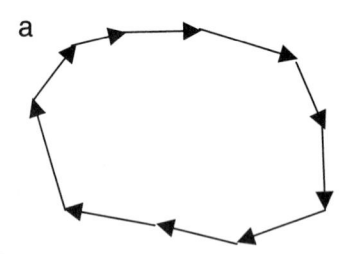

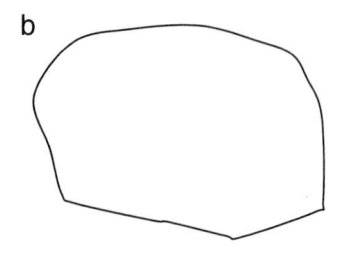

FIGURE 28 Boundary scanning: (a) segment contour and (b) generated continuous contour.

based on the fact that the scanner should be driven to follow the prescribed path as soon as possible, limited by available torque.

In Wu's tracking control strategy, the minimum time optimal control problem with specified path and limited control torque is formulated. The algorithm uses information about the curvature of the contour to determine the appropriate laser parameter to achieve the desired power density. A polygonal approximation of the contour, such as that obtained from slicing a faceted part model, is not accurate enough to support this scheme. Nevertheless, it is still possible that an appropriate continuous contour is obtained through smooth interpolation of the polygonal segment or adding an arc at sharp corners to allow near constant tracking speed, shown as Fig. 28.

3. Model-Based Scanning

Model-based scanning is characterized as adopting unfixed scanning directions compared to raster scanning style. It is proved that besides many other control parameters, the solidification sequence in each RP&M process will have an effect on the physical performance of the final part. For example, initial investigations [38] indicate that fabrication of a metal part with SLS will require local control of laser beam parameters, allowing these parameters to change from layer to layer or even within different areas in a given layer. Such model-based scanning is depicted conceptually in Fig. 29, where a part layer has been divided into several regions based on part quality predictions from a physical model of the process.

FIGURE 29 Model-based scanning.

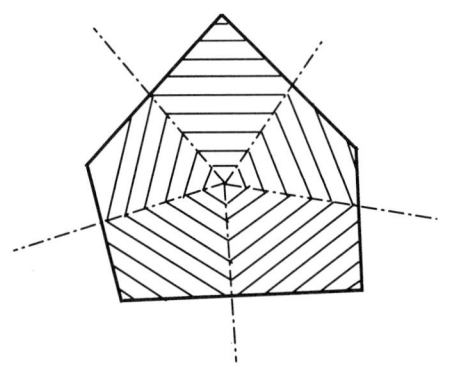

FIGURE 30 Spiral scanning with facilitating the heat expansion.

When describing intelligent slicing, Wozny [39] refers to spiral scanning, in which the center of the spiral is placed at the centroid of the polygonal slice, as shown in Fig. 30. Equiangular rays are extended from this point. An advantage of this approach is that the part is fabricated from the inside toward the outer boundary, which allows expansion due to the heat of the fabrication process to constantly move toward the unprocessed material. It appears that more accurate parts could be obtained in this manner.

Some RP&M processes, which directly build a mold shell prepared for casting rather than a part, need a particular scanning strategy different from other processes. The solidification happens within an area outside of the boundary in each layer. It is a more reasonable way of building a shell with a number of outward offsettings from the original boundary so that the mold made by this approach has a uniform thickness, which has an great effect on the transmission of gas and heat during casting. This characteristic is beneficial for obtaining a good performance from castings. A new algorithm [40] for obtaining the offset contours through a combination of finding the topological information of segments in a digitized image plane and calculating the endpoints of the contours by means of the intersection of two offset lines has been proposed. It has been proved that this method is efficient and robust no matter how complex the planar geometry is.

B. Two-Dimensional Contour Format

For many reasons, 2D slice data are of a valuable format. Some believe a 2D contour representation is more basic than a 3D solid model. At the primary level, each RP&M machine operates on the basis of stacks of 2D drawings. Two-dimensional contour software enables users to work efficiently with this data stream, thus solving special problems and enabling special applications. By tackling the interfacing problem at the contour level, contour software is able to solve all problems with bad STL files.

Many of the 2D contour formats differ in their details, but, in their present form, share common problems:

- *Flexibility.* They lack the possibility of being extended without breaking existing application programs. It is, perhaps, the major reason they will not obtain industry-wide acceptance and become *de facto* standards. A standard format for slices is a moving target, and changes will certainly be required.

- *Loss of information.* Like the STL format, using these formats will also result in loss of information. For example, it is not possible to represent normal vectors. The normal vectors along the contours can provide valuable information for some processes and pre- and post-processing algorithms.
- *Lack of user control.* They do not allow the sender to have complete control over the process. Unlike other, traditional manufacturing processes like NC milling, the user of an RP&M machine does not yet have control over all variables that influence the process by means of an open data exchange format.
- *Ambiguity.* The usage of (informal) English in the specification can lead to different interpretations and implementations; witness the current practice regarding previously mentioned "standards" like VDAFS.
- *Impractical assumptions.* Both formats require that the senders make a clear distinction between outer and inner contours, and contours cannot intersect in strange ways (e.g., they cannot exhibit self-intersections). These requirements demand a certain level of sophistication from CAD translators, and our current experience with 3D CAD data exchange formats (VDAFS, IGES, and STL) from various systems indicates this is usually not the case.
- *Process-dependent.* They are often not independent of fabrication processes. For instance, SLC formats developed by 3D Systems are biased toward fluid-based processes such as SLA.

Development in 2D formats in Europe is motivated in good measure by biomedical applications (implants, operation planning), as well as by reverse engineering applications that utilize laser and other scanning devices. Technical interests range from general boundary curve forms (beyond polylines) to more flexible file structures. Rather than tessellate a surface and then slice the tessellated surface, it will reduce error, produce better surfaces, and result in smaller files if the original surface is sliced (direct slicing) and the contour curves with polylines are then approximated.

The requirements for a flexible and vendor-independent format led to the development of the Common Layer Interface (CLI) format. The goal of CLI was a flexible format that applies to all RP&M technologies, permits user-specific data (such as patient orientation in CT scans), and allows data transfer among a wide range of applications. User-specific data are included in the Header Section. There is still some concern that CLI (also the 3D Systems slice format, SLC) is still not flexible enough to be a general file format. CLI seems to be biased toward fluid-based processes and dominated by medical scan data applications. An experimental data exchange format, called Layer Exchange ASCII Format (LEAF), addresses these and other shortcomings such as flexibility, loss of information, lack of user control, ambiguity, impractical assumptions, and process dependency. LEAF is an experimental tool for researchers for promoting standardization and is being developed further by researchers at the Fraunhofer Institute for Manufacturing, Engineering, and Automation in Stuttgart.

The HP/GL format previously discussed in this chapter is adopted in Japan frequently for representing 2D slice data. HP/GL is the *de facto* standard for 2D plotting, where the data are represented in a vector format: start point coordinates, end point coordinates, and pen up/down.

SLC is 3D Systems' contour data format for importing external slice data, and SLI is the company's machine-specific 2D format for the vector commands that control the laser beam.

The Cubital Facet List (CFL) format is based on a polygon-based representation consisting of n-sided polygons that can have multiple holes. The format avoids redundant vertex information and maintains topological consistency. CFL consists of a header and fields containing the total number of vertices (points) and facets in the object, a numbered sequence of vertex coordinates, numbered facets (with a number of holes), and pointers back to their respective vertices.

C. Common Layer Interface (CLI)

The CLI format was developed in a Brite EuRam project (Basic Research in Industrial Technologies for Europe/European Research on Advanced Materials) with the support of major European car manufacturers. It is a universal format for the input of geometry data to model fabrication systems based on RP&M. The CLI format is intended as a simple, efficient, and unambiguous format for data input to all 3D layer manufacturing systems, based on a two-and-a-half-dimensional layer representation. It is meant as a vendor-independent format for layer-by-layer manufacturing technologies.

The CLI file can be in binary or ASCII format. In a CLI format, the part is built by a succession of layer descriptions. The geometry part of the file is organized in layers in ascending order. Every layer is the volume between two parallel slices, and is defined by its thickness, a set of contours, and hatches (optically). Contours represent the boundaries of solid material within a layer, and are defined by polylines.

The CLI format has two kinds of entities. One is the polyline. A polyline is defined by a set of vertex points (x, y), connected contiguously in listed order by straight line segments. The polylines are closed, which means that they have a unique sense, either clockwise or counterclockwise. This sense is used in the CLI format to state whether a polyline is on the outside of the part or surrounding a hole in the part. Counterclockwise polylines surround the part, whereas clockwise polylines surround holes. This allows correct directions for beam offsetting.

The other is the hatch, which is a set of independent straight lines, each defined by one start point and one end point. One of the purposes of the hatch is to distinguish between the inside and outside of the part. The other is that hatches and open polylines are used to define support structures or filling structures, which are necessary for some 3D layer manufacturing systems like SLA, to obtain a solid model.

The advantages of the CLI format are presented as follows:

1. Since the CLI format only supports polyline entities, it is a simpler format than the HP/GL format.
2. The slicing step can be avoided in some applications.
3. Errors in layer information are much easier to correct than those in 3D information. Automated recovery procedures can be used, if required; and editing is also not difficult.

4. It is independent of vendors or fabrication machines, and requires only a simple conversion to the vendor-specific internal data structure of the machine.

The disadvantages of the CLI format include the following:

1. The CLI format only has the capability of producing polylines for the outline of a slice.
2. Although the real outline of the part is obtained by reducing the curve to segments of straight lines, the advantage over the STL format is lost.

The CLI format also includes layer information like the HP/GL format. However, the CLI format only has polyline entities, while HP/GL supports arcs, lines, and other entities. The CLI format is simpler than the HP/GL format and has been used by several RP&M systems. It is envisioned that the CLI format may become an industrial standard like STL.

D. Rapid Prototyping Interface (RPI)

The Rapid Prototyping Interface (RPI) format was designed by the Rensselaer Design Research Centre at Rensselaer Polytechnic [39,41]. It can be derived from currently accepted STL format data. The RPI format is capable of representing faceted solids, but it includes additional information about the facet topology. Topological information is maintained by representing each faceted solid entity with indexed lists of vertices, edges, and faces. Instead of explicitly specifying the vertex coordinates for each facet, a facet can refer to them by index numbers. This contributes to the goal of overall redundant information reduction.

The format is developed in ASCII to facilitate cross-platform data exchange and debugging. A RPI format file is composed of a collection of entities, each of which internally defines the data it contains. Each entity conforms to the syntax defined by the syntax diagram as shown in Fig. 31. Each entity is composed of an entity name, a record count, a schema definition, a schema termination symbol, and the corresponding data. The data are logically subdivided into records which are made up of fields. Each record corresponds to one variable type in the type definition.

The advantages of the RPI format include the following:

1. Topological information is added in the RPI format. As the result of this, flexibility is achieved. It allows users to balance storage and processing cost.
2. Redundancy in the STL is removed and the size of the file is reduced.
3. Format extensibility is made possible by interleaving the format schema with data as shown in Fig. 31. New entities can be added to the format and new variables can also be added to existing entities.
4. Representation of CSG primitives is provided, as are capabilities of representing multiple instances of both faceted and CSG solids.

The disadvantages of the RPI format are the following:

1. An interpreter which processes a format as flexible and extensible as the RPI format is more complex than that for the STL format.

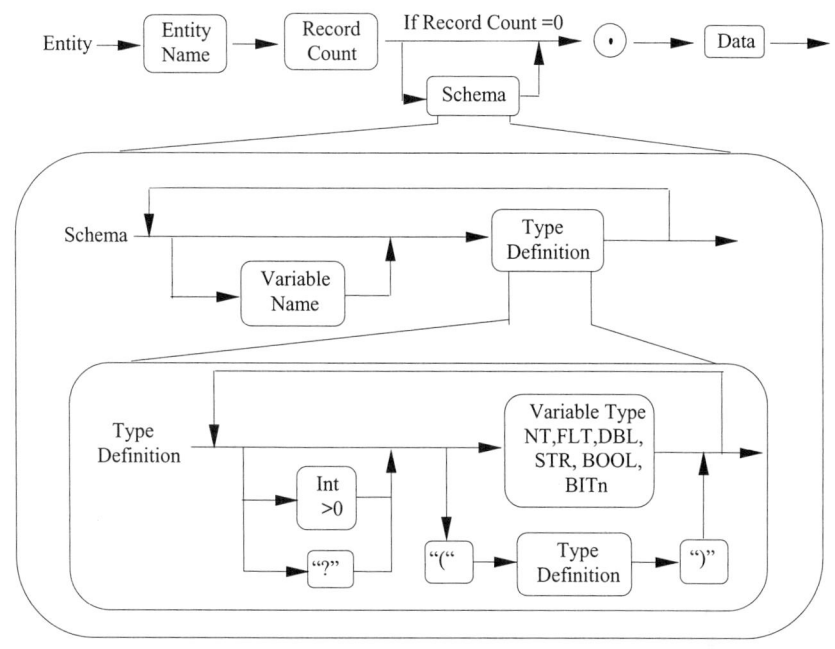

FIGURE 31 RPI format entity syntax diagram.

2. Surface patches suitable for solid approximation cannot be identified in the RPI format.

The RPI format offers a number of features unavailable in the STL format. The format can represent CSG primitive models as well as faceted models. Both can be handled with Boolean operators like union, intersection, and difference. Provisions for solid translation and multiple instancing are also provided. Process parameters, such as process types, scan methods, materials, and even machine operator instructions, can be included in the file. Faceted models are more efficiently represented as redundancy is reduced. The flexible format definition allows storage and processing cost to be balanced.

E. Layer Exchange ASCII Format (LEAF)

The LEAF, for Layer Exchange ASCII Format, was generated by the Helsinki University of Technology [42]. To describe this data model, LEAF borrows concepts from the object-oriented paradigm. At the top level, there is an object called the LMT-file (Layer Manufacture Technology file) that contains parts which in turn are composed of other parts. Ultimately, layers are composed of 2D primitives, and currently the only ones that are planned for implementation are polylines.

For example, an object of a given class is created. The object classes are organized in a simple tree as shown in Fig. 32. Attached to each object class is a collection of properties. A particular instance of an object specifies the values for each property. Objects inherit properties from their parents. In LEAF, the geometry of an object is simply one among several other properties.

LMT-file ⟶ Part ⟶ Layer ⟶ 2D Primitives

FIGURE 32 An object tree in LEAF.

In this example, the **object** is a LMT-file. It contains exactly one child, the object **P1**. **P1** is a combination of two parts, one of which is a support structure and the other is **P2**, again a combination of two others. The objects at the leaves of the tree—**P3**, **P4**, and **S**—must have been, evidently, sliced with the same z values so that the required operations, in this case **or** and **binary-or,** can be performed and the layers of **P1** and **P2** are constructed.

In LEAF, some properties, like **support-structure** and **open**, can also be attached to layers or even polyline objects, allowing the sender to represent the original model and the support structures as one single part. In Fig. 33, all parts inherit the properties of **object**, their ultimate parent. Likewise, all layers of the object **S** inherit the open property, indicating that the contours in the layers are always interpreted as open, even if they are geometrically closed.

Advantages of the LEAF format include the following:

1. It is easy to be implemented and used.
2. It is not ambiguous.
3. It allows for data compression and for a human-readable representation.
4. It is both CAD system and LMT process independent.
5. Slices of CSG models can be represented almost directly in LEAF.
6. The part representing the support structures can be easily separated from the original part.

The disadvantages of the LEAF format are the following:

1. A new interpreter is needed for connecting the 3D layer manufacturing systems.
2. The structure of the format is more complicated than that of the STL format.
3. The STL format cannot be translated into this format.

```
(LMT-file
(name Object) (radix 85) (units 1mm) ...
(Part  (name P1) ...
(binary-or (Part  (name S) (support-structure) (open) ...
            (Layer ...))
          (Part  (name P2) ...
             (or (Part    (name P3)) ...
                (Layer (name ...) (polyline ...)))
                (Part    (name P4) ...
                (Layer (name P4_L1) (polyline ...)))
             )
          )
)))
```

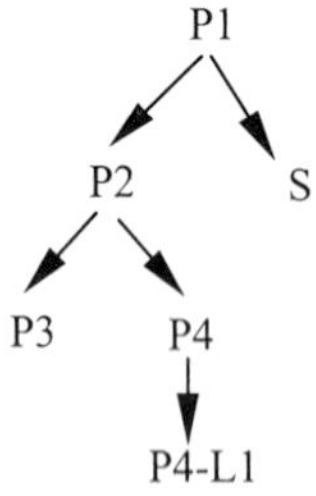

FIGURE 33 Instance tree in LEAF.

The LEAF format is described in several levels, mainly at a logical level using a data model based on object-oriented concepts, and at a physical level using a LISP-like syntax as shown in Fig. 33. At the physical level, the syntax rules are specified by several translation phases. Thus defined, it allows one to choose at which level interaction with LEAF is desirable, and at each level there is a clear and easy-to-use interface. It is doubtful if LEAF currently supports the needs of all processes currently available but it is a step forward in that direction.

F. SLC Format

The SLC file format (3D Systems, 1994) was generated by 3D Systems for representing cross-sectional information [43]. It is a $2^1/_2$D contour representation and also can be used to represent a CAD model. It consists of successive cross sections taken at ascending Z intervals in which solid material is represented by interior and boundary polylines. SLC data can be generated from various sources, either by conversion from solid or surface models or more directly from systems that produce data arranged in layers, such as from CT scanners.

The SLC format only contains the polyline that is an ordered list of X–Y vertex points connected continuously by each successive line segment. The polyline must be closed whereby the last point must equal the first point in the vertex list.

One of the strengths of the SLC format is that it is a simple representation of the solid object. In addition, the SLC format is directly accepted by rapid prototyping and manufacturing systems and does not need to be sliced in some cases.

However, the major weakness of the SLC format is that it can only approximately represent solid objects.

Through the comparison of several currently existing neutral formats and several proposed formats used for RP&M systems, it is clear that each format has its limitations in different aspects. Because of these, many efforts for improving the information process in RP&M and also for catching up with the latest development in engineering have been carried out. The next section will introduce these explorations, including solid interchange format, virtual reality modeling language, and volumetric modeling to support RP&M.

V. SOLID INTERCHANGE FORMAT (SIF): THE FUTURE INTERFACE

Several current RP&M research efforts are focused on the development of a future alternative data format for addressing the shortcomings of STL and for enabling data transfer for future advanced rapid manufacturing capabilities. This alternative data transfer mechanism is referred to as the Solid Interchange Format (SIF). To date, the SIF is a research topic only, with no current consensus or commercial implementation. Various proposals for possible SIF requirements, content, structure, data format, etc. have been submitted for consideration within the RP&M research community. There are a lot of universities contributing to the discussion of alternative data formats and development of SIF.

The solid interchange format will be based upon a precise, mathematical representation of the 3D part geometry. In addition to addressing the current limitations of STL, the data representation capabilities of SIF must accommodate expected capabilities of future RP&M systems, including the use of multiple materials, gradient material properties, part color specification, nonplanar build layers, explicit fiber directions, surface roughness, tolerance, and embedded foreign components. Also SIF is designed to have strong extensibility and additional annotation capabilities.

As with the proposed improvements to the STL-based data transfer, development and acceptance of an alternative RP&M data transfer mechanism will require support of both RP&M systems developers and CAD vendors. Modifications would be required within both CAD and RP&M vendor products to implement a new data interface. The proposed approach is to standardize an industry-consensus SIF through the ANSI/ISO process when the technical concepts have matured and RP&M industry support is formed. The basis for this representation might be provided by the ASIC save file format, since ASIC has been incorporated as the geometry engine for many commercially available geometric modeling systems.

Although it has been announced to be under development and liable to change, contents of the SIF/SFF (SFF here represents RP&M) already include four major categories: lexical conventions, grammar, semantics, and example, whose detail is available on the Web site of http://http.cs.berkeley.edu/~ jordans/sif/SIF_SFF.html.

Another language, L-SIF (Layered Solid Interchange Format), can be developed to describe $2\frac{1}{2}$D layers. Based on this standard, a slicer for generating the layered description from the 3D description can be developed. Other translators might be developed to perform certain transformations on layer-based data such as that obtained from laser digitizing measurements, CT, and MRI.

VI. VIRTUAL REALITY AND RP&M

A. Virtual Prototype and Rapid Prototype

Virtual reality (VR), until recently the preserve of the research labs, is gaining acceptance as a general potential tool. VR allows users to see and explore new products, plans, or concepts long before they exist in reality. It is likely that the uses for VR will coincide with applications that rapid prototyping systems have already been used for. Gibson *et al.* [44] have investigated both VR and PRM and concluded that it is a more efficient route for product development to combine each advantage. The primary use for a rapid prototyping system is not therefore in the qualitative assessment phase of product development. Also much more efforts are on making tooling processes to produce test parts and for short production runs. This is a much more important role for this technology to fill. Competitive marketing policies still dictate that physical models be created for purposes like tendering and user evaluation. VR, with its capacity to model real life, provides a practical replacement for rapid prototyping in this sense. A virtual prototype in VR has the potential of fulfilling at least four main functions, like visualization, verification, iteration, and optimization. There is no possibility of VR fulfilling the most important function, that of fabrication. The ideal product development environment is therefore a rapid prototyping base supported by CAD systems to supply the engineering detail while VR will be linked to the CAD systems for the consideration of aesthetic, communication and optimization.

SolidView, a software package for RP&M, designed to facilitate the preparation of STL files for RP&M, also contains the facilitation of 3D communication through the use of virtual prototypes. SoildView's viewing, measuring, and annotating capabilities allow the user to create an electronic design review using a virtual prototype. In conjunction with STL files, since each view has its own set of measurement and annotations, users can literally "walk around" the design, showing areas of change or special concern. Also furthermore, it is possible to share the virtual prototype, in the form of a specific file, to anyone on the Internet.

B. Virtual Reality Modeling Language (VRML)

The Virtual Reality Modeling Language (VRML) is a language for describing interactive 3D objects and worlds. VRML is designed to be used on the Internet, intranets, and local client systems. VRML is also intended to be a universal interchange format for integrated 3D graphics and multimedia. VRML may be used in a variety of application areas such as engineering and scientific visualization, multimedia presentations, entertainment and educational titles, Web pages, and shared virtual worlds. All aspects of virtual world display, interaction, and internetworking can be specified using VRML. It is the intention of its designers that VRML become the standard language for interactive simulation within the World Wide Web. VRML is based on the Open Inventor ASCII File Format from Silicon Graphics, Inc., which supports descriptions of computer graphics 3D scenes with polygonally rendered objects, lighting, materials, ambient properties, and realism effects. The first version of VRML allows for the creation of virtual worlds with limited interactive behavior. These worlds can contain objects that have hyperlinks to other worlds or data objects. When the user selects a link to a VRML document from within a correctly configured World Wide Web browser, a VRML viewer is launched for navigating and visualizing the Web. Future versions of VRML will allow for richer behaviors, including animation, motion physics, and real time multiuser interaction.

The Bremen Institute for Industrial Technology and Applied Work Science (BIBA) has opened a Web dialog on replacing the STL format with the Virtual Reality Modeling Language (VRML) format (http://www.biba.uni-bremen.de/users/bau/s2v.html). VRML will help to do the following:

• *Improve the communication and information exchange in the process chain.* As the different steps involved in the RP&M process chain are often done by different companies and even to meet different requirements, there is a need of communication and sharing information among different sites. By using a standard like VRML, which is not restricted to RP, many standard software tools, mostly independent from a specific hardware platform, are available, mostly as shareware.

• *Lower the barrier for RP & M application.* VRML can be used as a replacement for STL with a slight barrier. It has a node structure. When they are ever needed, RP-specific subnodes can easily be defined. By using VRML, all can be done with one standard. You do not have to buy several costly interfaces to your CAD package, or use a conversion service where you are not even sure whether you get it right the first time.

- *Open new markets.* VRML reaches the consumer market and therefore has enormous power in contrast to STL. When RP&M apply VRML right now, we can profit from developments done by others. As concept modelers like 3D Systems Actua and low- end "3D printers" appear, VRML opens the mass market to them.
- *VRML files are more compact than STL.* This is just because it uses a list of numbered points followed by a list of triangles (three numbers, order indicates surface normal direction). STL has a large overhead: For each triangle, not only are all 3D points given, the surface normal vector is included, too. It also makes verification and correction easier.

Advocates of replacing STL point out that VRML deals with more issues, including 3D extension of the World Wide Web and future 3D telecommunication and networking standards that could also become the standard interface for all design and manufacturing activities. This format will be applied for storing and viewing with a 3D Web browser before printing for telemanufacturing. Advocates claim that the adoption of VRML would make RP&M more accessible globally, but much is still left to do. VRML today provides a geometry-viewing capability but has not addressed engineering needs such as the creation of very complex geometries and the ability to use it in other analyses. Future versions of VRML are expected to include NURBS, but today, such geometry creates a heavy processing load. Additionally, software based on the VRML format is necessarily developed to realize the special information process for RP&M, such as support generation, slicing, and hatching.

VII. VOLUMETRIC MODELING FOR RP&M

Conventional solid modeling has focused on developing models of objects (known as solid models) based on their geometry and topology. These models do not possess material information and are homogeneous. However, due to new developments in the field of CAD/CAM (optimal design using homogenization, layered manufacturing, etc.), it is becoming increasingly important to model heterogeneous objects (objects with varying material/density distribution and microstructures). Preliminary work has been completed toward modeling objects made of a finite number of materials (objects with discretely varying material distribution) and objects composed of functionally gradient materials. Nowadays, solid models produced by most of the commercial CAD systems assume an homogeneous interior. RP&M technology has the exciting potential of prototyping solids with an inhomogeneous interior and/or a microstructured interior.

Furthermore, it will raise some interesting proposals while comparing the nature of geometric modeling (CAD) and physical modeling (manufacturing). As an incremental forming process, rapid prototyping and manufacturing technology fundamentally adds material piece-by-piece in order to build up shapes.

Unfortunately, neither solid modeling nor surface modeling has such a character as to analogize the additional forming process, even in principle. As a result, it unnecessarily increases the complexity of information processing by introducing slice and scanning vector generation, which can be regarded as an inverse procedure for stacking and layer generating in the building process.

When these flaws in the commonly used modeling systems are considered, it is apt to introduce a voxel-based modeling method for the RP&M field. Actually, voxel-based modeling is not a new concept in volume graphics, where it has another name, volumetric modeling. Kaufuman *et al.* [45] proposed that graphics is ready to make a paradigm shift from 2D raster graphics to 3D volume graphics with implications similar to those of the shift from vector to raster graphics. Volume graphics, voxelization, and volume rendering have attracted considerable research recently. The term "voxel" represents a volume element in volume graphics, just like the term "pixel" denotes a picture element in raster graphics. Typically, the volumetric data set is represented as a 3D discrete regular grid of voxels and commonly stored in a volume buffer, which is a large 3D array of voxels. A voxel is the cubic unit of volume centered at the integral grid point. Each voxel has numeric values associated with it, which represent some measurable properties or independent variables (e.g., color, opacity, density, material, coverage proportion, refractive index, even velocity, strength, and time) of the real object.

Unlike solid or surface modeling, volumetric modeling in discrete form makes it close to the idea of the piece-by-piece building process used in RP&M. In image-based systems, like SGC, successive layers of the part under construction are generated by the use of masks that either allow a light source to solidify a photopolymer under the exposed regions or deposit material on the exposed areas of the mask. Each mask is the image of the object's cross section, which is easily generated by taking out all the voxels that have the same Z-axis coordinate value as that desired. Although much of the current installed RP&M systems are vector-based, in which the sequential formation of the contours is by scanning the object's cross section and hatching is needed to obtain the interiors, image-based systems will dominate the market in the long term due to the perks of faster speed and independence of objects' geometric complexity. Furthermore, generation of scanning vectors from an image is still feasible if necessary.

It is the biggest disadvantage that a typical volume buffer occupies a large amount of memory. For example, for a moderate resolution of $512 \times 512 \times 512$ the volume buffer consists of more than 10^8 voxels. Even if we allocate only one byte per voxel, 128 Mbytes will be required. However, since computer memories are significantly decreasing in price and increasing in their compactness and speed, such large memories are becoming more and more feasible. Another drawback is the loss of geometric information in the volumetric model. A voxel-based object is only a discrete approximation of the original continuous object where the properties of voxels determine the object. In voxel-based models, a discrete shading method for estimating the normal from the context of the models is employed [46].

Chandru and Manohar [47] have proposed a system named G-WoRP, a geometric workbench for rapid prototyping, in which the voxel representation scheme (V-rep) provides an efficient interface among the various modules.

Several problems that are difficult using conventional geometry-based approaches have a simple solution using voxel models. These include estimation of mass properties, interference detection, tolerance calculation, and implementation of CSG operation. Further, voxel-based models permit the designer to analyze the object and modify it at the voxel level, leading to the design of custom composites of arbitrary topology. The generation of slices is made simple, and reverse engineering is greatly facilitated.

Presently, there are two approaches to generating an object in volumetric modeled data. The first source of volume data can be produced from a geometrical model, either closed surface or solid. The voxels are used to fill up the interior of the object with exact size and correct properties according to the accurate specification. It is obvious that the more voxels that are adopted, the less the presentation error is. Of course, increasing the number of voxels may need more space for storing and, in turn, cost more time to deal with. The second measure for building a voxel-based model is much like the process called reverse engineering with many examples of successful applications. Volumetric data sets are generated from medical imaging (e.g., CT, MRI, and ultrasonography), biology (e.g., confocal microscopy), geoscience (e.g., electron seismic measurements), industry (i.e., industrial CT inspection), and molecular systems (e.g., electron density maps) [47].

REFERENCES

1. Peter, P. S. *Data Structures for Engineering Software*. Computational Mechanics, USA, 1993.
2. Wholes, T. Rapid prototyping and tooling state of the industry. 1998 Worldwide Progress Report, RPA of SME, Michigan, 1998.
3. Johnson, J. L. *Principles of Computer Automated Fabrication*. Palatino Press, Irvine, CA, 1994.
4. Hull, C. W. Apparatus for production of three-dimensional objects by steorolithography. U.S. Patent, 4,575,330, 1986.
5. Jacobs, P. F. *Rapid Prototyping & Manufacturing*. Society of Manufacturing Engineers, 1992.
6. Bourell, D. L., Beaman, J. J., Marcus, H. L., and Barlow, J. W. Solid freeform fabrication—An advanced manufacturing approach. In *Proceedings of Solid Freeform Fabrication Symposium*, Austin, TX, August 12–14, 1991, pp. 1–7.
7. Levi, H. Accurate rapid prototyping by the solid ground curing technology. In *Proceedings of Solid Freeform Fabrication Symposium*, Austin, TX, August 12–14, 1991, pp. 110–114.
8. Sachs, E., Cima M., Cornie, J. *et al*. Three dimensional printing: Rapid tooling and prototypes directly from CAD representation. In *Proceedings of Solid Freeform Fabrication Symposium*, Austin, TX, August 6–8, 1990, pp. 52–64.
9. Lee, S. J., Sachs, E., and Cima, M. Powder layer deposition accuracy in powder based rapid prototyping. In *Proceedings of Solid Freeform Fabrication Symposium*, Austin, TX, August 9–11, 1993, pp. 223–234.
10. Nutt, K. Selective laser sintering as a rapid prototyping and manufacturing technique. In *Proceedings of Solid Freeform Fabrication Symposium*, Austin, TX, August 12–14, 1991, pp. 131–137.
11. Feygin M., and Hsieh, B. Laminated object manufacturing (LOM): A simple process. In *Proceedings of Solid Freeform Fabrication Symposium*, Austin, Texas, August 12–14, 1991, pp. 123–130.
12. Richardson, K. E. The production of wax models by the ballistic particle manufacturing process. In *Proceedings of the 2nd International Conference on Rapid Prototyping*, Dayton, OH, June 23–26, 1991, pp. 15–20.
13. Kochan, D. *Solid Freeform Manufacturing*. Elsevier, Amsterdam, 1993.

14. Greulich, M., Greul, M., and Pintat, T. Fast, functional prototypes via multiphase jet solidification. *Rapid Prototyping J.* **1**(1):20–25, 1995.
15. Reed, K., Harrvd, D., and Conroy, W. *Initial Graphics Exchange Specification (IGES)* version 5.0. CAD-CAM Data Exchange Technical Center, 1998.
16. Li, J. H. Improving stereolithography parts quality—Practical solutions. In *Proceedings of the 3rd International Conference on Rapid Prototyping,* Dayton, OH, June 7–10, 1992, pp. 171–179.
17. Famieson R., and Hacker, H. Direct slicing of CAD models for rapid prototyping. *Rapid Prototyping J.* **1**(2): 4–12, 1995.
18. Owen, J. *STEP: An Introduction.* Information Geometers, 1993.
19. Bloor, S., Brown, J., Dolenc, A., Owen J., and Steger, W. Data exchange for rapid prototyping, summary of EARP investigation. In *Presented at Rapid Prototyping and Manufacturing Research Forum,* University of Waraick, Coventry, October, 1994.
20. Swaelens B., and Kruth, J. P. Medical applications of rapid prototyping techniques. In *Proceedings of 4th International Conference on Rapid Prototyping,* Dayton, OH, June 14–17, 1993, pp. 107–120.
21. Vancraen, W., Swawlwns, B., and Pauwels, J. Contour interfacing in rapid prototyping—Tools that make it work. In *Proceedings of the 3rd International Conference on Rapid Prototyping and Manufacturing,* Dayton, OH, June 7–10, 1994, pp. 25–33.
22. Donahue, R. J. CAD model and alternative methods of information transfer for rapid prototyping systems. In *Proceedings of 2nd Internation Conference on Rapid Prototyping,* Dayton, OH, June 23–26, 1991, pp. 217–235.
23. Bohn J. H., and Wozny, M. J. Automatic CAD-model repair: Shell-closure. In *Proceedings of Solid Freeform Fabrication Symposium,* Austin, TX, August 3–5, 1992, pp. 86–94.
24. Makela, I., and Dolenc, A. Some efficient for correcting triangulated models. In *Proceedings of Solid Freeform Fabrication Symposium,* Austin, TX, August 9–11, 1993, pp. 126–132.
25. Leong, K. F., Chua, C. K., and Ng, Y. M. A study of stereolithography file errors and repair. Part 1. Generic Solution. *Int. J. Adv. Manufact. Technol.* (**12**):407–414, 1996.
26. Leong, K. F., Chua, C. K., and Ng, Y. M. A study of stereolithography file errors and repair. Part 2. Special Cases. *Int. J. Adv. Manufac. Technol.* (**12**):415–422, 1996.
27. Chua, C. K., Gan, G. K., and Tong, M. Interface between CAD and rapid prototyping systems. Part 2: LMI—An improved interface. *Int. J. Adv. Manufact. Technol.* **13**(8):571–576, 1997.
28. Chua, C. K., Gan, G. K., and Tong M. Interface between CAD and rapid prototyping systems. Part 1: A Study of existing interfaces, *Int. J. Adv. Manufact. Technol.* **13**(8):566–570, 1997.
29. Weiler, K. J. Topology, as a framework for solid modeling. In *Proceedings of Graphic Interface '84,* Ottowa, 1984.
30. Mortenson, M. E. *Geometric Modeling,* Wiley, New York, 1985.
31. Guduri, S., Crawford, R. H., and Beaman, J. J. A method to generate exact contour files for solid freeform fabrication. In *Proceedings of Solid Freeform Fabrication Symposium,* Austin, TX, August 6–8, 1992, pp. 95–101.
32. Guduri, S., Crawford, R. H., and Beaman, J. J. Direct generation of contour files from constructive solid geometry representations. In *Proceedings of Solid Freeform Fabrication Symposium,* Austin, TX, August 9–11, 1993, pp. 291–302.
33. Rock, S. J., and Wozny, M. J. Utilizing topological information to increase scan vector generation efficiency. In *Proceedings of Solid Freeform Fabrication Symposium,* Austin, TX, August 12–14, 1991, pp. 28–36.
34. Crawford, R. H., Das S., and Beaman, J. J. Software testbed for selective laser sintering. In *Proceedings of Solid Freeform Fabrication Symposium,* Austin, TX, August, 12–14, 1991, pp. 21–27.
35. Dolenc, A., and Makela, I. Slicing procedures for layered manufacturing techniques. *Comput. Aided Design* **26**(2):119–126, 1994.
36. Tyberg, J., and Bohn, J. H. Local adaptive slicing. *Rapid Prototyping J.* **4**(3):119–127, 1998.
37. Wu, Y-J. E., and Beaman, J. J., Contour following for scanning control in SFF Application: Control trajectory planning. In *Proceedings of Solid Freeform Fabrication Symposium,* Austin, TX, August 6–8, 1990, pp. 126–134.
38. Beaman, J. J. *Solid Freeform Fabrication: A New Direction in Manufacturing: With Research and Applications in Thermal Laser Processing.* Kluwer Academic, Dordrecht, 1997.

39. Wozny, M. J. Systems issues in solid freeform fabrication. In *Proceedings of Solid Freeform Fabrication Symposium,* Austin, TX, Aug. 3–5, 1992, pp. 1–15.
40. Du, Z. H. *The Research and Development on Patternless Casting Mold Manufacturing Directly Driven by CAD Model.* Tsinghua University, Ph.D dissertation, Beijing, China, 1998.
41. Rock, S. J., and Wozny, M. J. A flexible file format for solid freeform fabrication. In *Proceedings of Solid Freeform Fabrication Symposium,* Austin, Texas, August, 6–8, 1991, pp. 155–160.
42. Dolenc, A., and Melela, I. Leaf: A data exchanger format for LMT processes. In *Proceedings of the 3rd International Conference on Rapid Prototyping,* Dayton, OH, June 7–10, 1992, pp. 4–12.
43. 3D Systems, Inc., SLC File Specification, 3D System Inc. Valencia, VA, 1994.
44. Gibson, I., Brown, D., Cobb, S., and Eastgate, R. Virtual reality and rapid prototyping: Conflicting or complimentary. In *Proceedings of Solid Freeform Fabrication Symposium,* Austin, TX, Aug 9–11, 1993, pp. 113–120.
45. Kaufman, A., Cohen, D., and Yagel, R. Volume graphics. *IEEE Computer* **26**(7):51–64, 1993.
46. Kaufman, A. *Volume Visualization.* IEEE Computer Society Press, Los Alamitos, CA, 1990.
47. Chandru, V., and Manohar, S. G-WoRP: A geometric workbench for rapid prototyping. In *Proceedings of the ASME International Mechanical Engineering Congress,* 1994.

12
DATABASE SYSTEMS IN MANUFACTURING RESOURCE PLANNING

M. AHSAN AKHTAR HASIN

Industrial Systems Engineering, Asian Institute of Technology, Klong Luang, Pathumthani 12120, Thailand

P. C. PANDEY

Asian Institute of Technology, Klong Luang, Pathumthani 12120, Thailand

I. INTRODUCTION   417
II. MRPII CONCEPTS AND PLANNING PROCEDURE   418
   A. Manufacturing Resource Planning (MRPII): What It Is   418
   B. Hierarchical Manufacturing Planning and Control   419
III. DATA ELEMENT REQUIREMENTS IN THE MRPII SYSTEM   433
   A. Database of the MRPII System   433
   B. Data Storage and Retrieval in the MRPII System   438
   C. Information Transaction in MRPII   440
   D. Early-Stage Information Systems in Manufacturing Planning   443
   E. Information and Database Systems Centered around MRPII   445
IV. APPLICATION OF RELATIONAL DATABASE MANAGEMENT TECHNIQUE IN MRPII   452
V. APPLICATIONS OF OBJECT-ORIENTED TECHNIQUES IN MRPII   457
   A. Object-Oriented MRPII Modules   465
   B. Object-Oriented Inventory Control System   465
   C. Object-Oriented PAC System   467
   D. Object-Oriented Capacity Planning System   475
   E. Object-Oriented Bill of Materials   477
   F. MRPII as an Enterprise Information System   486
   G. Scopes of Object Orientation   492
REFERENCES   494

I. INTRODUCTION

The overall manufacturing system is composed of complex functions and activities. Most of the functions and activities are interrelated in some way. For production, a firm needs the following things [1,14,16]:

1. A variety of processes, machinery, equipment, labor, material, etc.
2. Relevant planning functions, which plan for the above items, in order to make use of them as efficiently and profitably as possible, and
3. Administrative functions as support activity.

To be profitable, not only are good machinery, equipment, or top quality materials necessary, but also good plans are a must. The company must efficiently and properly plan for the materials and resources, in order to ensure production of the right goods and components, in right amounts, at a right time, at an acceptable level of quality, and as economically as possible. For this purpose, an integrated resource planning system with the following major objectives is necessary: Efficient use of resources and materials, and good customer service.

A good materials and resource plan can contribute much to a company's performance, and thereby, profit. This truth has lead toward the development of the popularly known Manufacturing Resource Planning (MRPII), an integrated materials and resource planning system. Nowadays, MRPII is a very known and popular, though simple, tool, in the field of industrial materials management.

This chapter deals with the applications of database techniques in the MRPII system. Section II of the chapter discusses the MRPII concepts and its planning procedure, the next part (Section III) presents the requirements of data elements in the system, Section IV discusses applications of relational database management system, and the last part (Section V) deals with the applications of the object-oriented technique in the MRPII system.

II. MRPII CONCEPTS AND PLANNING PROCEDURE

A. Manufacturing Resource Planning (MRPII): What It Is

The Manufacturing Resource Planning, popularly known as MRPII, is basically an integrated materials management system. It has been defined by APICS (American Production and Inventory Control Society) as:

> A method for the effective planning of all the resources of manufacturing company. Ideally it addresses operational planning in units, financial planning in dollars, and has a simulation capability to answer 'what if' questions. It is made up of a variety of functions, each linked together: Business planning, Production planning, Master Production Scheduling (MPS), Material Requirements Planning (MRP), Capacity Requirements Planning (CRP), and execution systems for capacity and priority. Outputs from these systems would be integrated with financial reports, such as, the business plan, purchase commitment report, shipping budget, inventory production in dollars, etc. Manufacturing Resource Planning is a direct outgrowth and extension of MRP. Often referred to as MRPII (of closed loop MRP). [16, p. 228].

As defined above, the MRPII is a system that integrates several planning and execution steps, such as MPS, MRP, CRP, PAC and purchasing with the support from inventory, product structure of the goods, and other functions to provide necessary feedback in the earlier steps in a closed loop, in order to generate amount and timings of purchasing and manufacturing.

It is a computer-based materials planning system, sometimes also known as production and inventory planning and control system. This system introduced a shift from traditional two-bin or periodic inventory control policy to a time-phased discrete inventory policy.

The "closed loop MRP" provides information feedback that leads to the capability of plan adjustments and regeneration. The MRPII system provides some additional facilities, such as financial and accounting.

In the 1960s, a main-frame computer was necessary to run an MRPII system, but now, a Window-based PC or UNIX-based work station is sufficient to perform the job [14].

B. Hierarchical Manufacturing Planning and Control

In both short and long runs of plan generation and execution, the system must balance the needs against its capacity, at several hierarchical levels, with differing levels of information details and time spans. For instance, in the case of long-range planning decisions, the plan needs to identify overall business targets, possible areas of investment, market segments, and amount of investment. In the next stage, the mid-range plan, it should identify, in more detail, each product type with its amount in a specific time period. In the shortest version of the plan, it must prepare a plan that can show exact timings of production start and finish, detailed production schedule, resource allocation, etc. [1].

There are five levels in the overall manufacturing planning and control system, as shown in Fig. 1. The level of detail of plans increases from general categories to specific components, with a decrease in time span (planning horizon)

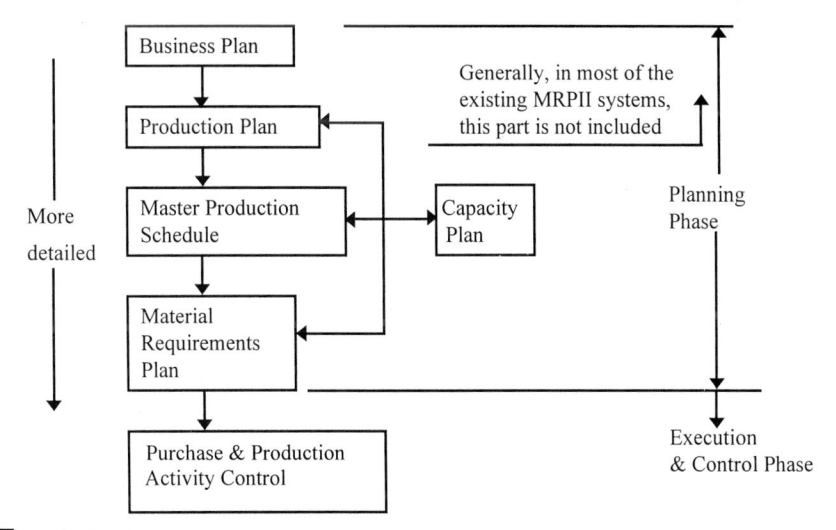

FIGURE 1 Levels of manufacturing planning.

from years to days, when we gradually move from top to bottom. At any level, the target is to find out what, when, and how much of a product or component to produce and/or purchase. Basically, a commercial MRPII system starts functionality from a *master production schedule* (MPS), which is built from two different functions of production plan, namely forecast and customer order.

The MRPII system begins with the identification of each component through a product structure, and then finds out the requirements along with the timings of all those components/subassemblies, based on forecast or customer order, in accordance with available stock on-hand. This misses a major requirement, which is the plans are not generated in accordance with available capacity. During order generation, to fulfill the requirements or production volume, it cannot consider the limitation of capacity of the plant. That is why the system is termed as an infinite capacity planning system.

Some of the major characteristics of this system are as follows:

1. The MRPII system is mostly applicable to make-to-stock, discrete, batch-oriented items. However, job shop, rate-based, and process manufacturing can also be accommodated with variants or enhancement.

2. The MRPII system is divided into separate modules, which have good interaction while preparing materials orders. The main modules are *forecast, bill of materials* (BOM) or *product structure,* MPS, *inventory, control, shop floor control* (SFC) or *production activity control* (PAC), *purchasing, sales* and *order processing, capacity management,* etc. The details of these modules or functions are discussed later.

3. The demand for finished goods, or end items, follows independent inventory, policies, like *economic order quantity* (EOQ), *re-order point* (ROP), or others, whereas demand for subassemblies, components, or raw materials is dependent on the demand for finished goods. The demand for end items are arranged in an MPS. The dependent demand can be calculated from this MPS by time phasing, and is of lumpy type. This calculation is managed by the *material requirements planning* (MRP) module of an overall MRPII system.

4. MRP is part of an overall resource planning (MRPII) system. The program, which generates the materials plan (i.e. orders), is known as the BOM explosion program. Since an MRPII system can prepare plans for all manufacturing resources, such as manpower and machines, including materials, it is popularly known as a *resource planning* system. The generation of a materials plan in accordance with capacity constraint is still not possible.

5. The orders are scheduled based on due dates and an estimated lead time. From the due dates, the order release dates are obtained by going backward, equal to lead time (known as lead time offsetting), in the production calendar. This scheduling process is known as backward scheduling.

6. An MRPII system is driven by MPS, which is derived from forecast, or *customer order,* or a *distribution requirements planning* (DRP) system.

The general structure of an MRPII system is shown in Fig. 2.

The MRPII system is modular, based on the functions/departments it serves. These modules share the manufacturing database, in order to generate combined materials plans for each department. The major modules are described below with their functionality.

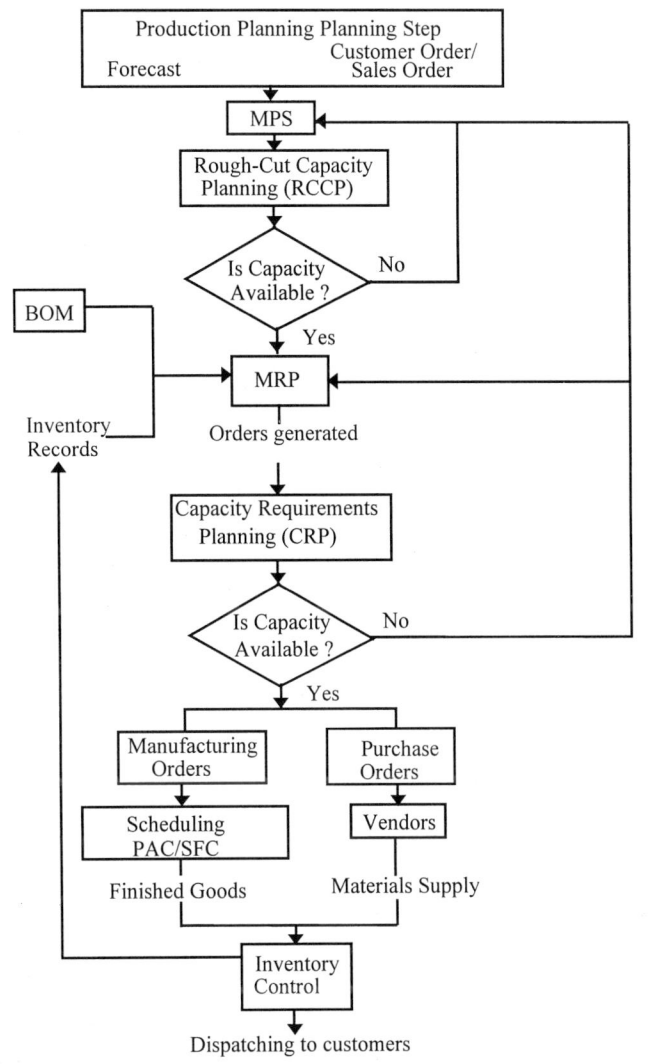

FIGURE 2 The closed loop system.

1. Bill of Materials

The *bill of materials* (BOM) of a product lists all the components, and sometimes the resources (such as labor), required to build a product. The BOM enables the planner to identify not only the components, but also their relationship in the final assembly.

There are several kinds of BOMs to facilitate different purposes. The most commonly used BOM is a tree-type structure. An example of a BOM of a product, a wooden table, is shown is Fig. 3. The major aspects of this BOM are explained as follows: The BOM shows a multilevel product structure, where components are arranged according to parent–component relationships. The part identification (Part ID) numbers are shown in parentheses just below the part name, inside the box. This information is necessary during explosion to

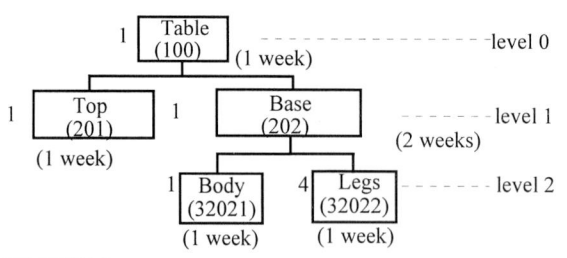

FIGURE 3 Tree-type product structure (BOM).

find out the requirements of the total amounts of the individual parts. The contents in parentheses, outside of the box, show the lead times in weeks. For manufacturing components, it is the manufacturing lead time, whereas it is the purchasing lead time for the purchasing component. A critical path is the line in the BOM that has the longest cumulative lead time. Here, it is 4 weeks, along Table–Base–Legs. This information is necessary during MRP explosion, to find out the total lead time required to manufacture a batch of products (Table). The order release dates for the item are found by subtracting the lead time from the order due date. This subtraction process is known as the *lead time offsetting* for *backward scheduling*. The numbers on the left-hand side of the box show the quantity required per (Q/per) assembly, which means number of components necessary to build one unit of the parent item.

The item at level zero is the table which is known as the *finished good*, or *end item*, and is sold to the customer. This is planned for production in the MPS and is said to have an "independent demand." Below this are the subassemblies and the components required to manufacture a table.

To facilitate easy display of this graphical BOM on a computer screen, it is generally converted to another format, known as indented BOM. The indented BOM of the Table is shown in Table 1.

The BOM in Fig. 3 is known as a multilevel BOM. When a subassembly is shown only one level down, then it is known as a single-level BOM. A single-level BOM for Table (Part ID 100) would be as shown in Fig. 4, where it can be said that "a Table (100) comprises two components, a Top (201) and a Base (202)," whereas the general expression of a "where-used" format of the BOM is the reverse presentation of that. For example, it can be said that "the Base (202) is an item, which is used to make one Table (100)."

TABLE I The Indented BOM

Manufacturing Bill of Material for Table, Part ID No. 100

Part ID no.	Part name	Quantity per assembly
100	Table	1
202	Base	1
32021	Body	1
32022	Legs	4
201	Top	1

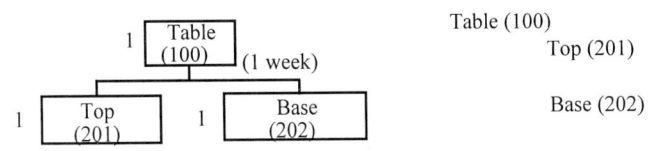

```
                                    Table (100)
         1   ┌─Table─┐
             │ (100) │ (1 week)         Top (201)
             └───┬───┘
         ┌───────┴───────┐              Base (202)
    1  ┌─Top─┐      1  ┌─Base─┐
       │(201)│         │(202) │
       └─────┘         └──────┘

         Tree Structure              Indented format
```

FIGURE 4 Single-level BOM.

There are several other variants of BOM presentation schemes [1], which are not elaborated here, as this chapter is not intended to include all possible aspects of the MRPII system.

2. Master Production Scheduling

The MPS is the next step in production planning. An estimation is done based on forecasting and/or customer orders/sales orders to identify the demand for a specific time horizon, which is transformed into an MPS. It is an input to the MRP explosion program, which translates the demand for end items to demand for individual components.

To resolve the differences between the MPS and the available production capacity, manual trial and error adjustment is applied. This process is called *rough-cut capacity planning* (RCCP), which is discussed later on.

In case of a make-to-stock item, the MPS is developed based on forecast. The completed finished goods are stored after production, and then sold to the customer from the stockroom. Any standard product, such as electronic goods (e.g., television sets), is of such kind. In case of make-to-order products, the finished goods are produced only when customers place orders. An MPS is developed using real customer orders, but input raw materials and some subassemblies can be procured and stored in advance based on forecast. This is known as job shop, which produces custom-tailored products, such as furniture. In case of assemble-to-order, the major subassemblies are produced in advance, based on forecast, and are kept in the stockroom. The finished goods are assembled from those stocked subassemblies, based on a *final assembly schedule* (FAS).

The MPS contains information on which, how much, and when to complete the production of finished goods. Generally, MPS is developed on a weekly or sometimes daily basis, known as a time bucket, with a total planning horizon at least equal to the critical path time of the product. The planning horizon is the time period for which an MPS is produced. It is done for a period of 3 months to 1 year.

Suppose that the historical demand proportion for two types of Tables, Office and House Table, is 50:50%. Table 2 shows a plan for a weekly time

TABLE 2 An MPS

Product	\multicolumn{12}{c}{Weeks}
	1	2	3	4	5	6	7	8	9	10	11	12
House	100	100	100	100	110	110	110	110	75	75	75	75
Office	100	100	100	100	110	110	110	110	75	75	75	75

```
0
|------|---------------|---------------|
| FROZEN |    SLUSHY    |  LIQUID ZONE  |
|------|---------------|---------------|
```

time periods ─────────→

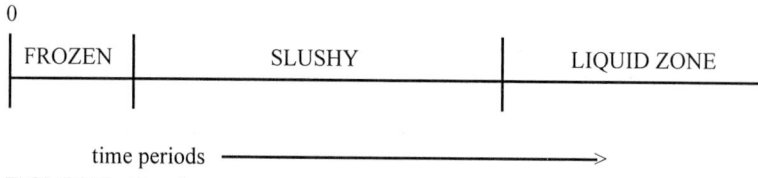

FIGURE 5 Time fences.

bucket and a planning horizon of three months. It is assumed that each month is comprises four weeks.

This MPS is still at the preliminary level, which requires adjustment in terms of capacity. The capacity planning section is given later on. Some terminology related to MPS are as follows

Delivery Promise. It is an amount not booked by any customer, and thus, is available to promise to customers. A delivery promise can be made on the *available to promise* (ATP) amount, where ATP = Beginning inventory + scheduled receipts − actual orders scheduled before next scheduled receipt.

Scheduled receipts. It is the order for which delivery is scheduled, but not yet fulfilled.

Time fences. As discussed earlier, the planning horizon is the time period, generally from 3 months to 1 year, for which the MPS is prepared. This may again be divided into separate zones, depending upon the level of certainty, as shown in Fig. 5 [1]. For the frozen zone, capacity and materials are committed to specific orders. Generally, no changes are allowed in this time period, thus is flagged as "Firm Planned." In the slushy zone, capacity and materials are committed to a reduced extent. Changes are allowed. The liquid zone is completely uncertain. No materials and capacity are committed for this time period [1].

3. Inventory Control

Inventories are those materials and supplies carried on hand by a business organization either for sale or to provide input to the production process [1]. There may be three types of inventories in a production company: Raw materials and subassemblies are materials purchased from the vendors, for use as inputs in the production process; work-in-process (WIP) inventories are partially processed materials in the production line; and finished goods are completed finished goods ready for sale to customers.

The inventory management is responsible for planning and controlling inventory. During planning, it decides the amount to be purchased or manufactured in one batch, known as lot size, and its timings.

It is necessary to classify the inventoried items in terms of their values based on Pareto analysis. This technique is known as ABC classification, which says that a relatively few items in number often constitute a large part in the total in terms of monetary value. It is usually found that the relationship between percentage dollar values of the items and corresponding numbers of items follow a pattern as shown in Fig. 6.

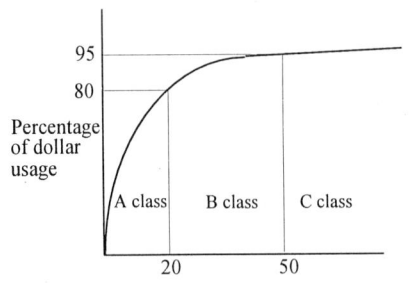

FIGURE 6 ABC Pareto curve.

A class items. Single-order inventory policy, and the Wagner–Whitin algorithm can be used to find out a refined lot size, or lot-for-lot (MRP) purchasing/production can be followed.

B class items. In this case, lot-for-lot (MRP) or a fixed lot size, obtained using EOQ or EPQ (*economic production quantity*), or the least total cost method can be followed.

C class items: In this case, bulk purchasing, fixed lot size, or the EOQ/two-bin system/periodic review system can be followed.

The MPS (or the finished good) is based on an independent inventory policy, whereas the MRP (or the lower-level components in the BOM of the finished good) is based on a dependent policy.

Independent policies. These policies find out the ordering size (volume) and timings of the finished goods. The most widely used policies in an MRPII system are EOQ/EPQ, order point system, lot-for-lot (MRP), etc.

Dependent policies. The components, raw materials, and subassemblies, which act as part of the finished good, do not have an independent demand of their own. The demand of these components depends on the demand of the finished goods. For example, the leg of a table is said to have dependent demand.

Lot-sizing rules, which are commonly used by MRPII professionals, are discussed below.

Lot-for-lot. Order size is exactly equal to the requirement in a time bucket. This is also known as MRP lot size.

Fixed lot. Irrespective of the requirement, a fixed lot or multiples of a lot are ordered to achieve minimum cost. EOQ, the most commonly used rule to determine a fixed lot, is discussed below.

The EOQ (or EPQ) formula tries to determine a lot size that offers minimum cost in terms of the above cost elements. Suppose that for Top of the Table, the order quantity is 400 units and the usage rate is 200 units per week, then Fig. 7 shows its inventory levels with time.

If the economic purchase quantity is Q (EOQ) per order, when each order costs Q for ordering an item, the item has an annual demand rate of D, and the unit purchase price is P at i percentage to carry the materials inside the

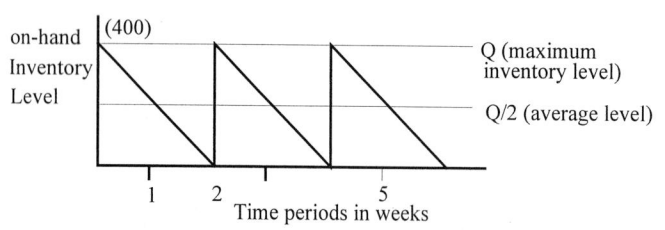

FIGURE 7 Inventory usage characteristics.

stockroom (i.e., inventory carrying, or holding cost), then

$$Q = \sqrt{\frac{2OD}{iP}}. \quad (1)$$

For example, if the purchasing price (P) of Top a Table is $10/unit, the ordering cost (Q) is $10 per order, the cost of carrying the inventory is estimated to be 20% (i.e., $i = 0.20$), and it has an annual demand of 10,000 units, then EOQ would be

$$Q = \sqrt{\frac{2 \times 10 \times 10000}{0.20 \times 10}} = 316 \text{ units}.$$

This amount is used as a fixed lot size in material requirements planning.

Although there are different variants of this EOQ policy, and different other policies as well, we will not discuss them all in this chapter.

4. Material Requirements Planning

The material requirements planning (MRP) prepares a schedule for the dependent components and raw materials in the BOM. On the basis of lead time for each component, it computes the timings and amount of these components. This process is known as *time phasing*. The MRP, having inputs from MPS, inventory, BOM, and open orders, finds the following:

1. *What items to order:* The process that identifies the items one by one, by going through the BOM level by level, is called MRP explosion.
2. *When to order:* From the target due date of requirements of the item, the calculation process that finds the order release dates, by calculating backward on the calendar, equal to lead time, is known as *lead time offsetting*. This scheduling process is called *backward scheduling*. Lead time is the time required to purchase or manufacture an item. This includes planning and order processing time, transportation time, materials inspection time, machine setup time, run or processing time, and queuing and moving time.
3. *How much to order.* This is calculated based on the amount in an MPS, on-hand inventory, and open order information. The MRP explosion program calculates this.

In some cases, the MRP should be able to regenerate the orders to satisfy any unforeseen situations on the shop floor, or in some other logistics functions.

Some terminology related to MRP calculation are discussed below [1].

Planned order. The orders generated by MRP explosion program and decided for execution are called planned orders. The order due date is termed as the *planned order receipt* date, and by lead time offsetting, the date on which the order should be released for execution is known as the *Planned Order Release* date.

Scheduled receipts. Scheduled receipts are orders placed on manufacturing or purchasing and represent a commitment and capacity at work centers allocated. Until the order is completed (closed), this order is termed an *open order*.

Gross and net requirement. Gross requirement is the total amount required for an item, computed from MPS, without considering on-hand inventory or open orders. Net requirements are calculated as

$$\text{Net requirements} = \text{Gross requirements} - \text{scheduled receipts} - \text{on-hand inventory.} \quad (2)$$

Table 3 shows the material requirements plan for the components of the finished good, Wooden Table.

TABLE 3   MRP Computation

Low level code	Item name		Past	1	2	3	4	5	6
0	Table	Gross requirement							70
		Scheduled receipt							
		On-hand	40	40	40	40	40	40	0
		Net requirement							30
		Planned order receipt							30
		Planned order release						30	
1	Top	Gross requirement						30	
		Scheduled receipt							
		On-hand	10	10	10	10	10	0	
		Net requirement						20	
		Planned order receipt						20	
		Planned Order Release					20		
1	Base	Gross requirement						30	
		Scheduled receipt							
		On-hand	10	10	10	10	10	0	
		Net requirement						20	
		Planned order receipt						20	
		Planned order release					20		
2	Body	Gross requirement					20		
		Scheduled receipt							
		On-hand	0	0	0	0			
		Net requirement					20		
		Planned order receipt					20		
		Planned order release				20			
2	Legs	Gross requirement					80		
		Scheduled receipt				70			
		On-hand	0	0	0		0		
		Net requirement					10		
		Planned order receipt					10		
		Planned order release				10			

TABLE 4 MRP for any Component, Lead Time 3 Weeks, Lot-for-Lot Lot Sizing

	PD	1	2	3	4	5	6	7	8
Gross requirements		4	10	18	0	10	8	0	15
Scheduled receipts			20						
Projected on-hand	20	16	26	8	8	0	0	0	0
Net requirements						2	8		15
Planned order receipts						2	8		15
Planned order release			2	8		15			

Periods, weekly time bucket

Note. PD means past date/due.

The procedure of calculation is as follows:

1. At level zero, the amount specified in the MPS is the gross requirement for Table. The net requirement is computed using Eq. (2). This is the planned order receipt. By offsetting the lead time of one week, the release time is found.

2. Next, at level 1, for Top and Base, the quantity per assembly is one in each case. Based on the planned order release amounts and time of Table, the gross requirements for both of them are found to be 30 on week 5. This means that the planned order release time and amount of a component at any level becomes the gross requirements for the next level component, when multiplied by the quantity per assembly, and offset by the lead time.

3. The computation continues down to level 2, and the same procedure applies.

In this example, the lot-for-lot lot sizing rule has been used. Examples of some other widely used rules are demonstrated in Tables 4 and 5.

Where it can be seen that the MRPs are different for the same MPS, depending upon the lot size rule.

There are several other variants of these MRP policies, which we do not intend to discuss in detail in this chapter [1,15,45].

Recent computerized MRPII systems have the capability of regenerating the planned orders in accordance with the changes in MPS. Two such procedures

TABLE 5 MRP, Lead Time 3 Weeks, Fixed Lot Size of 20 Units

	PD	1	2	3	4	5	6	7	8
Gross requirements		4	10	18	0	10	8	0	15
Scheduled receipts			20						
Projected on-hand	20	16	26	8	8	18	10	10	15
Net requirements						2			5
Planned order receipts						20			20
Planned order release			20			20			

Periods, weekly time bucket

Note. PD means past date/due.

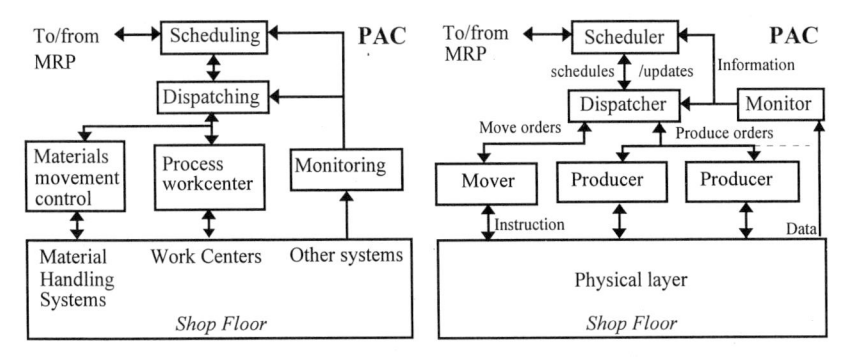

FIGURE 8 PAC System (Ref. 4, copyright Taylor & Francis).

are known: (i) *Net change MRP*, a procedure where only the changed orders are recalculated while others remain unchanged, and (ii) *regenerate MRP systems*, where all the orders are recalculated, in case of any change.

5. Production Activity Control

Production activity control (PAC), or alternatively known as *shop floor control* (SFC), describes the principles and techniques of planning and controlling the production during execution of manufacturing orders on the production floor [1,4]. It supports the following major functions:

- Scheduling,
- Dispatching,
- Monitoring,
- Control,
- Capacity management, and
- Physical materials arrangements.

The PAC functional elements and its model are shown in Fig. 8. After approval of the MRP generated orders, they are released as either purchasing orders for those components purchased from the vendors or manufacturing orders for those components manufactured on the shop floor. While the purchasing orders go to the purchasing department as *purchase request*, or *purchase requisition* (PR), the manufacturing orders are released to the shop floor.

One of the most important tasks of shop floor control is to assign priority to jobs, in order to prepare a *dispatching list* [1,4]. The dispatching list arranges the jobs in order to be processed at each work center according to a certain priority. A typical dispatch list is shown below:

Dispatch list
Work center: 5 **Work center ID: Assembly center**
Today: 16/9/98

Job No.	Part ID	Amount	Due date	Run time (hours)	Start date	Finish date
3151	1400	100	27/09/98	32.3	23/09/98	27/09/98
3156	1500	50	30/09/98	30.0	26/09/98	30/09/98
4134	1300	60	10/10/98	40.5	01/10/98	05/10/98

TABLE 6 Dispatching List in Accordance with the Priority Rules

Jobs	Number of days remained until due	Operation days required	Rank	EDD	CR
1000	9	7	1st	1001(2)	1001 (0.50)
1001	2	4	2nd	1010 (5)	1010 (0.83)
1003	8	5	3rd	1009 (7)	1000 (1.29)
1009	7	3	4th	1003 (8)	1003 (1.60)
1010	5	6	5th	1000 (9)	1009 (2.33)

There are several priority rules. The two most common rules are (i) *earliest due date* (EDD), where the job are arranged in a sequence of due dates, and (ii) *critical ratio* (CR), which is an index as

$$CR = \frac{\text{Due date} - \text{Present date}}{\text{Lead time Remaining}} = \frac{\text{Actual time remaining}}{\text{lead time remaining}}.$$

The priority schedules, prepared in accordance with the above two rules, are shown in Table 6.

Recently, information integration has gained momentum, leading toward CIM. The ESPRIT (European Strategic Program for Research in Information Technology) project is an attempt toward that. Out of several islands of automation in manufacturing, possibly PAC [4] is the best module, which requires integration of the most heterogeneous hardware systems. The problem is aggravated because of the closed architecture of CNC (*computer numerical control*) machines and other computer-controlled equipment, and nonimplementation of common 7-layer OSI communication protocol, such as MAP/TOP (Manufacturing Automation Protocol/Technical and Office Protocol). Additionally, PAC is highly a dynamic module, which goes through physical and logical changes frequently, because of changes in customer requirements, changes of equipment, disturbances, changes in product types, etc.

6. Capacity Management

Capacity management is responsible for determining the capacity needed to achieve the priority plan by planning and controlling the available capacity, and arranging for alternatives [1]. It verifies the feasibility of a materials plan, in varying the details at different levels, as shown in Figs. 9 and 10, in terms of resource capacity, where resources are the machines and equipment, and manpower. The capacity is measured in terms of man or machine hours. The capacity problem is still solved by the manual trial-and-error method.

Resource planning (RP) is concerned with long-range (say, for 2 or more years) capacity requirements against production planning. It roughly estimates the gross requirements of labour and machine hours for all or a group of products, for several years of operations. *Rough-cut capacity planning* (RCCP) includes a more detailed capacity requirements plan for individual products, over all weeks, and excludes the detailed shop floor scheduling and real time or unforeseen events. The *capacity requirements planning* (CRP), being the most

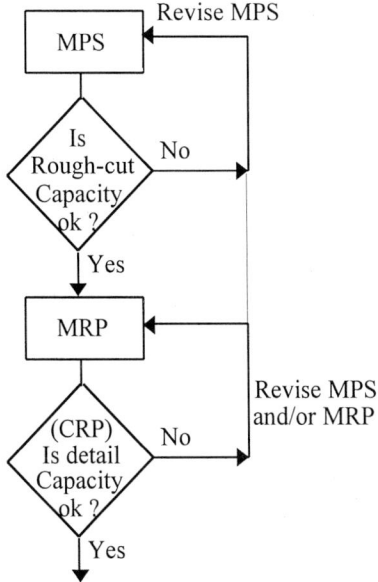

MANUFACTURING RESOURCE PLANNING

FIGURE 9 Capacity planning method.

detailed capacity planning stage, prepares detailed shop schedules, identifies alternative routing, etc. Generally, RP is not included here, and CRP is not supported by the MRPII systems. So, the following sections discuss only the RCCP method.

During RCCP, the work hours required to perform operations on a batch are verified against the available work hours during the same time period. If the available work hours are greater than or equal to the required hours, the MPS is accepted and approved. If not, then adjustments either to the MPS or to resource management is necessary, by the trial-and-error method.

For visual realization of overload or underload situations, load profiles are used for each work center and time period, and then necessary adjustments are done. For example, suppose that both House- and Office-type tables require the final painting work center, with the data provided in Table 7.

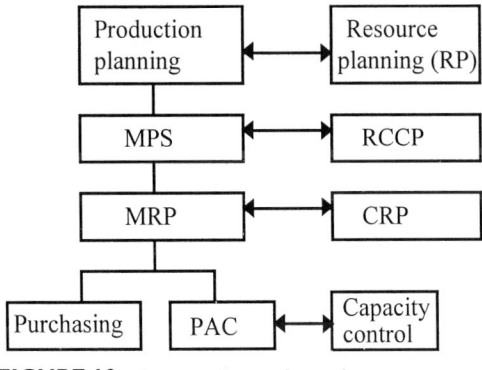

FIGURE 10 Capacity planning hierarchy.

TABLE 7 Required Man Minutes in Period 1

Table type	Production vol. (period 1)	Painting station Run time (min.)	Setup time (min.)	Total time (min.)
House	120	12	60	1500
Office	120	10	60	1260

Note. Total time required: 2760 minutes.

Similarly, suppose that for period 2, total required work minutes is 2000 minutes.

Against the above required work minutes, the available work minutes (man minutes) at that station is calculated as 1 worker, 5 working days per week, 1 shift per day, 8 hours per shift, 60 minutes per hour. Thus, the available man-minutes in periods 1 and 2 = $(5 \times 1 \times 8 \times 60) = 2400$ minutes.

Now, the load profile can be generated as shown in Fig. 11, where it is seen that the required capacity does not match the available capacity in each period. Some manual forward and backward adjustment may, thus, be necessary to keep the required capacity within the available capacity.

A shop calendar is maintained for finding the available work hours. With the assumption that each week comprises 40 work hours (excluding the provision of overtime), Table 8 is an example of a typical shop calendar.

7. Other Modules

Several other modules take part as "supporting modules" in the MRPII system, although they are not directly linked to the MRP explosion algorithm. They provide data as input only. Several modules, such as purchasing, sales, forecasting, accounting, costing, physical inventory verification, and distribution planning, exist within the MRPII system. As these modules do not take part in the algorithm directly, these are not discussed in detail, rather only the data elements that are input from these modules to the closed-loop MRP calculation are given in Section III of this chapter.

8. Operating Reports and Report Writers

Although, in manufacturing, a consolidated report has enormous necessity for management review and decision making, the users of MRPII, on many

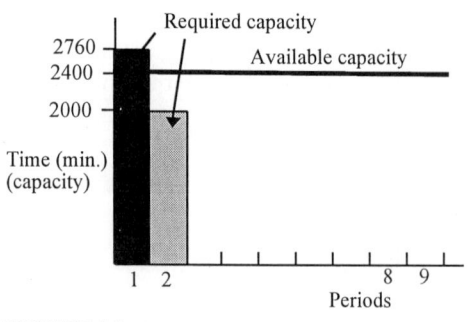

FIGURE 11 Load profile at painting station.

TABLE 8 An Example of a Shop Calendar

September 19xx												
Sunday		Monday		Tuesday		Wednesday		Thursday		Friday		Saturday	
										1	8	2	Nil
3	Nil	4	8	5	8	6	8	7	8	8	8	9	Nil
10	Nil	11	8	12	8	13	8	14	8	15	8	16	Nil
17	Nil	18	8	19	8	20	8	21	8	22	8	23	Nil
24	Nil	25	8	26	8	27	8	28	8	29	8	30	Nil

Note. Notation of calendar: | Date | Hours available |

occasions, neglect such reports simply because a typical MRPII produces so many reports that the need for additional ones seems to be limited. Moreover, the manufacturing databases are large and highly interrelated, which force the users to spend an enormous amount of computer time and hence, money too, on the production reports that cut across the subsystem boundaries [27,28].

An information center and ad hoc inquiry support task is normally required, and supported too in many MRPII systems, to satisfy special information needs. The problem again is the large and ever-increasing volume of manufacturing data collected and stored in large numbers of files in an MRPII system that must be processed for report generation. The problems of inquiry time, and thus cost, may be reduced in systems that provide summary databases or integrated inquiry and reporting facilities [28]. For example, Max Report Writer is an intelligent tool to help the user analyze information, stored in MRPII, in order to create ad hoc queries and reports. This has the capability to produce as much, or as little, information from the large manufacturing database as the user wants, without further programming [27].

III. DATA ELEMENT REQUIREMENTS IN THE MRPII SYSTEM

A. Database of the MRPII System

The center of an MRPII system is its large manufacturing planning and supporting database. The database may sometimes become so large that during implementation, only developing the database and verifying its accuracy may consume up to two-thirds of the total implementation time. A high degree of accuracy for all main data elements is a must for successful implementation. Many implementation attempts failed because of wrong plan generation from inaccurate databases. Additionally, once the system goes into operation, it becomes essential and a must to update the database on time. Otherwise, duplicate orders may be generated, wrong and false commitments to customers may be made, out-of-stock inventory situations may arise, etc.

In the earlier systems, the files of each distinct manufacturing and planning function were kept separately. As a result, when one file was changed, either the corresponding changes were not made in other functional files or duplicate efforts were necessary to keep all files consistent. As the functions of current computer-based MRPII systems are highly integrated, they maintain a single set of files. The appointed users can retrieve the information either as display or printout through standard reports. Numerous such built-in reports can be found in MRPII commercial packages, which in the background, uses a standard query system for the inquiries of the users.

Although the arrangement of data elements may vary from system to system, a typical system contains the following files:

Data input files
    Master data files
    Supporting data files
    Transaction (On-going/continuous) data file

Output files
    Manufacturing/purchasing order files
    Status (of different departmental) data files

1. Master Data Files

There are four master data files: *item master file* (IMF), *BOM file*, *work center file*, and *routing file*.

Item Master File

This is also known as the *part master record* (PMR) file, which contains the records of all parts/components, and even resources, required to build products. This file allows the planner to enter into the system the necessary part information, which may be categorized as the following:

Basic part information:

Part identification. A unique alphanumeric number which is used as a *key* to records. The ID may contain some group technology concepts in order to incorporate some feature qualifiers, such as design and manufacturing attributes, according to a similarity of features available among several components.

Descriptions. A lengthy character field to describe the name of the part, corresponding to the part ID.

User code. Although the above two items are common to any user, sometimes the users may differ as to which items they are interested in. For example, the accounting department may want to include packaging materials inside the BOM such that the cost of the packages may be automatically taken into account while calculating the total production cost of the product, whereas the design and engineering department is generally not interested in defining the packaging materials in the product design and BOM [45]. Similarly, the planning and the shop floor departments are generally interested in putting the tools as resources inside the BOM to facilitate capacity planning, but as it is not a part of the product design, the design department is not interested to include it. By having a user code with different levels and degrees of access, the needs of various interested groups can be served. The reports are also displayed or printed as per user code and other requirements.

Date added and obsoleted. The planner may be interested to keep records as to when the part was defined the first time, and afterward when the part would no longer be necessary for any reason, such as design change.

Several other items of information, sometimes tailored, may be necessary for some organizations not elaborated here [27,45].

Design and engineering information:

Drawing number. Necessary to relate the part ID to its drawing number.
Engineering status. Necessary to track the part in its complete life cycle.

In commercial packages, several other items of information are available as fields in the system database, such as units of measure (UOM), engineering change number, and revision number [27,45].

Low-level code. Level refers to the position where a part fits in the complete product structure. The recent MRPII software has the capability of determining the level of a component through a computation, known as *low-level coding,* specially when the same component appears at different levels in different products. It is not necessary for the planner to specify this; rather the software does this during data processing. In regenerative MRP systems, if explosion processing is simply done by calculating along the path through BOM hierarchies, it would, as a result, replan common components several times over. Here the low-level coding, a data processing mechanism, performs its role. It assigns each component a code that designates the lowest level of the component in any BOM on which it is found. The reason behind this is that MRP explosion processing is done level by level, from bottom to top in a tree, taking into account the total requirements of a component residing at a level [4].

Planning information:

Part type code. An essential field that determines whether a part is an in-house-built part or a purchased part to be supplied by a vendor, as well as whether a part is to be included as a finished good in the MPS or to be planned using ROP or another inventory policy.

In commercial packages, several other items of information are available as fields in the system database, such as manufacturer's part number, planned yield and scrap, etc. [27,45].

Bill of Materials File

This file describes the product structure, which is composed of parts described in the PMR. The records in this file each contain one parent–component relationship, with additional data, such as quantity per assembly, quantity code, BOM-type code, BOM level code, effectivity date, alternate part, lead time for assembly and lead time offset [27,45]. The search procedure for a component in the BOM, along with other information for the part, is explained later in this section.

Work Center File

The *work center* (WC) file and the *shop routing* file may reside under the PAC module. A WC is a single machine or a place, or a group of machines or places, that perform a particular operation on the shop floor. This is required to plan capacity and production schedules. Each WC must be defined by the required information, and must be identified by a unique number, known as the *WC identifier,* which is used as a key, with associated detailed description. Some other information (or data fields) that are necessary in this file include location, number of machines, number of workers, utilization rate, work hours assigned and available, smoothing factor, allowable queue, and overhead and labor rates (for costing) [27,45].

Shop Routing File

The shop routing describes the sequence of operations, with required WCs and tools, for producing a product. The routing should have an identifying number distinct from the number of the part being manufactured. This allows different parts to have the same shop routing [45]. A typical shop routing file may contain the following information (data elements):

Part ID (to link a routing to a particular part), operation sequence number, work center ID and descriptions, operation type (e.g., unit operation or batch operation), tool name and number, run time, setup time, planned scrap, etc. [27].

A standard shop routing is saved for a part. However, there are times when a particular manufacturing order may require some deviations from the standard one, due to specific reasons. In such a case, changes can be made in the standard file and then saved as an "order routing file," which indicates its application to a particular order only, whereas the standard file remains unchanged [27].

2. Supporting Data Files

Several other files contribute to the above master files to complete the system, depending upon the system's capability. Some major files are discussed, with their functionality and major data elements, below.

Cost Data File

This is used to input and review the cost-related data of a part, defined in IMF. Some major data elements are part ID (a key to IMF), part-type code, cost-type code (manually or automatically calculated), accounting-type code, unit of measure, costing date, direct material cost, direct labor cost, material and labor burdens, etc. [27]. Sometimes, a key to the *general ledger* (GL) accounting system is included in this file. Otherwise, a separate file that acts as an interface between closedloop MRP and a financial and cost accounting system/module may be introduced. The accounting system is also linked to different transaction files, such as materials purchase and sales, to exchange accounting data from/to accounts receivable (A/R) and accounts payable (A/P) files under an accounting system/module.

Inventory/Stock Files

There are two files associated with inventory control. The *stockroom data file* maintains information on available stockrooms in the company. Its data elements are a unique stockroom identification number and name, location, a code to flag whether it is a nettable (a permanent storage for regular transactions against usage) or nonnettable (a location for temporary storage, such as an inspection storage or a materials review board) stock, size/floor space, etc. The *inventory part data file* is necessary for linking part/component data in IMF to stockrooms where it is stored. It identifies the location (bin/shelve/rack/row/column) of parts in stockrooms (stockroom ID of stockroom data file), along with other inventory control information, such as lot size policy, order size, safety stock, lead time, physical cycle count code, and shelf life.

Purchase Files

These files link the part/component in IMF to its vendors, and other purchasing data/information. Several files may exist in a MRPII system to maintain these data/information. The *purchase part data file* maintains the basic purchasing information of a part if it is a purchased part. The data elements that may be found in this file are part ID (from IMF), purchasing lead times, purchaser's ID, UOM, etc. The *vendor data file* keeps the records, such as vendor ID and name, address, and FOB points, of all possible vendors/suppliers of input materials for the company. The *vendor part data file* identifies the relationships between parts/components and their suppliers (i.e., it shows what part can be purchased from what vendor, which means it basically provides a linkage between purchase part data file and vendor data file). It also provides price break down information for a part.

Sales Files

Two major files can be found in a MRPII system. The *sales part data file* identifies the MPS parts to be sold to the customers. It includes part ID (from IMF), sales price break down, taxation code, and sales UOM. The *customer file* keeps the records of permanent, potential, and past customers for future reference.

MRP File

This file contains information regarding a part's lot size policy in order to determine the amount to manufacture or purchase, and the lead time for backward scheduling. Additionally, it may include the planner's ID and name. Other information in this file are basically fed from other pertinent files, as given above.

Capacity Planning File

Although the current MRPII systems are unable to manage the CRP process, some systems provide connectivity with a third party scheduling software. This is beyond the scope of discussion in this chapter. However, some commercial MRPII systems provide only a RCCP module with limited capability. A RCCP module may contain two files for this process. The *shop calendar file* maintains a yearly calendar marked with weekly and other holidays, in order to exclude those days during backward scheduling. A *capacity maintenance file* may contain data on planned utilization of each work center, planned idleness of a machine for maintenance, etc.

For permanent data maintenance (input, display, print) purposes, in addition to the above major files, several other secondary/optional files, distributed in the pertinent modules, may be found in a system. Some examples of such secondary modules that may be found in a system are *quoting* (for quotation in bidding), *warranty tracking* (for efficient warranty process), *subcontracting* (for maintaining subcontract orders), *repetitive manufacturing* (in case of a repetitive environment, the module provides backflush capability against the received finished goods), *labor control* (to maintain labor/worker information), *management report writer* (to create summarized reports for management review), *lot tracking* (to track the products produced in a particular lot), etc. [27].

3. Transaction Data Files

In addition to the above files for permanent data maintenance, several other files are necessary for regular and ongoing continuous data inputs against all transactions. Some major transactional data files are discussed below along with their functionality.

Physical Inventory File

This file is utilized to store and retrieve information on a physical cycle count process. The file contains the records of inventory tag data, for use in cycle counts. Some important data elements in this file are tag number linked to part ID from IMF, quantity counted, name and ID of counting personnel, date of count, linked to stock ID from inventory module, etc.

Sales Order Entry File

Although the purchase orders are created automatically from the MRP explosion program, in case of urgency, the MRPII systems provide an additional file for entering a purchase order without any formal planning steps. This is the *unplanned purchase order file*, which includes part ID, vendor ID, line and delivery number, dates, quantity, price, etc.

To monitor and track the materials that are already purchased and waiting for reception or are in transit, a separate file, *reception record file* or *purchase order transit file*, is necessary to keep the records of amounts already arrived, the possible date of arrival, transportation mode, etc.

B. Data Storage and Retrieval in the MRPII System

In most of the traditional MRPII systems, the *record dictionary* and *pointer* [43] are used to identify and retrieve data, such as item/component/materials data from the BOM file, an example of a tree-type BOM of a Pen being given in Fig. 12, with the IMF, with selected fields, for the BOM being given in Table 9.

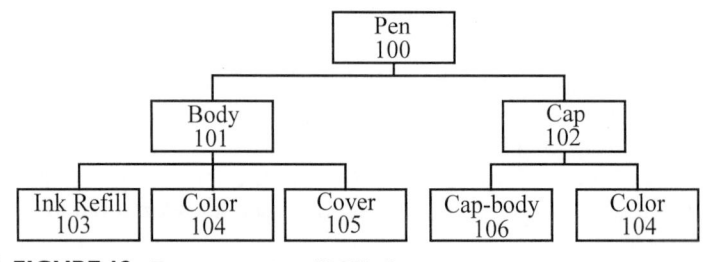

FIGURE 12 Tree presentation of BOM of pen.

MANUFACTURING RESOURCE PLANNING   439

TABLE 9   Item Master File (IMF) with Selected Fields

Record address	Part ID	Part name	Vendor, and (Mfg./Pur.)	First parent record	First component record
1	103	Ink Refill	TDCL (Pur.)		10
2	104	Color	TDCL (Pur.)		13
3	105	Cover	In-house (Mfg.)		16
4	102	Cap	In-house (Mfg.)	18	11
5	101	Body	In-house (Mfg.)	10	12
6	100	Pen	In-house (Mfg.)	12	
7	106	Cap-body	In-house (Mfg.)		15

As the part ID is a unique value for any component, it is used as the key to index and search data [43], as given in Table 10. The corresponding BOM file, with parent–component relationships and selected fields, is given in Table 11.

Now, if it is desired to find out the single-level BOM for subassembly Body (part ID 101) along with the information as to whether the component is a Purchased part or an inhouse Manufactured part, and if purchased, then the Vendor name, the record dictionary (Table 10) is searched. It is found that for this part (Body), the record address in IMF (Table 9) is 5. From Table 9, it is found that the pointer to the first parent record in BOM file (Table 11) is 10. When searched in the BOM file (Table 11) against the record number 10, it is found that the first component for Body (part ID 101) is 103 (Ink Refill). The pointer additionally indicates that the next component record can be found at address 13, which is the component with ID 104 (Color). The pointer at this record, in turn, indicates that the next component for this part is at record 16, where the component with ID 105 (Cover) is found. Thus, it is found that there are three components, with IDs 103, 104, and 105, for the parent part Body (ID 101). Additionally, the records at addresses 10, 13, and 16 give pointers to the IMF (Table 9) as 1, 2, and 3. When searched at record addresses 1, 2, and 3 in Table 9, the single-level BOM for subassembly Body (part ID 101) is established as shown in Table 12.

TABLE 10   Item Master, Indexed against Part ID (Key): Record Address Dictionary

Part ID (Key)	Record address
100	6
101	5
102	4
103	1
104	2
105	3
106	7

TABLE 11 BOM File with Pointers

Record No.	Parent (Part ID)	Component (Part ID)	Component next where-used	Parent's next component	Component's IMF record addr.
12	100	101		11	5
11	100	102			4
10	101	103		13	1
13	101	104	18	16	2
16	101	105			3
18	102	104		15	2
15	102	106			7

C. Information Transaction in MRPII

As mentioned earlier, the MRPII system, which is modular in construction and can be mapped one-to-one with the disparate departments of an organization, integrates the departmental operations into a single processing function, with the flexible option of handling the information of each department either independently or in an integrated fashion. The following sections discuss the information subsystems of the major functions/departments in the overall MRPII system.

1. Order Processing

When the customer wants to buy, he/she can place the order with the sales department (corresponding: Sales module of MRPII). This becomes the *customer order* in the next step of the MPS module of MRPII. In the case of make-to-stock items, the forecast amount and type of products become the MPS. In the case of a hybrid-type demand system, the direct customer order and forecast are combined together to produce the MPS. Then going through the complete MRPII algorithm, the orders are ultimately fulfilled from the finished good stockroom (corresponding: *inventory control* (IC) module of MRPII), by optionally updating the (A/R) of the accounting module of MRPII. This is shown in Fig. 13.

2. Purchasing Subsystem

The purchasing subsystem consists of those activities necessary to acquire raw materials and components for production and other purposes (see Fig. 14).

TABLE 12 Single-Level BOM for Body (Part ID 101)

Part ID	Part name	Vendor, and (Mfg./Pur.)
103	Ink refill	TDCL (Pur.)
104	Color	TDCL (Pur.)
105	Cover	In-house (Mfg.)

MANUFACTURING RESOURCE PLANNING

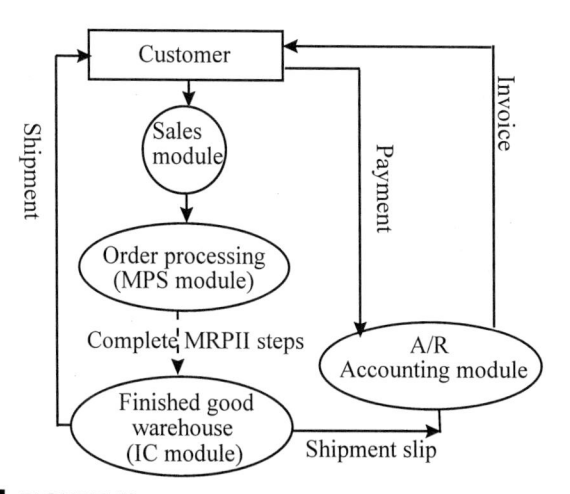

FIGURE 13 Order processing subsystem.

Generally, other requirements are fulfilled as "unplanned order" to combine with the regular manufacturing needs/orders, which are generated through the MRP explosion program. The later orders are known as "planned orders," which need approval in the computer system. All these are done in the MRP module of the MRPII system. The orders for purchasing are known as *purchase requests/requisitions* (PR) until those are assigned to particular vendors.

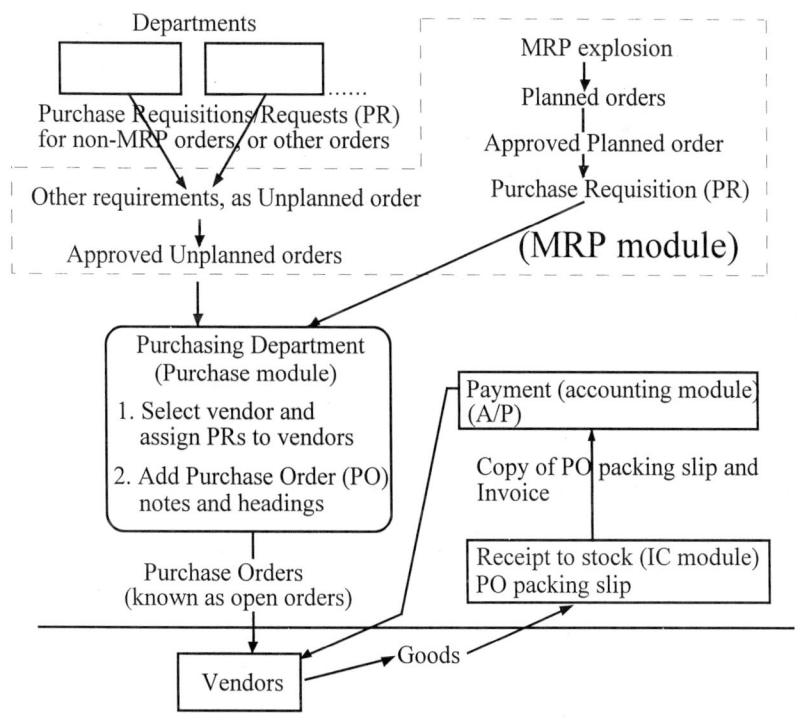

FIGURE 14 Purchasing function subsystem.

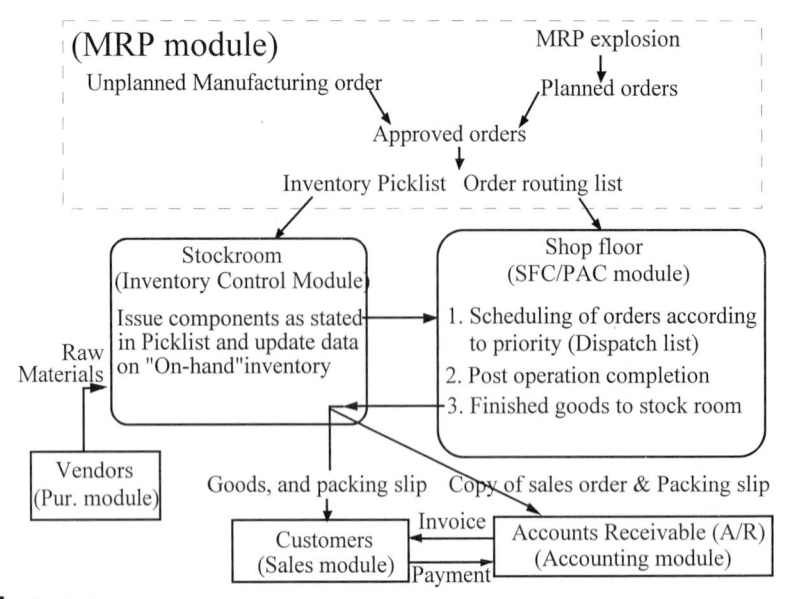

FIGURE 15 Manufacturing function subsystem.

A vendor database with all possible vendor lists are maintained, in the MRPII system, with their addresses, payment and shipment procedures, and possible price breakdowns. The complete process is known as *vendor scheduling*. Once a vendor is assigned to a particular PR and sent, the order status is changed from PR to *purchase order* (PO).

3. Manufacturing Subsystem

The manufacturing subsystem is responsible for generating and managing manufacturing orders (see Fig. 15). Generally, the orders are generated through the MRP explosion program, although some orders may be generated manually, as unplanned order. These orders need approval in the computer system. The manufacturing orders contain two vital lists, namely the *inventory pick list* and *shop routing list*. The inventory pick list lists all the raw materials and components needed to manufacture a particular product. The inventory people verify this list and then send the required materials to the shop floor through a menu item, "issue stock." At the same time, the shop routing list, which describes the requirements of operations, work centers, machines, tools, and sequence of operations to produce a particular product, is sent to the shop floor. After necessary prioritization, using some priority rules, a shop schedule is generated for maintaining the schedule within available capacity. Once production is complete for a particular order, the finished goods are sent to the *finished good stockroom* for shipment to the customers. When payment is also completed from the customer side, the accounting module describes the order as a "closed order".

The three functional subsystems described above are the most important subsystems, although there are several other functional subsystems in the complete MRPII system.

D. Early-Stage Information Systems in Manufacturing Planning

As different tasks in manufacturing planning became tedious, and need time-consuming iterative processes or trial-and-error solutions, there is no need to point out the importance of the role of computers in planning manufacturing resources, coupled with other related management functions. Over the years, several MISs (manufacturing information systems) have been developed for varied purposes, related to production resource planning, and in different details, basically to serve the same needs, an integrated resource planning for manufacturing. These MISs manage the information flow in parallel to resource flow, and establish functional connectivity between resources in different departments, where the resources may be machines and equipment, material, people, and money. The MRPII system is the most versatile of all such MISs.

The following section discusses some of the MISs [17] other than the MRPII system, since the MRPII system has been discussed in detail in earlier sections.

1. Computer-Aided Production Information System (CAPIS)

This system collects practical data through terminals located in work centers with on-line communication through (i) the production *scheduling and control* (SAC) system, to generate an optimum operation schedule, taking into account real shop conditions, which are then judged by the production planner, and (ii) *optimum seeking machining* (OSM), to know about the optimum working conditions of the machines and tools, taking into account the recorded basic engineering data from a file (see Fig. 16). This system, thus, focuses on generating operation schedules, based on machining and tool conditions, which is ultimately judged by people.

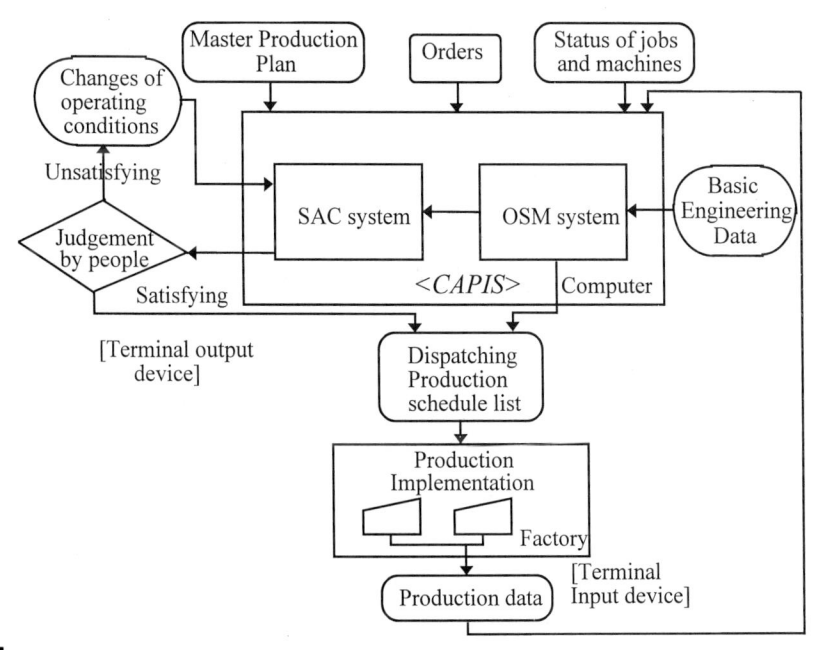

FIGURE 16 A general flow chart of the CAPIS system (Ref. 17, copyright Taylor & Francis).

The SAC performs simulations to find out the optimal schedule, which is then displayed at each work center by means of both visual display and/or printed instruction sheets.

It can be observed that although this on-line computer system is powerful in production scheduling, it lacks power in other functions of manufacturing, such as forecasting, linking forecast to MPS, which are complemented in the recent MRPII system.

2. Parts-Oriented Production Information System (POPIS)

This system is broader and one step closer to the MRPII system, in terms of functionality, than the CAPIS system. It consists of three modules—demand forecasting and production planning subsystem (Module I), parts production subsystem (Module II), and products assembly subsystem (Module III), all of which again consist of several submodules (see Fig. 17) [17].

The first module forecasts demand and sales, which is known as "primary information." It also manages data/information relating to the reception of

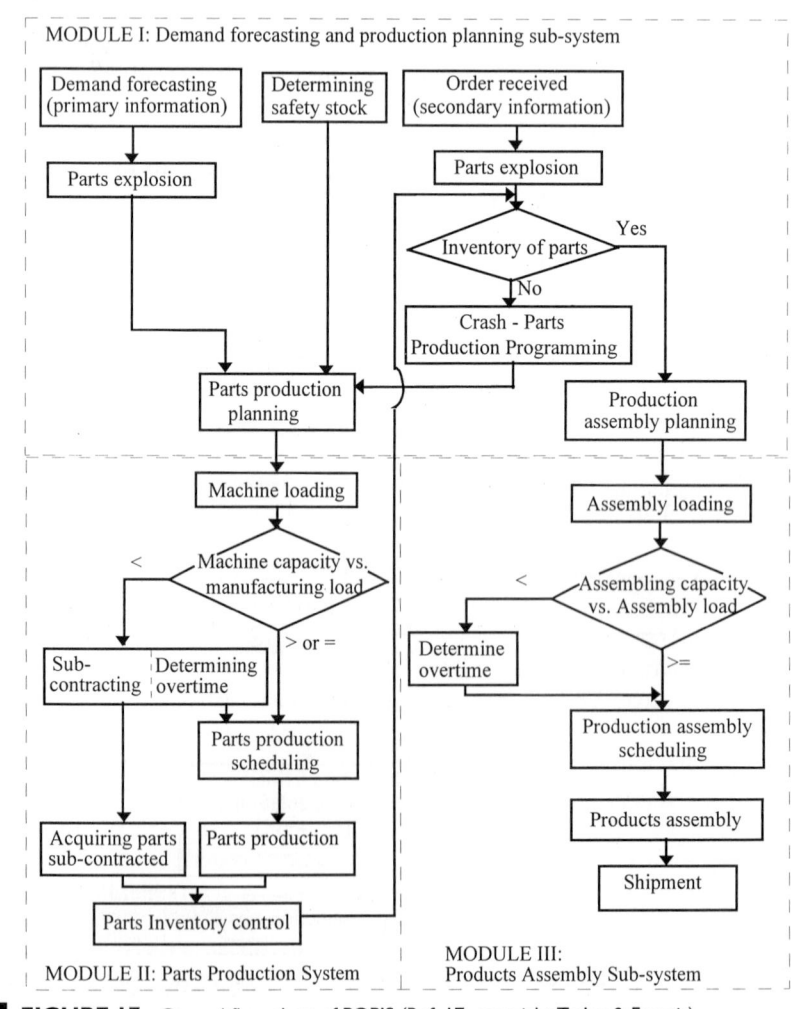

FIGURE 17 General flow chart of POPIS (Ref. 17, copyright Taylor & Francis).

orders, the determination of safety stock, and then the preparation of production plan, periodically, based on the primary information.

The second module, having input from the first module, prepares production schedule for the dependent parts (produced for stock) by properly sequencing them according to priority rules, and then manages the data/information of these produced parts along with the purchased parts as part of inventory control.

The third module, based on the information and data from the first module and materials along with information from the second module, prepares an assembly plan and executes the plan.

Although this computer-based information system has been proven to be useful for resource planning in manufacturing, it has not gained much popularity in today's manufacturing industries.

3. Communications-Oriented Production Information and Control System (COPICS)

This computer-integrated production information and management system was proposed by the International Business Machines Corporation as a concept of *management operating systems* (MOS) [17]. It deals with establishing a production plan based on forecast, and executing the plan as per capacity by purchasing raw materials and shipping the finished goods to customers. This is quite close to the idea of the current MRPII system.

This system introduced the idea of bill of materials of MRPII, from which an explosion is run to find out component requirements (see Fig. 18).

E. Information and Database Systems Centered Around MRPII

On several occasions, MRPII has been used as the center of a company-wide information system, sometimes leading toward the idea of *enterprise resource planning* (ERP), and *supply chain management* (SCM). Additionally, in several cases, the concepts of MRPII have been utilized to build customized information systems for companies. That means, these data and information systems can also be considered as a version of MRPII [13,18,23,25,37,54].

Although argumental, it can be stated that MRPII evolved toward ERP with the inclusion of several facilities, like electronic commerce and electronic data interchange, and toward supply/demand chain management with the inclusion of a network of companies who trade among themselves, either as a supplier or as a buyer. MRPII plays the central role of managing the data/information of resources in this connection (Fig. 19) [23].

The limitations of the MRPII system, either as an independent system or as a part of a company-wide information system, have also been complemented on several occasions by integrating information systems of other islands of manufacturing (see Fig. 20) [18,25,36].

From a survey, Meyer [25] identified four clusters of information for integration for manufacturing planning. These are: (i) internally oriented administrative systems, e.g., inventory status, purchasing, and accounting, (ii) market-oriented administrative systems, e.g., order entry, sales, forecasting, and distribution, (iii) internally oriented technical control systems, e.g., shop floor

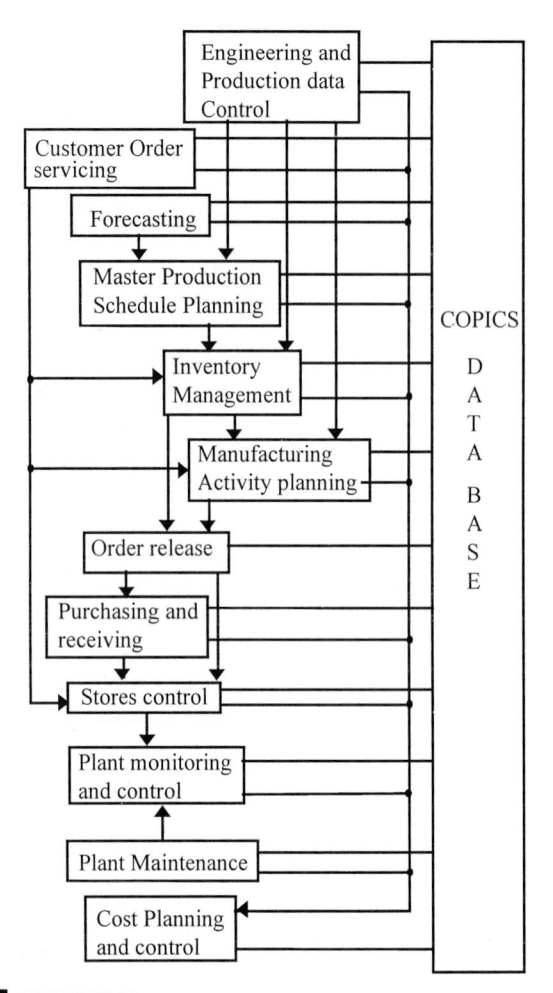

FIGURE 18 COPICS structure (Ref. 17, copyright Taylor & Francis).

control and quality reporting, and (iv) technical systems that link manufacturing to external groups and eventually the customer, e.g., design (CAD) and engineering. It can be noted that out of four clusters of information, three belong to the integrated MRPII system, where as only the last one is beyond the scope of MRPII. Meyer has shown this in a two-dimensional map, as seen in Fig. 21, where the islands of integration are linked with each other through a pivotal database, which is the MPS/MRP.

As opposed to the tradition of interfacing the databases of two systems, Hsu and Skevington [18] formulated a fundamental approach to the information integration of manufacturing enterprises, which includes MRPII as a key provider of data and information for several functions together for an enterprise. This approach entails the use of an intelligent metadatabase, which differs fundamentally from the strategies of both interfacing and a prevailing "super database management system." They applied the "feature" concept, traditionally known to be a technique for CAD/CAM integration, in the case of information modeling for all functions where MRPII takes a major part. This knowledge-

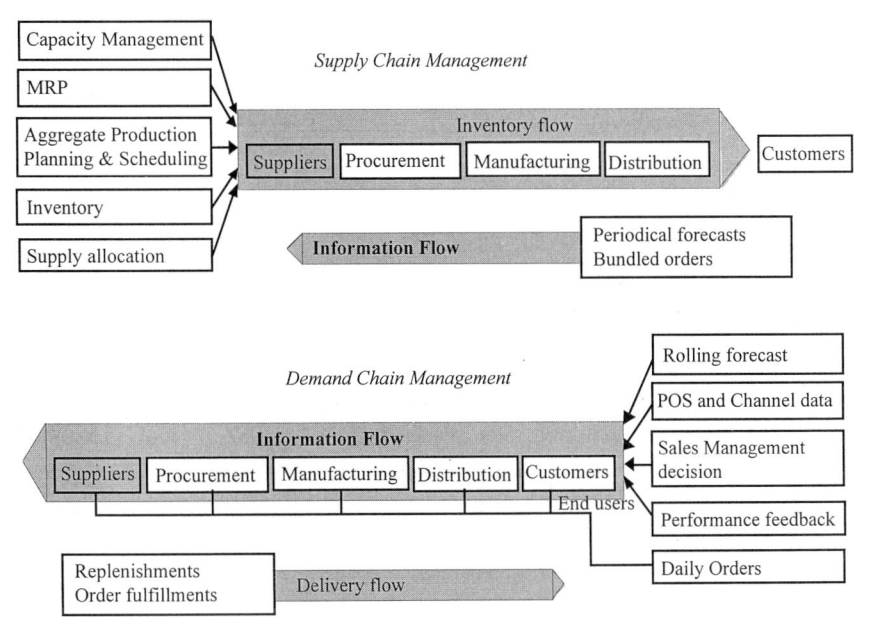

FIGURE 19 Information as driver for supply/demand chain (Ref. 23, copyright Taylor & Francis).

based enterprise information model has been termed as a metadatabase (see Fig. 22).

The authors also proposed an integrated system for computer-integrated manufacturing, specially between CAD/CAM, MRPII, and MRPII-related additional functions. The metadatabase serves as the core of the system residing in the kernel. The functional database, in conjunction with the metadatabase, constitutes the intelligent database system (DBS). The coordination is provided by a hierarchic control system. The application layer provides the system implementation for MRP.

As depicted in Fig. 23, the intelligent metadatabase plays the central role, which serves as an on-line repository of operational intelligence monitoring and supervises the flow of data across the system for real-time information.

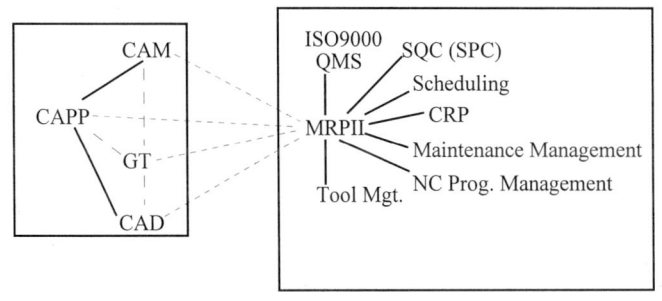

FIGURE 20 Systems Integration around MRPII. SQC, statistical quality control, includes SPC (statistical process control); QMS, quality management system, includes QA (quality assurance); CRP, capacity requirements planning; GT, group technology; CAPP, computer-aided process planning; CAD, computer-aided design; CAM, computer-aided manufacturing (Ref. 36, reproduced with permission from Inderscience Enterprises Limited).

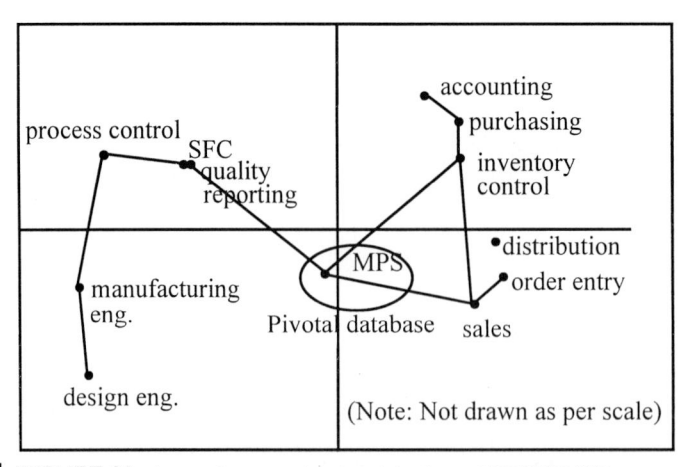

FIGURE 21 Integration around a pivotal database of MPS/MRP [25].

While the subsystems in this integrated database, such MRP, can function independently, its status and directories would be monitored by the metadatabase. The main difference in this system is that the conventional MRPII system's functional entities, such as orders and schedules, are converted to features, and the features and feature-based rules are then mapped onto data and knowledge representations. In this case, an object-oriented (or frame-based) representation for the feature hierarchy and dictionary is developed.

Harhalakis *et al.* [13] have also utilized the MRPII system's large database for further integration, to create an enhanced database system for a company. They are of the opinion that it is necessary to develop and share data from a variety of sources, specially the MRPII system. The authors have proposed the integration of MRPII with computer-aided design (CAD) and computer-aided process planning (CAPP), where they modeled and analyzed the system using Petri nets.

Since integrated information and databases have become the center of research in CIM, the MRPII system has been used to integrate CAD, CAPP,

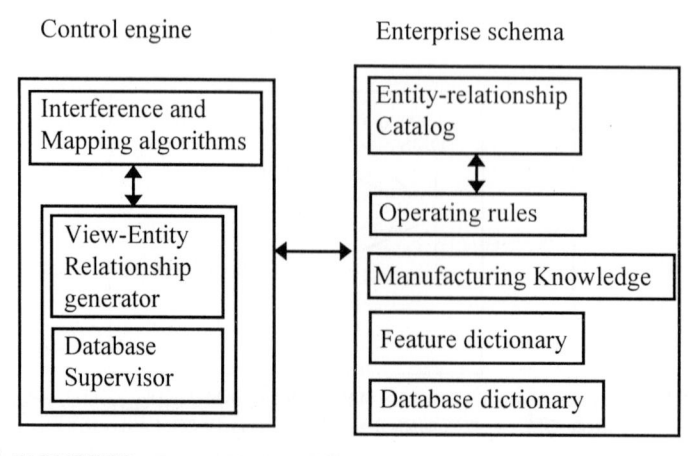

FIGURE 22 The metadatabase [18].

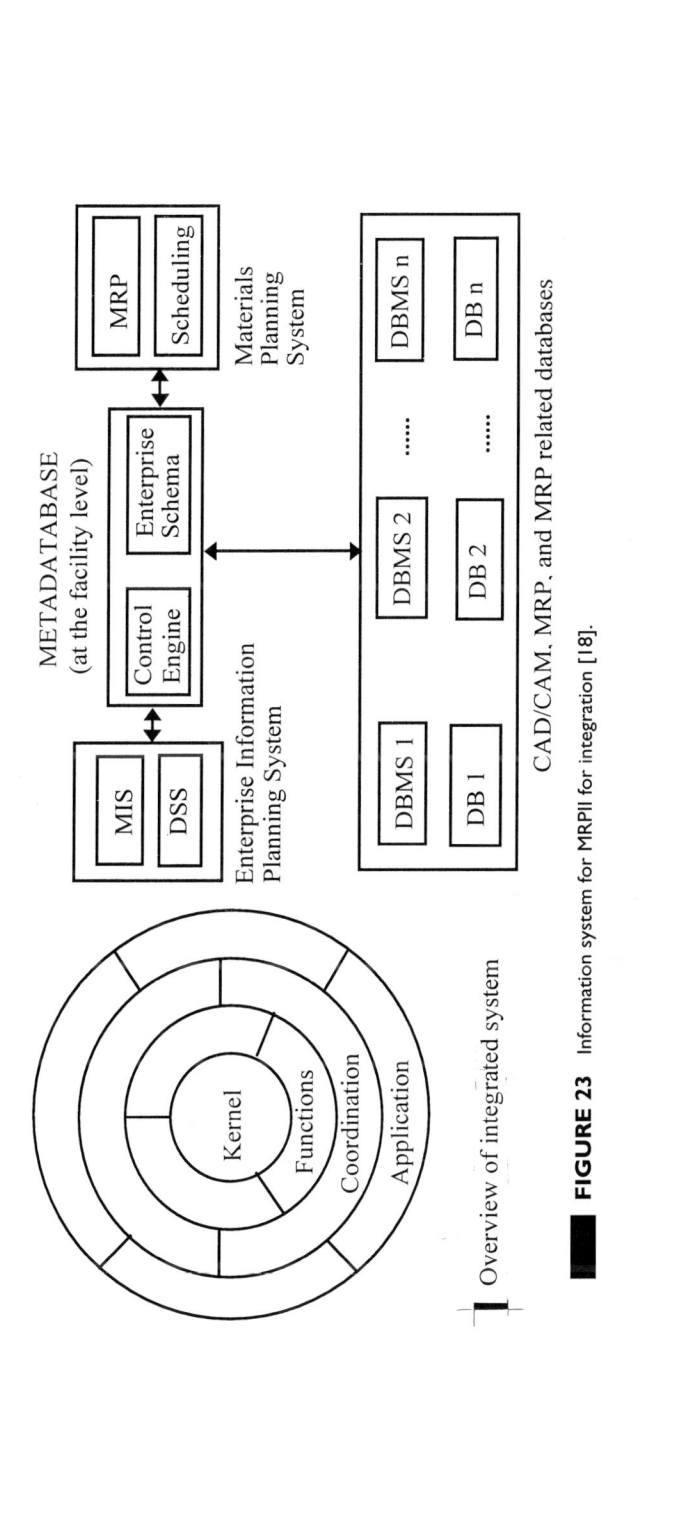

FIGURE 23 Information system for MRPII for integration [18].

TABLE 13 Common Data Records [13]

Part record		Part revision record	
CAD	**MRPII**	**CAD**	**MRPII**
Part number	Part number	Part number	Part number
Drawing number	Drawing number	Revision level	Revision level
Drawing size	Drawing size	Effectivity start date	Effectivity start date
BOM unit of measure	BOM unit of measure	Effectivity end date	Effectivity end date
—	Purchase inventory unit of measure	Status code	Status code
—	Unit of measure conversion factor	Drawing file name	—
—	Source code		
—	Standard cost		
—	Lead time		
Supersedes part no.	Supersedes part no.		
Superseded by part number	Superseded by part number		

Work center record	
MRPII	**CAPP**
ID number	ID number
Description	Description
Department	Department
Capacity (HR)	—
Rate code	—
Resource capacity	—
Dispatch horizon	—
Effectivity start date	Effectivity start date
Effectivity end date	Effectivity end date
Status code	Status code
—	Horse power
—	Speed range
—	Feed range
—	Work envelope
—	Accuracy
—	Tool change time
—	Feed change time
—	Speed change time
—	Table rotation time
—	Tool adjustment time
—	Rapid traverse rate

Routing record	
CAPP	**MRPII**
Routing number	Routing number
Part description	Part description
Unit of measure	Unit of measure
Operation number	Operation number
Operation description	Operation description
Work center ID no.	Work center ID no.
Setup time	Setup time
Machining time	—
Handling time	—
Run time	Run time
Feed	—
Speed	—
Depth of cut	—
Number of passes	—
—	Resource code
—	Begin date
—	End date
Status code	Status code

and MRPII through different DBMS approaches, as outlined by Harhalakis et al. [13]. As stated by the authors, the functional model of the proposed MRPII/BCAD/CAPP integrated system is based on the similarity of functions and the commonality of data among these three application modules. More specifically, Table 13 lists the data records the authors found common to the information subsystems [13].

To represent the functioning of the model, status codes for each entity are used to control the information flow and the status changes. The entities in question are part revision, routing, and work center. These are listed in Table 14.

TABLE 14 Status Codes [13]

Part revision status codes in MRPII, CAD, and CAPP

MRPII

R—"Released"	An active part, whose purchase or manufacture can be initiated in MRPII.
H—"Hold"	Under review, not to be used by MRPII.

CAD

W—"Working"	At a conceptual or preliminary stage, prior to approval, and not transmittable to MRPII.
R—"Released"	An active part, whose design has been finalized and approved.
H—"Hold"	Under review, pending approval, possibly with a new revision level. The part should not be used by any system.
O—"Obsolete"	The part is obsolete.

CAPP

W—"Working"	At a conceptual or preliminary stage, prior to approval.
R—"Released"	An active part, whose design has been finalized and approved.
H—"Hold"	Under review, pending approval, possibly with a new revision level.
O—"Obsolete"	The part is obsolete.

Routing status codes in MRPII and CAPP

MRPII

R—"Released"	An active routing, which is able to be passed down to the shop floor by MRPII.
H—"Hold"	Under review, not to be used by MRPII.

CAPP

W—"Working"	At a conceptual or preliminary stage, prior to approval, and not transmittable to MRPII.
R—"Released"	An active routing, whose process design has been finalized and approved.
H—"Hold"	Under review, pending approval, possibly with a new revision level. The routing should not be used by any system.
O—"Obsolete"	The routing is obsolete.

Work center status codes in MRPII and CAPP

MRPII

R—"Released"	An active work center.
H—"Hold"	Not to be used by MRPII.
D—"Delete"	A work center deleted from the system.

CAPP

W—"Working"	At a preliminary stage, work center details need to be entered in CAPP.
R—"Released"	An active work center, able to be used in process plans.
H—"Hold"	Under review, not to be used for process plans.
O—"Obsolete"	The work center is obsolete.

According to the authors [13], the Petri net theory has distinct advantages that enabled them to model an integrated database system around MRPII. The advantages are listed as: (i) its ability to model simultaneous events, (ii) its ability to represent conflicts, (iii) its potentiality to identify the status codes, using Petri net graphs, and (iv) its hierarchical modeling capability.

IV. APPLICATION OF RELATIONAL DATABASE MANAGEMENT TECHNIQUE IN MRPII

The past two decades have witnessed phenomenal change in the field of industrial engineering systems, which have expanded to include computer-based information. One tool regarding this is the *database management systems* (DBMS), particularly, relational DBMS. The relational data structure supported by a software is easier to conceptualize and manage some alternate data structures, and it allows greater flexibility in defining the data and their relationships [20].

Over the years, relational database techniques, as a tabular form, have been applied, and still now, are the most widely used in the MRPII system and its modules' design. The majority of existing commercial MRPII systems follows the relational approach. There have been reports of design efforts of MRPII and its modules using relational databases [29,35,54]. It must be stated that generating and managing, efficiently, the database of BOM is possibly the most difficult task among all the modules of MRPII. As such, the design of this module has attracted considerable attention from researchers.

Because of the large variety of products, which require several kinds of numerous resources for production, processing and response in a MRPII system become so high that ad hoc decision facilities become necessary, in place of the current situation where processing is done at a full level of detail all the time. The possibilities of abstraction and decomposition in a materials planning system, such as MRPII, becomes inevitable. Winter [54] proposed that a combination of metaplanning concepts with representation and processing capabilities provided by a relational DBMS is suitable for resolving the stated issue. Since a recent relational DBMS is capable of representing complex abstraction hierarchies, such databases can serve as an intelligent tool for the integration of different levels of information abstraction.

Hierarchical materials planning systems require the concepts of object abstraction. Abstraction can be applied to any object, such as machines, parts, or orders. The abstraction has five dimensions: aggregation, generalization, association, classification, and selection. A typical abstraction hierarchy is shown in Fig. 24 [54].

Winter proposed that objects, such as machines, manpower, and orders, as well as procedures that compute, govern, and link the objects, such as MPS, offsetting, and lot sizing, can be represented by data abstraction, and then represented by a relational view.

Although Winter [54] did not elaborate on the construction of abstract objects and their linkage methods through relational database management techniques, he presented the objects and procedures to show that they can be linked with relational techniques using different views of abstraction dimensions, such as aggregation, generalization, and selection.

MANUFACTURING RESOURCE PLANNING   **453**

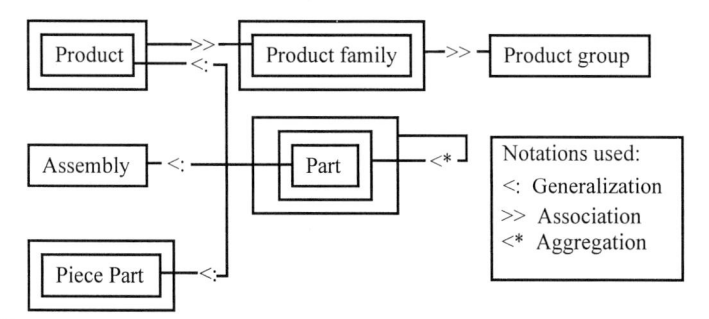

FIGURE 24 An overview of an abstraction hierarchy for a product structure (Ref. 54, reproduced with permission).

It is possible to represent all dimensions of abstraction in terms of relational views referring to physical relational tables or to other relational views. In order to explain this, it is assumed that piece parts are those parts, consumed by the production process, but are never outputs from a process (e.g., purchased parts, raw materials), subassemblies are those parts outputted from a process, but not the final product, and products are those parts not consumed by a process, but rather are the final outputs of a process. Figure 25 illustrates the aggregation view of subassembly, which is based on the "process" table, "BOM" table, and "piece part" table.

Figure 25 is graphically self-explanatory. The part ID of subassembly is obtained from that of the assembly process. The maximum lead times for the components (piece parts) required to build the subassembly are added together to find the lead time for a subassembly. The values of the components are multiplied by respective quantities to find the value of their subassembly. ABC classification of a subassembly is the minimum ABC position of its components [54].

The final product and its components can also be defined similarly. This way a complete aggregation hierarchy of BOM can be defined. Thus, it can be

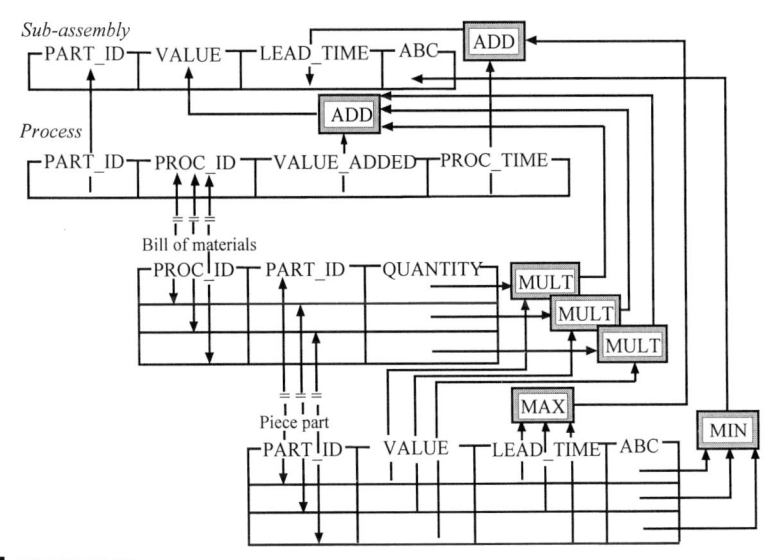

FIGURE 25 Aggregation view of subassembly (Ref. 54, reproduced with permission).

concluded that abstractions (of objects) can be represented as a relational view. Similarly, abstraction is possible in the case of many planning procedures.

Based on the fact that whenever a planning procedure can be represented by a series of relational operations that procedure can also be represented by a relational view, the Winter [54] illustrated how some MRP procedures can be represented as a relational view. The following discussion shows the netting procedure (which determines net requirements of materials or inventory) with a relational view.

A netting procedure requires a set of sequential operations (computations) using data from separate relational tables. Separate data tables for inventory and gross requirement can be created to perform those sequential computations (Fig. 26). In MRPII, net requirement represents the difference of amounts between current inventory on-hand (from the "inventory" table) and the gross requirement (from the "gross requirement" table). This has been shown as a relational view in Fig. 26. For each part, using an appropriate view, cumulative gross requirements should be found based on the gross requirements table. The amount of "inventory out" should be based on the on-hand inventory and cumulative gross requirement, whichever is least. (That is, if gross requirement is more than on-hand, an amount equal to gross requirement cannot be issued. In that case an amount equal to on-hand can be issued. On the other hand, if the on-hand amount is more than the cumulative gross requirement, then certainly an amount equal to the cumulative gross requirement should be released.) Whatever the abstraction level of parts, gross requirements, and inventory, the

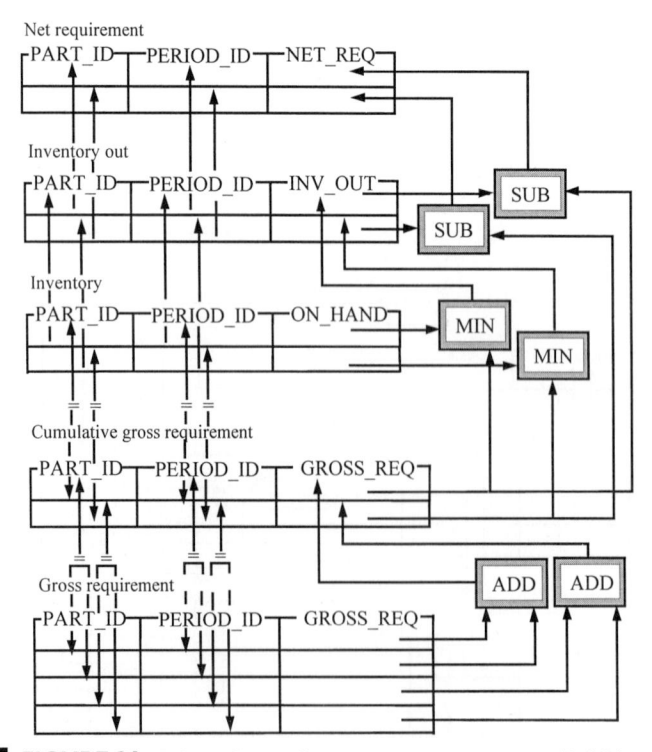

FIGURE 26 Relational view of net requirement computation (Ref. 54, reproduced with permission).

netting procedure is always feasible, and leads to net requirements at the same level of abstraction [54].

Similarly, several other MRPII procedures such as lot sizing, MRP explosion, and lead time offsetting, can also be represented in a relational view. Finally, a relational database system integrates the representation of abstraction hierarchies and planning procedures [54].

A prototype system, having database definition and processing in the relational DBMS Oracle V5. 1B, its SQL interface Oracle SQL*PLUS V2.1, and its C interface Oracle PRO*C V1.2, was developed. This system provides the facilities of normal materials planning, and additionally reusability and simulation. It is true that some of the complex planning procedures cannot be represented solely as a sequence of relational operations. Those were implemented in C programs. Database functions and relational operations were embedded in these procedural programs as high-level SQL commands. All base tables are loaded/unloaded via import/export procedures from a host-based MRP system that supports a hierarchical database model. The authors hoped that despite several drawbacks, continuing development of relational DBMS and the integration of database representation techniques and inferential processing will allow the application of the above concepts to more complex planning systems' design at a reasonable level of performance [54].

Olsen *et al.* [35] described the use of this approach in the case of customer-oriented products, which need a large number of variants. As a solution to the problem of managing a large number of product variants, if separate BOMs are created for each variant, the database would become so large that it would be impossible (and/or inefficient) to manage in the computer system. As a result, the authors suggested a generic structure of BOM. They designed this generic BOM using a relational database technique, but their approach is different from the traditional method of generic BOM. Earlier attempts to develop generic BOM have been directed toward either creating planning BOMs or improving the tabular structures only. As this technique has several limitations, including inflexibility, the authors proposed resolving it by the application of programming language notation [35], although there has been a report of the use of the object-oriented technique for this [7,8]. The authors, however, disagreed with the idea of object-oriented techniques for this purpose as it violates one requirement of describing components independently of their utilization.

Olsen *et al.* [35] proposed building generic BOM by utilizing some constructs, namely procedure concept, variables, input concept, and selection (case) statement, of programming languages. This has been termed as a procedure-oriented approach. In this approach, the variant or customer-specific product specification is established through input from the user. A prototype was tested on a PC under MS Windows. The programs were implemented with SQL Windows case tools from the Gupta Corporation.

The description of the generic BOM (GBOM) as a program enables the system to support the user in the product variant specification task by defining each component with header and body, which is stored as a database record. Variants are expressed simply through attributes.

Suppose that a "stool" has a component "seat," which may have three options of colors, namely red, blue, and white. The followings are the codes proposed by Olsen *et al.* [35].

```
component §400 is                component §200 is
    name("seat");                    name("stool");
    seatColor(red|blue|white)    end component;
end component;                   body §200 is
                                     include §400;
                                     include §500;
                                 end body;
```

In the above codes, a *procedure*, "component" has been illustrated. While the head identifies a component and presents its attributes, the body presents the goes-into relationships, i.e., BOM structure. Here, the head part of the component "seat" has a single attribute seatColor, which gives optional views of the component, i.e., may have different colors of red, blue, or white, based upon the user's selection. The other codes show it as a part of "stool" (ID: 200). The body part of the "seat" may be defined as shown in Fig. 27 [35].

In the Figure, the head part of codes for only cover (ID: 450) has been shown, although the seat is composed of cushion, chipboard, and cover. The heads of other components can be defined similarly. The codes show that the seat color may vary, depending upon the options of colors of cover, which may be selected by the user during variant creation. The attribute coverColor is, thus, used as a specification of the product variant. Further specifications with options in part features can be added, such as options of different seat sizes. The generic view of the complete procedure to create a specific BOM from the generic one is shown in Fig. 28 [35].

The system, in Fig. 28, has three tasks, Generic BOM Task (GBST), Product Variant Specification Task (PVST), and BOM Conversion Task (BCT). The GBST specifies the generic BOM for one or more products. At the stage of PVST, the attributes for a specific variant are given, in order to create a specific BOM for a particular product. At the step of BCT, each component variant referenced in the ABOM is replaced with a unique item number. The translation tables (TTAB) contain the necessary information for conversion from attribute values to component numbers [35].

The data structures, output from these three tasks, are: (i) The GBOM describes all components used in a BOM; (ii) ABOM describes a specific product variant; and (iii) NBOM describes the BOM in terms of indented BOM for use in a conventional information system, such as for use in commercial MRPII systems [35].

```
body §400 is                              component §450 is
    include §410;   ---- cushion              name("cover")
    include §420;   ---- chipboard            coverColor(red|blue|white);
    include §450 with;   ---- cover       end component;
        coverColor(seatColor);
    end include;
end body;
```

FIGURE 27 A GBOM view [35].

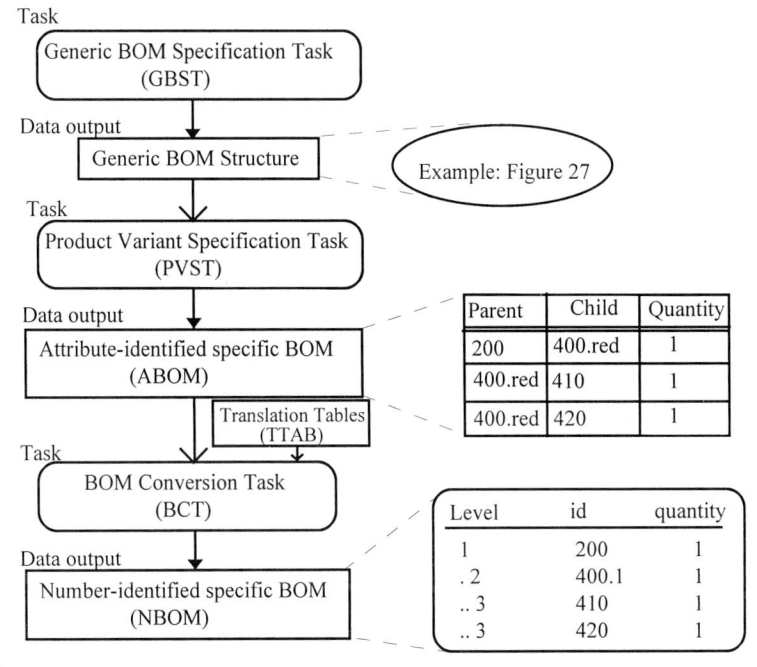

FIGURE 28 Procedure-oriented BOM generation [35].

V. APPLICATIONS OF OBJECT-ORIENTED TECHNIQUES IN MRPII

Many authors have discussed the weaknesses of traditional forms of database management techniques for MRPII and other similar systems. They are of the opinion that object technology may be helpful for solving many of the data management problems in complex manufacturing systems, composed of several planning functions, although it is fact that object technology also has some limitations [7,8,10–12,19,21,22,30,35,37,41,44,49,56–58].

As an MRPII system is composed of several planning and control functions, integration inside the MRPII system and its periphery for third party data connection is a vital requirement, and of interest too, as it contains a large volume of complex data. Each of these functions serves as an application module inside the system. It requires coordinated solutions to data management problems for not only individual application modules, but also for intermodule data exchange. The object paradigm, in many cases, has brought quite considerable success.

Out of several limitations of the traditional data management, a lack of data semantics is of particular importance. Thus, developing techniques for representing and using the semantics of data is key to realizing improvements in data management inside the MRPII system, and its integration with other manufacturing applications, such as quality management functions and maintenance scheduling.

Spooner *et al.* [47] discuss the research work at the Rensselaer Polytechnic Institute, which addressed the above problems with hybrid types of solutions. As the authors discuss, the desire to capture more of the semantics of data leads naturally to the use of data abstraction and object-oriented techniques to model and integrate data in a CIM environment. The authors present CIM as a system composed of design and engineering data and some production-related data, which is in fact an integrated MRPII system. Interestingly, the authors prescribe the use of object technology in the case of the first type of data, and the relational data technique for the MRPII-related functions. The logic behind this is explained:

> Data abstraction provides a means for organizing data into objects that are semantically meaningful to application systems. Object Oriented programming techniques enhance the semantic content of data by defining relationships, possibly with inheritance of properties for CIM applications [the authors here mean the engineering and design applications] because the fundamental principles behind it are the creation and manipulation of data objects, and these are exactly the activities done during typical engineering, design and manufacturing processes. The object paradigm also provides a flexible data model in which the complex data structures found in many design and manufacturing applications can be created and manipulated easily. This flexibility also helps in integration of the many applications in a typical CIM environment. [47, p. 144]

At the same time, the authors were of the opinion that other aspects of CIM, arguably the MRPII functions, having quite similar data, fit into the realm of traditional relational database technology. As a result, the CIM database management system was shown as a hybrid system, comprising object technology and relational data technology. This hybrid system was proposed as the ROSE Data Manager. The framework of this system, as shown in Fig. 29, contains a distributed object management component, which can be used to transfer data between an object database (design, engineering, etc.) and a relational database (MRPII functions).

In majority of the cases, the MRPII systems were built using the relational database management systems, although it has shortcomings in processing long-duration transactions, in storing images or large texture items, and in having complex data structures. Currently, the research direction in database management systems of MRPII (and other manufacturing systems, such as CAD and CAM) has moved from the relational database toward the object-oriented

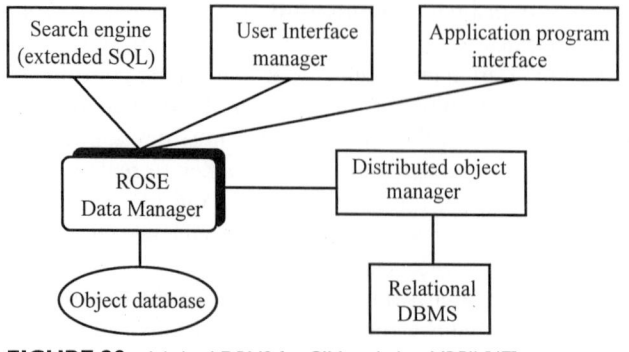

FIGURE 29 A hybrid DBMS for CIM, including MRPII [47].

database, which is capable of supporting complex data structures and network transactions [10].

Although *object-oriented database management systems* (OODMS) have proven to be very fruitful in many areas of MRPII, it has its own limitations as well. As discussed in Section II of this chapter, an ad hoc query is very essential in MRPII. As discussed by Du and Wolfe [10], it is difficult to declare a query in an OODMS. To query an object-oriented database (OOD), the user needs to navigate from one object to another through links. Also, so as not to violate the rule of encapsulation of object-oriented technology (OOT), the only way to access data is through designated methods in objects. Some commercial OODMSs, such as O2, ONTOS, ORION, Iris, and POSTGRES, support this ad hoc query facility, whereas others, such as Versant and Gemstone, do not possess that capability [10].

Zhou *et al.* [56] discuss the use of object technologies for information management in production planning and control (PPC). Although production planning and control do not exactly mean MRPII, they play a significant role in MRPII. Thus, on many occasions, the MRPII is termed as being similar to a production planning and control system. The authors present a distributed information management architecture, written in Visual C++ on a Windows NT platform, for PPC in a semiconductor manufacturing virtual enterprise, under the ESPRIT project (X-CITTIC). The Oracle 7 workgroup server has been used to build the databases, Iona's Orbix as ORB to link distributed information managers and applications, and ILOG for building the object servers, linking relational databases, and servers and building GUIs.

The authors describe some information/data, e.g., resource data, as local data, and other, such as customer orders, as global data. In this system every virtual enterprise unit connects to a local information manager (LIM), which holds all local data and serves local applications (e.g., local capacity models). Some units of the virtual enterprise may share one LIM. The authors cite an example: front end (FE) and back end (BE) wafer fabrications often share one production site and one shop floor control system and even some production resources. The global information manager (GIM), located at head quarters, maintains global data/information and is used by global applications (e.g., enterprise planner and controller). The communications between the information managers are performed using *object request broker* (ORB) with Internet inter-ORB protocol (IIOP) capability (Fig. 30).

Although of particular importance for further research on application of object-oriented technology in MRPII and PPC, the authors, however, do not elaborate how each of the elements of PPC were modeled using object technology, and how the functions of PPC (or modules of MRPII) interact with each other.

Park *et al.* [37] also report on a similar work on object-oriented production planning (aggregate) and control (PPC), as part of the *enterprise resource planning* (ERP) system. They present an object class extraction system in several steps through: (i) defining the object classes within the system using the Use Case approach, (ii) establishing relationships among the classes, (iii) establishing a hierarchical structure of classes, (iv) establishing event trace diagram, and (v) defining the detail attributes and operations about the object classes, although the last step is left for future work. The functions, which have been

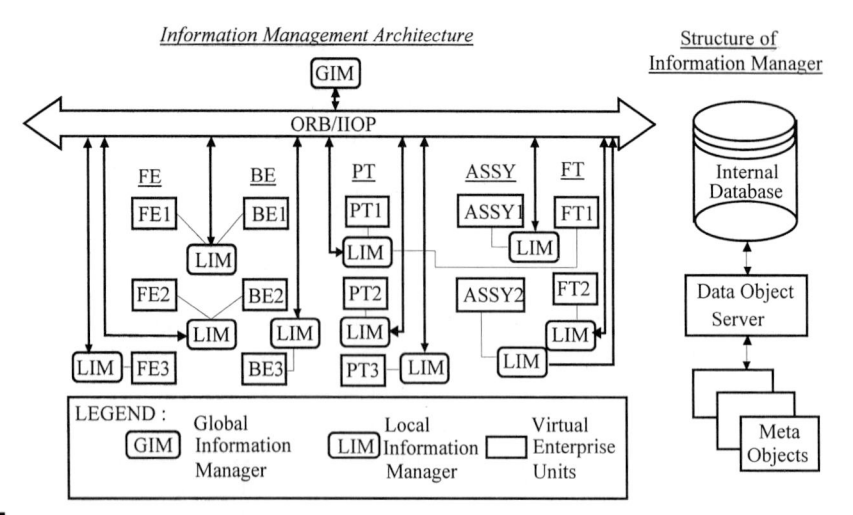

FIGURE 30 Virtual enterprise information management architecture [56].

covered in PPC systems, are scheduling and rescheduling, capacity requirements planning, inventory control at the factory level, dispatching, load monitoring, and process monitoring. The PPC system has been classified into the following object categories:

> Production objects
> > At factory level: factory level scheduling object, factory level rescheduling object, capacity requirements planning object, inventory control, factory level load monitoring object, dispatching object
> > At shop level: release control object, shop level load monitoring object, shop level scheduling object, shop level rescheduling object
> Database interface object
> > Oracle DB interface object, Informix DB interface object, file interface object
> User interface object as a database query translator
> > process progress indicator object
> > event generating object by user input data

In this study, the authors [37] further classify the PPC-related object classes into the following groups:

> Object class group associated with production plan function
> > manufacturing control object classes
> > manufacturing control interface object classes
> Object class group associated with production plan information
> > manufacturing data object class
> > manufacturing data interface object class
> > database interface object classes
> Object class group associated with user interface
> > user interface object classes

Work flow object class group object class
　manufacturing work flow object class
　manufacturing work flow engine object class
　event handler and equipment monitoring object classes

The above object classes and groups are shown in Fig. 31. The complete architecture was designed using the object patterns listed in Table 15.

Once the classes are defined and established, they can be extracted using the steps stated earlier. The authors used the Use Cases approach using the SELECT case tool for the process. The manufacturing control interface (MCI) object group has been classified into OrderManagement, LongTermPlanning, MidTermPlanning, ShortTermPlanning, RealTimeScheduling, PurchasingControl, InventoryControl, PcgInputOutputControl, and MfgInputOutputControl classes, the example of the extracted OrderManagement class with their interfaces being given in Table 16.

However, the details of how individual object classes, for instance, the components of the BOM, are defined and the relationships among the components are established; how one class is related to other classes for interdependent planning, for instance, how the MPS is linked to BOM, and how a process like MRP explosion takes place, are not explained [37].

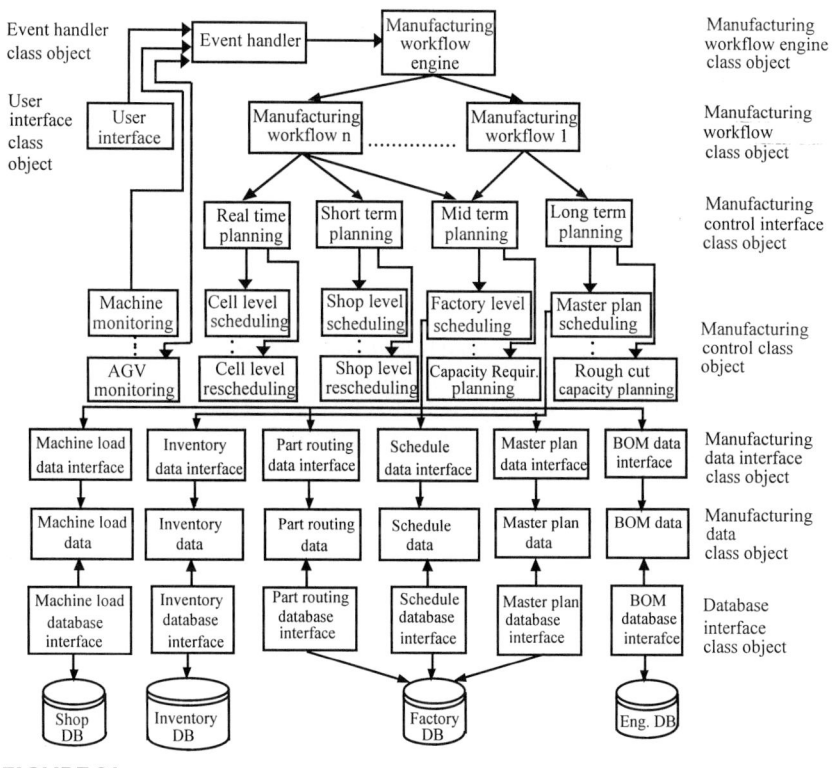

FIGURE 31 Object classes [37].

TABLE 15 Features of Patterns [37]

Pattern	Domain	Solutions
Functional object class pattern	Function-oriented system which is hard to extract objects	The individual function is regarded as a object class. The operations of the function are mapped into the member functions of object class.
Interface object class pattern	A various of objects needed for accessing other objects	Member functions generate interface object classes, calling for other objects consistently. As an example, work flow accesses other multiple objects using interface objects.
Multiple-strategy pattern	Algorithms utilized for object class member function	If one or more membership functions can be implemented using another type of algorithm, the abstracted object class is generated and constructs an object class including another type of algorithm under the abstract object class member functions. The work flows are accessing other multiple objects using interface objects.
Chained strategy pattern (structural pattern)	Algorithm utilized for object class member function generated through the multi strategy pattern	If the previously generated member functions of object class can be implemented using the multiple-strategy pattern, the objects are connected with the supplementary algorithm in the object class.

Ng and Ip [58] report on a case where the *enterprise resource planning* (ERP) system has been integrated with the real-time monitoring system (RTMS), in order to facilitate real-time data collection for planning and scheduling of manufacturing orders, etc., which, in turn, enhance abilities in the areas of production and material control, shop floor control, warehouse planning and control and other logistics functions. This is an enhanced MRPII system. The system was designed and implemented with a *distributed object-oriented technology* (DOOT), which increases system scalability, configurability, flexibility, reusability, and interoperability. For data collection, hard automation using sensors, bar code readers, *programmable logic controllers* (PLC), etc., were used. All relevant real-time shop floor data can be transferred to the ERP system in office bidirectionally. The schematic of the integrated system is shown in Fig. 32.

According to the authors, the ERP represents the application of newer information technology, which includes the move toward relational database

TABLE 16 OrderManagement MCI Class [37]

	Interface	MC class	Interface
OrderManagement	ExecOrderAccept( )	OrderAcception	OrderDataAccept(OrderData)
	ExecOrderCheck( )	OrderAvailabilityCheck	OrderDataCheck(OrderData)
	ExecDuedateEstimate( )	DuedataEstimation	OrderDataEstimate(OrderData)
	ExecOrderSequence( )	OrderSequencing	OrderDataSequence(OrderData)

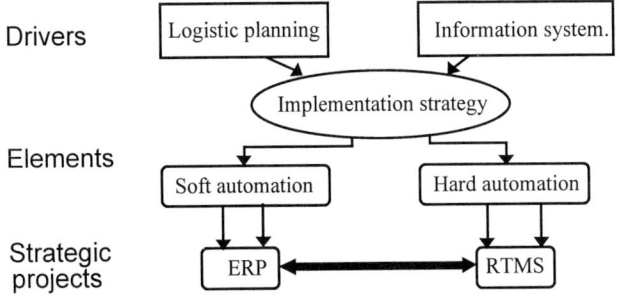

FIGURE 32 Integrated ERP system [58].

management systems (RDBMS), the use of a graphical user interface (GUI), open systems, and client-server architecture, to the MRPII model. The DOOT system architecture, presented by the authors, is divided into four domains: (i) presentation domain—it concentrates on the interaction with the user and managing the user interface; (ii) reporting domain—it is responsible for preparing reports, graphs, or queries; (iii) logic domain—it focuses on managing corporate resources (e.g., database tables) that users share, in particular the application logic; and (iv) database domain—it is a relational database server (e.g., Oracle, Informix, etc.) that manages the persistent storage of data; only the Logic domain can interact with the database domain. The presentation, reporting, logic, and database domains can be placed in different platforms and/or machines in a configurable manner, as shown in Figs. 32 and 33.

In Fig. 33, the *business object* is the conceptual image of the job-related object that the user deals with everyday. The model has two distinct layers: (i) the real object layer defines the user's conceptual view and belongs to the presentation domain, and (ii) the application layer defines the corporate resources view and belongs to the logic domain. The *business object model,* as defined by the object management group, represents the real-world business entities required in planning, for instance, a customer, a manufacturing or purchasing order, a finished good, or subassemblies. The application model is established as the *entity/relationship* (ER) model that defines business entities, their relationships, and attributes that preserve the integrity of the corporate information resources. The Business Object Model represents the user's view of the data

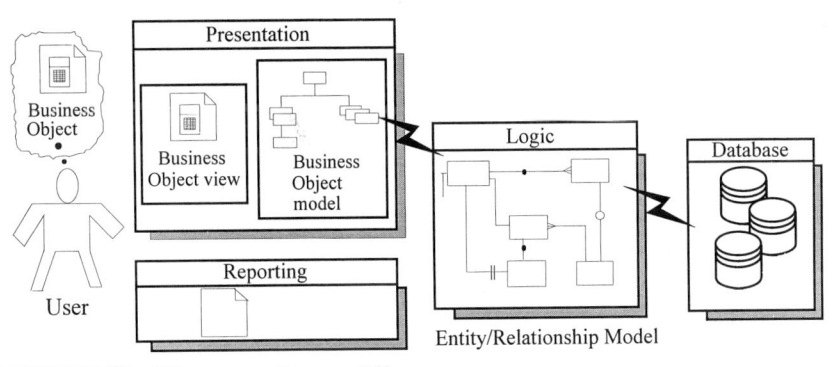

FIGURE 33 ERP system architecture [58].

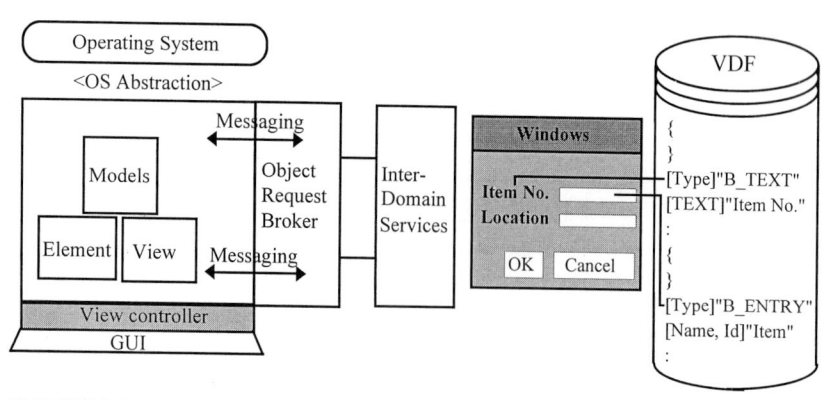

FIGURE 34 Presentation domain and VDF [58].

representation, and only a part of the overall E/R model, which a user deals with in the ERP system. Conceptually, the business object is a hierarchical composite object that has a root subject entity. For instance, a purchase order of an ERP/MRPII system is a form created and filled out from the purchase request, with associated information of a header, item names and IDs, vendor name, price, etc., whereas an E/R relationship model would show it as a combination of several entities interacting with it [58].

As Ng and Ip [58] explain, the presentation domain, responsible for managing the user interface and related matters, consists of three components, namely, *business object models, business object views,* and *business object elements*. The model, as the central control point of a business object, represents a hierarchical data collection, with a root object that identifies the business object. It is responsible for managing the data cache, requesting data from servers, updating the servers against transactions, and interacting with the user through the business object view. Each E/R represented in the business object model is implemented as a server object in the logic domain. The business object view is responsible for displaying the information, using GUI windows, as per user input/output through peripherals, without involving the server. The view layout is defined in ASCII format in a file, termed as the *view definition file* (VDF), as shown in Fig. 34.

The functions of the logic domain are to manage corporate data storage and retrieval, trigger event-driven processes, and provide program logic for the business operations. Its components are entities, relationships, transactions, and databases (Fig. 35). In this logic model, the main target is to establish the *entities object* and their *relationships object*. The hierarchical object model is shown in Fig. 36. The relationships manager in the logic domain is responsible for spreading the event-driven business processes, providing query methods for listing members of the relationship, assigning sequential keys to entity by querying the database, and resolving concurrency lock and registering interest. The transaction manager is responsible for managing the activities of the database, including data updating and consistency [58].

The reporting domain is responsible for presenting reports, graphs, and queries to the user on screen and printer through the Presenter, communicating

MANUFACTURING RESOURCE PLANNING

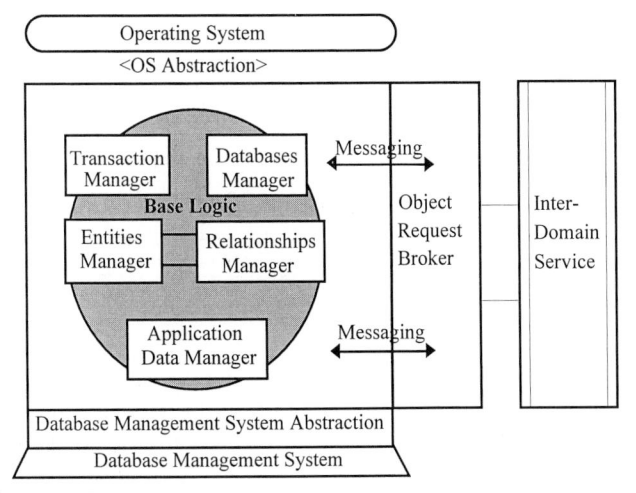

FIGURE 35 Logic domain [58].

with the logic domain through the database object to call the DBMS in order to perform SQL operations through the Extractor, and analyzing, calculating, and sorting operations for a report, and assimilating data.

A. Object-Oriented MRPII Modules

Development of object-oriented systems for individual modules/functions of MRPII system have been reported by several authors [7,8,11,12,44,49].

B. Object-Oriented Inventory Control System

Sinha and Chen [44] have suggested the object-oriented inventory control system using the hierarchical inventory management model, introduced by Browne [4]. The multilevel (inventory control) system has been designed utilizing the

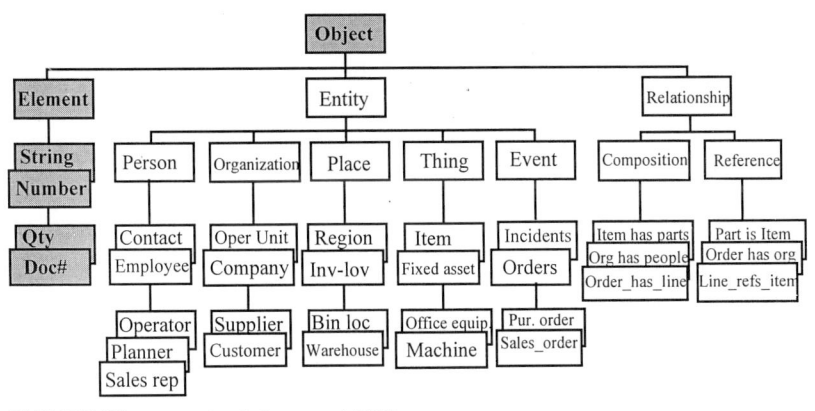

FIGURE 36 Hierarchical object model [58].

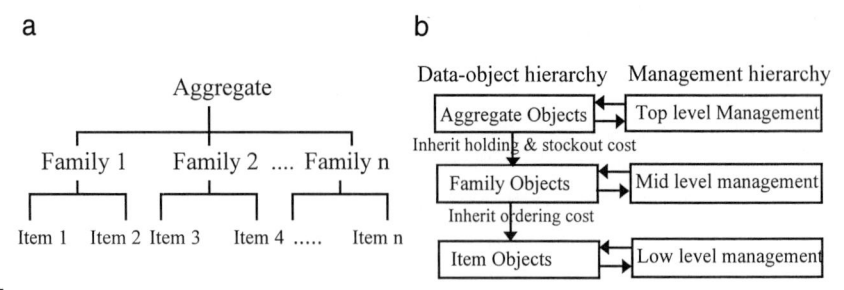

FIGURE 37 Object-oriented hierarchical inventory system: (a) inventory hierarchy and (b) inventory data-object hierarchy [44].

hierarchical parent–child inheritance relation of the object-oriented approach. In this hierarchical inventory system, it has been found that in a company, several similar individual inventoried Items may belong to a Family, and the Families, in turn, belong to the overall company's Inventory (termed here as Aggregate) (Fig. 37a).

The top level, which is decided by the top management to aim at the corporate financial and marketing goals, decides on inventory holding costs and stockouts, depending upon the level of customer service aimed at, which are the company's management policy variables. While decision analysis may be based upon sample inventory, the population consists of all inventoried items to form the object Aggregate. The second level of the hierarchy addresses the issues of inventory Family, which is a group of similar items based on ordering costs (and other characteristics when necessary). Decisions, such as order quantities, at this level may be based on an exchange curve, which is constructed using classical inventory parameters, the holding cost and ordering cost, in order to achieve an optimal point. The analysis may be based on a sample from the population, and then extended to the population to decide among others the ordering cost. The lowest level is the ultimate execution level to decide individual Item optimal quantities (may be EOQ), by inheriting the ordering cost, holding cost, and stockout [44].

The inheritance facility of object-oriented systems permits upper echelons to build on constraints to be observed by the lower levels. An example of Item and Family classes are shown below [44]:

>   Class Family
>   Attributes: Order_Cost, Holding_Cost,& others
>   End Family
>
>   Class Item inherit family
>   Attributes: Unit_Cost, Demand, and other
>   Function Inventory_Cost (X)
>   Inventory_Cost = (X/2)*Unit_Cost*Hold_Cost +
>   (Demand*365/X)*Order_Cost
>   End Inventory_Cost
>   End Item

In the above case, although the ordering and holding costs are not exported by Class Family, they are available within Item. Here, X represents the order quantity of an item.

It is observed that this object orientation in inventory eliminates the duplication of data storage of ordering and holding costs for individual items, as they are stored under Family or Aggregate. The authors have also developed, as a user interface, different objects for this inventory control system. These are system level objects, such as Print, Save_List, and Graph (Cost curve), and user level objects, which are described above (e.g., Item, Family, Aggregate [44]. From the success of this system, it is suggested that benefits of inheritance of object orientation can be utilized to develop other subsystems of MRPII, where many things are hierarchical in nature, e.g., (i) BOM, (ii) Aggregate planning and MPS, (iii) shop level, family level, and work center level scheduling, and (iv) capacity planning.

C. Object-Oriented PAC System

Reports also reveal that object-oriented systems for production activity control (PAC), or alternatively known as shop floor control, subsystem of the overall resource planning system, have also been developed.

Gausemeier *et al.* [11] report a case of successful development and implementation of such an object-oriented PAC system, integrated with other modules of MRPII. In this respect, it must be noted that the MRPII system's PAC module is limited in its functionality, thereby, needing additional third party development of a detailed PAC system, and integration with it for full-fledged operation, or customized needs of control.

Gausemeier *et al.* [11] are of the opinion that although the material flow in the shop floor has reached a high level of automation, information processing related to that has not yet achieved that level. With differences between job processing situations and environments in different shops, disturbances (e.g., accidental events), and corresponding capacity changes in a single shop, and with ever-changing customer requirements from time to time, the PAC system must be flexible enough to accommodate those changes. Additionally, it must be noted that the PAC subsystem is one of the areas of a manufacturing information system (another, for instance, is the BOM-designed integrated system) that must deal with complex databases, because of the presence of heterogeneous types of hardware systems. Thus, these areas need special attention regarding system development and maintenance. Several authors [11,12] have advocated that object-oriented systems can be best utilized to deal with such complex requirements (Fig. 38).

Gausemeier *et al.* [11] also opine that the PAC system needs to fulfill three special requirements, such as, flexibility for requirement change from time to time, a coordinated communication structure for integrating different devices, and efficient scheduling and rescheduling capability in cases of disturbances and overloads. This can be best satisfied by object orientation. Without detailing the object structures and patterns, Gausemeier *et al.* [11] give a brief outline of the system as given below.

Gausemeier *et al.* [11] draw an analogy between the basic construction and operation principles of natural objects (or organisms) and manufacturing

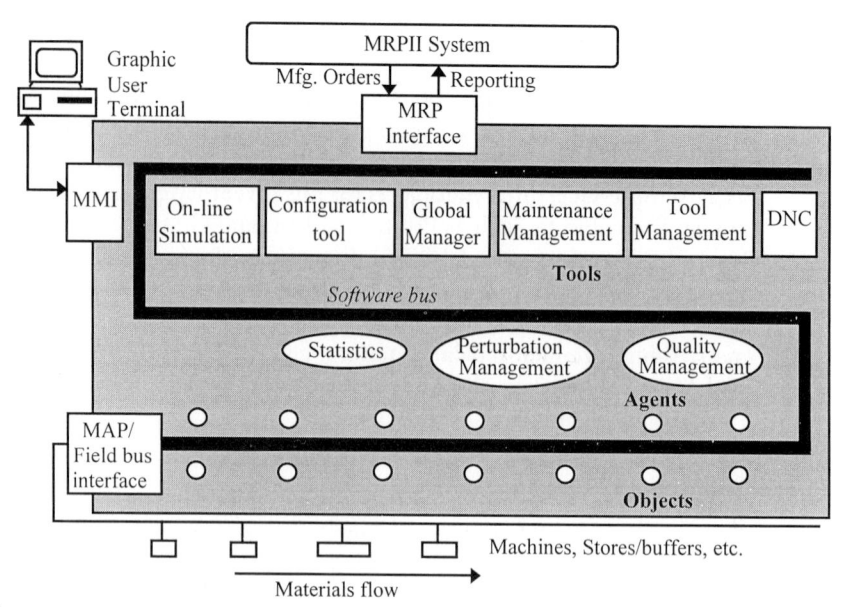

FIGURE 38 A PAC system integrated with MRP [11].

systems. As the authors say,

> Complex organisms are based on organs, controlled by the nervous system, which is in fact a network of communication between organs. Each organ has specialized functions and operates autonomously. The organs are again composed of several specialized cells, though the cells belonging to an organ perform the same basic functions. The entire organic system is managed and coordinated by the communication network, the nervous system. [11]

Similar concepts can be applied to the PAC system, which should be composed of functional elements, such as a machine or a conveyor belt, and a communication network. These basic functional elements are the manufacturing objects (MO), as accepted by Gausemeier *et al*. These MOs need to be scheduled, rescheduled, and monitored. For instance, to complete an order, a sequence of MOs need to developed, and then materials need to be directed along this sequence of MOs. When some additional information, or intelligence, is added to the real-world manufacturing objects by propagating the knowledge of the planner or scheduler, as algorithm or rule, it is termed as an *intelligent object* (IO). A *global manager* (GM), similar to the organic nervous system, is created to coordinate and manage the tasks of these IOs. This GM serves the communication between this enhanced PAC module and the MRPII system (as shown in Fig. 38). The IO is built using the object-oriented principle. As is necessary in an object, an IO encapsulates data and methods. Every IO has methods for scheduling, controlling, and monitoring [11].

The GM provides all information to the IOs for scheduling. The IOs contain different scheduling algorithms, as methods. When jobs are released from MRP to the PAC module, all suitable production devices compete for the job. Once the IOs calculate grades of competing devices, the one with the highest score is selected for the operation. This is some kind of priority fixing mechanism. The results of the scheduling are set into the time schedule which exists for every IO. In cases of disturbances, which is quite common in any shop, the IO first tries to fix it using strategies and procedures encapsulated in the method. In case, it goes beyond the method, the operator is informed through dialogues [11].

Grabot and Huguet [12] also presented an object-oriented PAC system development method at Aerospatiale. The authors opine similarly to Gausemeier *et al.* that a PAC module changes from time to time, because of the changes of jobs of different customers, disturbances in the shop, expansions in shop size, inclusion and exclusion of resources, i.e., in general, because of factory dynamics. This makes the development process of a PAC module and subsequent integration with an MRPII system difficult, time consuming, and costly. The authors are of the opinion that object-oriented technology, with the ability to reuse past experience by utilizing reference models, can be of tremendous help in this regard.

The authors consider a PAC system composed of PAC modules, which communicate among themselves and with other external systems. There may be several types of modules in a PAC system, depending upon the workshop characteristics. The authors found several such modules, three of them being given in Fig. 39, as example. These modules can be organized through a hierarchic or distributed structure. The design of a PAC system depends on the association of these modules. Once they are defined, the activities involved in corresponding functions associated with each must be described. The functions,

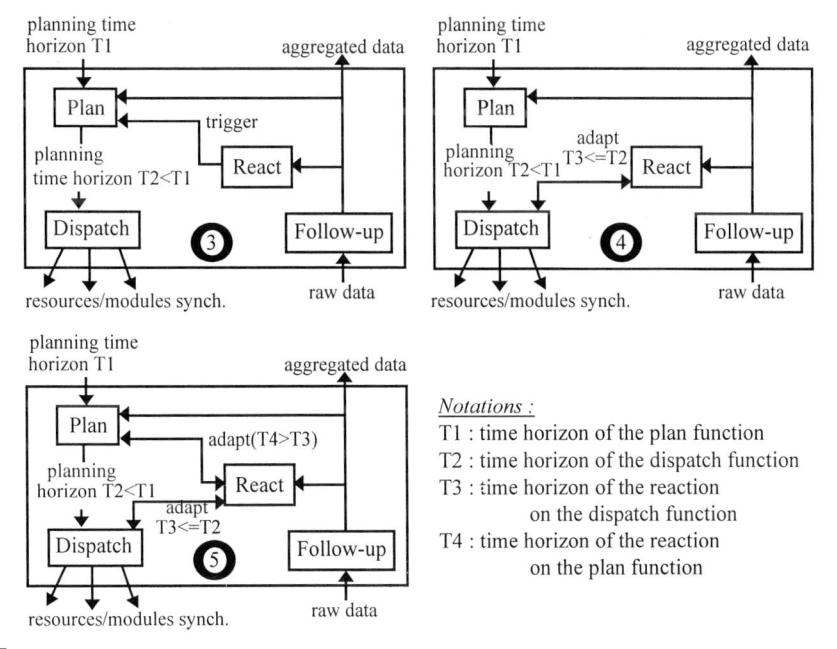

FIGURE 39 Selected typology of PAC modules [12].

associated with these modules are:

- *Plan*. It considers the general plan required in executing the activities of the workshop. The plan function can be ensured manually by the scheduler or a software. In case of the Kanban type of production control, no software is necessary.
- *Dispatch*. It coordinates the resources at the workshop. It releases either a list of jobs to perform or a list of activities/operations to be performed under a job.
- *Follow-up*. It collects all the results provided by sensors, as well as requests from outside of the PAC unit, and then transmits them to other functions of the PAC unit, other PAC modules.
- *React*. It allows an adaptation of the decision made by the Plan function. It generally does not act on the whole plan, but rather on a part of it that may vary according to the global time horizon of the reaction level [12].

Grabot and Huguet [12] use the HP FUSION method for the design of an object-oriented PAC system. It follows the steps given below [12]:

1. Analysis (description of what the system does)

- *Object model (OM) development*. Object formalism (instantiation, decomposition, inheritance) is added to the entity relationship diagrams. An example of an OM is given in Fig. 40.
- *Interface*. System interfaces are determined to know about the relationship with the environment.
- *Interface model development*. The life-cycle model defines allowable sequences of interactions with the environment; and the operation model defines the semantics of each system operation in the interface. An example of an interface model to show links between the workshop and its environment, which is termed here as a scenario, is shown in Fig. 41.
- Checking the completeness and consistency of the model.

1. Design

- *Object interaction graphs (OIG)*. These are developed to show the exchanges (and their sequences) of messages between objects (an example is shown for dispatch manager in Fig. 42).
- *Visibility graph*. These are developed to show the structure that enables communication of the *object-oriented* (OO) system.
- *Class description*. It is the initial codification phase required for describing the internal and external interfaces.
- *Development of inheritance graphs*.
- *Updating of class descriptions*.

1. Implementation. It involves codification, optimization, inspection, and testing.

In this method, Grabot and Huguet [12] use state-chart formalism to model the internal behavior of the classes. They focus on the reusability of past reference models to develop new system in a shorter time. They propose some building bricks, or components, for reuse. The components are gathered in functional groups, as shown in Fig. 43.

MANUFACTURING RESOURCE PLANNING

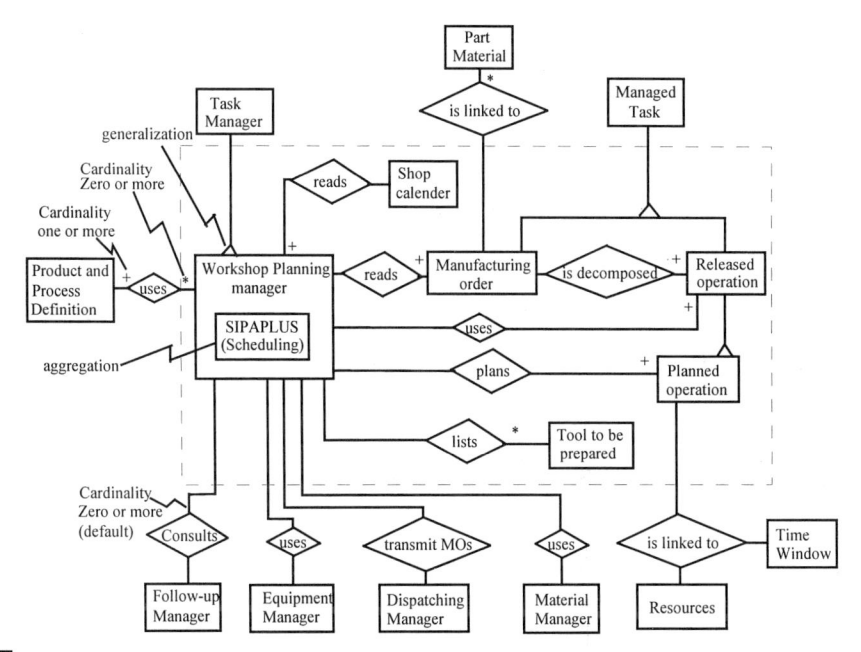

FIGURE 40 An object model of the PAC module components [12].

The OM and OIG of the FUSION method have been suggested for describing each component, whereas the state-chart formalism has been suggested for describing the internal behavior of the classes (i.e., dynamic model). Two case tools, FUSION softcase and Paradigm Plus, have been tested and proven to be useful. The authors are of the opinion that reusability is an essential requirements in the case of PAC system development, which can be ensured by developing first the generic components and then by efficiently managing object and object pattern (component) libraries [12].

Smith and Joshi [46] present an object-oriented architecture for the *shop floor control* (SFC) system, though under the CIM environment. It must be noted that SFC is a dynamic module of MRPII, which is a collection of physical and conceptual objects, when viewed from the OO point, such as orders (to be competed), parts (to be manufactured and/or assembled), machines, equipment, material handling systems (e.g. conveyor belt, forks, robots), and people. The target of OO SFC is to create suitable objects with necessary behavior with their attributes, and methods for interaction among objects, in order to complete the production as per plan generated by the MRPII system, be it as a stand alone island, or under a CIM environment.

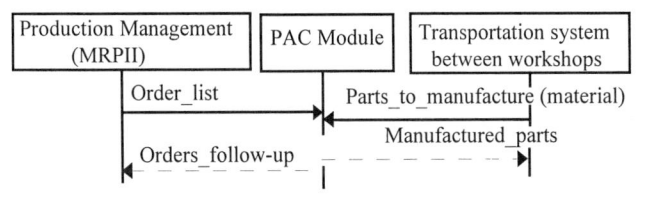

FIGURE 41 An affectation scenario of manufacturing orders [12].

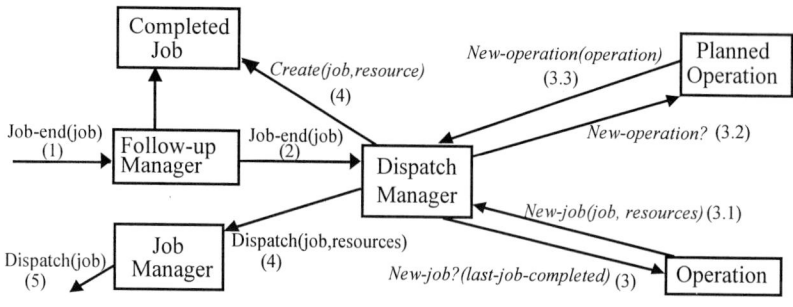

FIGURE 42 A partial view of an object interaction graph of "dispatch manager" [12].

Smith and Joshi [46] have defined the organization of an SFC system as hierarchical, with three levels—shop, workstation, and equipment—in order to improve controllability and make it generic. The equipment level provides a view of physical machines on the shop floor. The authors have created several objects at the equipment level. Out of these objects, which are of particular importance in the case of SFC for MRPII, are *material processing machines* (MP) consisting of the machines, inspection devices, etc. that autonomously processes a part, *material handling machines* (MH) for intraworkstation part movement functions (e.g., loading, unloading, processing machines, and *material transport machines* (MT) for interworkstation part movement functions (e.g., transporting parts from one station to another). At the workstation level, a workstation is considered as a set of equipment level objects and additionally some other objects, such as a part buffer. The shop floor level, composed of workstation objects, is responsible for managing part routing and reporting shop status to other modules.

This SFC system developed a shop floor equipment controller class, consisting of communications and storage classes. These aspects mostly relate to the information integration of CIM hardware systems, which is beyond the scope of this chapter. However, the system has also introduced scheduling as part of the OOSFC (object-oriented SFC) information system, which has direct relevance to MRPII's PAC aspect. The control cycle (function) has been presented as a sequence of activities having the pseudo-codes (thus, generic)

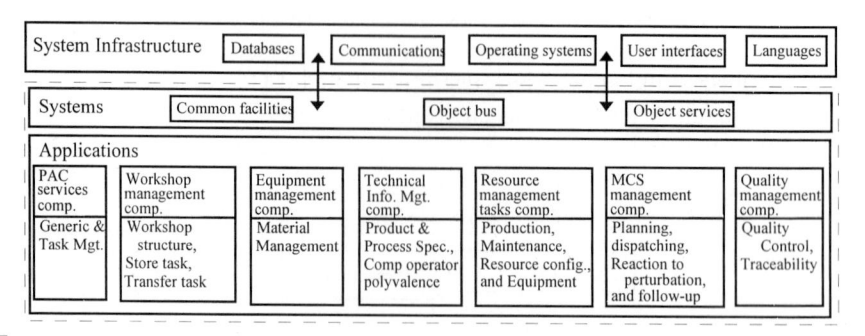

FIGURE 43 PAC development architecture, proposed by Grabot and Huguet [12].

as follows [46]:

>   wait for startup message
>   read configuration information
>   do until shutdown message received
>   call scheduler
>   call task executor
>   read messages
>   update system states
>   enddo
>   write configuration information
>   shutdown

The separate calls of execution and scheduling in the above codes of the SFC system have kept scheduling separate from execution. While "execution" is responsible for determining whether a particular action is valid, and performing it if valid, "scheduling" is responsible for determining an efficient sequence of actions. The scheduler is responsible for placing task request records in the task queue. The task executor, after examining the records, executes the tasks if the preconditions (such as, if machine is idle) are met. By separating the scheduling and execution functions, different scheduling algorithms can be "plugged-in" to the controller, depending on the production requirements. The system has been implemented in C++ [46].

Moriwaki *et al*. [26] have developed an object-oriented scheduling system. Although the system is real-time and has special reference to FMS and autonomous distributed manufacturing, the concept of the system is well applicable to the MRPII system in general. The study first discusses the architecture of autonomous distributed manufacturing systems (for FMS), and then its real-time scheduling system. Since the architecture of FMS is beyond the scope of this chapter, the following section discusses only the scheduling function as it has direct relevance to MRPII's PAC module.

A monitoring system has an important role in this scheduling system, as it needs to monitor and inform the SFC system of the needs for real-time scheduling. The status of the objects is changed according to the status data transmitted from the monitoring system. Thus, the objects are autonomous. The conflicts between objects are resolved through negotiation. The ultimate manufacturing processes are done according to the schedules determined in the system. It considers only machining processes, and not any assembly or transportation process, and is based on the assumptions that the process plans and machining times of individual work pieces are fixed [26].

Figure 44 shows the objects, their attributes, and methods. The objects are classified into four classes—work pieces, process plans of the work pieces, equipment, and operations. The objects representing the work pieces include three classes of objects—part type, lot, and the part. While the "part type" object represents the kinds of part, the "lot" object represents individual lots of that part type, and the "part" object corresponds to individual work pieces in the lot. The "equipment" class is represented by the objects of equipment type and equipment. The process plans of individual part types are established by the process objects and preference relations objects. The operation objects give the

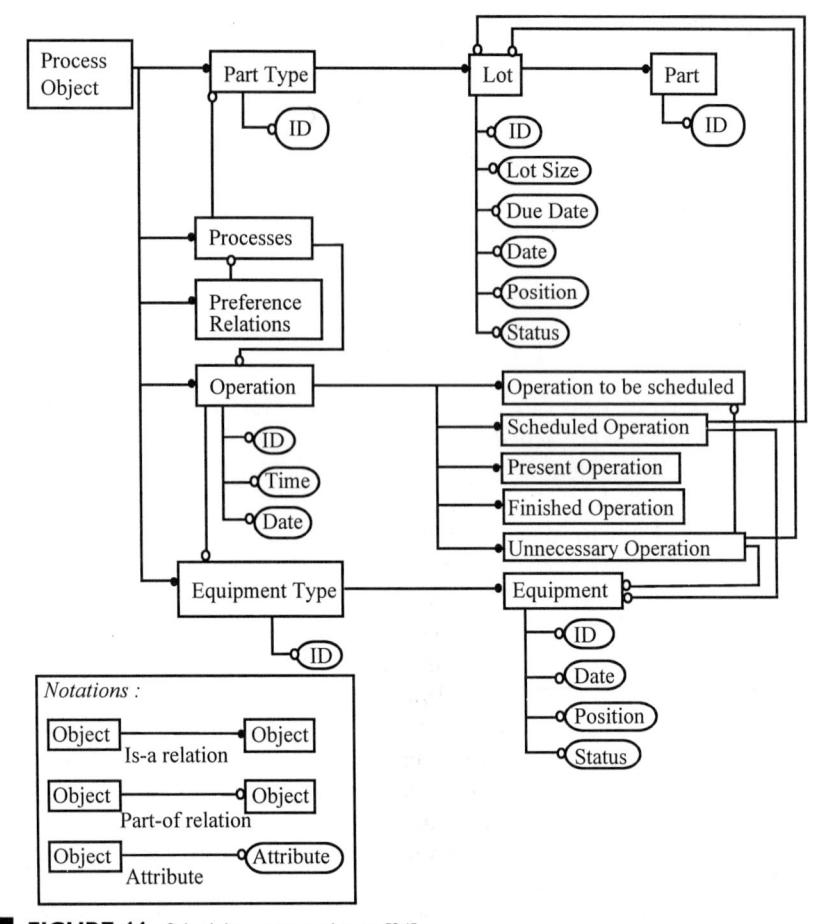

FIGURE 44 Scheduling system objects [26].

relations among the processes of the part types and feasible "equipment type" that can perform the operation. An example of such processes, operations, and their preference relations of part types A and B is shown in Fig. 45. In this figure, a_i and b_j are the processes, and the arcs are the preference relations among the processes. Each process has been defined as a set of alternative operations available (e.g., a_{ik}, b_{jm}), which specify a feasible type of machining cells ("equipment" and "equipment type" objects) [26].

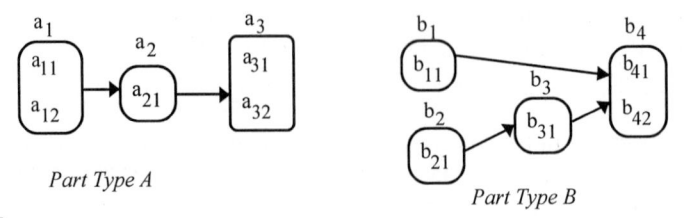

FIGURE 45 Preference relations between processes [26].

MANUFACTURING RESOURCE PLANNING 475

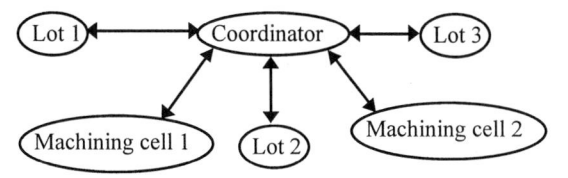

FIGURE 46 Negotiation through coordinator [26].

The schedules of individual machining cells ("equipment") and lots are determined by selecting a suitable operation of that lot, and by loading the selected operation to a suitable machining cell. The start and finish times are specified accordingly. Then the scheduled operations of that lot are performed by the cells ("equipment"). Therefore, the status of the operations are changed as the scheduling progresses. Five possible statuses are given in Fig. 44. In this system, each machining cell (an "equipment" object) can select a suitable operation to perform and determine start and finish times of the operation. On the other hand, each lot can also select and determine a schedule. In some cases, conflicts may arise when several cells select the same operation of a particular lot. A negotiation that is established by creating another object, "coordinator," as shown in Fig. 46, is necessary. A summarized version of the complete scheduling is shown in Fig. 47. A prototype system in Smalltalk was developed [26].

D. Object-Oriented Capacity Planning System

Capacity planning is an aspect of scheduling, which in turn is an aspect of PAC of MRPII. Since it presents some additional information, when described in detail, this is considered separately in many cases in commercial systems. Thus, it is presented separately in this chapter too.

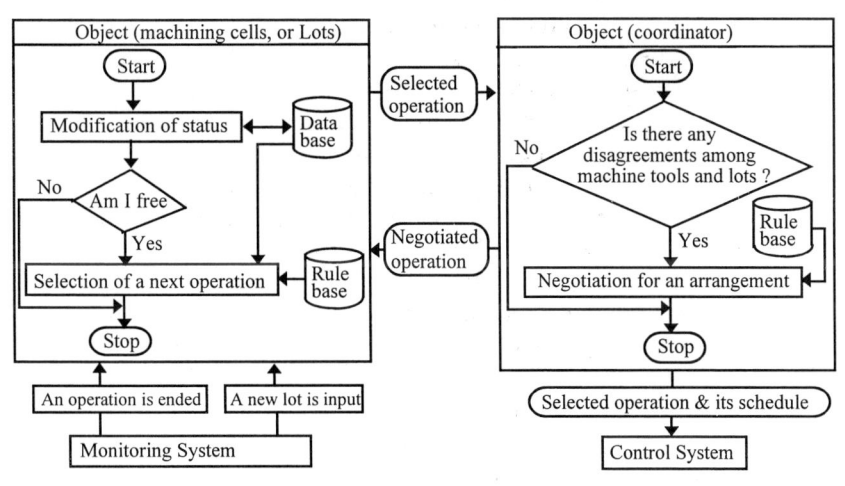

FIGURE 47 Scheduling process [26].

Ulrich and Durig [50] present a capacity planning and scheduling system, using object-oriented technology. It is known that these two functions together aim at achieving a production schedule on the time axis (time horizon) consuming (available) resources.

In order to ensure reusability of objects, a three-level OO system is suggested as follows [50]:

Universal platform. It provides a universal base (library) of available objects that are quite generic and, thus, applicable to several kinds of application areas/functions.

Specific platform. This becomes more specific to a functional application area (e.g., capacity planning). The objects are defined based on the field/function in addition to the universal ones.

Individual supplements. For a field (such as capacity planning), individual realizations need supplements to the specific platform. It may be an individual capacity planning solution for a particular case, whereas the specific platform defines the capacity planning method in general.

Three basic elements, as listed below, are identified as describing the problem at a very high level of abstraction for the specific platform [50].

Resources. It represents capacity of resources, such as machines and labor.

Planning items. These are the production orders, generated internally, or ordered externally.

Time axis. It shows a shop calendar on a continuous time axis.

The following two data administration techniques for administering a set of objects of the same kind that belong to a collection are developed: (i) Open administration, which enables the user to have access to these objects and can perform normal database operations, and (ii) hidden administration, which does not allow the user to have access to these objects, and the administration is performed automatically by the system [50].

The consumption resources comprise consumption elements, which perform the acts of consumption, for which a hidden data administration is necessary to manage those "acts." Each resource administers its adjoined consumption elements according to a well-defined pattern, e.g., intervals and areas. A link to the shop calendar helps to perform that along the time axis. A scheduling of the consumption elements along the time axis according to the defined pattern determines the availability of resources [50].

This kernel of resources and consumption elements, administered by the data administration technique, is linked to the production process environment for consumption (Fig. 48). Production factors, such as machines and labors, comprise resources, represented by workload or the available material for consumption to the production process. The planning items utilize the consumption elements, which are allocated to resources. The user manages these directly, using open data administration [50].

In order to demonstrate the use of individual supplement object classes, a particular task of capacity-oriented time scheduling of production orders for the period of 1 week to 3 months (i.e., short term planning) for final assembly

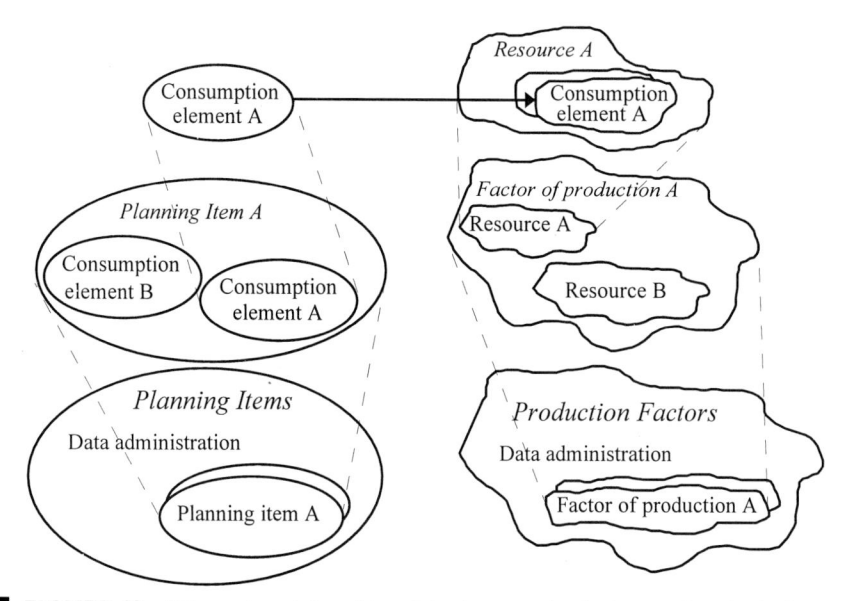

FIGURE 48 Object-oriented view of the relation between planning items and production factors [50].

has been illustrated. For this situation, the hierarchies of abstract objects for specific platforms and individual supplements are given in Table 17. The classes in italics are additional for individual supplements. For every customer order, a number of elementary orders may exist, which act as internal production orders, and are released to fulfill a specific customer request. A new class "production order" is introduced as an individual supplement class, comprising "customer order" and "planning item". The "planning item" contains all general methods for performing planning activities within the scheduling process. The new subclass "elementary order" inherits all these methods, in addition to some supplementary methods for this specific application [50].

E. Object-Oriented Bill of Materials

Several authors [7,8,49] have reported successful development of an OOBOM (object-oriented BOM) system, narrating its advantages. On the other hand Olsen *et al.*, [35] disagree. According to Olsen *et al.*, although the power of an OO approach is recognized in general, the composite object hierarchy and inheritance features are not advantageous for modeling product structures. The reason behind this is that in an OO system, the components inherit the features of their parents, which violate the requirement of describing components independently of their utilization.

Trappey *et al.* [49] state that a conventional BOM structure, which manages data in relational database management style, cannot satisfy the needs requested by all departments in a company. In this respect, they mention several limitations, such as rigidity of data structure, inability to describe behavioral relations, and difficulty in changing data description. They advocate that the object-oriented programming (OOP) concept can design a BOM (OOBOM)

TABLE 17 Specific Platform and Individual Supplement Classes [50]

Specific platform	Specific platform and supplement

Object
  Model
    Production planning model
      Element of production
        Factor of production
        Planning item
        Process data
        Calendar
      Data-administration
        Open administration
          Calendar administration
          Production order administration
          Planning item administration
          Process data administration
        Hidden administration
          Resources
            Interval covering resource
            Area covering resource
      Element of consumption
        Interval covering element
        Area covering element
	Object
	  Model
	    Production planning model
	      Element of production
	        Factor of production
	          Assembly line
	        Production order
	          Customer order
	        Planning item
	          Elementary order
	        Process data
	          Bill of Materials
	          Production parameters
	        Calendar
	      Data-administration
	        Open administration
	          Calendar administration
	          Production order admin.
	            Customer order admin.
	            Elementary order admin.
	          Production factor administration
	            Assembly line admin.
	          Process data administration
	            Bill of materials admin.
	            Production parameter admin.
	        Hidden administration
	          Resources
	            Interval covering resource
	            Area covering resource
	      Element of consumption
	        Interval of consumption
	        Interval covering element
	          Production element
	          Setup element
	          Blocking element
	        Area covering element

	Parts view and controller

View
  Production planning view
    One-dimensional view
    Two-dimensional view
Controller
  Production planning controller
    One-dimensional controller
    Two-dimensional controller
	View
	  Production planning view
	    One-dimensional view
	      Assembly line view
	    Two-dimensional view
	Controller
	  Production planning controller
	    One-dimensional controller
	      Assembly line controller
	    Two-dimensional controller

efficiently to complement the limitations of the conventional BOM system. The authors develop a prototype OOBOM in a Smalltalk environment.

Trappey *et al.* [49] suggest that a BOM may consist of the following classes and subclasses:

Part class
    MfgPart. Parts to be manufactured in-house
        Routing. Describes the information in process sheets, such as operation number, operation description, and material required.
        Packaging. Specifies the packaging information of a manufactured part, such as container or size.
    ProcPart. Parts to be procured
        ProcCo. Records the information relevant to the supplier of a procured part, such as coName (company name), coAddr (address), FOB points, price, and telephone numbers.

The Part class is in fact a meta class, which is an abstraction of components, subassemblies, and products. The definition of an object is encapsulated in the "instant variables" of its class. For example, "Part" has instant variables, such as partName, partNo, parents, type, and attributes. While the "MfgPart" inherits the variables from "Part," it may have additional variables of its own, such as children (subassemblies), consumableTool, packaging, routing, and cadLink. The attributes of a part can be used to describe objects of different collections. The attributes instance variable is a dictionary data type and stores key-value data pairs. The authors cite an example of a turnbuckle where diameter is a parameter. If it has a value of 10, then the list "(diameter 10)" is described as a pair data in the attributes variable of "Part" [49].

The OOBOM [49] stores the data entities of objects, in both a logical (a data entity is a logical representation) and a physical (a table or a record) representation. A data dictionary is responsible for (i) managing and controlling the data, which stores the logical relationship among data entities and relationships between an object and its attributes, and (ii) managing relationships in a physical database among tables and between a table and its columns.

In the OOBOM system [49], the classes for transaction objects are all the subclasses of the "BomRecord" class, which serves as the data dictionary. It has been defined as the subclass of "Model." The "BomRecord" has the following a set of global variables:

LibPart Dic. Records all existing standard parts in the categorized sets.
LibraryCategory. Lists all part categories.
PartRecord. Lists all existing parts, and all part definitions are encapsulated in PartRecord by the part names.
ProductCategory. Stores the categories of final products.
ProductCategoryDic. Lists all final products organized by product categories.

The hierarchy is shown below [49]:

```
Object ()
  Model ('dependents')
    BomRecord ('model')
    BOMPrint ('selProduct' 'selType' 'maxLength')
    NodeTree ('buttonSel' 'onPart' 'myWindow' 'myComposite'
              'compositeSet' 'lineComposite' 'howManyNode')
    PartLibrary ('libSel' 'libSet' 'partSel' 'partSet')
    PartWindow ('dealPart' 'itemSel' 'itemSet' 'valueSet' 'valueSel'
                'parentSel' 'childSel')
    ProductBrowser ('categorySelectOn' 'finalProductSelectOn'
                    'finalProductSet' 'textMode')
```

The BOMPrint, NodeTree, PartLibrary, PartWindow, and ProductBrowser classes manipulate the transaction management via the MVC (model–view–controller) paradigm of Smalltalk. While doing this, each uses its own window interface, as shown in Fig. 49, and described below [49]:

PartWindow. It supports the basic operations on part data, such as part creation, modification, and query. It is invoked by all other windows to support part data entry and editing.

ProductBrowser. It provides users with functions for browsing the final products in the BOM database. It can invoke a BOM tree to define or edit a product structure. Indented BOM can also be shown.

PartLibrary. It manages all standard parts by grouping them in categories.

BOMTree. It shows the assembly structure of a product.

Authors [Trappey *et al.*] [49] also advocate that this OOBOM system can further be extended to integrate engineering data management system (maybe MRPII) and CAD/CAM as well.

Chung and Fischer [8] gave an outline of the structure and a data model of an OOBOM. They also demonstrated the use of the proposed architecture by developing a prototype system through coding in C++ language. The authors are of the opinion that a structure of BOM is in fact an abstraction hierarchy

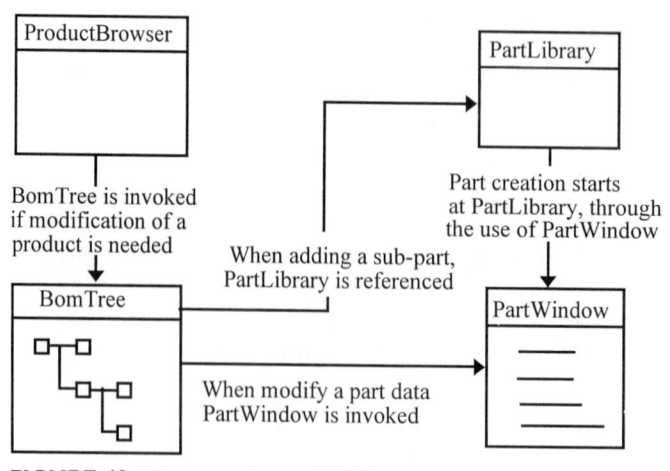

FIGURE 49 The transaction model [49].

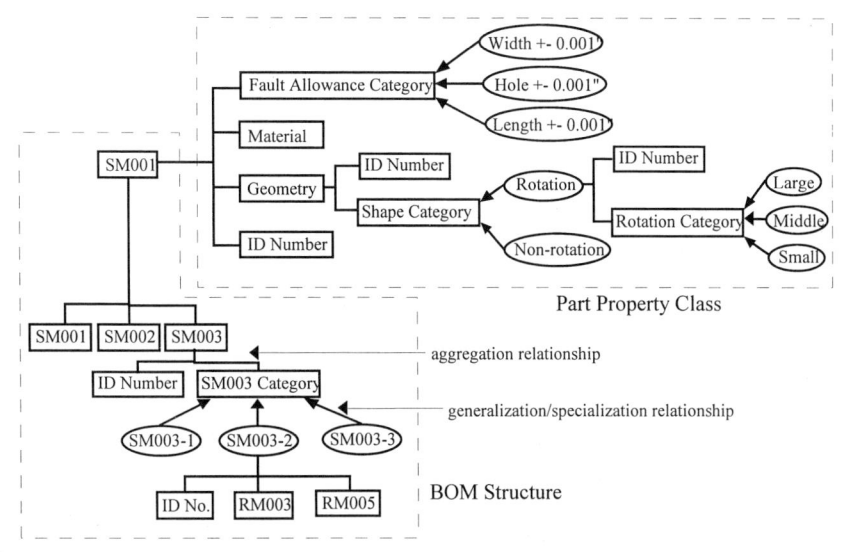

FIGURE 50 Example of aggregation/generalization in an OOBOM system [8].

of an OO data model, and thus, the conceptual data model of OOBOM can be mapped onto the abstraction and inheritance architectures of an OO data model. The conceptual data model integrates the semantic relationships, such as References, Referenced-by, Owns, Owned-by, Composed-of, and Part-of, with object orientation concepts.

In an OOBOM system, the parts, which are assembled together to form a subassembly, can have aggregation semantic relationships, i.e., is-part-of relationship, where the subassembly is termed an aggregation object and the parts that go into subassembly are called the component objects. For instance, in Fig. 50, SM003 is an aggregation object and ID number and SM003 Category are the component objects. A generalization relationship, i.e., is-kind-of relationship, is used to define generic part objects from their possible categories or options. For instance, in Fig. 50, Rotation and Nonrotation are the categories of the generic object Shape Category. SM003-1 is a possible option of SM003; thereby, it is having a specialization relationship, which is the converse of a generalization one [8].

The authors propose two classes of objects, namely the BOM class, which simply defines the physical and logical relationships between components in the hierarchy of BOM, and the Part Property class, which defines the properties, such as shape, color, and material, of the parts in the BOM class (Fig. 50 and 51).

They opine that this classification is similar to E-class (entity class) and D-class (domain class) of an OSAM database respectively. The BOM objects may reference (Reference semantic relationship) the properties in the Part Property class. The Own semantic relationship can be used to generate/delete/change/modify an individual object to maintain engineering changes that happen frequently in production organizations. While a BOM object may contain a set of instances created by the user of the OOBOM database, the property object does not contain the user-created instances. The property object is only a property that specifies the data type and/or a permissible range of values [8].

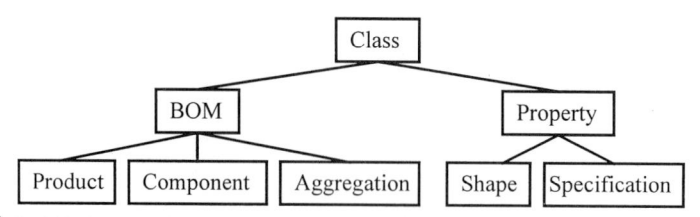

FIGURE 51 Class hierarchy, as used in Fig. 50 [8].

An object in the BOM class can get property information of the Property class via Referencing (R), Generalization (G), Own (O), and Aggregation (A) relationships. When referencing is needed, an attribute (which is a character string that is the unique identification of the referenced object, or an address pointer to the object) that establishes reference to another object is created, thereby creating a relationship between two objects. Communications between objects are established by sending messages through the execution of methods and utilization of defined semantic relationships. Since several objects may try to have a lot of communications, a control mechanism is necessary to simplify that. The OOBOM allows a relationship and communication between objects when, and only when, one object has an attribute that is a reference to another object. The relationships are shown in Fig. 52. In the case of referencing, the messages

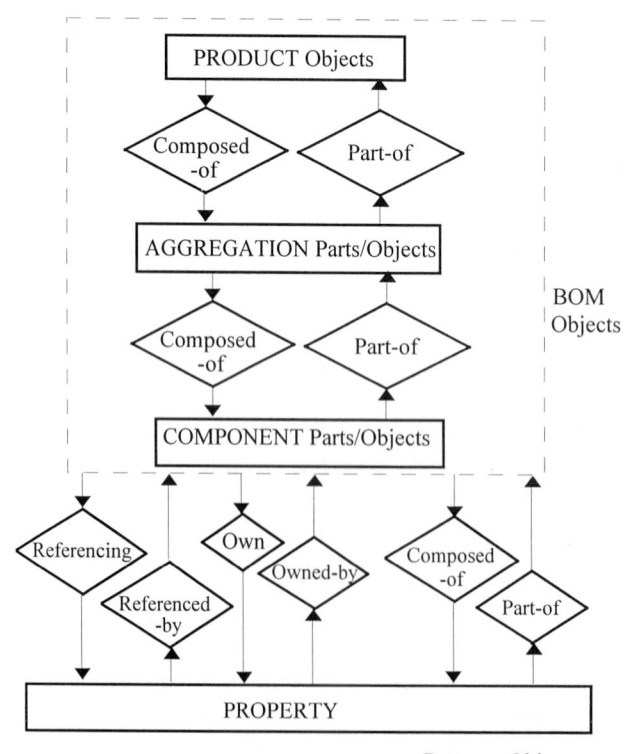

FIGURE 52 Relationships in a BOM hierarchy [8].

associated with a Referencing relationship are sent by the BOM object, and any message associated with the Referenced-by relationship are sent by the property object. The existence of a Referenced-by relationship means that a property object contains a list of all the BOM objects that reference the property object [8].

In an Aggregation relationship (Fig. 52), messages associated with composed-of relationships are sent from parent to child, whereas messages associated with part-of relationships are sent from child to parent. In an MRPII environment, there may be frequent engineering changes. In such a situation, decomposed components need to be updated if their parent is modified. In an Own relationship, BOM object may own another object, which may be a property object as well. The owner object can order the destruction of the owned object and can perform operations, like resetting the values of the owned objects' attributes. An example of an Own relationship is the creation and maintenance of BOM and property objects [8].

Chung and Fischer [8] have listed possible attributes of both BOM and property classes. The example of a property object is given in Table 18.

In another previous occasion, Chung and Fischer [7] illustrate the use of an object-oriented database system, using ORION, a commercial OO database system of Itaska, for developing BOM for use in the MRPII system. ORION is a distributed database system. As such, the object identity also needs the site identifier of the site in which the object is created. Being opposed to the traditional idea of using a relational database system for BOM, the authors mention

TABLE 18 Property Object Description [8]

CLASS NAME	P-RM005
DOCUMENTATION	Properties of BOM Object RM005
CLASS ATTRIBUTES	
Superclass	PROPERTY
Subclass	None
Class category	Property
OBJECT IDENTITY	Object Identifier
DATA ATTRIBUTES	Lead-Time, Make-or-Buy, Cost, Safety-Stock, Stock-on-Hand, etc.
RELATIONSHIP METHODS	
Referenced-by-Relationship	All BOM Objects
Owned-by-Relationship	RM005
Part-of-Relationship	P-SM001, P-SM003
OTHER METHODS	Query (Query methods are used to search and retrieve properties.), Check (Check and/or reset methods can be exploited to modify and initialize the values of the part attributes.), Reset, Display (It controls the display of the details and is necessary for linking with query, check, and reset methods.)
END CLASS	

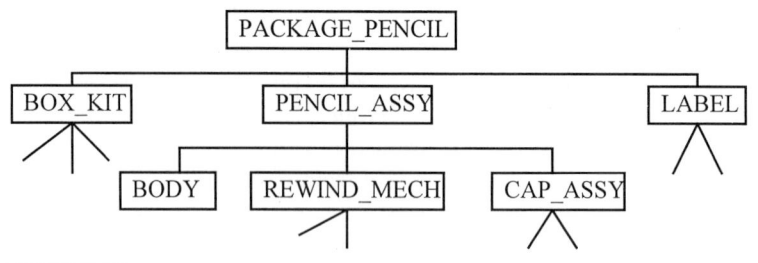

FIGURE 53 An example of a BOM [7].

several limitations, and advocate the use of OODB instead. The authors opine that unlike relational data models, an OO data model allows the design of an application in terms of complex objects, classes, and their associations, instead of tuples and relationships. This characteristic of the OO technique is highly desirable in a BOM system, as a BOM is a complex composite object.

Aggregation is useful and necessary for defining part–component hierarchies, and is an abstraction concept for building the composite objects from the component objects. It must be remembered that BOM is a hierarchy that relates parent–component relationships, and several components are logically (logically during the modeling stage and, later on, physically on the shop floor) assembled together to form a composite object. During operation of the BOM module in the MRPII system, it may be necessary to perform some operations (such as deletion, addition, storage management) in the entire BOM, considering it as a single logical unit. In the OOBOM proposed by Chung and Fischer [7], the BOM has a composite object hierarchy with an is-part-of relationship between parent and component classes, and this composite object may be treated as a single logical unit, and thus fulfills the requirement.

Fig. 53 is an example of a PACKAGE_PENCIL object class, having component object classes of BOX_KIT, PENCIL_ASSY, and LABEL. The PENCIL_ASSY is again composed of several component classes. Thus, the BOM shown has a hierarchy of object classes that can form a composite object hierarchy.

The detailed information on the PENCIL_ASSY object class is shown in Table 19.

The components in a BOM require a unique component identifier. This (in the form of an object identifier) is created automatically in ORION, without the designer's interference, while instantiating an object. The object identifier is used to facilitate the sharing and updating of objects. The uniqueness of an identifier allows a direct correspondence between an object in the data representation and a subassembly in BOM.

During creation of a BOM, each part is defined independently, and then dependency relationships are established between parts and components defining parent–component relationships. In the case of OOBOM, objects are created independently, but then dependency relationships between object instances are established. An example of such a BOM for PACKAGE_PENCIL is in Fig. 54. There exists the aggregation relationship between the component instances associated with PACKAGE_PENCIL. For example, each PACKAGE_PENCIL

TABLE 19 PACKAGE_PENCIL Object Class [7]

PACKAGE_PENCIL CLASS

Class name	PENCIL_ASSY
Object identity	OID
Documentation	Parts for PACKAGE_PENCIL, part supplier, part description, part material, part specification,
Superclass	PACKAGE_PENCIL
Subclass	BODY, REWIND_MECH, CAP_ASSY
Attributes	Lead time, safety stock, quantity on hand, quantity per, assembly time, machines_and_tools.
Methods	display, change_part, add_part, delete_part, manufacturing_techniques, material_requirement_planning, machining_process, inventory_control.

instance owns specific instances of component classes PENCIL_ASSY, BOX_KIT, and LABEL [7].

In an industry, sometimes a planning BOM [39,40] is necessary, when there are several options against a particular part. For example, METAL_CASE type BOX_KIT may have two options, that made of iron and that made of copper (Figs. 54a and 54b). In the OOBOM [7], this type of situation has been dealt with efficiently using the concept of generic instance and version instance. In Fig. 54b, METAL_CASE may have a generic instance, which may have two options of iron and copper, known as version instance. In Fig. 54c, the M292 model is a generic instance of PACKAGE_PENCIL class, whereas M292-1 is a particular version instance for M292. In Fig. 54a, M292 is a model of PACKAGE_PENCIL, in which the BOX_KIT may be of metal type,

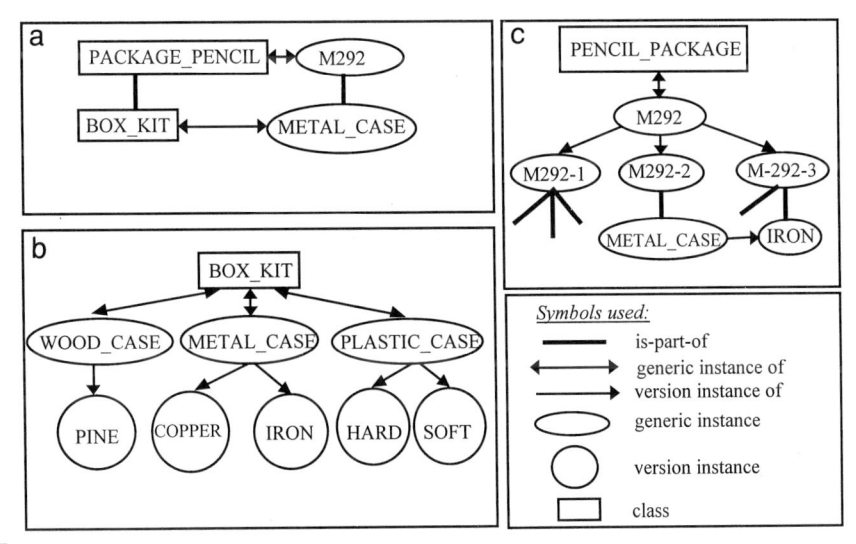

FIGURE 54 Hierarchy of object classes and instances [7]. (a) Composite link between generic instances. (b) Hierarchy of version and generic instances of BOX_KIT. (c) Object version hierarchy.

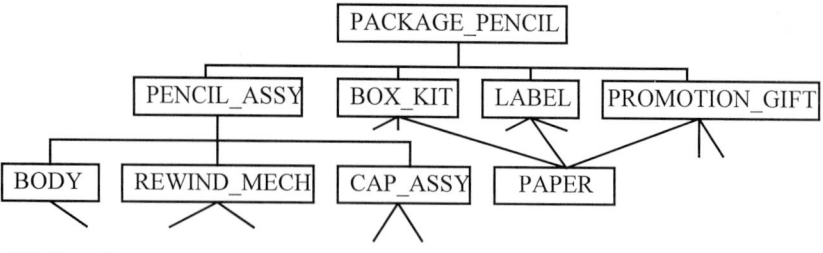

FIGURE 55 An example of multiple inheritance [7].

i.e., METAL_CASE. Again, M292 may have several options, like M292-1 and M-292-2. Thus, M-292 is a generic instance of PACKAGE_PENCIL, and METAL_CASE is a generic instance of BOX_KIT. The generic instance may be used to reference objects (e.g., iron) without specifying in advance the particular version needed. Changes in the definition of a class must be propagated to its generic instances unless a new generic or version instance is explicitly created.

When part/component is used to assemble several parents in a BOM, there arises the situation of multiple inheritance, as shown in Fig. 55. In this situation, there may be name conflicts, which have been resolved by arranging (user-defined or default ordering) the order of the parent class for each component class. In this example, the order of parent classes for the component class PAPER is BOX_KIT, LABEL, and PROMOTION_GIFT (this is an object class to promote sells). However, this order can be changed by the user, based on requirement. In the case of name conflicts arising from the inheritance of instance variables and methods, one must add new instance variables or modify the name in a class lattice composed of the conflicting component classes [7].

Chung and Fischer [7] suggest that certain numerical algorithms should be added to the OOBOM system, in the form of rule-based procedures, to facilitate integration of OOBOM with the MRP system, which needs to perform calculations for MRP. The authors also suggest that for graphical display, Pascal language may be used for pixel-based graphic operations. However, several other issues need to be addressed.

F. MRPII as an Enterprise Information System

On many occasions, OO information systems have been modeled, where MRPII played either the central role of a company-wide information system or a major role in it. [22,57].

An information system is considered a vital ingredient of a computer-integrated manufacturing (CIM) system. An efficient design of an information system, based on data of different islands of information, is thus a must.

Ngwenyama and Grant [57] present a case study for modeling an information system involving MRPII as the center part. The primary reason for using object-oriented paradigm is the recognition that the OO approach offers powerful, but simple, concepts for representing organizational reality and the system designer's ideas about the system. They identified three levels of abstraction in OO modeling: (i) organizational, (ii) conceptual, and (iii) technical, as shown in Table 20.

TABLE 20 Conceptual Framework for Information Modeling [57]

Levels of modeling	Object-oriented concepts		
	Objects	Messages	Methods
Organizational	Business process	Information flows	Business procedures
	Business activities	Physical flows	Decision making procedures
	Organizational roles		
	Information views		
Conceptual	Information handling	Data flows	Information processing procedures
	Processes		Communication procedures
	Communication processes		
	Data		
	Subject databases		
Technical	Information systems	Data flows	Application programs
	Database structures		Operating procedures
	Hardware		
	Systems software		
	Communication system		

Ngwenyama and Grant [57] develop the information system using seven conceptual models. The procedure for deriving a model is as follows: (i) identify candidate objects, (ii) classify them as active or passive, (iii) define their characteristics, (iv) define the methods they enact with or which operate on them, (v) define the messages that they send or receive, and (vi) construct the diagrams. The models are shown in Fig. 56.

The object of the *global model* is to capture, at the highest level of abstraction, the interactions among the organization system and/or subsystems. This shows the primary information links (messages). Developing the global model requires the definition of major operating systems, also considered objects, embedded in the enterprise without regard to artificial boundaries, such as departments. The MRPII system and its modules have the central role of linking several business activities at this level. Next, the *business model* decomposes each subsystem (i.e., objects) into its set of related activities/processes. These can be further divided into individual tasks. Later, the information flow

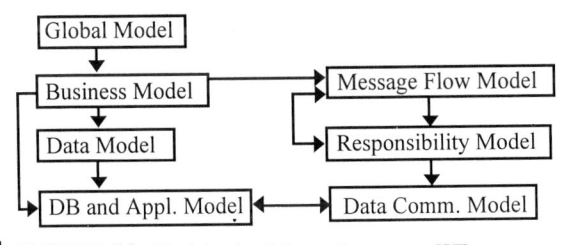

FIGURE 56 Models of an information system [57].

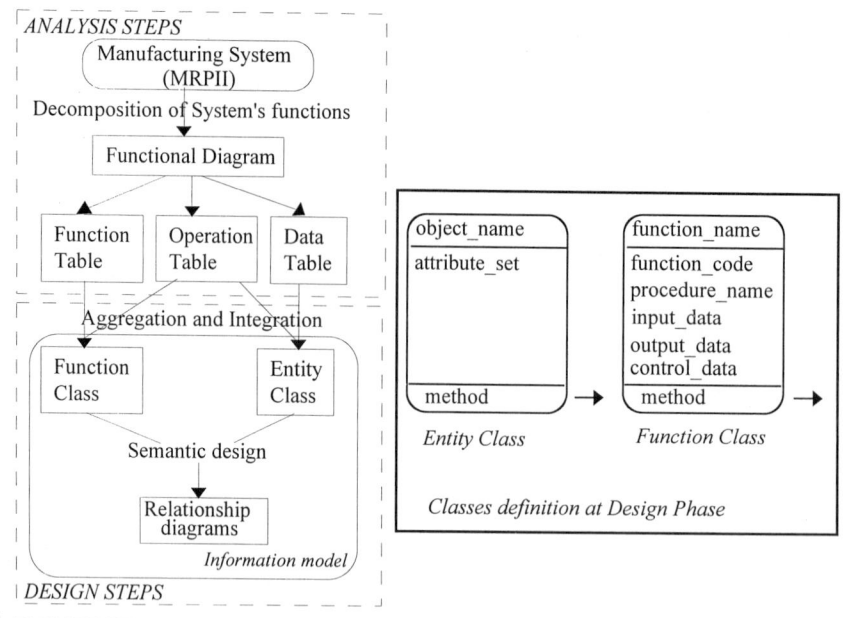

FIGURE 57 OOMIS Methodology [22].

(messages) received or generated by such activities/functions/tasks at different levels of abstraction are described in the *message flow model*. The *responsibility model* documents the role of responsibility for information processing at various levels of organization. It documents which objects (such as machines and individuals) have access or control over what messages. Then the conceptual design of constructing the detailed architecture starts, which is done through the *data model, database and application model,* and *data communication model*. The names of these three models describe their roles and functionalities. However, the authors did not give any detail of the data construction of each of the entities or objects of any system (e.g., MRPII).

Kim *et al.* [22] present an object-oriented information modeling technique for MIS, which is in fact the MRPII system. In place of existing methodologies, like IDEF and GRAI, the authors develop a new technique, known as *object-oriented modeling for manufacturing information system* (OOMIS), which uses a representational scheme, class, for integrating manufacturing (MRPII) functions and data. The OOMIS consists of two steps, analysis and design, as in Fig. 57 [22].

In the analysis phase, the complete manufacturing (MRPII) system is decomposed into its functions. The functional diagram in Fig. 58 shows three such functions of the complete MRPII system. These are again divided into subfunctions, up to specific small interacting unit functions, which can perform fundamental and simple operations. The functional diagram in Fig. 59 shows the next level decomposition for inventory control function (module of MRPII) as seen in Fig. 58 [22].

From the proven psychological fact that it is difficult to grasp more than five to seven distinct concepts at a time, this OOMIS methodology suggests decomposing a function into not more than six subfunctions at a level. Then,

MANUFACTURING RESOURCE PLANNING 489

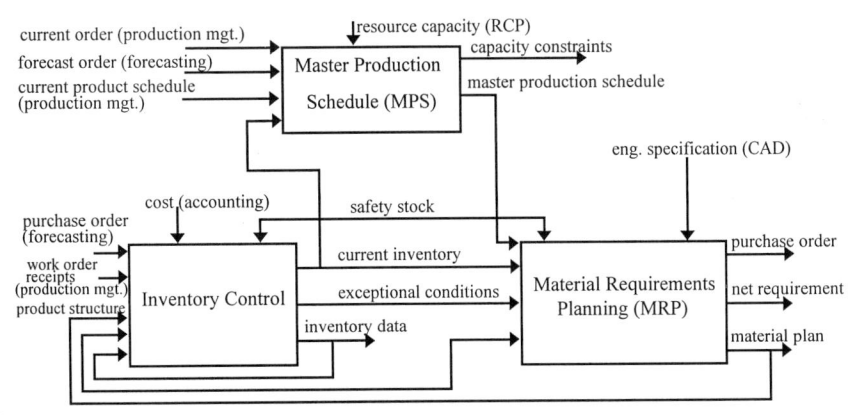

FIGURE 58 Partial functional diagram of MRPII system [22].

similar to the IDEF technique, the functional diagrams are prepared indicating inputs, outputs, and control mechanism, as shown in Figs. 58 and 59. In the diagrams, information and materials must be distinguished by their different logistic properties. The functional diagrams are converted into a function table giving some additional information, like function code and procedure name. The function table for inventory control function is shown in Table 21a. The function code includes some codes for indicating decomposition level and order. The data table represents output data of the functional diagrams. This data may be modified and referenced by other functions, since the complete system's functions are highly interrelated and interacting, as is the case of MRPII. A data table contains function name and code received respectively from the functional diagram and table; attribute_name, which is a part of the manufacturing data and represents the output data name literally; attribute_of, which is the entire manufacturing data; and a description of attribute. Next in the hierarchy is the operation table, which describes how a manufacturing function handles its operations. The operation table for inventory control function is shown in Table 21b. The operations in the operation table are the aggregated set of processes or procedures of the unit functions, which become the class methods later in the design phase [22].

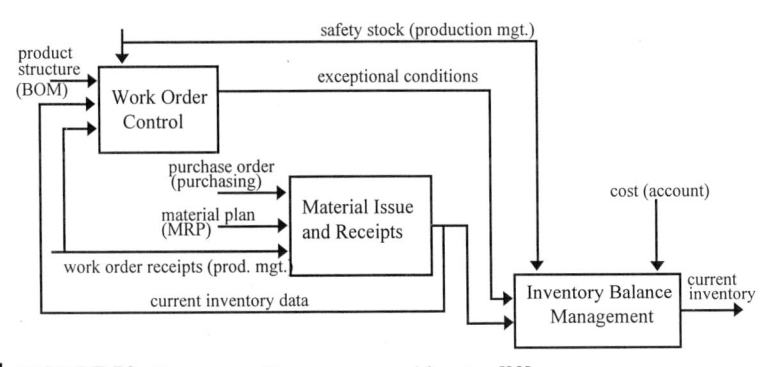

FIGURE 59 Decomposed inventory control function [22].

TABLE 21 Function and Operation Tables for Inventory Control [22]

(a) Function name: inventory_control

function code: F7

procedure name: i_c_proc

input data: material plan (MRP)
        purchase order (purchasing)
        work order receipts (production mgt.)
        product structure (BOM)

output data: current inventory status

control data: cost (account)
        safety stock (production mgt.)

(b) Function name: inventory_control   **Function code: F7**

Operation	Description
inventory_trans	Process all inventory translation on line
report_inventory	Report current inventory status
material_receipt	Update received material
work_order_proc	Process work orders and report material issue
proc_bom	Make part list from work order

In the design phase, the tables obtained in the analysis phase are translated into an object-oriented information system (such as for MRPII) using OOMIS. The aggregation and integration process converts the function, operation, and data tables into a class dictionary having two types of classes, namely function class and entity class (Fig. 57). As example, a part of the class dictionary is shown in Table 22. Here, the operations of inventory control function (Table 21b) have been used to define the methods of the classes of Table 22. While the function class describes the properties of the MRPII functions, the entity class describes the data. The class dictionary can be translated into a specific data dictionary of OODBMS. The semantic relationships (aggregation, generalization, unidirectional and bidirectional synchronous and asynchronous interaction) are used to describe class relationships. Figure 60 illustrates the aggregation hierarchy of the classes of Table 22 [22].

The aggregation process is carried out by identifying common concepts in the function, operation, and data tables. The attribute_name tuples of the data tables, which have the same attribute_of field, are aggregated to represent a manufacturing datum whose name is attribute_of. If the function tables have the same input and control data, these are merged together, where the merged function table contains the output data that are related to each function table. This combined table can refer to the operation tables, which are then related to each function table, to choose a suitable method for organizing the function table. Then the integration process is carried out to resolve

MANUFACTURING RESOURCE PLANNING

TABLE 22 A Part of the Class Dictionary [22]

fn_name: work_order_control	obj_name: work_order	obj_name: inventory_date
fn_code: F7.1 proc_name: w_o_c_proc in_data: work_order 　　　　BOM_info 　　　　inventory_data out_data: exceptional_conditions con_data: safety_stock	product_id: batch_id: priority: order_date: due_date: completion_date quantity: cost: BOL_no: Routing:	product_id: part_id: on-hand: lead_time: lot_size: on_order: location: raw_material_type: alternative:
work_order_control	update	update_inventory_status
obj_name: production_info	**obj_name: part_info**	**obj_name: BOM_info**
product_id: production_name: description: version_no: uom: part_info: BOM_no: BOL_no:	part_id: material_code: process_plan_no: NC_prog_no: GT_code: drawing_no:	BOM_no: product_id: part_id: quantity: uom: assembly_instruction:
update	update	add_bom modify_bom

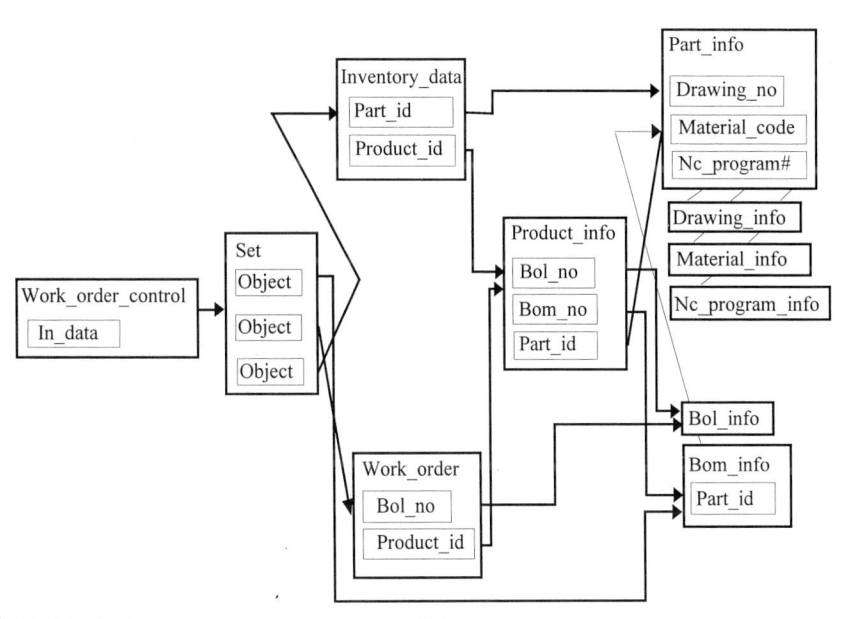

FIGURE 60 Aggregation hierarchy of classes [22].

conflicts in the aggregated tables. During this, each table is compared with other tables to identify and remove conflicts between corresponding components [22].

The function class represents the characteristics of the manufacturing (MRPII here) function. Methods of this class describe the operations of the function. The attributes of the class are function code, procedure name, source function, and manufacturing entities, which are the function's input, output, and control data. Entity class describes the physical properties of the manufacturing (here, MRPII) data (or entities). The methods of this class come from the operation tables, and are responsible for calculating the values of the manufacturing data or evaluating the status of the function [22].

If a new function is necessary in the system (here MRPII), it can easily be designed by selecting the suitable classes from the existing class dictionary. In case there is no such class, new classes may be designed by describing the properties of the function [22].

Huarng and Ravi [19] are of the opinion that object orientation provides the modeler the liberty of representing interactions between object behaviors. This makes it possible to understand the dynamics of information flow. It must be noted that several modules of MRPII, such as BOM and PAC, are highly dynamic, particularly in a make-to-order environment, which in turn, makes the information flow dynamic. Each function in an organization is composed of a sequence of activities, or in other words, each function is a cycle of activities. Such is the case for MRPII as well. For example, order generation can be represented as a sequence of behaviors of the following objects: gross requirement, inventory on-hand, open order.

G. Scopes of Object Orientation

Although object orientation has got momentum in research in the areas of manufacturing, including MRPII, its application has also been defined to be confined within the boundary of some specific areas.

Nof [32,33] assesses what can and cannot be expected to be accomplished from the promising object orientation in manufacturing systems engineering. It simplifies the burdensome complexity of manufacturing, including planning and control and software development. It provides intuitive clarity, discipline, and flexibility essential in the functions of manufacturing. *Object-oriented programming* (OOP) can increase a programmer's productivity. It is also flexible to subsequent modifications. Although most of the MRPII functions do not contain complex data structures, some modules, such as PAC, BOM generation, and its (optionally) graphical display, indeed need a complex data structure. In such a case, object orientation is favorable. *Object-oriented control* (OOC) and object-oriented modeling also provide distinct advantages, such as modularity of modeling and logic requirements, direct and intuitive mapping of real objects to software objects, and minimization of efforts of software development through reusability. As discussed earlier, these are specially useful in the case of PAC system design. Table 23 lists some manufacturing objectives, which includes functions of MRPII, and the possibility of object orientation.

With the increase in the abilities of computations and extended functions in the MRPII system, customer expectations are also increasing. Software

TABLE 23 Affinity Mapping between Functions and OO Premises [32,33*]

Objectives	Object-orientation promises
Produce well-defined, repeatable, interchangeable parts and products	Classifies objects in hierarchical structures, having data and attributes encapsulated
Manufacture by process and assembly plans	Applies assembly structures and a high level of abstraction
Based on methods for defining process operations and manufacturing services	Methods define operations and services inside an object and pass it through messages
Design complex products and process their elements	Specifies complex systems by their elementary object components
Combine information and materials processing to create end products	Combines data and process model together in one object
Depend on consistent and systematic plans	Represents consistently and systematically natural reality and human thinking
Communicate and integrate among multiple functions	Communicates by messages, polymorphism, and corresponding operations
Have a culture of clear, ordered, stable processes and procedures	Model stability, clarity, and flexibility due to minimal dependency between objects
Rapidly adapt to change	Reusability minimizes effort to rewrite codes

*Copyright Taylor & Francis.

developers are providing these additional functions as much as possible with minimal effort. Sometimes data textual elements, graphics, and even knowledge are also introduced together in a single system. In many cases, object orientation has been successful in minimizing cost of development by minimizing effort. Table 24 lists some complexities in the MRPII systems [32,33].

Nof [32,33] finds object orientation of particular advantage in the case of several manufacturing functions, which dominantly includes MRPII, although it has some limitations too, which include a high run-time cost among others. However, the author in conclusion hopes that the limitations will be relaxed by emerging and future capabilities.

Wang and Fulton [53] report on a case of manufacturing information system development. Although it is an MIS in general, it contains many MRPII functions, though not in a disciplined way as in MRPII. Earlier the system was developed using a relational DBMS. Later the system was developed using

TABLE 24 Increasing Complexity in Manufacturing Software [32,33*]

Information level	Examples of manufacturing applications (MRPII)
Data	All modules of MRPII
Graphics	Bill of Materials (Some MRPII systems)
Information	All modules of MRPII
Knowledge	Sometimes, scheduling, forecasting, etc.
What-if simulation	Production flow analysis, lead time determination

*Copyright Taylor & Francis.

OODMBS. The reasons behind this are the limitations of RDBMS and the corresponding advantages of OODBMS. As stated, a relational data model has several drawbacks including a lack of semantic expression, a limitation of supporting heterogeneous data types, a difficulty in representing complex objects, and an inability to define a dynamic schema, whereas these are overcome in object-oriented design and OODBMS. Thus, object orientation has been highly recommended for such manufacturing information systems (e.g., MRPII).

REFERENCES

1. Arnold, J. R. T. *Introduction to Materials Management*. Prentice-Hall, Englewood Cliffs, NJ, 1991.
2. Berio, G. *et al*. The M*-object methodology for information system design in CIM environments. *IEEE Trans. Systems Man Cybernet.* 25(1):68–85, 1995.
3. Bertrand, J. W. M., and Wortmann, J. C. Information systems for production planning and control: Developments in perspective. *Production Planning and Control* 3(3):280–289, 1992.
4. Browne, J. Production activity control—A key aspect of production control. *Int. J. Prod. Res.* 26(3):415–427, 1988.
5. Browne, J., Harhen, J., and Shivnan, J. *Production Management Systems: A CIM Perspective*. Addison–Wesley, Reading, MA, 1989.
6. Chang, S.-H. *et al*. Manufacturing bill of material planning. *Production Planning and Control* 8(5):437–450, 1997.
7. Chung, Y., and Fischer, G. W. Illustration of object-oriented databases for the structure of a bill of materials (BOM). *Comput. Indust. Eng.* 19(3):257–270, 1992.
8. Chung, Y., and Fischer, G. W. A conceptual structure and issues for an object-oriented bill of materials (BOM) data model. *Comput. Indust. Engrg.* 26(2):321–339, 1994.
9. Dangerfield, B. J., and Morris, J. S. Relational database management systems: A new tool for coding and classification. *Int. J. Oper. Production Manage.* 11(5):47–56, 1991.
10. Du, T. C. T., and Wolfe, P. M. An implementation perspective of applying object-oriented database technologies. *IIE Transactions*, 29(9):733–742, 1997.
11. Gausemeier, J. *et al*. Intelligent object networks—The solution for tomorrow's manufacturing control systems. In *Proceedings of the 3rd International Conference on Computer Integrated Manufacturing*, Singapore, 11–14 July, 1995, pp. 729–736.
12. Grabot, B., and Huguet, P. Reference models and object-oriented method for reuse in production activity control system design. *Comput. Indus.* 32(1):17–31, 1996.
13. Harhalakis. G. *et al*. Development of a factory level CIM model. *J. Manufact. Systems* 9(2):116–128, 1990.
14. Hasin, M. A. A., and Pandey, P. C. MRPII: Should its simplicity remain unchanged? *Indust. Manage.* 38(3):19–21, 1996.
15. Higgins, P. *et al. Manufacturing Planning and Control: Beyond MRPII*. Chapman & Hall, New York, 1996.
16. Higgins, P. *et al*. From MRPII to mrp. *Production Planning and Control* 3(3):227–238, 1992.
17. Hitomi, K. *Manufacturing Systems Engineering*. Taylor & Francis, London, 1979.
18. Hsu, C., and Skevington, C. Integration of data and knowledge in manufacturing enterprises: A conceptual framework. *J. Manufact. Systems* 6(4):277–285, 1987.
19. Huarng, A. S., and Krovi, R. An object-based infrastructure for IRM. *Inform. Systems Manage.* 15(2):46–52, 1998.
20. Jackson, D. F., and Okike, K. Relational database management systems and industrial engineering. *Comput. Indust. Engrg.* 23(1–4):479–482, 1992.
21. Kemper, A., and Moerkotte, G. Object-oriented database management: Application in engineering and computer science. Prentice–Hall, Englewood Cliffs, NJ, 1994.
22. Kim, C. *et al*. An object-oriented information modeling methodology for manufacturing information systems. *Comput. Indust. Engrg.* 24(3):337–353, 1993.

23. Korhonen, P. et al. Demand chain management in a global enterprise—Information management view. *Production Planning and Control* 9(6):526–531, 1998.
24. Kroenke, D. *Management Information Systems.* Mitchell McGraw–Hill, New York, 1989.
25. Meyer, A. De. The integration of manufacturing information systems. In *Proceedings of the International Conference on Computer Integrated Manufacturing,* Rensselaer Polytechnic Institute, Troy, New York, May 23–25, 1988, pp. 217–225.
26. Moriwaki, T. et al. Object-oriented modeling of autonomous distributed manufacturing system and its application to real time scheduling. In *Proceedings of the International Conference on Object-Oriented Manufacturing Systems,* Calgary, Alberta, Canada, 3–6 May, 1992, pp. 207–212.
27. *Micro-Max User Manual.* Micro-MRP, Foster City, CA, 1991–1992.
28. *MRPII Elements: Datapro Manufacturing Automation Series.* McGraw-Hill, Delran, NJ, 1989.
29. Nandakumar, G. The design of a bill of materials using relational database. *Comput. Indust. Engrg.* 6(1):15–21, 1985.
30. Naquin, B., and Ali, D. Active database and its utilization in the object-oriented environment. *Comput. Indust. Engrg.* 25(1–4):313–316, 1993.
31. Nicholson, T. A. J. Beyond MRP—The management question. *Production Planning and Control* 3(3):247–257, 1992.
32. Nof, S. Is all manufacturing object-oriented? In *Proceedings of the International Conference on Object-Oriented Manufacturing Systems,* Calgary, Alberta, Canada, 3–6 May, 1992, pp. 37–54.
33. Nof, S. Y. Critiquing the potential of object orientation in manufacturing. *Int. J. Comput. Integr. Manufact.* 7(1):3–16, 1994.
34. Ojelanki, K. N., and Delvin, A. G. Enterprise modeling for CIM information systems architectures: An object-oriented approach. *Comput. Indust. Engrg.* 26(2):279–293, 1994.
35. Olsen, K. A. et al. A procedure-oriented generic bill of materials. *Comput. Indust. Engrg.* 32(1):29–45, 1997.
36. Pandey, P. C., and Hasin, M. A. A. A scheme for an integrated production planning and control system. *Int. J. Comput. Appl. Technol.* 8(5/6):301–306, 1995.
37. Park, H. G. et al. An object oriented production planning system development in ERP environment. *Comput. Indust. Engrg.* 35(1/2):157–160, 1998.
38. Pels, H. J., and Wortmann, J. C. Modular decomposition of integrated databases. *Production Planning and Control* 1(3):132–146, 1990.
39. Ramalingam, P. Bill of material: A valuable management tool: Part I. *Indust. Manage.* 24(2):28–31, 1982.
40. Ramalingam, P. Bill of material: A valuable management tool: Part II. *Indust. Manage.* 25(1):22–25, 1983.
41. Ranganathan, V. S., and Ali, D. L. Distributed object management: Integrating distributed information in heterogeneous environment. *Comput. Indust. Engrg.* 25(1–4):317–320, 1993.
42. Ranky, P. G. *Manufacturing Database Management and Knowledge-Based Expert Systems.* CIMware, Addingham, England, 1990.
43. Seymour, L. *Data Structures,* Schaum's Outline Series in Computers. McGraw–Hill, New York, 1997.
44. Sinha, D., and Chen, H. G. Object-oriented DSS construction for hierarchical inventory control. *Comput. Indust. Engrg.* 21(1–4):441–445, 1991.
45. Smith, S. B. *Computer-Based Production and Inventory Control.* Prentice–Hall, Englewood Cliffs, NJ, 1989.
46. Smith, J., and Joshi, S. Object-oriented development of shop floor control systems for CIM. In *Proceedings of the International Conference on Object-Oriented Manufacturing Systems,* Calgary, Alberta, Canada, 3–6 May, 1992, pp. 152–157.
47. Spooner, D., Hardwick, M., and Kelvin, W. L. Integrating the CIM environment using object-oriented data management technology. In *Proceedings of the International Conference on Computer Integrated Manufacturing,* Rensselaer Polytechnic Institute, Troy, New York, May 23–25, 1988, pp. 144–152.
48. Starmer, C., and Kochhar, A. K. Fourth generation languages based manufacturing control systems—Lessons from an application case study. *Production Planning and Control* 3(3):271–279, 1992.

49. Trappey, A. J. C. *et al.* An object-oriented bill of materials system for dynamic product management. In *Proceedings of the 3rd International Conference on Computer Integrated Manufacturing,* Singapore, 11–14 July, 1995, pp. 629–636.
50. Ulrich, H., and Durig, W. Object-oriented realization of planning tools for production planning and control. In *Proceedings of the International Conference on Object-Oriented Manufacturing Systems,* Calgary, Alberta, Canada, 3–6 May, 1992, pp. 158–167.
51. Van Veen, E. A., and Wortmann, J. C. Generative bill of materials processing systems, *Production Planning and Control* 3(3):314–326, 1992.
52. Van Veen, E. A., and Wortmann, J. C. New developments in generative BOM processing systems. *Production Planning and Control* 3(3):327–335, 1992.
53. Wang, C.-Y., and Fulton, R. E. Information system design for optical fiber manufacturing using an object-oriented approach. *Int. J. Comput. Integr. Manufact.* 7(1):61–73, 1994.
54. Winter, R. E. A database approach to hierarchical materials planning. *Int. J. Oper. Production Manage.* 10(2):62–83, 1990.
55. Wortmann, J. C. Flexibility of standard software packages for production planning and control. *Production Planning and Control* 3(3):290–299, 1992.
56. Zhou, Q. *et al.* An information management system for production planning in virtual enterprises. *Comput. Indust. Engrg.* 35(1/2):153–156, 1998.
57. Ngwenyama, O. K., and Grant, D. A. Enterprise modeling for CIM Information systems architectures. An object-oriented approach. *Comput. Indust. Engrg.* 26(2):279–293, 1994.
58. Ng, J. K. C., and Ip, W. H. The strategic design and development of ERP and RTMS. *Comput. Indust. Engrg.* 34(4):777–791, 1998.

13
DEVELOPING APPLICATIONS IN CORPORATE FINANCE: AN OBJECT-ORIENTED DATABASE MANAGEMENT APPROACH

IRENE M. Y. WOON
MONG LI LEE

School of Computing, National University of Singapore, Singapore 117543

I. INTRODUCTION 498
II. FINANCIAL INFORMATION AND ITS USES 499
    A. Financial Statements 500
    B. Using the Financial Statements 502
    C. Financial Policies 503
III. DATABASE MANAGEMENT SYSTEMS 505
    A. Components of a DBMS 505
    B. Capabilities of a DBMS 506
    C. Data Models 507
IV. FINANCIAL OBJECT-ORIENTED DATABASES 508
    A. General Concepts 509
    B. Object Modeling 510
    C. Modeling Financial Policies 513
V. DISCUSSION 515
    REFERENCES 516

Financial information systems has evolved from spreadsheets to simple database systems where data are stored in a central repository, to today's sophisticated systems that integrate databases with complex applications. The object-oriented paradigm promises productivity and reliability of software systems through natural modeling concepts and cleaner and extensible designs while database management systems offer necessary capabilities such as persistence, integrity, and security. In this paper, we propose a unified framework for modeling both financial information and policies. A financial information system can be modeled and implemented using the object-oriented model. This forms the basis for exploratory and complex business data analysis and strategic decision-making support. In addition, we will illustrate that the object-oriented approach also provides a uniform representation for expressing financial policy formulation.

I. INTRODUCTION

In the early 1980s, a number of integrated financial spreadsheets–graphics–word processing, e.g., Symphony and Excel, were used to capture, analyze, and present the financial information of a company. The main problem with such packages was their inability to automatically update links; when financial data in one spreadsheet were changed, then many related spreadsheets would have to be updated manually by the user to ensure the correctness of the financial reports. As a consequence, interest in databases as a medium for storing financial data grew.

As the amount of data multiplies, the many features offered by a database management system (DBMS) for data management, such as reduced application development time, concurrency control and recovery, indexing support, and query capabilities, become increasingly attractive and ultimately necessary. In addition, consolidating data from several databases, together with historical and summary information can create a comprehensive view of all aspects of an enterprise. This is also known as data warehousing. The data warehouse facilitates complex and statistical analysis such as:

- On-line analytic processing (OLAP), which supports a multidimensional model of data and *ad hoc* complex queries involving group-by and aggregation, and
- Exploratory data analysis or data mining where a user looks for interesting patterns in the data.

Systems that were specifically developed for use by the financial community included SAP, Peoplesoft, and Oracle Financials, which had Oracle or Sybase as its data repository.

Research into artificial intelligence provided the impetus for the development of products that embed human expertise into financial software programs. The expert's knowledge was typically represented in the form of a production rule in the form: observation → hypothesis. FINSIM Expert [1] is one such system used to analyze financial information for various purposes, e.g., credit analysis and investment analysis. Real-world "expert" systems would typically marry a traditional database with a knowledge base in which was encoded the expert's cognitive processes, to allow access to financial data. This was the early precursor to deductive databases. Research into deductive databases is aimed at discovering efficient schemes for uniformly representing assertions and deductive rules and for responding to highly expressive queries about the knowledge base of assertions and rules.

In many application domains, complex kinds of data must be supported. Object-oriented (OO) concepts have strongly influenced efforts to enhance database support for complex types. This has led to the development of object database systems. An important advantage of object database systems is that they can store code as well as data. Abstract data type methods are collected in the database, and the set of operations for a given type can be found by querying the database catalogs. Operations can be composed in *ad hoc* ways in query expressions. As a result, the object-oriented DBMS is like a software repository, with built-in query support for identifying software modules and combining operations to generate new applications. Data consistency is preserved as the DBMS provides automatic management of constraints, which include user-defined operations.

The features of the financial domain that make this technique appealing are:

• Financial data have a relationship to one another, which can be naturally expressed in the object-oriented modeling notation.
• Within the framework of generally accepted financial accounting principles, accountants are free to choose from a number of alternative procedures to record the effects of an event. The encapsulation feature in the object-oriented approach allows these different procedures to be modeled such that the applications used are not affected.
• Financial data requirements vary for different industries and for different companies within the same industry, which is also supported by the encapsulation feature in the object-oriented approach.

The remainder of this paper is organized as follows. Section II gives a quick tutorial in finance covering various relevant aspects such as financial statements and their definition and use such as in implementing financial policies. This will give the reader an appreciation of the domain area with a view to understanding fragments of the model shown in later sections. Section III provides an introduction to database management systems covering its components, capabilities, and data models. Readers well versed in finance and/or databases may choose to skip the appropriate section(s). In Section IV, we show how the data in the financial statements may be modeled using the OO paradigm. In addition, we demonstrate how financial policies, which can be expressed in terms of financial statement information, may be modeled.

II. FINANCIAL INFORMATION AND ITS USES

Peter and Jane thought they could make a lot of money selling musical shoes. They soon found out, however, that to make money, they first had to have money. For a start, they needed money to buy machinery that would make these shoes from raw materials of leather, plastic, rubber, bells, sound cards, etc., money to buy the raw materials, and money to rent premises to house the shoe-making machinery. They decided to cut manpower costs by doing everything themselves. Money from their piggy banks was not enough, so they decided to approach some banks for a loan. Luckily for them, Peter's uncle was the Chairman of the Board of a small bank—so they received a small loan at very favorable rates. Peter and Jane were ecstatic—with this loan, they could start making their shoes and selling it. To cut down on marketing costs, they settled on buying a second-hand van and selling their shoes door-to-door.

In the language of finance, Peter and Jane have made investments in assets such as inventory of raw materials, shoes, and machinery. The loan they have taken out is referred to as a liability; they represent obligations that would have to be met, i.e., the loan must be repaid. They expect to do this by selling the shoes at a profit. Business grew beyond their expectations. To meet demands for their product, they had to expand their operations, buying more equipment, renting

TABLE 1 Peter and Jane's Balance Sheet as at 27.03.1999

Assets	(£000s)	Liabilities	(£000s)
Current		*Current*	
Cash	100	Accounts Payable	300
Accounts Receivables	400	Total current liabilities	300
Inventories	500		
Total current assets	1000	*Long-term*	
		Bank Loans	1700
Fixed		Total long-term liabilities	1700
Net Value of Equipment	1000		
Net Value of Vans	1000	Shareholder's fund	1000
Total fixed assets	2000		
Total assets	3000	Total liabilities	3000

bigger premises, hiring more workers, etc. To finance all these investments, they decided to incorporate their business and float some shares to the public, i.e., in return for funds, members of the public became joint owners of the firm.

The value of Peter and Jane's business can be recorded and reflected in simple financial models. We will look at three of these: the balance sheet, the income statement, and the cash flow statement.

A. Financial Statements

Table 1 shows Peter and Jane's balance sheet. The balance sheet gives a financial picture of the business on a particular day.

The assets that are shown on the left-hand side of the balance sheet can be broadly classified as current and fixed assets. Fixed assets are those that will last a relatively long time, e.g., shoe-making machinery. The other category of assets, current assets, comprises those that have a shorter life-span; they can be converted into cash in one business operating cycle, e.g., raw materials, semi-finished shoes/parts of shoes, and unsold finished shoes. An operating cycle is defined as a typical length of time between when an order is placed and when cash is received for that sale. Whether an asset is classified as current or fixed depends on the nature of the business. A firm selling vans will list it (a van) as a current asset, whereas Peter and Jane using vans to deliver goods will list it as a fixed asset. The liabilities represents what the firm owes, e.g., bank loans and creditors, and this is shown on the right-hand side of the balance sheet. Just as assets were classified based on their life span, so are liabilities. Current liabilities are obligations that must be met in within an operating cycle while long-term liabilities are obligations that do not have to be met within an operating cycle. Also shown on the right-hand side of the balance sheet is the shareholder's fund, e.g., money received from the issuance of shares.

The balance sheet shows the values of fixed assets at its net value, i.e., the purchase price less accumulated depreciation. Depreciation reflects the accountant's estimate of the cost of the equipment used up in the production process. For example, suppose one of the second-hand vans bought at £500 is estimated to have 5 more useful years of life left and no resale value beyond that.

TABLE 2 Peter and Jane's Income Statement for 1.7.1998–30.3.1999

	(£000s)
Revenues	
Sales	3000
Expenses	
Cost of goods sold	(1800)
Admin and selling expenses	(500)
Depreciation	(200)
Profit/loss	
Earnings before interest and taxes	500
Interest expense	(100)
Pretax income	400
Taxes	(150)
Net income	250

According to the accountant, the £500 cost must be apportioned out as an expense over the useful life of the asset. The straight-line depreciation method will give £100 of depreciation expense per year. At the end of its first year of use, the van's net value will be £500 − £100 = £400 and at the end of its second year of use, its net value will be £500 − £200 = £300, and so on.

Table 2 gives the income statement of Peter and Jane's business for the past year. Rather than being a snapshot of the firm at a point in time, the income statement describes the performance of the firm over a particular period of time, i.e., what happened in between two periods of time. It shows the revenues, the expenses incurred, and the resulting profit or loss resulting from its operations. Details of income and expenses shown in the statement differ according to the firm, industry, and country.

The last financial model is called the cash flow statement. This shows the position of cash generated from operations in relation to its operating costs. Consider some typical cash flows: cash outflows in the purchase of raw materials, payment of utilities and rents, cash inflows when debtors pay or bank loans are activated. This statement shows the operating cash flow, which is the cash flow that comes from selling goods and services. This should usually be positive; a firm is in trouble if this is negative for a long time because the firm is not generating enough cash to pay its operating costs. Total operating cash flow for the firm includes increases to working capital, which is the difference between the current assets and current liabilities. The total operating cash flow in this case is negative. In its early years of operations, it is normal for firms to have negative total cash outflows as spending on inventory, etc., will be higher than its cash flow from sales.

Profit as shown in the income statement is not the same as cash flow. For instance, sales on the income statement will tend to overstate actual cash inflows because most customers pay their bills on credit. The cash flow statement shown in Table 3 is derived from the balance sheet and the income statement. In determining the economic and financial condition of a firm, an analysis of the firm's cash flow can be more revealing.

TABLE 3 Peter and Jane's Cash Flow Statement for 1.7.1998–30.3.1999

Cash flows from operations	(£000s)
Earnings before interest and taxes	500
Depreciation	200
Taxes	(150)
	450
Increases to working capital	(700)
Total operating cash flows	(250)

B. Using the Financial Statements

Managers and shareholders of a firm rely on the financial information given in the financial statements to perform many tasks such as reporting profit, computing tax, evaluating investment options, analyzing performance, appraising the values of assets, and designing financial strategies. However, financial information is only useful when they are interpreted correctly. A variety of standard techniques can be employed to do this. Typically, the trend of absolute historical figures, the trend of certain ratios (the proportion of one financial variable to another), and the sources and uses of funds are analyzed.

An analysis of the periodical series of absolute financial figures is undertaken in order to draw attention to changes that have taken place, identifying trends and regular changes due to trade cycles, and irregular fluctuations which denote instability and greater risks. This initial analysis provides a rough indicator of the condition of the firm. The analysis of a firm's ratios involves a more detailed scrutiny of the financial statements. There are several reasons why ratio analysis is used. Isolated figures mean very little on their own. For example, does an increase in sales indicate that the firm is better off? Surely not, if its costs are increasing on a larger scale. Thus, significant pieces of data need to be logically related, if their meaning is to be interpreted correctly. Ratio analysis also allows for meaningful comparisons within a firm over time, against other firms and against the industry as a whole. Individual ratios are grouped into different categories, each representing a financial concept, such as liquidity, profit, risk, and growth, that is deemed relevant in characterizing a firm's financial condition and performance. Comparing a firm's ratios against those for the industry as a whole (industry average) allows one to judge whether the firm is adequate in some area. There are various categorization schemes and some variation in the definition of the ratios. For instance, some authors, e.g., Van Horne [2] recommend that the inventory turnover ratio be computed from the cost of goods sold and average inventory while others, e.g., Miller [3] prefer to use sales and end-of-year inventory values.

Typical ratio categories are:

1. *Liquidity ratios* indicate a firm's ability to meet its daily obligations. It is possible for a firm to be profitable and yet fail if it is unable to settle its short-term debts. Examples are the ratio of current assets to current liabilities, the

ratio of all current assets except inventory to current liabilities, and the ratio of cost of goods sold to average inventory.

2. *Activity ratios* are constructed to measure how effectively a firm's assets are being managed. The idea is to find out how quickly assets are used to generate sales. Examples are the ratio of total operating revenues to average total assets, and the ratio of total operating revenues to average receivables.

3. *Debt ratios* show the relative claim of creditors and shareholders on the firm and thus indicate the ability of a firm to deal with financial problems and opportunities as they arise. A firm highly dependent on creditors might suffer from creditor pressure, be less of a risk-taker, and have difficulty raising funds; i.e., it will have less operating freedom. Examples are the ratio of total debt to total shareholders' fund, the ratio of total debt to total assets, and the ratio of total debt to total shareholders' fund.

4. *Coverage ratios* are designed to relate the financial charges of a firm to its ability to service them, e.g., the ratio of interest to pretax profit.

5. *Profitability ratios* indicate the firm's efficiency of operation. Examples of ratios measuring profitability are the ratio of profit to sales, the ratio of profit to total assets, and the ratio of profit to shareholders' funds.

C. Financial Policies

The total value of a firm can be thought of as a pie (see Fig. 1). Initially, the size of the pie will depend on how well the firm has made its investment decision. The composition of the pie (usually known as capital structure) depends on the financing arrangements. Thus, the two major classes of decisions that financial managers have to make are investment and financing.

A major part of the investment decision is concerned with evaluating long-lived capital projects and deciding whether the firm should invest in them. This process is usually referred to as capital budgeting. Although the types and proportions of assets the firm needs tends to be determined by the nature of the business; within these bounds, there will many acceptable proposals that the firm may need to consider. Many rules can be employed to decide which ones to select, e.g., NPV rule, payback rule, the accounting rate of return rule, internal rate of return rule, profitability index, and capital asset pricing model.

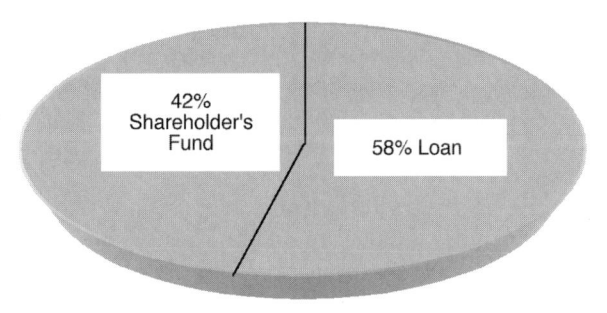

FIGURE 1 Pie model of a firm.

After a firm has made its investment decisions, it can then determine its financing decisions. This is what Peter and Jane have done—they identified their business, worked out what they needed, and then looked for ways to raise money for what they needed to start up the business. Thus, financing decisions are concerned with determining how a firm's investments should be financed. In general, a firm may choose any capital structure it desires: equity, bonds, loans, etc. However, the capital structure of the firm has a great impact on the way in which the firm pays out its cash flows. There are many theories put forward to suggest the optimal capital structure of a firm [4,5].

From the examination of the domain area of investment and financing decisions, it can be seen that there are many theories and methods supporting various arguments as to what policies financial managers should pursue to ensure that the firm achieves growth and profitability. Each theory/method has its own assumptions, shortcomings, and advantages. This paper will not attempt to model any of these theories or methods. Instead it will look at the implementation of these policies and demonstrate how they can be modeled so that the object-oriented implementation can be automatically generated.

Some examples of policy implementations are:

- Capital budgeting (investment).
    1. Fund capital expenditures from profit only.
    2. Expected return on investment $>= X\%$.
    3. Total operating revenues to average inventory ratio $= X \ldots Y$.
    4. The market value of any individual stock cannot exceed $X\%$ of total account.

- Capital structure (financing).
    1. Debt $<= X$ times share capital.
    2. Interest expense $> X$ times of operating cash flow.
    3. Debt–equity ratio $= X \ldots Y$.
    4. Liquidity ratio $>= X$.

Policies are thus implemented as rules of thumbs, giving targets to be achieved or indicators to monitor. These targets could be expressed as values, ranges of values, and upper and lower bounds of values that ratios or variables must have. These targets could be absolutes or benchmarked to some other ratio/variable in a firm and could be derived from comparison with some industry average or derived from comparison with the past year's data, etc. They have an impact of increasing/decreasing funds flow within the firm by controlling investments made or changing the financial structure of their firm.

In this section, we have shown that financial policies are expressed as target values for ratios or financial variables to satisfy. These values are derived from the financial statements, which in turn record and assign values to events and operations that occur within a firm (such as accepting orders, producing goods, and delivering goods). This section sets the scene for the rest of the paper and allows the reader to appreciate examples given in subsequent sections.

III. DATABASE MANAGEMENT SYSTEMS

Given the rapid growth of data and the wide recognition of data as a valuable organizational asset, it is increasingly important for an organization to manage the amount of data and extract useful information in a timely manner. Databases and database technology have become indispensable in many areas where computers are used such as business, engineering, medicine, law, education, and library science. A database is basically a collection of data that describes the activities of one or more related organizations. For example, a sales database may contain information about customers (such as their customer number, name, address, person to contact, credit limit), products (product code, description, price, amount sold), and retail outlets (name, monthly turnover). Relationships, such as which products are popular with particular customers and retail outlets, may also be captured in the database.

A DBMS is a software designed to facilitate the processes of defining, constructing, and manipulating databases for various applications. Defining a database involves specifying the types of data to be stored in the database, together with detailed descriptions of each type of data (also known as the meta-data). Constructing the database involves storing the data itself on some storage medium that is controlled by the DBMS. Manipulating a database includes querying the database to retrieve specific data (such as "retrieve the products sold by outlet A"), updating the database to reflect changes in the miniworld (such as "increase the price of new product B"), and generating reports from the data.

The data in a DBMS is traditionally viewed at three levels:

- *Internal level*. Data are organized physically on a storage medium, which involves the ordering and encoding of field values, the ordering and size of records, and access methods or indexes of the data.
- *Conceptual level*. This is the data modeling level, which captures the abstract representation of the data in a schema.
- *External level*. Applications at this level may impose additional constraints on the data and their semantics.

The process of creating a database for an application typically goes top-down through these three levels, from the external to the conceptual, and then to internal designs.

A. Components of a DBMS

Figure 2 shows the architecture of a typical DBMS. Records of data and meta-data are usually stored on storage devices such as disks and tapes. The disk space manager is responsible for managing the available disk space in units of a page (4 Kbytes or 8 Kbytes). Requests to allocate, deallocate, read, and write pages are carried out by this layer. When a data record is needed for processing, it is fetched to main memory from the disk. The file manager determines the page on which the record resides; access methods or indexes may be used to facilitate fast identification of the required page. The buffer manager, which partitions the available memory into a collection of pages called a buffer pool,

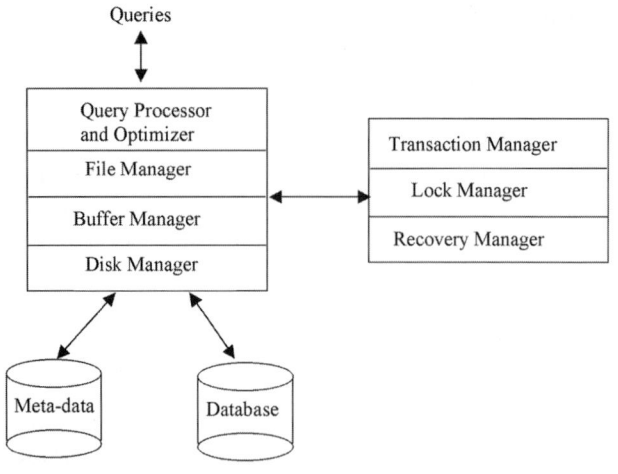

FIGURE 2 Components of a DBMS.

fetches the requested page to the buffer from the disk. When a user issues a query, the query optimizer uses information about how the data are stored to generate an efficient execution plan.

In order to provide concurrency control and crash recovery in the DBMS, the disk space manager, buffer manager, and file manager must interact with the transaction manager, lock manager, and recovery manager. The transaction manager ensures that transactions (or user programs) request and release locks on data records according to some protocol and schedules the transaction executions. The lock manager keeps track of requests for locks while the recovery manager maintains a log of changes and restores the system to a consistent state after a crash.

B. Capabilities of a DBMS

Using a DBMS to manage data offers many advantages. These include:

- *Persistence*. Large volumes of data can be managed systematically and efficiently as a DBMS utilizes a variety of sophisticated techniques to store and retrieve data. Persistence due to permanent storage of data is important to many applications.
- *Data independence*. The DBMS provide an abstract view of the data, which insulate application programs from the details of data, representation, and storage.
- *Control of data redundancy*. When several users share the data, centralizing the administration of data can minimize redundancy, without which an undesirable inconsistency in data and wastage of storage space can occur.
- *Data integrity and security*. The DBMS can enforce compliance to known constraints imposed by application semantics. Furthermore, it can restrict access to different classes of users.
- *Data availability and reliability*. In the event of system failure, the DBMS provides users access to as much of the uncorrupted data as possible. It also has the ability to recover from system failures without losing data (crash recovery).

The DBMS provides correct, concurrent access to the database by multiple users simultaneously.

- *High-level access.* This is provided by the data model and language which defines the database structure (also known as schema) and the retrieval and manipulation of data.
- *Distribution.* Multiple databases can be distributed on one or more machines, and viewed as a single database is useful in a variety of applications. This feature is crucial especially when databases in the different departments of an organization may have been developed independently over time and the management now needs an integrated view of the data for making high-level decisions.

This list of capabilities is not meant to be exhaustive but it serves to highlight the many important functions that are common to many applications accessing data stored in the DBMS. This facilitates quick development of applications that are also likely to be more robust than applications developed from scratch since many important tasks are handled by the DBMS instead of being implemented by the application.

C. Data Models

A central feature of any DBMS is the data model upon which the system is built. At the conceptual level of a DBMS architecture, the data model plays two important roles. First, the data model provides a methodology for representing the objects of a particular application environment, and the relationships among these objects (the conceptual or semantic role). Second, the data model is structured to allow a straightforward translation from the conceptual schema into the physical data structures of the internal level of the DBMS (the representational role).

Many commercial DBMS today such as DB2, Informix, Oracle, and Sybase are based on the relational data model proposed by [6]. At that time, most database systems were based on either the hierarchical model [7] (IBM's IMS and SYSTEM-2000) or the network model [8] (IDS and IDMS). The hierarchical and network models are strongly oriented toward facilitating the subsequent implementation of the conceptual schema. This is because, historically, the physical structure of a DBMS was designed first, and then a data model was developed to allow conceptual modeling on the particular physical design. Thus, the hierarchical data model is based on underlying tree-oriented data structures, while the network model is based on ring-oriented data structures. The use of the hierarchical and network data models in the semantic role is thus burdened with numerous construction roles and artificial constraints.

On the other hand, the relational data model is simple and elegant: a database is a collection of one or more relations, and each relation is a table with rows and columns. The tabular representation of data allows the use of simple, high-level languages to query the data. Despite its attractive simplicity, however, the relational model must be enhanced to fulfil the two roles of a conceptual level data model. In pursuit of discovering semantic enhancements to the relational model, a rich theoretical foundation about data dependencies and normalization was produced [9].

Database design is a complex process, and research into database design methods has developed the idea of using two distinct data models at the conceptual level. An enhanced conceptual data model would provide an effective means of describing the database application environments. A representational data model would be employed for efficient translation of a schema into physical data structures. Thus, the hierarchical, network, or relational data model could be employed as a representational data model. The DBMS would provide a user-invisible translation between the conceptual schema and the representational schema. Therefore, database applications are able to declare and reference data as viewed in the conceptual schema. Conceptual data modeling of an application is often carried out using semantic data models such as the object-oriented model and the entity–relationship (ER) model. Note that the object-oriented model is used in Objectstore and Versant, but there are no database systems that support the ER model directly, although an ER model description of data can be translated into a collection of relations if we want to use a relational DBMS.

The ER approach [10] incorporates the concepts of entity types and relationship sets, which correspond to structures naturally occurring in information systems. An entity is an object that exists in our minds and can be distinctly identified. Entities can be classified into different entity types; each entity type contains a set of entities, each satisfying a set of predefined common properties or attributes. A relationship is an association among two or more entities. Relationships can be classified into different relationship sets; each relationship set contains a set of relationships, each satisfying a set of attributes. The structure of a database organized according to the ER approach can be represented by a diagrammatic technique called an entity–relationship diagram (ERD).

The objected-oriented (OO) paradigm gained prominence in the 1990s. OO concepts such as classes and inheritance are a powerful tool for modeling the real world. The advantages of relationship modeling, extensibility and easy maintenance provided by this technology, were quickly recognized by the database community. This led to the development of object-oriented databases. An object-oriented database combines object-orientation with database capabilities. Opinion is divided, however, as to what particular features and characteristics it should possess. Atkinson *et al.* [11] give the mandatory features that define an object-oriented database system. From the DBMS perspective, it must have persistence, secondary storage management, concurrency, recovery, and *ad hoc* query facility. From the OO perspective, it must support complex objects, identity, encapsulation, types or classes, inheritance, overriding with late binding, extensibility, and computational completeness. Note that some of these features deal with implementation and performance issues rather than facet modeling.

IV. FINANCIAL OBJECT-ORIENTED DATABASES

As financial information is so crucial in running a business, there has always been an interest in developing data models [12–14] that will capture the key characteristics of the domain. In this section, we will introduce some fundamental OO modeling concepts. Subsequently, we will apply these concepts to the financial domain. A comprehensive exposition of the OO method and its modeling and application can be found in [15,16].

A. General Concepts

The object-oriented approach views software as a collection of discrete objects that incorporates both structure (attributes) and behavior (operations). This is in contrast to conventional software development where data and behavior are loosely connected.

An object is defined as a concept, abstraction, or tangible object with well-defined boundaries and meaning for the problem at hand. Examples of objects are customer John Doe, Order No 1234, or a pair of shoes stock no 12345 B-PRI. All objects have an identity and are distinguishable. This means that two objects are distinct even if they have the same attributes, e.g., two pairs of shoes of the same color, style, and weight with the same stock number. The term "identity" means that objects are distinguished by their inherent existence and not by the descriptive properties they may have.

An object is an encapsulation of attributes and operations. Encapsulation separates the external interface of an object from the internal implementation details of the object. The external interface is accessible to other objects and consists of the specifications of the operations that can be performed on the object. The operations define the behavior of the object and manipulate the attributes of that object. The internal implementation details are visible only to the designer. It consists of a data section that describes the internal structure of the object and a procedural section that describes the procedures that implement the operations part of the interface. This means that the implementation of an object may be changed without affecting the applications that use it. For example, the cost of a pair of shoes can be measured by different methods, such as average cost, LIFO, and FIFO. If the firm decides to change its costing method for shoes, the encapsulation feature ensures that no changes will have to be made to any application that requires the unit cost for a pair of shoes.

A class is an abstraction that describes properties that are important to the application. Each class describes a set of individual objects, with each object having its own value for each attribute but sharing the attribute names and operations with other objects in the class. The objects in a class not only share common attributes and common operations, they also share a common semantic purpose. Even if a van and a shoe both have cost and size, they could belong to different classes. If they were regarded as purely financial assets, they could belong to one class. If the developer took into consideration that a person drives a van and wears shoes, they would be modeled as different classes. The interpretation of semantics depends on the purpose of each application and is a matter of judgement.

Figure 3 shows that objects such as Leather and Shoe can be abstracted into an Inventory Item class with attributes, Description, Quantity on Hand, and Unit Cost. Operations that manipulate the attributes include Issue Stock (which reduces the Quantity on Hand when the raw material is required for the

	Objects		Inventory Item Class
Leather – Batch No XXX			**Attributes**
			Description
Leather – Batch No XYZ		Abstract	Quantity on Hand
		⇒	Unit Cost
Shoe SNo: 12345 B-PRI		into	**Operations**
			Issue Stock
Shoe SNo: 12346 B-PRI			Write-off Stock

FIGURE 3 Objects and classes.

assembly process), Write-off Stock (which sets the value of Quantity on Hand to 0 when the goods are considered damaged and unusable).

Note that the Inventory Item Class includes raw materials (as in leather and rubber) and finished products (shoes). Hence we can design classes such as Raw Materials and Products, which are refinements of Inventory Item.

B. Object Modeling

To define an object model for any domain, the following logical activities will have to be carried out:

1. Identify the objects and classes and prepare a data dictionary showing the precise definition of each.
2. Identify the association and aggregation relationships between objects.
3. Identify the attributes of the objects.
4. Organize and simplify the object classes through generalization.

These activities are logical as in practice; it may be possible to combine several steps. In addition, the process of deriving an object model is rarely straightforward and usually involves several iterations.

The object modeling technique consists of three models, each representing a related but different viewpoint of the system:

1. the object model, which describes the static structural aspect,
2. the dynamic model, which describes the temporal behavioral aspect, and
3. the functional model, which describes the transformational aspect.

Each model contains references to other models; e.g., operations that are attached to objects in the object model are more fully expanded in the functional model. Although each model is not completely independent, each model can be examined and understood on its own.

1. Object Model

The object model describes the structure of the objects in the system—their identity, their relationships to other objects, their attributes, and their operations. The object model is represented graphically with object diagrams

DEVELOPING APPLICATIONS IN CORPORATE FINANCE 511

Invoice Line		**Inventory Item**
Description Quantity Delivered Unit Price	●── shows ──	Description Quantity in Hand Unit Cost
Calculate total price		Issue Stock Write-off Stock

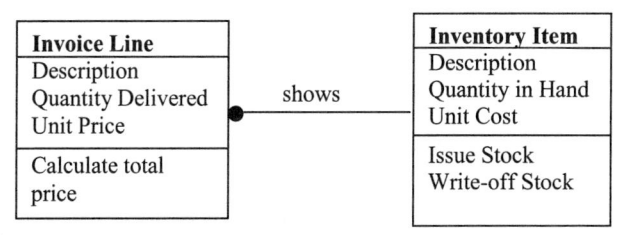

FIGURE 4 Association relationship.

containing object classes. Classes are arranged into hierarchies sharing common structure and behavior and are associated with other classes. Classes define attribute values carried by each object and the operations that each object performs or undergoes. It is thus the framework into which the dynamic and functional model may be placed.

Objects and object classes may be related to other objects in several ways. They could be dependent on one another in which case the relationship is known as an *association*. Associations may be binary or tenary or of higher order and are modeled as bidirectional. These links may also express the multiplicity of the relationship, either 1-1, 1-to-many, or many-to-many. For example the association between an Inventory Item and an Invoice Line is 1-to-many because an inventory item may appear on several invoice lines. The solid ball in Fig. 4 denotes the multiplicity of the Inventory Item objects in the Invoice Line class.

The second type of relationship is *aggregation*, which expresses a "part–whole," or a "part-of" relationship in which objects representing the components of something are associated with an object representing the entire assembly. An obvious example from Peter and Jane's firm is the components that go into making a shoe, e.g., leather, rubber, bells, and thread. Another example is shown in Fig. 5, where an invoice is composed of its individual invoice lines. A small diamond drawn at the assembly end of the relationship denotes aggregation. The Invoice class has a Status attribute which gives the state of the object. We will elaborate on this in the next section on dynamic models.

Generalization is the relationship between a class and its more refined classes. It is sometimes referred to as a "is-a" relationship. For example, Current Asset is the generalization for Cash, Inventory Item, and Accounts Receivables. Current Asset is called the superclass while Cash, Inventory Item, and

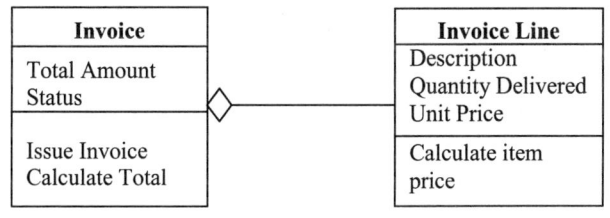

Invoice		**Invoice Line**
Total Amount Status	──◇──	Description Quantity Delivered Unit Price
Issue Invoice Calculate Total		Calculate item price

FIGURE 5 Aggregation relationship.

```
                    ┌─────────────────────┐
                    │  Current Asset      │
                    ├─────────────────────┤
                    │  Opening Balance    │
                    │  Total To Date      │
                    ├─────────────────────┤
                    │  Calculate Total    │
                    └─────────────────────┘
```

┌──────────────┐   ┌────────────────────┐   ┌──────────────────────┐
│   Cash   │   │ Inventory Item   │   │   Accounts   │
├──────────────┤   ├────────────────────┤   │ Receivables (A/R)   │
│ Currency   │   │ Description   │   ├──────────────────────┤
├──────────────┤   │ Quantity in Hand │   │ Name   │
│ Convert   │   │ Unit Cost   │   │ Credit limit   │
└──────────────┘   ├────────────────────┤   │ Credit Terms   │
                   │ Issue Stock   │   ├──────────────────────┤
                   │ Write-off Stock   │   │ Update Credit Terms │
                   └────────────────────┘   │ Categorize A/R   │
                                            │ Age A/R   │
                                            └──────────────────────┘

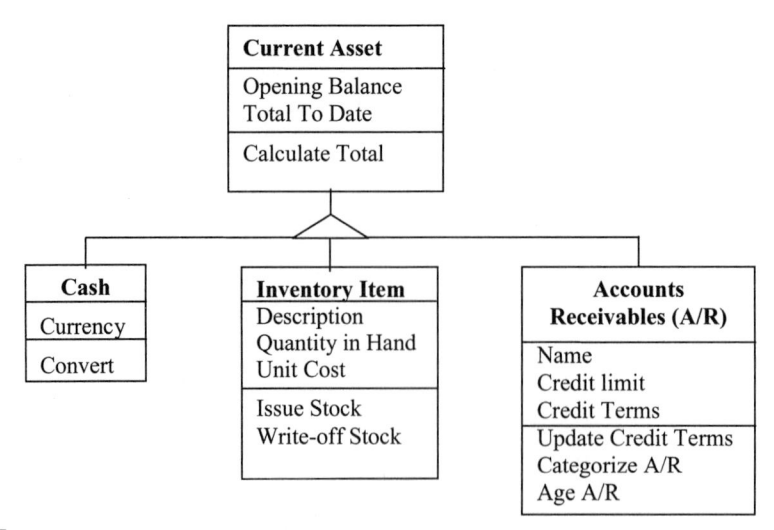

FIGURE 6 Generalization relationship.

Accounts Receivables are called subclasses. Each subclass inherits all the attributes and operations of its superclass in addition to its own unique attributes and operations. Figure 6 shows how this relationship is depicted. The subclass Accounts Receivables has attributes Name, Credit Limit, and Credit Terms for its customers and operations Update Credit Terms and Categorize A/R, which determines good and bad payers. In addition to its own class attributes and operations, objects of Account Receivables will also inherit the attributes and operations of Current Asset.

This ability to factor out common attributes of several classes into a common class and to inherit the properties from the superclass can greatly reduce repetition within design and programs and is one of the advantages of object-oriented systems.

2. Dynamic Model

The dynamic model describes those aspects of a system concerned with time and order of operations. It captures the control aspect of the system that describes the sequences of operations as they occur regardless of what the operation does, what they operate on, and how they are implemented. The dynamic model is represented graphically with state diagrams. Each state diagram shows the state and the event sequences permitted in a system for one class of objects. Figure 7 shows the state diagram for an invoice. When a customer takes goods on credit, he will be issued an invoice. At this point in time, the invoice is deemed to be outstanding. At some point in time, the customer may pay. If payment is not received within the credit period granted to him, the invoice is said to be overdue. When the customer makes full payments, the accounts will be adjusted to reflect this (i.e., the customer's debts are reduced and the amount of cash increases), and the customer will be issued a receipt. The firm might decide to write-off the invoice if the customer subsequently goes bankrupt or it becomes uneconomical to pursue the customer for paying.

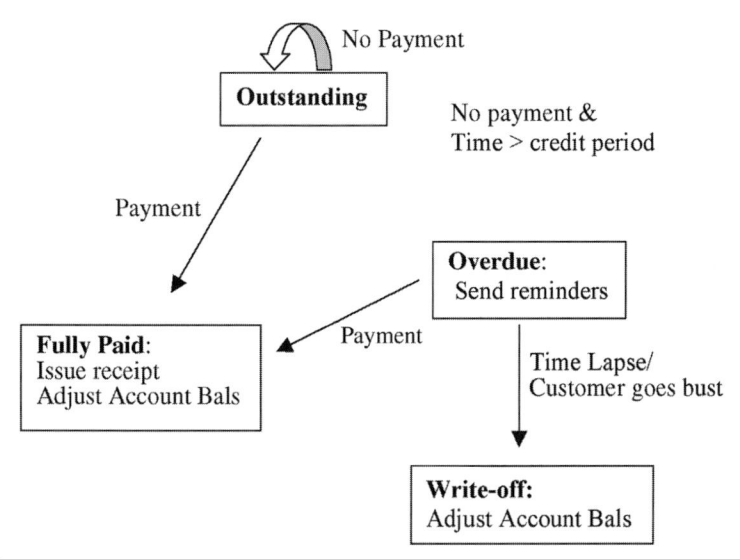

DEVELOPING APPLICATIONS IN CORPORATE FINANCE   513

FIGURE 7 State diagram for an invoice.

3. Functional Model

The functional model describes those aspects of a system concerned with transformation of values—functions, mapping, constraints, and functional dependencies. The functional model captures what the system does regardless of how and when it is done. The functional model may be represented with data flow diagrams that show the dependencies between the inputs and the outputs to a process. Functions are invoked as actions in the dynamic model and are shown as operations on objects in the objection model. An example of an operation on Invoice (see Fig. 7) is "Issue receipt." The inputs to this process are the invoice details, such as its number and customer name, and its corresponding payment details, and its output is the receipt that is sent to the customer.

C. Modeling Financial Policies

In the previous section, we have shown how the OO paradigm can be used to model financial information. Entities such as customers, customer orders, suppliers, requisition orders, and employees can be intuitively modeled as objects and classes. Based on these classes, events and operations that occur in the daily routine of running a firm such as Peter and Jane's can also be modeled. In this section, we will examine how financial policies may also be modeled using the OO approach.

We view financial data as a class that is a generalization of the Balance Sheet, Income statement, and Cash Flow Statement classes. The accounts' hierarchy of each of the financial statements can be directly mapped as superclasses and subclasses. For example, the Balance Sheet class is a superclass of the Asset, Liability, and Shareholders' Fund classes, and the Asset class is in turn a superclass of the Current Asset and the Fixed Assets classes. Financial policies can therefore be modeled as a class that interacts with the Financial Data class.

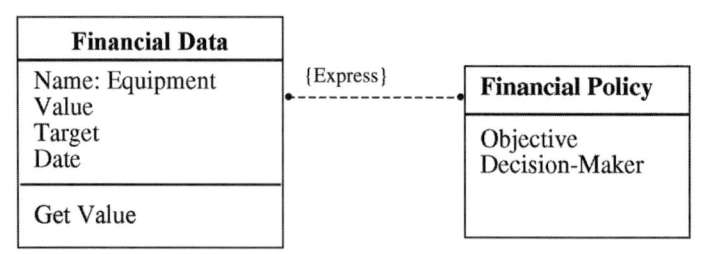

```
┌─────────────────────────────┐
│     Financial Data          │                    ┌─────────────────────────┐
├─────────────────────────────┤    {Express}       │    Financial Policy     │
│ Name: Equipment             │•---------------•   ├─────────────────────────┤
│ Value                       │                    │ Objective               │
│ Target                      │                    │ Decision-Maker          │
│ Date                        │                    │                         │
├─────────────────────────────┤                    └─────────────────────────┘
│ Get Value                   │
└─────────────────────────────┘
```

FIGURE 8 Constrained links and attributes.

However, to model financial policies, two other concepts are needed:

- Constraints on objects and attributes, and
- Derived objects and attributes.

Constraints are functional relationships between two or more components (objects, classes, attributes, links, and associations) of an object model. A constraint limits the value that a component can assume. Constraints on attributes are shown in braces, positioned near the constrained class. Constraints on classes are shown as a dotted line connecting the constrained class to the class it depends on. For example, to model a policy where the firm is only able to purchase new equipment if it has made profit in the previous years, we constrain the attribute Target of the financial class Equipment to the value "Financial Data. Value > 0" where "Financial Data. Value" denotes the attribute Value of the financial class Profit. This constraint may be explicit as shown in Fig. 8, or it may also be embedded in the operations (see next example). Since not all financial data are used to make policy decisions, but are only certain key indicators, we also have a constraint on the Financial Data class.

A derived object is defined as a function of one or more objects, which in turn may be derived. The derived object is completely determined by other objects and ultimately the derivation tree terminates with base objects. The notation for a derived object is a slash or diagonal line (on the corner of the box). For example, Financial Ratio is a derived class since its value is obtained from dividing one financial component by another. Note that these financial components may themselves be derived classes or financial data class. Figure 9

```
              Class                                  Instance of the Class

┌─────────────────────────┐             ┌─────────────────────────────────────┐
│ /   Financial Ratio     │             │ /    Financial Ratio                │
├─────────────────────────┤             ├─────────────────────────────────────┤
│ Name                    │             │ Name: Liquidity Ratio               │
│ /Numerator              │             │ /Numerator: Current Assets          │
│ /Denominator            │             │ /Denominator: Current Liabilities   │
│ Value                   │             │ Value                               │
│ Target                  │             │ Target                              │
├─────────────────────────┤             ├─────────────────────────────────────┤
│ Compute Ratio           │             │ Compute Ratio                       │
│ Compute Value           │             │ Compute Value                       │
│ Get Target              │             │                                     │
└─────────────────────────┘             └─────────────────────────────────────┘
```

FIGURE 9 Derived classes and attributes: A class and an instance of the class.

shows the attributes and operations for a Financial Ratio class and an instance of this class.

Constraints on derived objects can be embedded in the operations. For example, most firms require their liquidity ratio to be within a certain range to ensure that they are well positioned to handle business emergencies. However, the value for the liquidity ratio is usually obtained by a trend analysis of the past 10 years or by comparing with the industry norm. This requires complex statistical computations and the constraint is better expressed procedurally in the operations such as Get Target in Fig. 9.

To conclude, we see that the OO approach provides a uniform and systematic way in which financial information and policies are modeled. This facilitates the automatic implementation of a financial database management system through the use of commercially available tools and products such as ObjectTeam and Intelligent OOA.

V. DISCUSSION

A database management system offers many capabilities and handles important tasks that are crucial to applications accessing the stored data. The object-oriented technology provides a framework for representing and managing both data and application programs. It is a promising paradigm to solve the so-called impedance mismatch: the awkward communication between a query language and a programming language that results when developing applications with a database system. We have seen how the financial domain can be sensibly modeled using object-oriented concepts. The object-oriented approach also removes the gap between an application and its representation. It allows the designer to model the real world as closely as possible, which can be mapped directly to design and implementation constructs.

Financial information can be viewed at two levels. At one level, we look at the raw data that are associated with routine events and operations such as sales, invoices, and payments. At another level, we abstract and generalize the raw financial data to analyze and interpret them. It is quite apparent from the examples given in Section IV that the basic financial data associated with the routine events and operations in a firm can be adequately represented by the OO modeling notation. Basic financial data associated with the routine events and operations in a firm can be abstracted to a higher level through the class hierarchy, which allows strategic decisions and policy formulations. For example, policy statements could be expressed in terms of financial ratios that are derived from financial statements, which are composed of basic financial data. The encapsulation feature proves useful as the composition of financial classes such as Asset and Liability varies for different industries. For example, the Current Asset class will have objects such as inventory items for the trading and manufacturing industry that will not exist in the service industry such as banks. Instead, the Current Asset class in the banking industry will have objects such as investment items, which include marketable securities, government bonds, and fixed deposits. In the same way, the key indicators used to implement financial policies may be modified without affecting the application program. Object-oriented database systems are also extensible as we can extend its capabilities by adding new classes to the system when the need arises.

We can also model financial policies using rules and formal methods. Rules are predominantly used in expert systems and deductive databases. It is a problem-solving approach that uses rules to encode the heuristic and search strategies to infer new knowledge from the database of facts. The expression of the policy statement in rules may be quite natural but presents problems in updating especially when the number of rules grows. If we use formal methods [17], then each policy is precisely defined using some notations such as the Z notation and the Vienna Development Method. However, the tools support for the implementation of these specifications is inadequate. Furthermore, both these techniques are not suitable for modeling financial information. On the other hand, the OO approach focuses on objects and organizes domain knowledge around these objects and their relationships. It presents a seamless way for modeling financial information and policies.

REFERENCES

1. Klein, M., FINSIM Expert: A KB/DSS for financial analysis and planning. In *EUROINFO '88: Concepts for Increased Competitiveness* (H. J. Bullinger, E. N. Protonotaris, D. Bouwhuis, and F. Reim, Eds), 908–916. North-Holland, Amsterdam, 1988.
2. Van Horne, J. C. *Financial Management and Policy*. 11th ed. Prentice–Hall, Englewood Cliffs, NJ, 1998.
3. Miller, D. E. *The Meaningful Interpretation of Financial Statements: The Cause and Effect Ratio Approach*. Am. Management Assoc., New York, 1996.
4. Myers, S. C. The capital structure puzzle. *J. Finance,* 39:575–592, 1984.
5. Smith, C. Raising capital: Theory and evidence. In *The Revolution on Corporate Finance* (J. Stern and D. Chew, Jr, Eds.), 2nd ed. Blackwell, Oxford, 1992.
6. Codd, E. F. A relational model of data for large shared data banks. *Commun. ACM* 13(6): 377–387, 1970.
7. Tshichritzis, D. C., and Lohovsky, F. H. Hierarchical database management. *ACM Comput. Surveys* 8(1):105–123, 1976.
8. Taylor, R., and Frank, R. CODASYL database management systems. *ACM Comput. Surveys* 8(1):67–104, 1976.
9. Maier, D. *Theory of Relational Databases*. Computer Science Press, Rockville, MD, 1983.
10. Chen, P. P. The entity-relationship model: Toward a unified view of data. *ACM Trans. Database Systems* 1(1):166–192, 1976.
11. Atkinson, M., Bancilhon, F., Dewitt, D., Dittrich, K., Maier, D., and Zdonik, S. The object-oriented database system manifesto, deductive and object-oriented databases, 223–240. Elsevier Science, Amsterdam, 1990.
12. Lieberman, A. Z., and Whinston, A. B. A structuring of an event accounting information system. Accounting Rev. (April):246–258, 1975.
13. Haseman, W. D., and Whinston, A. B. Design of a multi-dimensional accounting system. *Accounting Rev.* (January):65–79, 1976.
14. Everest, G. C., and Weber, R. A relational approach to accounting models. *Accounting Rev.* (April): 340–359, 1977.
15. Booch, G. *Object-Oriented Analysis and Design with Applications,* 2nd ed. Addison-Wesley, Reading, MA, 1994.
16. Rumbaugh, J., Jacobson, I. and Booch, G. *The Unified Modeling Language Reference Manual*. Addison–Wesley, Reading, MA, 1999.
17. Woon, I. M. Y., and Loh, W. L. Formal derivation to object-oriented implementation of financial policies. *Int. J. Comput. Appl. Technol.* 10(5/6):316–326, 1997.

14
SCIENTIFIC DATA VISUALIZATION: A HYPERVOLUME APPROACH FOR MODELING AND RENDERING OF VOLUMETRIC DATA SETS

SANGKUN PARK

Institute of Advanced Machinery and Design, Seoul National University, Seoul 151-742, Korea

KUNWOO LEE

School of Mechanical and Aerospace Engineering, Seoul National University, Seoul 151-742, Korea

I. INTRODUCTION 518
   A. Volume Visualization 518
   B. Volume Graphics 518
   C. Volume Modeling 519
   D. Multiresolution Modeling 519
   E. Scattered Data Modeling 519
   F. Feature Segmentation 520
II. REPRESENTATION OF VOLUMETRIC DATA 520
   A. Introduction to Hypervolume 520
   B. Mathematical Representation of a Hypervolume 521
   C. Main Features and Application Areas of a Hypervolume 523
III. MANIPULATION OF VOLUMETRIC DATA 525
   A. Derivatives of a NURBS Volume 525
   B. Generation of a NURBS Volume 527
   C. Gridding Methods of Scattered Data 536
IV. RENDERING METHODS OF VOLUMETRIC DATA 538
V. APPLICATION TO FLOW VISUALIZATION 540
   A. Related Works 540
   B. Application Examples 541
   C. Feature Segmentation 544
VI. SUMMARY AND CONCLUSIONS 546
   REFERENCES 547

I. INTRODUCTION

Scientific data visualization aims to devise algorithms and methods that transform massive scientific data sets into valuable pictures and other graphic representations that facilitate comprehension and interpretation. In many scientific domains, analysis of these pictures has motivated further scientific investigation.

A remarkable work on scientific visualization as a discipline started in 1987, which was reported by the National Science Foundation's Advisory Panel on Graphics, Image Processing, and Workstations [1]. The report justified the need for scientific visualization and introduced the short-term potential and long-term goals of visualization environments, and emphasized the role of scientific visualization in industrial fields.

The IEEE Visualization conference series has been a leading conference in scientific visualization since 1990, and its importance has grown within ACM's SIGGRAPH conference. Many researchers and practitioners get together at the annual Eurographics Workshop on Visualization in Scientific Computing. Similarly, hundreds of conferences and workshops in the world have developed the theme. Also numerous journals and books worldwide involved in computer science, physical science, and engineering now devote themselves, in part or in full, to the topic.

Recent work in scientific visualization has been stimulated by various conferences or workshops as described above. It mainly includes topics in volume visualization, volume graphics, and volume modeling. Also it also covers the following topics: multiresolution modeling, scattered data modeling, and feature segmentation. Now we will introduce key aspects of each topic below, commenting on the current status of work or requirements.

A. Volume Visualization

Volume visualization found its initial applications in medical imaging. The overall goal of volume visualization is to extract meaningful information from volumetric data. Volume visualization addresses the representation, manipulation, and rendering of volumetric data sets without mathematically describing surfaces used in the CAD community. It provides procedures or mechanisms for looking into internal structures and analyzing their complexity and dynamics. Recent progresses are impressive, yet further research still remains.

B. Volume Graphics

As an emerging subfield of computer graphics, volume graphics is concerned with the synthesis, manipulation, and rendering of 3D modeled objects, stored as a volume buffer of voxels [2]. It primarily addresses modeling and rendering geometric scenes, particularly those represented in a regular volume buffer, by employing a discrete volumetric representation. The primary procedure for its representation needs voxelization algorithms that synthesize voxel-based models by converting continuous geometric objects into their discrete voxel-based representation.

Volume graphics is insensitive to scene and object complexities, and supports the visualization of internal structures. However, there are several problems associated with the volume buffer representation, such as memory size, discreteness, processing time, and loss of geometric representation. That is, volume graphics must consider such issues as geometric accuracy, minimality, effectiveness/efficiency, and representation and rendering quality (for example, 3D antialiasing). Nevertheless, by offering a comprehensive alternative to traditional surface graphics, volume graphics has the potential of developing into a major trend in computer graphics.

C. Volume Modeling

Volume modeling is often referred to by some authors as the process of identifying and synthesizing objects contained within a 3D data set, very regular and dense 3D image data obtained by a scanning instrument. The term "volume modeling" in a more general sense may be used to mean the methods for representing and modeling the attributes of 3D objects and their internal structures. It is worth noting the internal structures. Most geometric modeling methods have often assumed object interiors to be homogeneous. A solid modeling system is a typical example. Thus, the internal structure of an inhomogeneous object should be represented or modeled by a mathematical formulation or other techniques, which is a part of the major goals aimed for by volume modeling.

In the past several years, a tremendous amount of research and development has been directed toward these volume models, but there has been very little work on developing the volume models that feed a rendering pipeline for scientific visualization.

D. Multiresolution Modeling

Multiresolution models can capture a wide range of levels of detail of an object and can be used to reconstruct any one of those levels on demand. These levels of detail of multiresolution models allow us temporarily to filter out detailed information for faster or interactive visualization or other analysis purposes. This is the case, for example, that a faster zooming process allows us to enhance the opportunity of interactivity. In addition, multiresolution models can assist in geometric processing algorithms. For example, collision detection or volume intersection computations are often iterative and require reasonably good initial approximations. An outstanding approach to multiresolution modeling is the use of wavelet methods. Muraki [3] discussed some aspects of tensor product methods in the 3D case.

E. Scattered Data Modeling

The term "scattered data" means nonuniform distributions of the data and irregularities in the data, contrary to data that lies at regular Cartesian (or rectilinear) grids. For most applications, the data of interest is not available on a nice regular grid. Rather, it is arbitrarily located in a spherical or volumetric domain. Many applications have troubles with these types of data, but have solved these problems as follows: a modeling function that fits the scattered data is first found, and then the function is sampled on the type of grid. These sampling outputs are often passed onto a rendering procedure in which a 3D array would be used as a data structure.

Further research is needed to develop accurate, efficient, and easily implemented modeling methods for very large data sets. In particular, we are interested in estimating and controlling errors. Well-known approaches for scattered data modeling are the modified quadratic Shepard (MQS) [4], volume splines [5,6], multiquadric [5,6], and volume minimum norm network (MNN) [7]. See the references for more details on these methods.

F. Feature Segmentation

The term, "segmentation" has been defined as the process of identifying which pixels or voxels of an image belong to a particular object, such as bone, fat, or tissue in medical applications. Now it includes the extraction of intrinsic data characteristics or meaningful objects from given original data, and so is often referred to as feature extraction or segmentation.

Generally, the features are application-dependent, and so the mechanisms for characterizing them must be flexible and general. Some researchers expect that a certain mathematical model will make it possible to detect the feature objects and/or represent them. Also others expect that expert system technology will do.

Scientific data visualization has acquired increased interest and popularity in many scientific domains. It mainly takes aims at devising mathematical principles, computational algorithms, and well-organized data structures, which do transform massive scientific data sets into meaningful pictures and other graphic representations that improve apprehension or inspiration. To achieve these goals, many visualization tools and techniques have appeared and been integrated to some degree within a system. Few systems, however, fully meet their users' various needs for visualization, and system developers are not allowed to construct general visualization tools without considering a data dimensionality and distribution or other intrinsic data characteristics, i.e., domain-dependent features.

The crucial factor of these difficulties arises basically from a lack of mathematical models that represent a wide range of scientific data sets and realize all standard visualization procedures such as volumetric modeling, graphical representation, and feature segmentation within a unified system framework.

In this chapter, we describe a mathematical model necessary for establishing a foundation for the evolving needs of visualization systems as mentioned above, and demonstrate its usefulness by applying it to data sets from computational fluid dynamics.

II. REPRESENTATION OF VOLUMETRIC DATA

A. Introduction to Hypervolume

To understand the internal structures or the relationships implied by scientific data sets, we first should describe their shapes, which represent a three-dimensional geometric object or a region of interest in which physical phenomena occur. Also to visualize these phenomena at a given time, we must explain the scene's appearance at that time.

For all of them, we suggest a *hypervolume*, as a mathematical formulation, which is based on a higher dimensional trivariate and dynamic NURBS (nonuniform rational B-splines) representation [8–10]. The term "higher dimensional" presents no dependence of data dimensionality, and "trivariate and dynamic" implies the capabilities of describing an evolving physical object in spatial and temporal coordinates, respectively. NURBS, as a well-known interpolating function, plays a key role in transforming a discrete data set into a continuous world.

The hypervolume consists of two different models that are independent of each other. One is the *geometry volume*, which defines 3D geometric objects, such as inhomogeneous materials or a region of interest in which physical phenomena occur, covered by the scientific data sets. The other is the *attribute volume*, which describes scalar- or vector-valued physical field variables, such as pressure, temperature, velocity, and density, as functions of four variables, i.e., the three positional coordinates and time. It also can include the graphical variables, such as color and opacity. The combination of these two volumes can provide all the geometric, physical, and graphical information for representing, manipulating, analyzing, and rendering scientific data sets. The relevant procedure will be explained later in detail.

B. Mathematical Representation of a Hypervolume

The mathematical formulation of the geometry volume of a hypervolume, which is a tensor product of NURBS of order ku in u direction, kv in v direction, kw in w direction, and kt in t direction, is a three-dimensional, quadvariate vector-valued piecewise rational function of the form

$$G(u,v,w,t) = \frac{\sum_{i=0}^{nu}\sum_{j=0}^{nv}\sum_{k=0}^{nw}\sum_{l=0}^{nt} h_{ijkl} G_{ijkl} N_i^{ku}(u) N_j^{kv}(v) N_k^{kw}(w) N_l^{kt}(t)}{\sum_{i=0}^{nu}\sum_{j=0}^{nv}\sum_{k=0}^{nw}\sum_{l=0}^{nt} h_{ijkl} N_i^{ku}(u) N_j^{kv}(v) N_k^{kw}(w) N_l^{kt}(t)}. \tag{1}$$

$\{G_{ijkl} = (x_{ijkl}, y_{ijkl}, z_{ijkl})\} \subset \mathbf{R}^3$ forms a tridirectional control grid in the three-dimensional rectangular space, $\{h_{ijkl}\}$ are the weights, and $\{N_i^{ku}(u)\}$, $\{N_j^{kv}(v)\}$, $\{N_k^{kw}(w)\}$, and $\{N_l^{kt}(t)\}$ are the normalized B-spline basis functions defined on the knot vectors

$$\mathbf{u} = \{u_i\}_{i=0}^{nu+ku} = \{\bar{u}_0, \ldots, \bar{u}_{ku-1}, \bar{u}_{ku}, \ldots \ldots, \bar{u}_{nu}, \bar{u}_{nu+1}, \ldots, \bar{u}_{nu+ku}\}$$

where $\bar{u}_0 = \cdots = \bar{u}_{ku-1}$ and $\bar{u}_{nu+1} = \cdots = \bar{u}_{nu+ku}$,

$$\mathbf{v} = \{v_j\}_{j=0}^{nv+kv} = \{\bar{v}_0, \ldots, \bar{v}_{kv-1}, \bar{v}_{kv}, \ldots \ldots, \bar{v}_{nv}, \bar{v}_{nv+1}, \ldots, \bar{v}_{nv+kv}\}$$

where $\bar{v}_0 = \cdots = \bar{v}_{kv-1}$ and $\bar{v}_{nv+1} = \cdots = \bar{v}_{nv+kv}$,

$$\mathbf{w} = \{w_k\}_{k=0}^{nw+kw} = \{\bar{w}_0, \ldots, \bar{w}_{kw-1}, \bar{w}_{kw}, \ldots \ldots, \bar{w}_{nw}, \bar{w}_{nw+1}, \ldots, \bar{w}_{nw+kw}\}$$

where $\bar{w}_0 = \cdots = \bar{w}_{kw-1}$ and $\bar{w}_{nw+1} = \cdots = \bar{w}_{nw+kw}$,

$$\mathbf{t} = \{t_l\}_{l=0}^{nt+kt} = \{\bar{t}_0, \ldots, \bar{t}_{kt-1}, \bar{t}_{kt}, \ldots \ldots, \bar{t}_{nt}, \bar{t}_{nt+1}, \ldots, \bar{t}_{nt+kt}\}$$

where $\bar{t}_0 = \cdots = \bar{t}_{kt-1}$ and $\bar{t}_{nt+1} = \cdots = \bar{t}_{nt+kt}$.

Also note that the parameters, u, v, and w, in Eq. (1) represent three positional coordinates in the four-dimensional parameter space of the geometry volume, and the parameter t is used for the time coordinate.

To get more understandable interpretation for Eq. (1), we can rewrite it as

$$\mathbf{G}(u,v,w,t) = \frac{\sum_{i=0}^{nu}\sum_{j=0}^{nv}\sum_{k=0}^{nw} h_{ijk}\left(\sum_{l=0}^{nt} h_l \mathbf{G}_{ijkl} N_l^{kt}(t)\right) N_i^{ku}(u) N_j^{kv}(v) N_k^{kw}(w)}{\sum_{i=0}^{nu}\sum_{j=0}^{nv}\sum_{k=0}^{nw} h_{ijk}\left(\sum_{l=0}^{nt} h_l N_l^{kt}(t)\right) N_i^{ku}(u) N_j^{kv}(v) N_k^{kw}(w)}, \quad (2)$$

where $h_{ijkl} = h_{ijk}h_l$, and it follows that

$$\mathbf{G}(u,v,w,t)$$
$$= \frac{\sum_{i=0}^{nu}\sum_{j=0}^{nv}\sum_{k=0}^{nw} h_{ijk}\left(\sum_{l=0}^{nt} h_l \mathbf{G}_{ijkl} N_l^{kt}(t)\right) N_i^{ku}(u) N_j^{kv}(v) N_k^{kw}(w)}{\left(\sum_{l=0}^{nt} h_l N_l^{kt}(t)\right)\left(\sum_{i=0}^{nu}\sum_{j=0}^{nv}\sum_{k=0}^{nw} h_{ijk} N_i^{ku}(u) N_j^{kv}(v) N_k^{kw}(w)\right)}$$

$$= \frac{\sum_{i=0}^{nu}\sum_{j=0}^{nv}\sum_{k=0}^{nw} h_{ijk}\left(\frac{\sum_{l=0}^{nt} h_l \mathbf{G}_{ijkl} N_l^{kt}(t)}{\sum_{l=0}^{nt} h_l N_l^{kt}(t)}\right) N_i^{ku}(u) N_j^{kv}(v) N_k^{kw}(w)}{\sum_{i=0}^{nu}\sum_{j=0}^{nv}\sum_{k=0}^{nw} h_{ijk} N_i^{ku}(u) N_j^{kv}(v) N_k^{kw}(w)}. \quad (3)$$

Therefore, we obtain

$$\mathbf{G}(u,v,w,t) = \frac{\sum_{i=0}^{nu}\sum_{j=0}^{nv}\sum_{k=0}^{nw} h_{ijk}\mathbf{G}_{ijk}(t) N_i^{ku}(u) N_j^{kv}(v) N_k^{kw}(w)}{\sum_{i=0}^{nu}\sum_{j=0}^{nv}\sum_{k=0}^{nw} h_{ijk} N_i^{ku}(u) N_j^{kv}(v) N_k^{kw}(w)}, \quad (4)$$

where

$$\mathbf{G}_{ijk}(t) = \frac{\sum_{l=0}^{nt} h_l \mathbf{G}_{ijkl} N_l^{kt}(t)}{\sum_{l=0}^{nt} h_l N_l^{kt}(t)}. \quad (5)$$

From Eq. (4), we know that it has dynamic behavior since the control grid term in Eq. (4), which is Eq. (5) or simply a NURBS curve, describes a spatial movement or deformation as the parameter t ($=$ time) elapses. Also if we set the control grid term be constant at all elapsed time, then Eq. (4) describes only the static geometric object; that is, it does not contain dynamic behavior information. The static geometry volume is often referred to as a NURBS volume, which has the form

$$\mathbf{V}(u,v,w) = \frac{\sum_{i=0}^{nu}\sum_{j=0}^{nv}\sum_{k=0}^{nw} h_{ijk}\mathbf{V}_{ijk} N_i^{ku}(u) N_j^{kv}(v) N_k^{kw}(w)}{\sum_{i=0}^{nu}\sum_{j=0}^{nv}\sum_{k=0}^{nw} h_{ijk} N_i^{ku}(u) N_j^{kv}(v) N_k^{kw}(w)}. \quad (6)$$

Similar to Eq. (1), the attribute volume of a hypervolume can be expressed by

$$\mathbf{A}(u,v,w,t) = \frac{\sum_{i=0}^{nu}\sum_{j=0}^{nv}\sum_{k=0}^{nw}\sum_{l=0}^{nt} h_{ijkl}\mathbf{A}_{ijkl} N_i^{ku}(u) N_j^{kv}(v) N_k^{kw}(w) N_l^{kt}(t)}{\sum_{i=0}^{nu}\sum_{j=0}^{nv}\sum_{k=0}^{nw}\sum_{l=0}^{nt} h_{ijkl} N_i^{ku}(u) N_j^{kv}(v) N_k^{kw}(w) N_l^{kt}(t)} \quad (7)$$

from which we obtain

$$\mathbf{A}(u,v,w,t) = \frac{\sum_{i=0}^{nu}\sum_{j=0}^{nv}\sum_{k=0}^{nw} h_{ijk}\mathbf{A}_{ijk}(t) N_i^{ku}(u) N_j^{kv}(v) N_k^{kw}(w)}{\sum_{i=0}^{nu}\sum_{j=0}^{nv}\sum_{k=0}^{nw} h_{ijk} N_i^{ku}(u) N_j^{kv}(v) N_k^{kw}(w)}, \quad (8)$$

where

$$\mathbf{A}_{ijk}(t) = \frac{\sum_{l=0}^{nt} h_l \mathbf{A}_{ijkl} N_l^{kt}(t)}{\sum_{l=0}^{nt} h_l N_l^{kt}(t)}. \tag{9}$$

The attribute volume in Eq. (8) is also a quadvariate, i.e., u, v, w spatially and t temporally, vector-valued piecewise rational function, of which the order is the same as that of the geometry volume in Eq. (1). Note that Eq. (7) is also a tensor product of the nonuniform rational B-spline of order ku, kv, kw, and kt in the u, v, w, and t direction respectively.

$\{\mathbf{A}_{ijkl}\} \subset \mathbf{R}^a$ forms a tridirectional control grid in the a-dimensional application space. For a fluid flow application, $\mathbf{A}_{ijkl} = (\rho_{ijkl}, \mathbf{V}_{ijkl}, e_{ijkl})$ is defined in this chapter where $\rho \in \mathbf{R}^1$ is a flow density, $\mathbf{V} \in \mathbf{R}^3$ is a flow velocity, and $e \in \mathbf{R}^1$ is an internal energy per unit mass.

Finally, a hypervolume can be derived simply from Eqs. (1) and (7) by the following procedures. We assume that the orders, ku, kv, kw, kt, the weight h_{ijkl}, the number of control vertices along each direction, nu, nv, nw, nt, and the knot vectors, $\mathbf{u}$, $\mathbf{v}$, $\mathbf{w}$, $\mathbf{t}$ of two volumes, i.e., Eqs. (1) and (7), are identical. Also we substitute $\binom{\mathbf{G}_{ijk}(t)}{0}$ for $\mathbf{G}_{ijk}(t)$ in Eq. (4) and also $\binom{0}{\mathbf{A}_{ijk}(t)}$ for $\mathbf{A}_{ijk}(t)$ in Eq. (8), and then perform the vector sum of the two results. From this summation, we obtain our goal of a hypervolume. That is,

$$\frac{\sum_{i=0}^{nu} \sum_{j=0}^{nv} \sum_{k=0}^{nw} h_{ijk} \binom{\mathbf{G}_{ijk}(t)}{0} N_i^{ku}(u) N_j^{kv}(v) N_k^{kw}(w)}{\sum_{i=0}^{nu} \sum_{j=0}^{nv} \sum_{k=0}^{nw} h_{ijk} N_i^{ku}(u) N_j^{kv}(v) N_k^{kw}(w)} \tag{10}$$

$$+ \frac{\sum_{i=0}^{nu} \sum_{j=0}^{nv} \sum_{k=0}^{nw} h_{ijk} \binom{0}{\mathbf{A}_{ijk}(t)} N_i^{ku}(u) N_j^{kv}(v) N_k^{kw}(w)}{\sum_{i=0}^{nu} \sum_{j=0}^{nv} \sum_{k=0}^{nw} h_{ijk} N_i^{ku}(u) N_j^{kv}(v) N_k^{kw}(w)} \tag{11}$$

$$= \frac{\sum_{i=0}^{nu} \sum_{j=0}^{nv} \sum_{k=0}^{nw} h_{ijk} \binom{\mathbf{G}_{ijk}(t)}{\mathbf{A}_{ijk}(t)} N_i^{ku}(u) N_j^{kv}(v) N_k^{kw}(w)}{\sum_{i=0}^{nu} \sum_{j=0}^{nv} \sum_{k=0}^{nw} h_{ijk} N_i^{ku}(u) N_j^{kv}(v) N_k^{kw}(w)}. \tag{12}$$

Also it follows that

$$\mathbf{H}(u, v, w, t) = \frac{\sum_{i=0}^{nu} \sum_{j=0}^{nv} \sum_{k=0}^{nw} h_{ijk} \mathbf{H}_{ijk}(t) N_i^{ku}(u) N_j^{kv}(v) N_k^{kw}(w)}{\sum_{i=0}^{nu} \sum_{j=0}^{nv} \sum_{k=0}^{nw} h_{ijk} N_i^{ku}(u) N_j^{kv}(v) N_k^{kw}(w)}, \tag{13}$$

where

$$\mathbf{H}_{ijk}(t) = \binom{\mathbf{G}_{ijk}(t)}{\mathbf{A}_{ijk}(t)}. \tag{14}$$

C. Main Features and Application Areas of a Hypervolume

The main features of the hypervolume proposed in this chapter are summarized as follows:

• This volume makes it possible to analyze the physical phenomena structure at any arbitrary position in a continuous physical domain when only discrete scientific data are given.

- This volume has the properties of convex hull, local control, and affine invariance under geometric transformations such as translation, rotation, parallel, and perspective projections and can utilize other useful techniques developed in the CAGD (computer-aided geometric design) literature, because this model is based on a NURBS representation.
- The geometric volume, which describes a physical domain in the parametric form, provides many differential elements such as arc length, surface area, and volume element, which are often required to calculate numerically any physical or interesting feature for a feature-based visualization.
- The attribute volume, which describes field variables in the parametric form, provides various expressions for the derivative operators such as gradient, divergence, curl, and Laplacian, in connection with the geometry volume.
- This volume allows existing visualization techniques to visualize a physical phenomena structure without changing their internal system structure, and makes it possible to implement and enhance a feature-based visualization.
- This volume permits multiple physical domains. That is, a set of hypervolumes can be dealt with from the decomposed physical domains in a systematic way.
- This volume enables us to represent/manage both the spatial and the temporal domains. That is, the independent parameters, u, v, and w, of a hypervolume govern a physical domain at an instant time t, and a parameter t is used to record the time history of this physical domain. For example, in the case of flow visualization, this volume can describe a complex physical motion in a turbulent flow domain with a time history.

The hypervolume presented in this chapter can be applied to many physical situations where interesting objects are evolving as time elapses. Note that these situations typically have been described by numerical computations or experimental measurements, and recorded into scientific data sets. Some of the applications include:

- the description of 3D geometric objects when they do not have movement or deformation and their internal physical properties or field variables do not vary as time elapses (e.g., the description of homogeneous solids standing fixed),
- the description of the spatial movement or deformation of 3D geometric objects of which internal physical properties are constant along time (e.g., the description of a rigid body motion of inhomogeneous materials),
- the description of historic records of physical field variables when 3D geometric objects in which physical phenomena occur do not vary (e.g., the description of water flowing into a fixed space), and
- the description of dynamics of 3D geometric objects with varying physical field variables as time elapses (e.g., the description of gas movement as its internal properties are varying).

Expressing these situations in terms of two constituent volumes of a hypervolume, we simply state that:

- both the geometric volume and the attribute volume are static,
- the geometric volume is static but the attribute volume is dynamic,

SCIENTIFIC DATA VISUALIZATION **525**

- the geometric volume is dynamic but the attribute volume is static, and
- both the geometric volume and the attribute volume are dynamic.

Note that "static" means no change along time while "dynamic" denotes any alteration as time elapses.

III. MANIPULATION OF VOLUMETRIC DATA

We introduce the derivatives of a hypervolume that are required as an elementary function in most numerical computations, especially in the computation of differential elements or derivative operators for advanced functionality. We also discuss two different generation algorithms of a hypervolume. Using these generation methods, we can obtain an actual instance of a hypervolume model from a given original data set without depending on the data dimensionality and distribution. Then we introduce several gridding methods that enable a hypervolume to handle scattered data. For a simple description, we use a NURBS volume instead of a hypervolume. A simple extension allows us to construct complete algorithms for a hypervolume, since a hypervolume comes from a NURBS volume.

A. Derivatives of a NURBS Volume

We begin by recalling the *Leibniz* rule, a more general version of the product rule for differentiation,

$$\frac{\partial^p}{\partial x^p}\{f_1(x) \cdot f_2(x)\} = \sum_{r=0}^{p} \binom{p}{r} \left\{\frac{\partial^r}{\partial x^r} f_1(x)\right\} \cdot \left\{\frac{\partial^{p-r}}{\partial x^{p-r}} f_2(x)\right\}, \tag{15}$$

where

$$\binom{p}{r} = \frac{p!}{r!(p-r)!}.$$

For clarity, let us introduce the differentiation notation

$$\frac{\partial^{a+b+c}}{\partial u^a \partial v^b \partial w^c} V(u, v, w) = D_u^a D_v^b D_w^c V(u, v, w) \tag{16}$$

and denote a NURBS volume by

$$V(u, v, w) = \frac{\sum_{i=0}^{nu} \sum_{j=0}^{nv} \sum_{k=0}^{nw} h_{ijk} V_{ijk} N_i^{ku}(u) N_j^{kv}(v) N_k^{kw}(w)}{\sum_{i=0}^{nu} \sum_{j=0}^{nv} \sum_{k=0}^{nw} h_{ijk} N_i^{ku}(u) N_j^{kv}(v) N_k^{kw}(w)} = \frac{\Omega(u, v, w)}{h(u, v, w)}. \tag{17}$$

From Eqs. (16) and (17), we can obtain

$$\frac{\partial^r \Omega}{\partial w^r} = D_w^r \Omega(u, v, w) = D_w^r \{V(u, v, w) \cdot h(u, v, w)\}. \tag{18}$$

Substituting the *Leibniz* rule into Eq. (18) yields

$$D_w^r\{V(u,v,w) \cdot h(u,v,w)\} = \sum_{k=0}^{r} \binom{r}{k} D_w^{r-k} V D_w^k h$$

$$= D_w^r V \cdot h + \sum_{k=1}^{r} \binom{r}{k} D_w^{r-k} V D_w^k h \quad (19)$$

and thus

$$D_w^r V = \frac{1}{h}\left[D_w^r \Omega - \sum_{k=1}^{r} \binom{r}{k} D_w^{r-k} V D_w^k h\right], \quad (20)$$

which is the rth partial derivative of a NURBS volume with respect to w. Next, the qth partial derivative of Eq. (20) with respect to v is given by

$$D_v^q D_w^r V = D_v^q \left[\frac{1}{h}\left\{D_w^r \Omega - \sum_{k=1}^{r}\binom{r}{k} D_w^{r-k} V D_w^k h\right\}\right]$$

$$= \frac{1}{h}\left\{D_v^q\left(D_w^r \Omega - \sum_{k=1}^{r}\binom{r}{k} D_w^{r-k} V D_w^k h\right) - \sum_{j=1}^{q}\binom{q}{j} D_v^{q-j} D_w^r V D_v^j h\right\}$$

$$= \frac{1}{h}\left\{\begin{array}{l} D_v^q D_w^r \Omega - \sum_{k=1}^{r}\binom{r}{k}\sum_{j=0}^{q}\binom{q}{j} D_v^{q-j} D_w^{r-k} V D_v^j D_w^k h \\ - \sum_{j=1}^{q}\binom{q}{j} D_v^{q-j} D_w^r V D_v^j h \end{array}\right\}. \quad (21)$$

Finally, the pth partial derivative of Eq. (21) with respect to u is given by

$$D_u^p D_v^q D_w^r V = D_u^p\left[\frac{1}{h}\left\{\begin{array}{l} D_v^q D_w^r \Omega - \sum_{k=1}^{r}\binom{r}{k}\sum_{j=0}^{q}\binom{q}{j} D_v^{q-j} D_w^{r-k} V D_v^j D_w^k h \\ - \sum_{j=1}^{q}\binom{q}{j} D_v^{q-j} D_w^r V D_v^j h \end{array}\right\}\right]$$

$$= \frac{1}{h}\left[D_u^p\left\{\begin{array}{l} D_v^q D_w^r \Omega - \sum_{k=1}^{r}\binom{r}{k}\sum_{j=0}^{q}\binom{q}{j} D_v^{q-j} D_w^{r-k} V D_v^j D_w^k h \\ - \sum_{j=1}^{q}\binom{q}{j} D_v^{q-j} D_w^r V D_v^j h \end{array}\right\} - \sum_{i=1}^{p}\binom{p}{i} D_u^{p-i} D_v^q D_w^r V D_u^i h\right].$$

Thus we obtain

$$D_u^p D_v^q D_w^r V = \frac{1}{h}\left[\begin{array}{l} D_u^p D_v^q D_w^r \Omega \\ - \sum_{k=1}^{r}\binom{r}{k}\sum_{j=0}^{q}\binom{q}{j}\sum_{i=0}^{p}\binom{p}{i} D_u^{p-i} D_v^{q-j} D_w^{r-k} V D_u^i D_v^j D_w^k h \\ - \sum_{j=1}^{q}\binom{q}{j}\sum_{i=0}^{p}\binom{p}{i} D_u^{p-i} D_v^{q-j} D_w^r V D_u^i D_v^j h \\ - \sum_{i=1}^{p}\binom{p}{i} D_u^{p-i} D_v^q D_w^r V D_u^i h \end{array}\right], \quad (22)$$

which is the pth, qth, and rth partial derivatives of a NURBS volume with respect to u, v, and w, respectively. Note that we can compute $D_u^p D_v^q D_w^r \Omega(u, v, w)$ and $D_u^p D_v^q D_w^r h(u, v, w)$ in Eq. (22) by using the *deBoor* algorithm [11].

B. Generation of a NURBS Volume

In this section, we consider two simple algorithms for a NURBS volume generation. The first algorithm belongs to the generation of an interpolated volume and the second is for swept volumes, all of which are based on NURBS parametric form.

1. Interpolated Volume

We describe how to construct a NURBS volume by an interpolation method, which will be presented in detail below, with a volumetric data distributed over a regular Cartesian or curvilinear grid. If the volumetric data are not available on a grid configuration, we need to go through the gridding process and produce an array of values from original data.

The geometry volume of a hypervolume can be generated by the simple extension of the same interpolation algorithm applied to the NURBS volume, if we have time series information of the volumetric data. Similarly the attribute volume can be constructed.

For a better understanding of the interpolation algorithm, we assume all homogeneous coordinates (i.e., weight values) have unit values, and thus the rational form of a NURBS volume is reduced to the simpler nonrational form. That is, with an assumption, $h_{ijk} = 1$, and a relation, $\sum_{i=0}^{nu} N_i^{ku}(u) = \sum_{j=0}^{nv} N_j^{kv}(v) = \sum_{k=0}^{nw} N_k^{kw}(w) = 1$, the NURBS volume in Eq. (6) can be written as

$$V(u, v, w) = \sum_{i=0}^{nu} \sum_{j=0}^{nv} \sum_{k=0}^{nw} V_{ijk} N_i^{ku}(u) N_j^{kv}(v) N_k^{kw}(w). \quad (23)$$

Note that we need to use the rational form of Eq. (23), i.e., Eq. (6), if we have an analytical shape [12]. For example, in analyzing or visualizing a pipe flow, the pipe's geometry, which has the shape of a cylinder, cannot be represented by a nonrational form.

Now, we are given a $(nu + 1) \times (nv + 1) \times (nw + 1)$ number of grid points and our goal is to build a trivariate piecewise nonrational function given in Eq. (23) that interpolates the grid data. The nonrational B-spline volume in Eq. (23) can be written as

$$V(u, v, w) = \sum_{i=0}^{nu} \left(\sum_{j=0}^{nv} \left(\sum_{k=0}^{nw} V_{ijk} N_k^{kw}(w) \right) N_j^{kv}(v) \right) N_i^{ku}(u)$$

$$= \sum_{i=0}^{nu} \left(\sum_{j=0}^{nv} C_{ij}(w) N_j^{kv}(v) \right) N_i^{ku}(u) \quad (24)$$

$$= \sum_{i=0}^{nu} S_i(v, w) N_i^{ku}(u).$$

In Eq. (24), $C_{ij}(w)$ and $S_i(v, w)$ are referred to as a control curve and a control surface, respectively, and are defined as

$$\mathbf{C}_{ij}(w) = \sum_{k=0}^{nw} \mathbf{V}_{ijk} N_k^{kw}(w) \tag{25}$$

$$\mathbf{S}_i(v, w) = \sum_{j=0}^{nv} \mathbf{C}_{ij}(w) N_j^{kv}(v). \tag{26}$$

Now we will determine the knot vectors of $\mathbf{V}(u, v, w)$, $\mathbf{u} = \{u_i\}_{i=0}^{nu+ku}$, $\mathbf{v} = \{v_j\}_{j=0}^{nv+kv}$, and $\mathbf{w} = \{w_k\}_{k=0}^{nw+kw}$. Consider a k-directional data array $\{\mathbf{P}_{ijk}\}_{k=0}^{k=nw}$ for each $i = 0, \ldots, nu$ and $j = 0, \ldots, nv$. First, we compute $\{w_{ijk}\}_{k=0}^{k=nw+kw}$ with each k-directional data array by using the parameterization technique introduced by Hartley and Judd [13]. Then we compute w_k by

$$w_k = \frac{\sum_{i=0}^{nu} \sum_{j=0}^{nv} w_{ijk}}{(nu+1)(nv+1)}. \tag{27}$$

Similarly, u_i and v_j can be computed as

$$u_i = \frac{\sum_{j=0}^{nv} \sum_{k=0}^{nw} u_{ijk}}{(nv+1)(nw+1)}, \qquad v_j = \frac{\sum_{k=0}^{nw} \sum_{i=0}^{nu} v_{ijk}}{(nw+1)(nu+1)}. \tag{28}$$

From the knot vectors computed, we compute the Greville abscissa [14] (ξ_i, η_j, ζ_k), corresponding to the grid data $\mathbf{P}_{ijk}$; they are given by

$$\xi_i = \frac{u_{i+1} + u_{i+2} + \cdots + u_{i+ku}}{ku}, \quad i = 0, \ldots, nu$$

$$\eta_j = \frac{v_{j+1} + v_{j+2} + \cdots + v_{j+kv}}{kv}, \quad j = 0, \ldots, nv \tag{29}$$

$$\zeta_k = \frac{w_{k+1} + w_{k+2} + \cdots + w_{k+kw}}{kw}, \quad k = 0, \ldots, nw.$$

Now, with the Greville abscissa $\{(\xi_i, \eta_j, \zeta_k)\}$ computed in Eq. (29) and the grid data set $\{\mathbf{P}_{ijk}\}$, we compute $\{\mathbf{V}_{ijk}\}$ such that

$$\mathbf{V}(\xi_i, \eta_j, \zeta_k) = \sum_{i=0}^{nu} \left(\sum_{j=0}^{nv} \left(\sum_{k=0}^{nw} \mathbf{V}_{ijk} N_k^{kw}(\zeta_k) \right) N_j^{kv}(\eta_j) \right) N_i^{ku}(\xi_i)$$

$$= \sum_{i=0}^{nu} \left(\sum_{j=0}^{nv} \mathbf{C}_{ij}(\zeta_k) N_j^{kv}(\eta_j) \right) N_i^{ku}(\xi_i) \tag{30}$$

$$= \sum_{i=0}^{nu} \mathbf{S}_i(\eta_j, \zeta_k) N_i^{ku}(\xi_i) = \mathbf{P}_{ijk}, \tag{31}$$

where

$$\mathbf{C}_{ij}(\zeta_k) = \sum_{k=0}^{nw} \mathbf{V}_{ijk} N_k^{kw}(\zeta_k) \tag{32}$$

$$\mathbf{S}_i(\eta_j, \zeta_k) = \sum_{j=0}^{nv} \mathbf{C}_{ij}(\zeta_k) N_j^{kv}(\eta_j). \tag{33}$$

SCIENTIFIC DATA VISUALIZATION

First, we calculate unknown $S_i(\eta_j, \zeta_k)$ from known P_{ijk} in Eq. (31). Then in Eq. (33), unknown $C_{ij}(\zeta_k)$ is computed from $S_i(\eta_j, \zeta_k)$. Finally, we find a goal V_{ijk} from the computed $C_{ij}(\zeta_k)$ in Eq. (32).

For $j = 0, \ldots, nv$ and $k = 0, \ldots, nw$, the system of $(nv+1) \times (nw+1)$ equations in Eq. (31) is given by

$$\sum_{i=0}^{nu} S_i(\eta_0, \zeta_0) N_i^{ku}(\xi_i) = P_{i00}$$

$$\sum_{i=0}^{nu} S_i(\eta_0, \zeta_1) N_i^{ku}(\xi_i) = P_{i01}$$

$$\cdots$$

$$\sum_{i=0}^{nu} S_i(\eta_0, \zeta_{nw}) N_i^{ku}(\xi_i) = P_{i0nw}$$

$$\sum_{i=0}^{nu} S_i(\eta_1, \zeta_0) N_i^{ku}(\xi_i) = P_{i10}$$

$$\sum_{i=0}^{nu} S_i(\eta_1, \zeta_1) N_i^{ku}(\xi_i) = P_{i11}$$

$$\cdots$$

$$\sum_{i=0}^{nu} S_i(\eta_1, \zeta_{nw}) N_i^{ku}(\xi_i) = P_{i1nw}$$

$$\cdots\cdots$$

$$\sum_{i=0}^{nu} S_i(\eta_{nv}, \zeta_0) N_i^{ku}(\xi_i) = P_{inv0}$$

$$\sum_{i=0}^{nu} S_i(\eta_{nv}, \zeta_1) N_i^{ku}(\xi_i) = P_{inv1}$$

$$\cdots$$

$$\sum_{i=0}^{nu} S_i(\eta_{nv}, \zeta_{nw}) N_i^{ku}(\xi_i) = P_{invnw}.$$

From the system of equations above, we can see that $S_i(\eta_j, \zeta_k)$ is a control net of a control curve that interpolates the $\{P_{ijk}\}$ along the u direction. Similarly, for $k = 0, \ldots, nw$ and $i = 0, \ldots, nu$, the system of $(nw+1) \times (nu+1)$ equations in Eq. (33) is given by

$$\sum_{j=0}^{nv} C_{0j}(\zeta_0) N_j^{kv}(\eta_j) = S_0(\eta_j, \zeta_0)$$

$$\sum_{j=0}^{nv} C_{1j}(\zeta_0) N_j^{kv}(\eta_j) = S_1(\eta_j, \zeta_0)$$

$$\cdots$$

$$\sum_{j=0}^{nv} \mathbf{C}_{nuj}(\zeta_0) N_j^{kv}(\eta_j) = \mathbf{S}_{nu}(\eta_j, \zeta_0)$$

$$\sum_{j=0}^{nv} \mathbf{C}_{0j}(\zeta_1) N_j^{kv}(\eta_j) = \mathbf{S}_0(\eta_j, \zeta_1)$$

$$\sum_{j=0}^{nv} \mathbf{C}_{1j}(\zeta_1) N_j^{kv}(\eta_j) = \mathbf{S}_1(\eta_j, \zeta_1)$$

$$\cdots$$

$$\sum_{j=0}^{nv} \mathbf{C}_{nuj}(\zeta_1) N_j^{kv}(\eta_j) = \mathbf{S}_{nu}(\eta_j, \zeta_1)$$

$$\cdots\cdots$$

$$\sum_{j=0}^{nv} \mathbf{C}_{0j}(\zeta_{nw}) N_j^{kv}(\eta_j) = \mathbf{S}_0(\eta_j, \zeta_{nw})$$

$$\sum_{j=0}^{nv} \mathbf{C}_{1j}(\zeta_{nw}) N_j^{kv}(\eta_j) = \mathbf{S}_1(\eta_j, \zeta_{nw})$$

$$\cdots$$

$$\sum_{j=0}^{nv} \mathbf{C}_{nuj}(\zeta_{nw}) N_j^{kv}(\eta_j) = \mathbf{S}_{nu}(\eta_j, \zeta_{nw}).$$

From the system of equations above, we can see that $\mathbf{C}_{ij}(\zeta_k)$ is a control net of a control curve that interpolates the $\mathbf{S}_i(\eta_j, \zeta_k)$ along the v direction. Again, the system of $(nu + 1) \times (nv + 1)$ equations in Eq. (32) for $i = 0, \ldots, nu$ and $j = 0, \ldots, nv$ is given by

$$\sum_{k=0}^{nw} \mathbf{V}_{00k} N_k^{kw}(\zeta_k) = \mathbf{C}_{00}(\zeta_k)$$

$$\sum_{k=0}^{nw} \mathbf{V}_{01k} N_k^{kw}(\zeta_k) = \mathbf{C}_{01}(\zeta_k)$$

$$\cdots$$

$$\sum_{k=0}^{nw} \mathbf{V}_{0nvk} N_k^{kw}(\zeta_k) = \mathbf{C}_{0nv}(\zeta_k)$$

$$\sum_{k=0}^{nw} \mathbf{V}_{10k} N_k^{kw}(\zeta_k) = \mathbf{C}_{10}(\zeta_k)$$

$$\sum_{k=0}^{nw} \mathbf{V}_{11k} N_k^{kw}(\zeta_k) = \mathbf{C}_{11}(\zeta_k)$$

$$\cdots$$

$$\sum_{k=0}^{nw} \mathbf{V}_{1nvk} N_k^{kw}(\zeta_k) = \mathbf{C}_{1nv}(\zeta_k)$$

$$\bullet \bullet \bullet \bullet$$

$$\sum_{k=0}^{nw} \mathbf{V}_{nu0k} N_k^{kw}(\zeta_k) = \mathbf{C}_{nu0}(\zeta_k)$$

$$\sum_{k=0}^{nw} \mathbf{V}_{nu1k} N_k^{kw}(\zeta_k) = \mathbf{C}_{nu1}(\zeta_k)$$

$$\bullet \bullet \bullet$$

$$\sum_{k=0}^{nw} \mathbf{V}_{nunvk} N_k^{kw}(\zeta_k) = \mathbf{C}_{nunv}(\zeta_k).$$

From the system of equations above, we can see that $\mathbf{V}_{ijk}$ is a control net of a control curve that interpolates the $\mathbf{C}_{ij}(\zeta_k)$ along the w direction. Therefore, the $\mathbf{V}_{ijk}$ is a control net or grid of a control volume that interpolates the $\{\mathbf{P}_{ijk}\}$ along each parametric direction.

2. Swept Volume

Now we address the topic of sweeping a section surface along an arbitrary guide (= trajectory) curve. Denote the guide curve by $\mathbf{G}(w)$ and the section surface by $\mathbf{S}(u, v)$ as shown in Fig. 1. The procedure for generating a swept volume from $\mathbf{G}(w)$ and $\mathbf{S}(u, v)$ shown in Fig. 1 is as follows:

(a) Input the guide curve $\mathbf{G}(w)$, one point $\mathbf{P}$ located on both $\mathbf{G}(w)$ and $\mathbf{S}(u, v)$, and the section surface $\mathbf{S}(u, v)$.

(b) Arrange $\mathbf{G}(w)$ and $\mathbf{S}(u, v)$ to have the same configuration as shown in Fig. 1. That is, the normal vector of $\mathbf{S}(u, v)$ is directed along the tangent vector of $\mathbf{G}(w)$. The normal vector of $\mathbf{S}(u, v)$ is calculated by the cross product of the u and v directional tangent vectors of $\mathbf{S}(u, v)$.

(c) Compute the Greville abscissa, which is often referred to as node values, of $\mathbf{G}(w)$ and also those of $\mathbf{S}(u, v)$ in both directions, u and v.

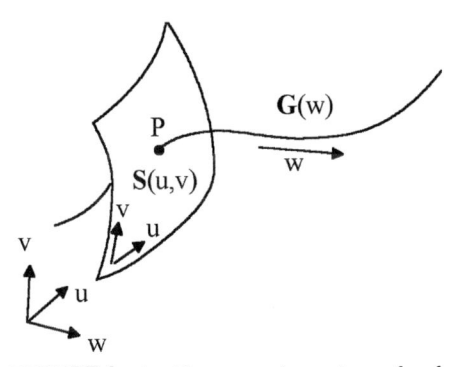

FIGURE 1 A guide curve and a section surface for sweeping.

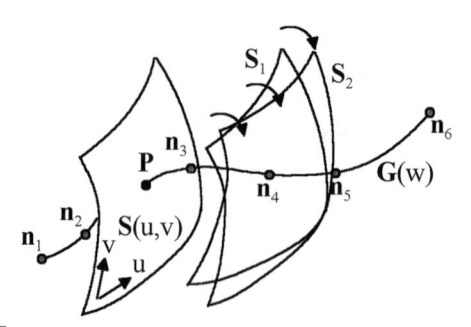

FIGURE 2 Transformations of a section surface in sweeping.

(d) Compute the Greville points (= node points) of $G(w)$ evaluated at the Greville abscissa and also the tangent vectors at the same positions. For a better understanding, see Fig. 2, which illustrates six node points, $n_1, n_2, n_3, n_4, n_5, n_6$ of $G(w)$ when $G(w)$ has six control points. In addition, compute the tangent vector of $G(w)$ at the point, P.

(e) Transform the section surface, $S(u, v)$, by translation and rotation through two steps as follows: The first step is to translate $S(u, v)$ by $(n_1 - P)$. The second step is to rotate $S(u, v)$ translated in the first step. Here, the rotational axis is determined from the cross product of two tangent vectors, one being the tangent vector of $G(w)$ at position P and the other being that at position n_1. The rotational angle is measured from these two tangent vectors, and the center of rotation is n_1. In addition, we evaluate the node points of the transformed $S(u, v)$ at the Greville abscissa of $S(u, v)$ already calculated in step (c), and save the results together with position n_1.

(f) Transform $S(u, v)$ resulting from step (e) by a process similar to step (e). That is, move the $S(u, v)$ by $(n_2 - n_1)$ and then rotate $S(u, v)$ by the angle between two tangent vectors, one being the tangent vector of $G(w)$ at position n_1 and the other being that at position n_2. Here the rotational axis is calculated from the cross product of these tangent vectors, and the rotation center is n_2. In addition, evaluate and save the node points of the transformed $S(u, v)$ at the Greville abscissa already calculated in step (c). The same procedure is repeated until the node points of the transformed $S(u, v)$ are computed at the last node point of $G(w)$. Figure 2 illustrates S_1, the section surface after translating from n_3 to n_4, and S_2, the section surface after rotation by the angle between two tangent vectors of $G(w)$ at positions n_3 and n_4. Through the processes described above, we can get the node points distribution in the u and v directions along the w directional node position.

(g) Now we can get the control grid (or regular control point set) for generating a swept volume by using the interpolated method described in the previous section, where the Greville abscissa (or node values) from step (c) and the node points from steps (e) and (f) are used as input data. The knot vectors along the u and v directions of a swept volume are the same as those of the section surface $S(u, v)$ and the w-directional knot vector of a swept volume is the same as that of the guide curve $G(w)$.

Note that the procedure for constructing extruded volumes and revolved ones can be easily derived from the swept volume algorithm described above.

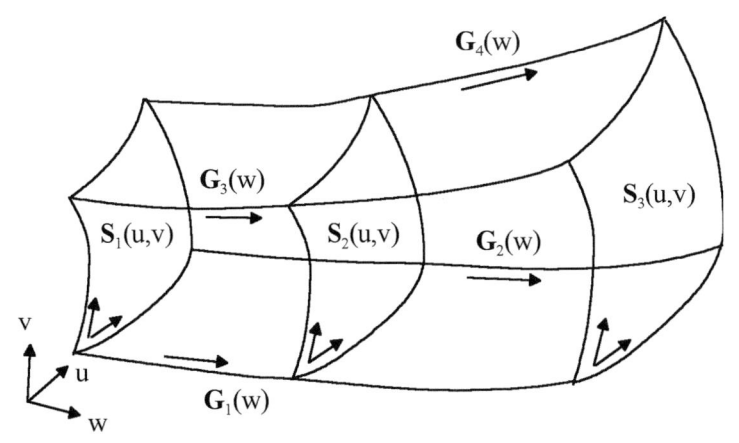

FIGURE 3 Four guide curves and three section surfaces for a swept volume.

The extruded volume can be viewed as a special case of swept volume when the guide curve $G(w)$ is a straight line. Similarly the revolved volume can be generated if $G(w)$ is a circular arc or a circle.

Furthermore, we will present another algorithm for constructing a swept volume in a situation different from that described above. Its configuration is shown in Fig. 3. That is, four guide curves, $G_1(w)$, $G_2(w)$, $G_3(w)$, and $G_4(w)$, and n section surfaces, $S_1(u, v)$, $S_2(u, v)$, ..., $S_n(u, v)$, are used to define the swept volume. Note that only three section surfaces are shown in Fig. 3. The detail procedure is described as follows:

(a) Input four guide curves $G_1(w)$, $G_2(w)$, $G_3(w)$, and $G_4(w)$ and n section surfaces, $S_1(u, v)$, $S_2(u, v)$, ..., $S_n(u, v)$. See Fig. 3 for $n = 3$.

(b) Arrange the four guide curves to have the same direction as that shown in Fig. 3. All section surfaces are also adjusted to have the same configuration, and their normal vectors are directed toward the same direction as the four guide curves as shown in Fig. 3.

(c) Reparameterize the four guide curves such that the parameter for each curve ranges from 0.0 to 1.0. Similarly, reparameterize all the section surfaces such that each surface has a parameter range 0.0 to 1.0 along the u and v directions.

(d) Raise the degree of the guide curves of lower degree such that the four guide curves have the same degree, and insert proper knots such that each curve has the same knot vector.

(e) Raise the degree of section surfaces of lower degree such that all the section surfaces have the same degree along the u and v directions, and insert proper knots such that each surface has the same knot vectors along u and v directions.

(f) For the ith section surface, take the following procedures: Find t_1, t_2, t_3, t_4 such that $G_1(t_1) = S_i(0,0)$, $G_2(t_2) = S_i(1,0)$, $G_3(t_3) = S_i(0,1)$, and $G_4(t_4) = S_i(1,1)$. If t_1, t_2, t_3, t_4 are not same, then for the jth guide curve ($j = 1,2,3,4$), split $G_j(w)$ at $w = t_j$, resulting in two splitted curves, $G_j^0(w = 0 : t_j)$ and $G_j^1(w = t_j : 1)$, and then reparameterize $G_j^0(w = 0 : t_j)$ and $G_j^1(w = t_j : 1)$ such that they have the parameter range $[0, (t_1 + t_2 + t_3 + t_4)/4]$ and $[(t_1 + t_2 + t_3 + t_4)/4, 1]$, respectively.

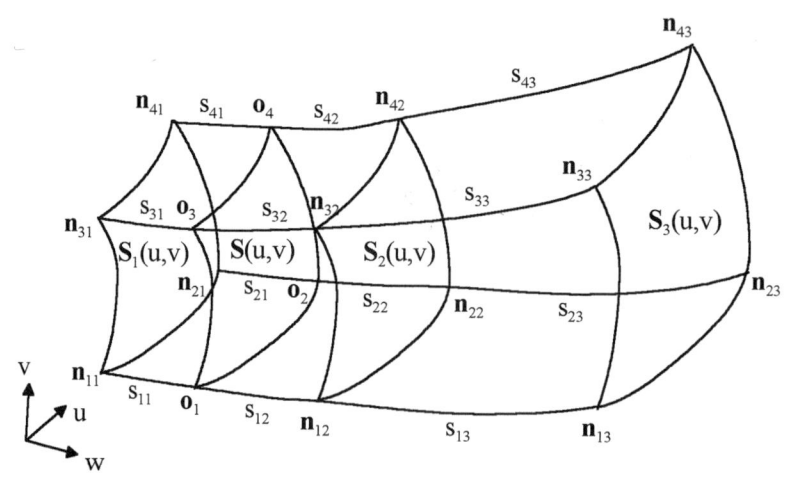

FIGURE 4 A configuration for transforming section surfaces.

Note that each of the four corner points of the ith section surface lies on the corresponding guide curve at the same parameter value, $(t_1 + t_2 + t_3 + t_4)/4$ ($= t_m$), which means that $S_i(0,0) = G_1(t_m)$, $S_i(1,0) = G_2(t_m)$, $S_i(0,1) = G_3(t_m)$, and $S_i(1,1) = G_4(t_m)$. Thus t_m is the common Greville abscissa (= node value) of each guide curve, and the four corner points are the node points of the corresponding guide curves.

(g) Transform all the section surfaces to form a single merged surface located at the new node points of the four guide curves at which the section surfaces are not originally located. Figure 4 shows the configuration for this transformation.

Let us denote the new node points by o_1, o_2, o_3, o_4, where o_i is the node point of $G_i(w)(i = 1,2,3,4)$, which can be computed in step (f). Also we denote by n_{11}, n_{12}, n_{13} the node points of $G_1(w)$ at which the section surfaces have originally been located. Similarly, the node points of $G_2(w), G_3(w)$, and $G_4(w)$ are denoted by $n_{21}, n_{22}, n_{23}, n_{31}, n_{32}, n_{33}$, and n_{41}, n_{42}, n_{43}, respectively. Now, we compute s_{11}, s_{12}, s_{13}, which are arc lengths between o_1 and n_{11}, n_{12}, n_{13} along $G_1(w)$. Similarly, we compute $s_{21}, s_{22}, s_{23}, s_{31}, s_{32}, s_{33}$, and s_{41}, s_{42}, s_{43} along $G_2(w), G_3(w)$, and $G_4(w)$, respectively.

The transformation consists of two steps. One is the transformation of each section surface. That is, in Fig. 4, $S_1(u, v), S_2(u, v)$, and $S_3(u, v)$ are transformed into $S_1^*(u, v), S_2^*(u, v)$, and $S_3^*(u, v)$ such that the four corner points of each transformed surface are located at o_1, o_2, o_3, and o_4. The details of the transformation will be illustrated later in Fig. 5. The other step is the weighted sum of $S_i^*(u, v)$. First, we will explain the weighted sum. In Fig. 4, we compute the weighting factor s_i of each section surface $S_i(u, v)$ by

$$s_1 = \frac{1}{\frac{s_{11} + s_{21} + s_{31} + s_{41}}{4}}, \quad s_2 = \frac{1}{\frac{s_{12} + s_{22} + s_{32} + s_{42}}{4}},$$

$$s_3 = \frac{1}{\frac{s_{13} + s_{23} + s_{33} + s_{43}}{4}}$$

SCIENTIFIC DATA VISUALIZATION

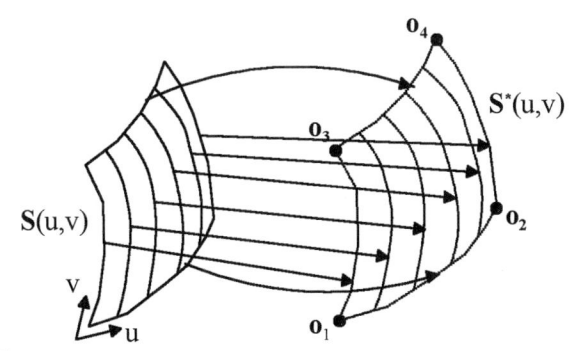

FIGURE 5 Transformation of u- and v-ray curves obtained from a section surface.

from which we know that the weighting factors are determined from the inverse of the average distance between the new node points o_1, o_2, o_3, o_4 and each section surface $S_i(u, v)$. Thus, by using the weighting factors, we compute the single merged surface $S(u, v)$ by

$$S(u, v) = \frac{s_1 S_1^* + s_2 S_2^* + s_3 S_3^*}{s_1 + s_2 + s_3}.$$

Now, we will explain the transformation from $S_i(u, v)$ to $S_i^*(u, v)$ with Fig. 5. For the ith section surface, take the following procedures:

(1) Compute the u-directional node values of $S_i(u, v)$ and then compute the v-ray curves, isoparametric curves along the v direction at each of the u-directional node values. Here, we know that the number of v-ray curves is equal to that of the u-directional node points.

(2) Compute the u-ray curves and iso parametric curves along the u direction, at the staring and ending v parameters of $S_i(u, v)$. Again we know that the number of the u-ray curves is two.

(3) Move the two u-ray curves to the positions o_1, o_2 and o_3, o_4. That is, move both ending points of the lower u-ray to the positions o_1 and o_2, and the upper u-ray to o_3 and o_4, while preserving the tangent vectors of each of the u-ray curves at its end points during the movement. Then evaluate the two u-ray curves at the u-directional node values already calculated in step (1).

(4) Move each of the v-ray curves into two corresponding node points, one being calculated from the upper u-ray and the other from the lower in step (3), while preserving the tangent vectors of the v-ray curve at its end points during the movement. This movement process is applied to all v-ray curves positioned at the u-directional node points.

(5) Compute $S_i^*(u, v)$ by interpolating the node points of the v-ray curves obtained in step (4).

(h) By using the interpolated volume method, we obtain the control grid of a swept volume from the initial section surfaces and their transformed surfaces obtained in step (g). Note that the u- and v-knot vectors of the swept volume are equal to those of anyone of the section surfaces, and the w-knot vector is equal to that of anyone of the guide curves.

C. Gridding Methods of Scattered Data

Many researchers have tried to construct methods for creating structured or unstructed grids from scattered data points. Some methods involve unstructured grids or meshes being dependent on the distribution of the scattered data points. In two dimensions, this would be a method for triangulating a set of scattered points in a plane [15]. The rendering process of the triangular meshes determines the color of each pixel in the image by applying bilinear interpolation to the data value at each node. Although the original data are preserved, the sparseness of the data points results in a pseudo-colored distribution that is difficult to interpret. That is, it is possible to incorrectly visualize the spatial distribution of the data.

Other methods attempt to create new data distributions from the original data for their actual visualization. Most of the methods construct a structured grid configuration, which has a regular Cartesian or curvilinear grid type, calculated from the original scattered data. This section serves only as a very brief introduction to the topic.

The simplest approach, called the "nearest-neighbor gridding" method, is to create a Cartesian grid from the ungridded point data by the following procedure. First, we calculate the smallest box that minimally covers the spatial distribution of the data. Second, a Cartesian (or regular) grid configuration is constructed from the box and stored into n-dimensional arrays. The n-dimensional arrays consist of common 3D spatial grids and 1D model fields, e.g., temperature, pressure, and velocity. These array types of data structure can be found in the Vis-5D system [16], which uses 5D rectangles organized as 2D arrays of 3D spatial grids. The 2D arrays are indexed by time and by model field. Next, we find the nearest point to each grid point in the resultant grid configuration. Finally, we assign that grid point the original point's value, as shown in Fig. 6. Figure 6 illustrates the case where only three grid points are related. Such a technique has a positive side that it preserves the original data values, while the rendering results might not satisfy qualitative display requirements because the discrete spatial structure is preserved.

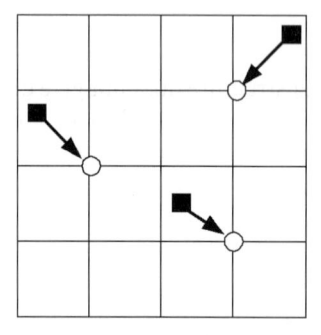

■ original point
○ grid point

FIGURE 6 Nearest neighbor gridding method.

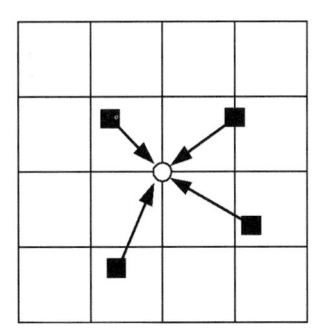

■ original point
○ grid point

FIGURE 7 Weighted average gridding method.

A potentially more appropriate method, and certainly more accurate than the simple method aforementioned, uses the concept of weighted averaging as shown in Fig. 7. The governing procedures are as follows: First, we compute the smallest box enveloping the original data spatially, and create a Cartesian grid configuration, saved into n-dimensional arrays. These steps are similar to those explained above. Next, for each grid point in the grid configuration, we calculate the weighted average of the scalar values of the original m data points spatially nearest to that grid point. Here, we should obtain a weighting factor applied to each of the m values, that is, $w_i = f(d_i)$, where $d_i (i = 1, \ldots, m)$ is the distance between the grid point and the ith point in the original data points. Figure 7 illustrates a case for $m = 4$. Depending on the characteristics of application fields, we can choose one of various weighting functions. The weighting function $w = d^{-2}$ is commonly recommended in most applications. Note that this approach is based on Shepard's method [17], and many advanced techniques [10] such as radial basis function methods, FEM methods, and multistage methods are still under development.

We need only a scatter data interpolation function for modeling or analyzing the spatial distribution of scattered data, while for effective visualization of the data, it is necessary to perform the meshing or gridding process and produce a 3D array of values or more dimensional arrays from original data. It is worthwhile noting that this gridding process is necessary, not sufficient. The reason comes from that the array data structure does not give directly new values at arbitrary positions in a continuous field and thus new meaningful objects cannot be extracted. For example, streamlines or stream surfaces in a steady fluid flow cannot be extracted. In order to achieve a goal of qualitative visualization or new feature segmentation, we need a more continuous process or a new interpolating function that efficiently computes continuous data fields from the discrete grid distribution. We expect that the hypervolume suggested in this chapter enables us to realize the continuous process significantly. That is, the interpolated volume method in the previous section will provide a way of obtaining the continuous field from the discrete grid points, and from the interpolated volume, the computation for the extraction of any feature objects, and their rendering implementation will be realized in an efficient manner.

Some practical examples of feature segmentation will be illustrated in the next section.

IV. RENDERING METHODS OF VOLUMETRIC DATA

We discuss several volumetric rendering methods for visualizing a three- or more dimensional data set to enhance the structural comprehension of the data set significantly. One of the most commonly used rendering methods is the direct volume rendering algorithm, e.g., ray casting [18] or splatting [19]. Also the tiny cube [20,21], hexahedron [22], and vanishing cube [20,21] methods are well known as visualization techniques of multivariable function objects.

The tiny cube method creates a number of small cubes (or boxes) to be placed in the spatial domain of the data set. These boxes are commonly distributed in a gridded structure, as shown in Fig. 8, with a uniform gap between boxes in each direction, i.e., the u, v, and w directions in the gridded distribution. The faces of these boxes are then rendered by color information calculated from the function values of the volume model used for representing the volumetric data. Here we can use $\mathbf{H}(u, v, w)$ or hypervolume in Eq. (13) as the volume model. It should be noted that the images displayed by this method become difficult to interpret if the number of boxes in each direction is greater than 15.

The hexahedron method is similar to the tiny cube method above. In this method, we assume that the gap distance between boxes is zero, and use the function values at the volume centers of some of the boxes in order to produce the images of the boxes. In this case, a box placed in the interior can be visible if the boxes between the interior box and the viewer are not turned on.

In the vanishing cube method, we create equally spaced planes in each direction instead of the boxes. That is, we create three rectangles for each grid point in the governing volume model, as shown in Fig. 9. Each of the rectangles is colored using bilinear interpolation of the values of the volume model at

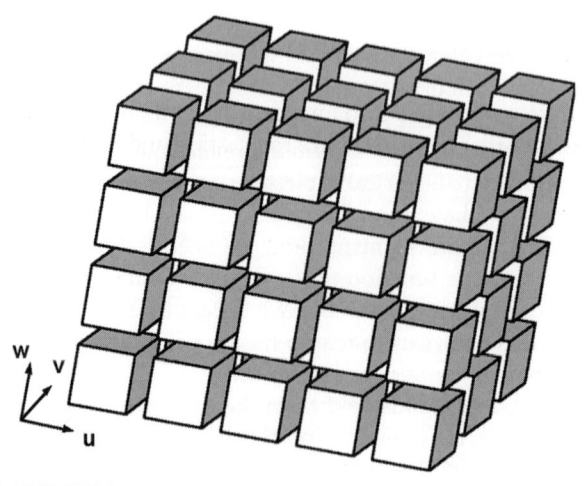

FIGURE 8 Tiny cube method.

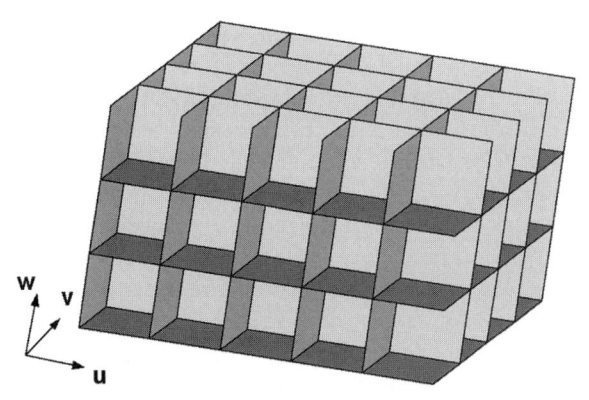

FIGURE 9 Vanishing cube method.

its four vertices. By using this method, the interior planes can be viewed if the exterior planes are rendered as partially transparent. In real practice, the number of planes embedded in the volume model cannot be too large.

Direct volume rendering involves "shooting" rays through an object. To simplify the required summation or integration process [23], the object is usually divided into a large number of uniformly sized boxes called *voxels*. Then for each voxel, the voxel intensity and its gradient magnitude should be calculated in order to classify and render the data set. The classification requires calculating an optical density value for each voxel in the data set, called opacity. The opacity is often used to put a stress on any meaningful surfaces or boundaries between different materials. Typically, the opacities are calculated from either voxel intensities or a combination of voxel intensities and gradient information. Once the data set is classified and the opacity and color are computed, we obtain two new voxel data sets, a color and an opacity data set. Then we simply determine the color and opacity on sampling points (generally not on voxel positions) by commonly trilinear interpolation, but this step may lower the quality of the image. As an alternative, we may directly compute the color and opacity on the sampling positions without using interpolation during the rendering process. However, this step may increase the complexity of the algorithm and require more computational processes. Finally, the rendering images are constructed by using several rendering techniques. The major distinction between the techniques is the order in which the voxels are processed to generate an image, and they are grouped into image–order and object–order algorithms. Examples of image-order algorithms are ray casting and Sabella's method [24]. The splatting algorithm [19], V-buffer algorithm [25], and slice shearing algorithm [26] belong to object–order algorithms. Note that these methods require a voxelization algorithm or an octree structure [18] as a preprocessing step, and have a disadvantage that they are computationally intensive in any case.

As a generalization of the direct volume method, a method based on linear transport theory has been proposed [23]. In this method, the rays are replaced by virtual (light) particles moving through the data field. These particles interact with the 3D field data (which is represented by grid points) and collect information about the light intensity for screen display. The general transport theory model for volume rendering is given by the integro-differential equation. The evaluation of this model requires very expensive computations, and thus techniques such as Monte Carlo simulation, series expansions, and rendering algorithms on massively parallel machines [27] are usually applied with this model. It should be mentioned that the data value and its derivatives at the evaluation points are currently computed by trilinear interpolation, which sometimes may produce incorrect information and should be improved to reduce computational inaccuracy.

Finally, we remark that most of the rendering algorithms have mainly focused on the construction procedures that produce graphic images, not a volume representation. We expect that the volume representation can reduce the amount of computation for rendering images. In fact, too much computation is required for rendering images in the direct volume rendering methods. The volume representation also provides a great deal of information for the improvement of the rendering quality. We suggest that a hypervolume as the volume representation will play a great role in the enhancement of the rendering algorithms. Main features of the hypervolume were listed in detail in the previous section.

V. APPLICATION TO FLOW VISUALIZATION

A. Related Works

Visualizing 3D fluid flow fields has long been a part of fluid dynamics research. Since the 19th century, an experimental flow visualization for showing the patterns resulting from the injection of ink, smoke, or particles in a fluid has been performed. Current computer-aided visualization techniques also basically simulate this experimental visualization scheme.

We can categorize these flow visualization techniques according to the data dimensionality we wish to visualize—scalar, vector, and tensor—or by the object dimensionality to be visualized—points, curves, surfaces, and volumes—or by the scope of the domain of interest—local and global. Reviews of prior works in the classification can be found in [28,29]. In general, common visualization techniques such as arrow plots, streamlines [30], and particle traces work well for 2D applications, while advanced visualization techniques such as stream surfaces [31], tensor probes [32], vector field topology [33,34], and hyperstreamlines [35] are useful for visualizing the velocity field of 3D data sets. In some cases, cutting planes can be effective for viewing slices of 3D data. For example, the flow around an airplane wing may be well displayed using the cross sections of the wing.

These visualization techniques produce colorful and sometimes even beautiful images. However, there are still problems in the visualization of the vector and the tensor fields. The main reason is the inexistence of a flexible volumetric representation that feeds a variety of flow visualization techniques introduced above and makes it possible to analyze the initial flow data more intuitively and productively for the creation of effective 3D graphical presentations.

In most cases, measured or simulated volume data are typically represented as raw data with no prior definition of interesting objects to be visualized. Thus, it is difficult to provide CFD (computational fluid dynamics) researchers with a feature-based visualization, which is increasingly required in order to reduce graphical complexity, increase information contents, and detect complex flow structures intuitively. Feature segmentation, which means the extraction of important characteristics from a data set, is needed for further analysis and interpretation and also is required as a preliminary step for an effective feature-based flow visualization. Vector field topology techniques [33,34] and mathematical morphology techniques [36] are well known as examples of feature segmentation, and iconic representations [28,29,37] are often used for displaying feature data already extracted from a data set. In most cases, this feature segmentation successfully describes the characteristics of a fluid flow field and provides elementary information for further analysis in a continuous computational space referred to as a curvilinear coordinate system. However, they have only a discrete data set as an input resource. That is, they have a large problem in that positional coordinate values and field variables' values at arbitrary positions in a continuous physical domain should be derived from the discrete raw data in the domain.

In the visualization program PLOT3D [38], as in many such packages, the values of field variables within each cell are interpolated by a trilinear function at the computational space coordinates of each query point. Here, very expensive computation is required to convert each query point in physical space into its computational space representation. For this step, the neighboring grid points of the query point should be first searched. The computational loads on the searching problem greatly limit the speed of the global visualization. Note that this basic step is frequently executed as an elementary routine for any visualization. In the basic step introduced above, which can be found in most existing visualization techniques, we can find two problems. One is the computational inaccuracy induced by the trilinear interpolation using a product of the fractional displacements of the query point along each computational space dimension within a grid cell as the relative contribution of each vertex of the grid cell. The other is the computational inefficiency caused by searching the neighbors of the query point directly from a raw data at every time step as already explained. There exists tradeoffs between the two problems. If a higher-order interpolating function is used for the improvement of the accuracy, it requires more additional neighbors of a query point and thus more expensive computational loads.

Now, we will describe the practical examples of a hypervolume as a new volumetric data representation for accurately analyzing 3D vector fields in scientific visualization and supporting all information necessary for the creation of effective 3D graphical presentations. This representation allows a unified mathematical basis to be used as a general framework in the visualization systems. This representation is also independent of any visualization technique being used, and thus is immediately applicable to many current systems. The usefulness of the data representation proposed in this paper will be demonstrated with simple examples of feature segmentation.

B. Application Examples

We have applied a hypervolume to several flow visualization examples. We considered the visualization of the streamlines or stream surfaces for various flow fields. First, a hypervolume is constructed by using the interpolation technique

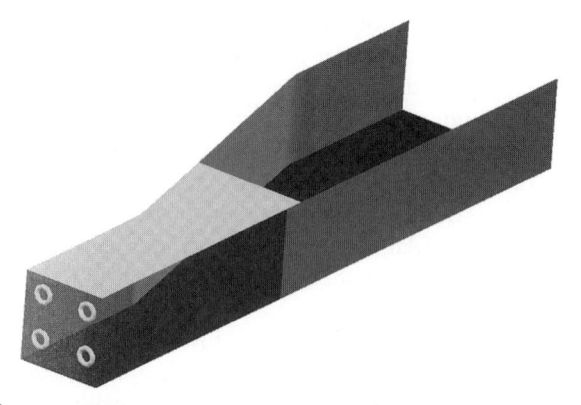

FIGURE 10 A rectangular duct geometry. Reprinted from S. Park and K. Lee, (1997) with permission from Elsevier Science.

developed in this chapter. Then the streamlines or stream surfaces are computed by a procedure to be explained later under Feature Segmentation (see next section). In addition, the pressure as an additional field variable is concurrently derived from the generated hypervolume using the laws of physics. Finally, the computed results are displayed with various different sizes and colors, which map the computed numerical values to the visual images on a computer screen.

Our first example is an internal flow in a rectangular duct as shown in Fig. 10, where several planes are removed to show the duct geometry in detail. Figure 11 shows the four streamtubes in the duct. Note that the starting seed curves of the streamtubes are four circles of the same radius, and the displayed color and radius of the streamtubes indicate the magnitude of flow velocity and the flow pressure, respectively.

Our second example illustrates the capabilities of multiple hypervolumes applied to decomposed flow domains as shown in Fig. 12. Figure 13 shows a

FIGURE 11 Four streamtubes in a rectangular duct where color and radius indicate the flow velocity and pressure, respectively. Reprinted from S. Park and K. Lee, (1997) with permission from Elsevier Science.

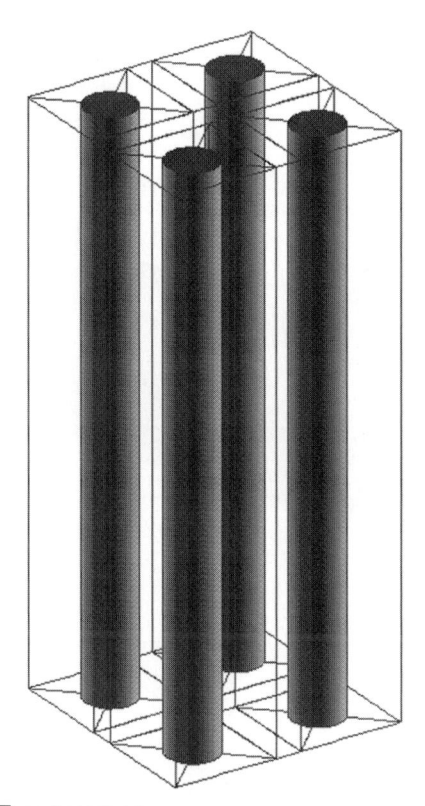

FIGURE 12 Decomposed flow domains in a tube bank. Reprinted from S. Park and K. Lee, (1997) with permission from Elsevier Science.

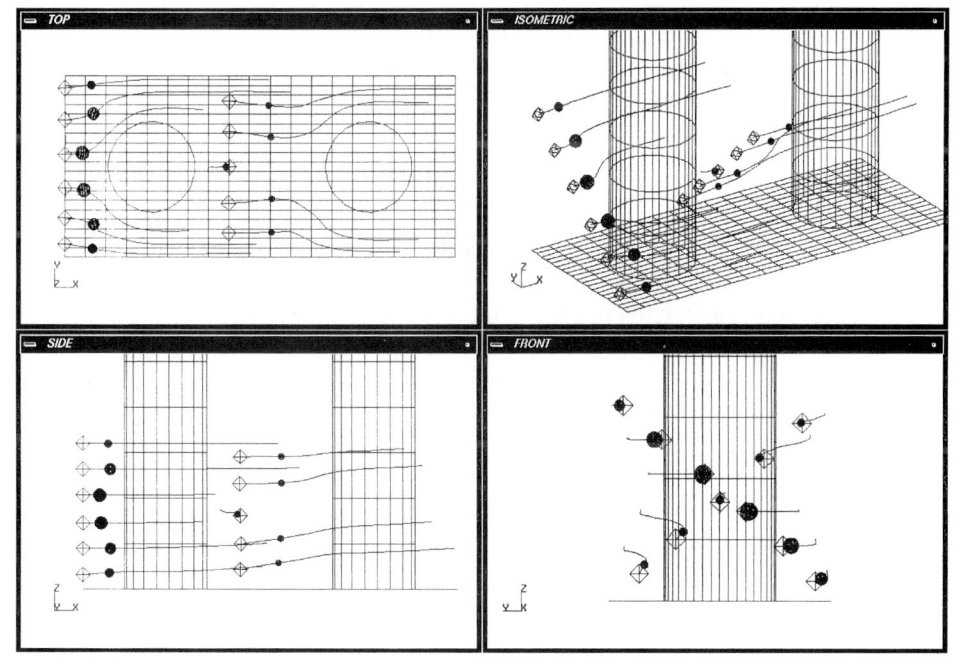

FIGURE 13 Streamlines in a tube bank where the diameter of the particles indicates the pressure. Reprinted from S. Park and K. Lee, (1997) with permission from Elsevier Science.

FIGURE 14 Six streamtubes in a tube bank where color and radius indicate the flow velocity and pressure, respectively. Reprinted from S. Park and K. Lee, (1997) with permission from Elsevier Science.

frame at an instant when particles, having left their start points, are located at specific positions along their trajectories. In the figure, the diameter of the particles indicates the instantaneous pressure along the path. Figure 14 shows the six streamtubes in the tube bank in Fig. 12.

Our third example presents the stream surfaces around an airplane wing as shown in Fig. 15. The starting curve is a line, and the line becomes curved along its trajectory in the figure. Note that the color indicates the relative magnitude of a flow velocity.

C. Feature Segmentation

In this section, we will show how a streamline is generated from the hypervolume as an example of feature segmentation. This example will show the capabilities of our hypervolume for a feature-based visualization. As is well known, a streamline in a steady fluid velocity field is a trajectory of a single small particle injected into the flow. The streamline, being integral curves, gives insight into the global structure of the velocity vector field and serves as a basic element for other flow visualizations; e.g., a stream surface can be seen as a set of streamlines. The streamline in a steady state can be computed by

$$\mathbf{x} = \mathbf{x}_0 + \int_0^t \mathbf{v}\, dt, \qquad \mathbf{v} = \mathbf{v}_0 + \int_0^t \mathbf{a}\, dt \qquad (34)$$

using a velocity vector field $\mathbf{v}(t)$ and an initial seed point $\mathbf{x}_0(t_0)$

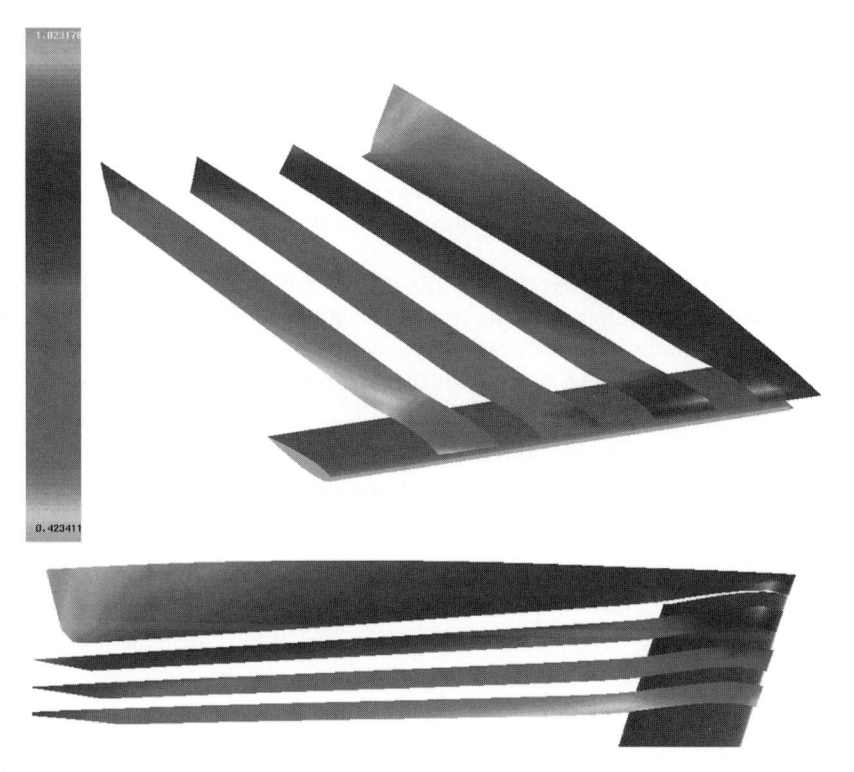

FIGURE 15 Four stream surfaces around an airplane wing where color indicates the flow velocity. Reprinted from S. Park and K. Lee, (1997) with permission from Elsevier Science.

If we assume that the acceleration **a** in Eq. (34) is constant during Δt, then the streamline equation in Eq. (34) can be rewritten as

$$\Delta \mathbf{x} = \mathbf{v}\Delta t + \frac{1}{2}\mathbf{a}(\Delta t)^2. \tag{35}$$

Thus, we can get the streamline if we can compute the term **a** in Eq. (35). The acceleration **a** can be expressed by the velocity **v**, the partial derivatives $\partial \mathbf{v}/\partial u$, $\partial \mathbf{v}/\partial v$, $\partial \mathbf{v}/\partial w$, and the contravariant basic vectors ∇u, ∇v, ∇w as follows.

Since

$$\mathbf{a} = \frac{d\mathbf{v}}{dt} = \frac{\partial \mathbf{v}}{\partial u}\frac{\partial u}{\partial t} + \frac{\partial \mathbf{v}}{\partial v}\frac{\partial v}{\partial t} + \frac{\partial \mathbf{v}}{\partial w}\frac{\partial w}{\partial t}$$

where

$$\frac{\partial u}{\partial t} = \frac{\partial u}{\partial x}\frac{\partial x}{\partial t} + \frac{\partial u}{\partial y}\frac{\partial y}{\partial t} + \frac{\partial u}{\partial z}\frac{\partial z}{\partial t} = \nabla u \cdot \mathbf{v},$$

$$\frac{\partial v}{\partial t} = \frac{\partial v}{\partial x}\frac{\partial x}{\partial t} + \frac{\partial v}{\partial y}\frac{\partial y}{\partial t} + \frac{\partial v}{\partial z}\frac{\partial z}{\partial t} = \nabla v \cdot \mathbf{v},$$

and

$$\frac{\partial w}{\partial t} = \frac{\partial w}{\partial x}\frac{\partial x}{\partial t} + \frac{\partial w}{\partial y}\frac{\partial y}{\partial t} + \frac{\partial w}{\partial z}\frac{\partial z}{\partial t} = \nabla w \cdot \mathbf{v}$$

the acceleration **a** is given by

$$\mathbf{a} = (\nabla u \cdot \mathbf{v})\frac{\partial \mathbf{v}}{\partial u} + (\nabla v \cdot \mathbf{v})\frac{\partial \mathbf{v}}{\partial v} + (\nabla w \cdot \mathbf{v})\frac{\partial \mathbf{v}}{\partial w}. \quad (36)$$

Here we can easily get ∇u, ∇v, ∇w from the geometry volume and **v**, $\partial \mathbf{v}/\partial u$, $\partial \mathbf{v}/\partial v$, $\partial \mathbf{v}/\partial w$ from the attribute volume suggested in this chapter. Note that the parameters, u, v, and w represent three positional coordinates in the parameter space of a hypervolume.

Therefore, we can compute $\Delta \mathbf{x}$ during a time interval Δt from Eqs. (35) and (36). Note that if the time interval Δt decreases, the assumption that **a** is constant during the Δt is reasonably valid and so we can obtain a more realistic streamline during Δt. Finally, the streamline over a full domain of a fluid flow can be easily obtained as follows:

(1) Find (u_0, v_0, w_0) such that $\mathbf{G}(u_0, v_0, w_0) = \mathbf{x}_0$, where $\mathbf{x}_0$ is an initial seed point and $\mathbf{G}(u, v, w)$ is the geometry volume suggested in this chapter. Note that the Newton–Raphson method for solving this nonlinear equation is applied to form

$$\left[\frac{\partial \mathbf{F}(u_i, v_j, w_k)}{\partial u} \frac{\partial \mathbf{F}(u_i, v_j, w_k)}{\partial v} \frac{\partial \mathbf{F}(u_i, v_j, w_k)}{\partial w}\right] \begin{bmatrix} u_{i+1} - u_i \\ v_{j+1} - v_j \\ w_{k+1} - w_k \end{bmatrix} = [-\mathbf{F}(u_i, v_j, w_k)],$$

where $\mathbf{F}(u, v, w) = \mathbf{G}(u, v, w) - \mathbf{x}_0 = 0$.

The Greville abscissa of the control point distanced nearly from the given $\mathbf{x}_0$ is chosen as the initial guess. The convergence is achieved when the differences of $\Delta u = u_{i+1} - u_i$, $\Delta v = v_{j+1} - v_j$, and $\Delta w = w_{k+1} - w_k$ are under the user-supplied parametric tolerance and the value of $\|\mathbf{F}(u_i, v_j, w_k)\|$ is also under the user-supplied spatial tolerance.

(2) Compute **v** at (u_0, v_0, w_0) directly from $\mathbf{A}(u, v, w)$, where $\mathbf{A}(u, v, w)$ is the attribute volume suggested in this chapter.

(3) Compute **a** at (u_0, v_0, w_0) by using Eq. (36) in which each term can be calculated from $\mathbf{G}(u, v, w)$ and $\mathbf{A}(u, v, w)$.

(4) Compute $\Delta \mathbf{x}$ from **v**, **a**, and a given Δt by using Eq. (35), and then obtain $\mathbf{x} = \mathbf{x}_0 + \Delta \mathbf{x}$.

(5) Assign $\mathbf{x}_0$ to $\mathbf{x}$ and repeat step (1).

VI. SUMMARY AND CONCLUSIONS

Most existing visualization systems provide a variety of functionalities concerned with the following major subjects: data models, rendering algorithms, and graphical presentation. A data model involves describing a discrete grid distribution or an unstructured mesh with a native form or data structure, depending on the type, dimensions, and organization of the data. From this data model, a rendering algorithm extracts interesting objects and/or computes their color and opacity values by interpolation. Then a graphical presentation displays these rendering data on a typical computer screen with some graphic techniques aimed at producing realistic images. Most visualization systems follow these ordered procedures where it is worth noting that only a data model allows a wide range of visualization possibilities.

Despite many needs for a data model to build a flexible visualization system and support various application developments, a very powerful data model has not yet been established. The data model should describe adequately the full range of data used, allow a simple evaluation for rendering purposes, and derive all the required data, e.g., higher-order derivative data, from the given data set without additional computations. These requirements or expectations will be sufficiently satisfied if the hypervolume proposed in this chapter is chosen.

We have suggested the hypervolume model as a mathematical representation for modeling and rendering volumetric data, and have described two methods for creating a volume model, depending on the spatial distribution of volumetric data. The interpolated volume method can be applied to the gridded distribution of volumetric data, and the swept volume method can be utilized for volumetric modeling of the cross-sectional distribution of data sets. We have also introduced several gridding methods for scattered volumetric data, from which we can obtain discrete grid points to be directly used in the interpolated volume method. In addition, we have mentioned several rendering methods of volumetric data, all of which can be implemented with a hypervolume.

We are currently verifying that the hypervolume can provide a mathematical framework for the analysis of integrated, multidisciplinary simulations that involve interactions between disciplines such as fluid dynamics, structural dynamics, and solid mechanics. The hypervolume model presented in this chapter has a contribution in these senses.

REFERENCES

1. McCormick, B. H., DeFanti, T. A., and Brown, M. D. (Eds.). "Visualization in Scientific Computing." *Computer Graphics* 21(6): Nov. 1987.
2. Kaufman, A., Cohen, D., and Yagel, R. Volume graphics. *Computer* 26(7):51–64, 1993.
3. Muraki, S. Volume data and wavelet transform. *IEEE Comput. Graphics Appl.* 13(4):50–56, 1993.
4. Franke, R., and Nielson, G. Smooth interpolation of large sets of scattered data. *Internat. J. Numer. Methods Engrg.* 15:1691–1704, 1980.
5. Franke, R., and Nielson, G. Scattered data interpolation and applications: A tutorial and survey. In *Geometric Modeling: Methods and Their Application* (H. Hagen and D. Roller, Eds.), pp. 131–160. Springer-Verlag, Berlin, 1990.
6. Nielson, G. *et al.* Visualization and modeling of scattered multivariate data. *IEEE Comput. Graphics Appl.* 11(3):47–55, 1991.
7. Nielson, G. A method for interpolating scattered data based upon a minimum norm network. *Math. Comp.* 40:253–271, 1983.
8. Casale M. S., and Stanton, E. L. An overview of analytic solid modeling. *IEEE Comput. Graphics Appl.* 5:45–56, 1985.
9. Lasser, D. Bernstein–Bezier representation of volumes. *Comput. Aided Geom. Design* 2:145–149, 1985.
10. Lasser, D., and Hoschek, J. *Fundamentals of Computer Aided Geometric Design*. A K Peters, Wellesley, MA, 1993.
11. de Boor, C. *A Practical Guide to Splines*. Springer-Verlag, New York, 1978.
12. Tiller, W. Rational B-splines for curve and surface representation. *IEEE Comput. Graphics Appl.* 3:61–69, 1983.
13. Hartley, P. J., and Judd, C. J. Parametrization and shape of B-spline curves for CAD. *Comput. Aided Design* 12:235–238, 1980.
14. Farin, G. *Curves and Surfaces for Computer Aided Geometric Design*, pp. 150–151. Academic Press, San Diego, 1990.

15. Agishtein, M. E., and Migda, A. A. Smooth surface reconstruction from scattered data points. *Comput. Graphics (UK)* **15**(1):29–39, 1991.
16. Hibbard, W., and Santek, D. The VIS-5D system for easy interactive visualization. In *Proceedings of Visualization 90* (A. Kaufman, Ed.), pp. 28–35. IEEE Comput. Soc. Press, Los Alamitos, CA, 1990.
17. Shepard, D. A two dimensional interpolation function for irregular spaced data. In *Proceedings 23rd ACM National Conference*, pp. 517–524, 1968.
18. Levoy, M. Efficient ray tracing of volume data. *ACM Trans. Graphics* **9**:245–261, 1990.
19. Westover, L. Footprint evaluation for volume rendering. *Comput. Graphics* **24**(4):367–376, 1990.
20. Nielson, G. M., and Hamann, B. Techniques for the visualization of volumetric data. In *Visualization '90* (A. Kaufman, Ed.), pp. 45–50. IEEE Comput. Soc. Press, Los Alamitos, CA, 1990.
21. Nielson, G. M., Foley, Th. A., and Hamann, B., Lane, D. Visualizing and modeling scattered multivariate data. *IEEE Comput. Graphics Appl.* **11**:47–55, 1991.
22. Pajon, J. L., and Tran, V. B. Visualization of scalar data defined on a structured grid. In *Visualization '90* (A. Kaufman, Ed.), pp. 281–287. IEEE Comput. Soc. Press, Los Alamitos, CA, 1990.
23. Krüger, W. The application of transport theory to visualization of 3D scalar data fields. *Comput. Phys.* (July/Aug): 397–406, 1991.
24. Sabella, P. A rendering algorithm for visualizing 3D scalar fields. *ACM Comput. Graphics* **22**:51–58, 1988.
25. Upson, C., and Keeler, M. V-BUFFER: Visible volume rendering. *ACM Comput. Graphics* **22**:59–64, 1988.
26. Lacroute, P., and Levoy, M. Fast volume rendering using a shear-warp factorization of the viewing transformation. *Comput. Graphics* **28**(4):451–458, 1994.
27. Krüger, W., and Schroder, P. Data parallel volume rendering algorithms for interactive visualization. *Visual Comput.* **9**:405–416, 1993.
28. Hesselink, L., and Delmarcelle, T. Visualization of vector and tensor data sets. In *Frontiers in Scientific Visualization* (L. Rosenblum et al., Eds.). Academic Press, New York, 1994.
29. Delmarcelle, T., and Hesselink, L. A unified framework for flow visualization. In *Engineering Visualization* (R. Gallagher, Ed.). CRC Press, Boca Raton, FL, 1994.
30. Kenwright, D., and Mallinson, G. A streamline tracking algorithm using dual stream functions. In *Proceedings of Visualization '92*, pp. 62–68. IEEE Comput. Soc. Press, Los Alamitos, CA, 1992.
31. Hultquist, J. P. M. Constructing stream surfaces in steady 3D vector fields. In *Proceedings of Visualization '92*, pp. 171–178. IEEE Comput. Soc. Press, Los Alamitos, CA, 1992.
32. de Leeuw, W. C., and van Wijk, J. J. A probe for local flow field visualization. In *Proceedings of Visualization '93*, pp. 39–45. IEEE Comput. Soc. Press, Los Alamitos, CA, 1993.
33. Helman, J., and Hesselink, L. Visualizing vector field topology in fluid flows. *IEEE Comput. Graphics Appl.* **11**:36–46, 1991.
34. Globus, A., Levit, C., and Lasinski, T. A tool for visualizing the topology of 3D vector fields. In *Proceedings of Visualization '91*, pp. 33–40. IEEE Comput. Soc. Press, Los Alamitos, CA, 1991.
35. Delmarcelle, T., and Hesselink, L. Visualizaing second-order tensor fields with hyperstreamlines. *IEEE Comput. Graphics Appl.* **13**:25–33, 1993.
36. Silver, D., and Zabusky, N. J. Quantifying visualizations for reduced modeling in nonlinear science: Extracting structures from data sets. *J. Visual Commun. Image Represent.* **4**:46–61, 1993.
37. Kerlick, G. D. Moving iconic objects in scientific visualization. In *Proceedings of Visualization '90* (A. Kaufman, Ed.), pp. 124–130. IEEE Comput. Soc. Press, Los Alamitos, CA, 1990.
38. Buning, P. G., and Steger, J. L. Graphics and flow visualization in CFD. In *AIAA 7th CFD Conference*, Cincinnati, OH, AIAA Paper 85-1507-CP, pp. 162–170, 1985.
39. Park, S., and Lee, K. High-dimensional trivariate NURBS representation for analyzing and visualizing fluid flow data. *Computers and Graphics* **21**(4):473–482, 1997.

15 THE DEVELOPMENT OF DATABASE SYSTEMS FOR THE CONSTRUCTION OF VIRTUAL ENVIRONMENTS WITH FORCE FEEDBACK

HIROO IWATA

Institute of Engineering Mechanics and Systems, University of Tsukuba, Tsukuba 305-8573, Japan

   I. INTRODUCTION   550
      A. Haptic Interface   550
      B. Issues in Haptic Software   552
  II. LHX   554
      A. Basic Structure of LHX   554
      B. Implementation of LHX   556
      C. Haptic User Interface   557
 III. APPLICATIONS OF LHX: DATA HAPTIZATION   557
      A. Basic Idea of Haptization   557
      B. Methods of Haptization   559
      C. Volume Haptics Library   561
 IV. APPLICATIONS OF LHX: 3D SHAPE DESIGN USING AUTONOMOUS VIRTUAL OBJECT   563
      A. Shape Design and Artificial Life   563
      B. Methods for Interaction with Autonomous Virtual Objects   564
      C. Direct Manipulation of Tree-Like Artificial Life   564
      D. Manipulation of Autonomous Free-Form Surface   565
  V. OTHER APPLICATIONS OF LHX   570
      A. Surgical Simulator   570
      B. Shared Haptic World   570
      C. HapticWeb   571
 VI. CONCLUSION   571
      REFERENCES   571

I. INTRODUCTION

It is well known that sense of touch is inevitable for understanding the real world. Force sensation plays an important role in the manipulation of virtual objects. A haptic interface is a feedback device that generates skin and muscle sensation, including sense of touch, weight, and rigidity. We have been working in research on haptic interfaces in virtual environments for a number of years. We have developed various force feedback devices and their applications. In most cases of haptic interfaces, software of a virtual environment is tightly connected to the control program of force displays. This problem is a hazard for development of further applications of haptic virtual environments. In 1991, we started a project for the development of a modular software tool for a haptic interface. The system was called VECS at the time. We have been improving the software tools to support various force displays and their applications [3,4,6]. Our latest system is composed of seven modules: the device driver of force display, haptic renderer, model manager, primitive manager, autonomy engine, visual display manager, and communication interface. The system is called LHX, named for library for haptics. Various types of force displays can be plugged into LHX. This chapter introduces techniques and applications in the development of a database system for haptic environments using LHX.

A. Haptic Interface

A haptic interface, or force display, is a mechanical device that generates reaction forces from virtual objects. Research activities into haptic interfaces have been rapidly growing recently, although the technology is still in a state of trial-and-error. There are three approaches to implement an haptic interface: tool handling-type force display, exoskeleton-type force display, and object-oriented-type force display. We have developed prototypes in each category.

1. Tool Handling-Type Force Display

Tool handling-type force display is the easiest way to realize force feedback. The configuration of this type is similar to a joystick. Virtual world technology usually employs glove-like tactile input devices. Users feel anxious when they put on one of these devices. If the glove is equipped with a force feedback device, the problem is more severe. This disadvantage obstructs practical use of the haptic interface. Tool handling-type force display is free from being fitted to the user's hand. Even though it cannot generate force between the fingers, it has practical advantages.

We developed a 6-DOF (degree-of-freedom) force display which has a ball grip [5]. The device is called "HapticMaster" and is commercialized by Nissho Electronics Co. (Fig. 1). The HapticMaster is a high-performance force feedback device for desktop use. This device employs a parallel mechanism in which a top triangular platform and a base triangular platform are connected by three sets of pantographs. The top end of the pantograph is connected with a vertex

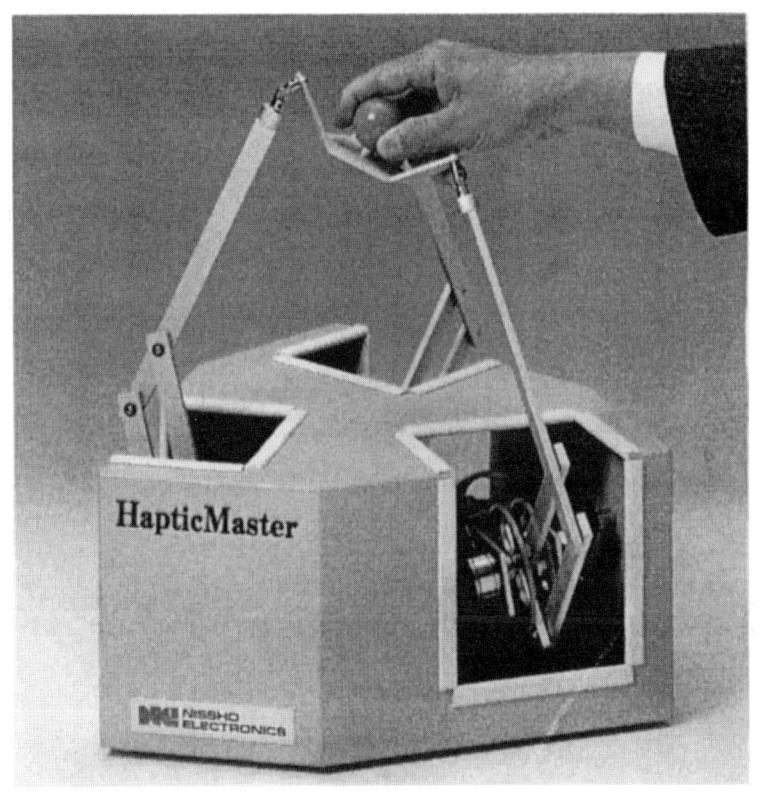

CONSTRUCTION OF VIRTUAL ENVIRONMENTS

FIGURE 1 HapticMaster.

of the top platform by a spherical joint. This compact hardware has the ability of carrying a large payload. Each pantograph has three DC motors.

The grip of HapticMaster can be replaced to fit specialized applications. A simulator of laparoscopic surgery, for example, has been developed by attaching a real tool for surgery on the top plate of the HapticMaster.

2. Exoskeleton-Type Force Display

In the field of robotics research, master manipulators are used in teleoperation. Most master manipulators, however, have large hardware with high costs, which restricts their application areas. In 1989, we developed a compact master manipulator as a desktop force display [2]. The core element of the device is a 6-DOF parallel manipulator, in which three sets of pantograph link mechanisms are employed. Three actuators are set coaxially with the first joint of the thumb, forefinger, and middle finger of the operator.

We improved the device by increasing the degrees-of-freedom for each finger. We have developed a new haptic interface that allows 6-DOF motion for three independent fingers: thumb, index finger and middle finger [12]. The device has three sets of 3-DOF pantographs, at the top of which three 3-DOF gimbals are connected. A thimble is mounted at the end of each gimbal. The thimble is carefully designed to fit the finger tip and is easy to put on or take

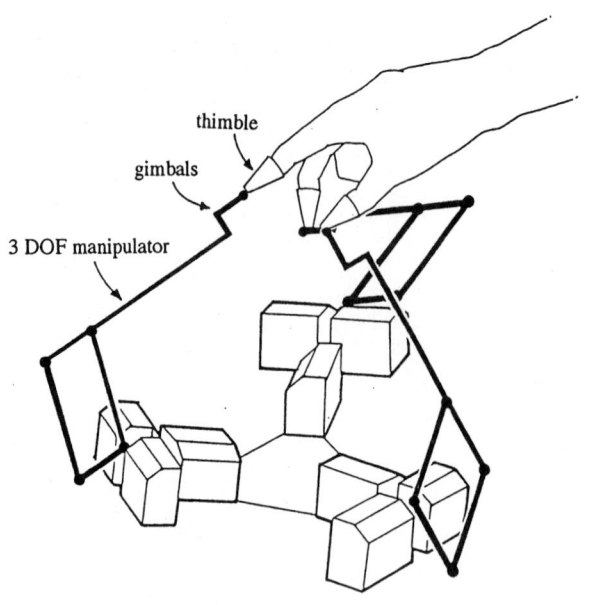

FIGURE 2 Force display for three fingers.

off. The device applies 3-DOF force at each finger tip. The user can grasp and manipulate virtual objects by their three fingers. Figure 2 illustrates the mechanical configuration of the device. This device is easily realized by replacing the top platform of the HapticMaster with three gimbals with thimbles.

3. Object-Oriented-Type Force Display

Object-oriented-type force display is a radical idea of design of a haptic interface. The device moves and deforms to present shapes of virtual objects. A user of the device can make contact with a virtual object by its surface. It allows natural interaction as compared to that of exoskeleton and tool handling type. However, it is fairly difficult to implement. Furthermore, its ability to simulate virtual objects is limited. Because of these characteristics, object-oriented type is effective for specific applications. We focused on 3D shape modeling as an application of our object-oriented-type force display. We have developed a prototype named Haptic Screen [13]. The device employs an elastic surface made of rubber. An array of actuators is set under the elastic surface. The surface deforms by the actuators. Each actuator has force sensors. Hardness of the surface is made variable by these actuators and sensors. Deformation of a virtual object occurs according to the force applied by the user. Figure 3 illustrates the mechanical configuration of the Haptic Screen.

B. Issues in Haptic Software

Software tool for development of a virtual environment is one of the key technologies in the field of virtual reality. There are commercially available software tools such as WorldToolKit, dVS, and Super Scape VRT [7–9]. Those softwares are not designed to support a haptic interface.

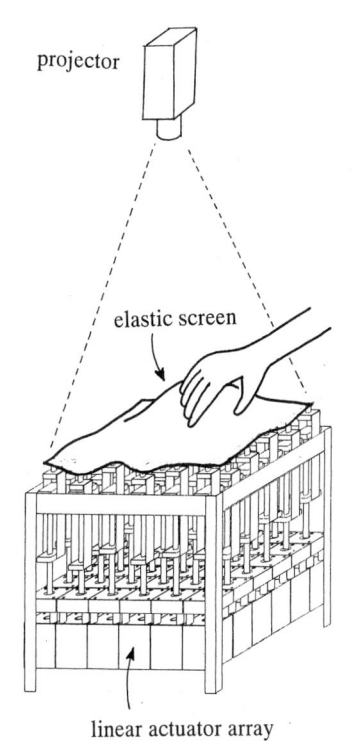

FIGURE 3 Haptic Screen.

Recently research on haptic interfaces has been growing rapidly, although software for a haptic interface is at an early state. Sensable Device developed GHOST as a software tool for their commercial haptic interface named PHANToM [11]. Another example of haptic software is found in the work by the University of North Carolina at Chapel Hill. They developed Armlib, which supports the PHANToM and ARGONE remote manipulator [10].

Issues in haptic software can be summarized in the following aspects, and LHX is designed to deal with these issues:

(1) *Wide applicability of the mechanical configuration of a haptic interface.* The PHANToM and ARGONE remote manipulator have similar mechanisms. The design of a haptic interface has wide valuation as to the mechanical configuration as discussed later. One of the focuses of LHX is how to support various configurations of a haptic interface.

(2) *Construction of a haptic user interface.* Haptic software should support easy construction of a user environment. LHX has primitives for construction of a user interface with force feedback.

(3) *Network capability.* Collaboration in virtual space is one of the major applications of virtual reality. LHX has network capability for constructing a haptic virtual environment shared by multiple users.

(4) *Connection with visual display.* In most applications, a haptic interface is connected to a visual display. LHX includes a visual display interface.

II. LHX

A. Basic Structure of LHX

In order to deal with the issues in haptic software discussed in the previous section, LHX is composed of seven modules: a device driver of force display, a haptic renderer, a model manager, a primitive manager, an autonomy engine, a visual display manager, and a communication interface. By dividing these modules, force displays and virtual environments are easily reconfigured. Figure 4 shows the basic structure of LHX.

Functions of those modules are as follows:

1. Device Driver

A device driver manages sensor input and actuator output for a haptic interface. Various types of haptic interface can be connected to LHX by changing the device driver. We developed a device driver of above-mentioned force displays so that they can be connected to LHX.

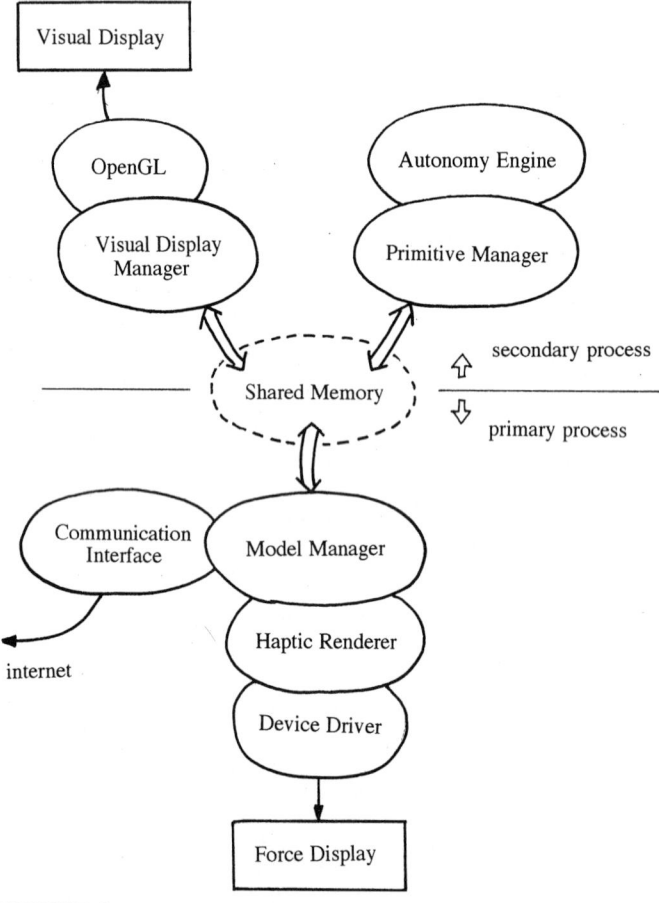

FIGURE 4 Basic structure of LHX.

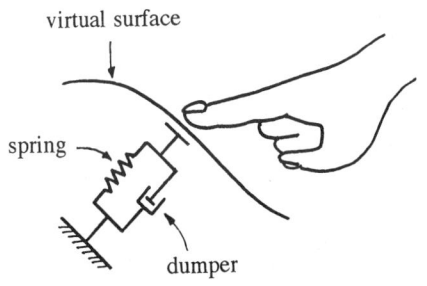

FIGURE 5 Surface haptic renderer.

2. Haptic Renderer

Currently rendering means generation of a visual image. However, force sensation also needs rendering. Hardness, weight, and viscosity of virtual objects are generated by haptic rendering. We have developed a software package for haptic rendering. Haptic render of LHX has three categories according to three types of force displays:

a. Tool Handling-Type Renderer

LHX supports two haptic renders: surface renderer and volume renderer. Surface renderer is implemented by a spring and dumper model (Fig. 5). Volume renderer is implemented by mapping voxel data to force and torque (Fig. 6).

b. Exoskeleton-Type Renderer

Exoskeleton-Type force display applies force to multiple fingers. A renderer of this category is composed of multiple surface renderers of tool handling type.

c. Object-Oriented-Type Renderer

An object-oriented-type renderer determines the stiffness of the surface of Haptic Screen according to the physical model of the virtual object.

3. Model Manager

A model of virtual objects is implemented in the model manager module of LHX. The shapes and attributes of virtual objects are defined in this module.

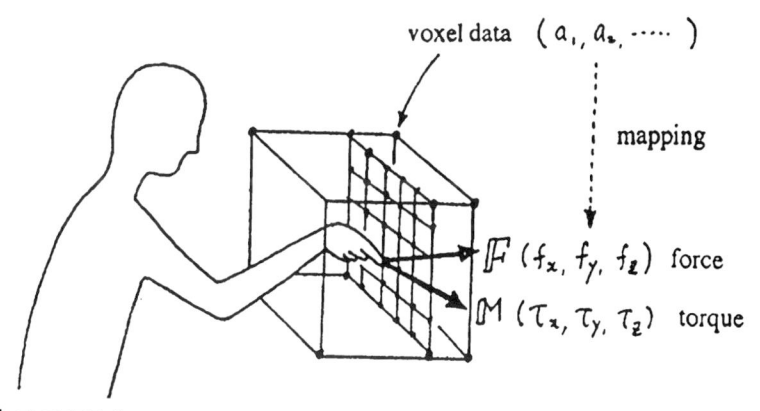

FIGURE 6 Volume haptic renderer.

Users of the LHX program determine the methods for interaction between the virtual objects and the operators.

4. Primitive Manager

Primitives of virtual objects are stored in the primitive manager. Primitives include cube, sphere, cylinder, free-form surface, and 3D voxels. Haptic icons for the user interface are also included. This module supervises the ID code of each primitive. Users of LHX interactively generate or erase primitives. Working primitives are placed in shared memory.

5. Autonomy Engine

An autonomy engine determines the behavior of virtual objects. Physical laws of the virtual world are contained in this module. Gravity, elasticity, and viscosity are currently implemented. Collisions between primitives are detected in real time. This module defines "time" of a virtual environment. The time of a virtual environment increases independently from the user. This function enables autonomous growth of virtual objects.

6. Communication Interface

LHX has a network interface by which multiple force displays are connected to each other. Multiple users can simultaneously interact in the same virtual environment. This function enables easy construction of a groupware program. LHX supports TCP/IP so that the system can use the existing Internet.

7. Visual Display Manager

The visual display manager generates graphic images of a virtual environment. This module translates the haptic model into OpenGL format. HMD, stereo shutter glasses, and a spherical screen are supported as visual displays.

B. Implementation of LHX

LHX is currently implemented in SGI and Windows NT workstations. Considering the connection of a haptic interface to a visual image generator, SGI and Windows NT workstations are the most promising platforms. C++ is used for its implementation. Since our force displays are interfaced with PCs, the device driver module is implemented in a PC. The host workstation and PC are connected by RS-232C.

LHX is composed of two processes: visual feedback and force feedback. The visual feedback process runs the visual display manager, primitive manager, and autonomy engine. The force feedback process runs the other modules. Shared memory is used for communication between these processes. The required update rate of force feedback is much higher than that of visual feedback. Images can be seen continuously at an update rate of 10 Hz. On the other hand, force feedback requires 40 Hz at least. In LHX the force feedback process has a higher priority than the visual feedback process. LHX enables a high update rate of force display in a complex virtual environment.

FIGURE 7 Haptic icon.

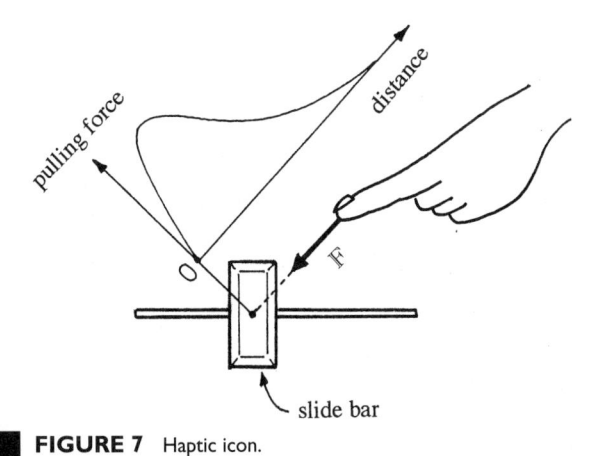

C. Haptic User Interface

Unlike a conventional 2D user interface, operation in a 3D virtual environment is complicated. It is usually difficult to point a button, which is floating in 3D space. We therefor have developed 3D icons with force feedback. When the user's hand comes close to a haptic icon, it is pulled toward the center of the icon. Figure 7 indicates the pulling force around a haptic icon. The user does not need to point the button precisely due to this pulling force, so that the performance of the pointing task is improved.

Primitives of LHX include haptic icons for user interface. Figure 8 shows a typical user interface of LHX. The user of the system sees his/her virtual hand, virtual objects, and virtual control panels. Virtual control panels include buttons or slide bars. In Fig. 8, four buttons are located on the left-hand side and a slide bar is located on the right. A virtual object seen at the center is a free-form surface. Command input and parameter settings are done through these devices. If the virtual hand comes close to these buttons, the hand is pulled toward the center of the buttons by force display. This applied force assists the user to operate the control panels. If the user grasps the button, the color of the button changes and the command is inputted.

III. APPLICATIONS OF LHX: DATA HAPTIZATION

A. Basic Idea of Haptization

Scientific visualization is a major application area of virtual reality. The recent evolution of computer graphics technology enables real-time interactive presentation of scientific data. Simulations and scientific experiments often produce data in the form of a large number of values within a three-dimensional coordinate space. This information is often hard to comprehend in numerical form. Volume visualization is a powerful tool for investigators of those data.

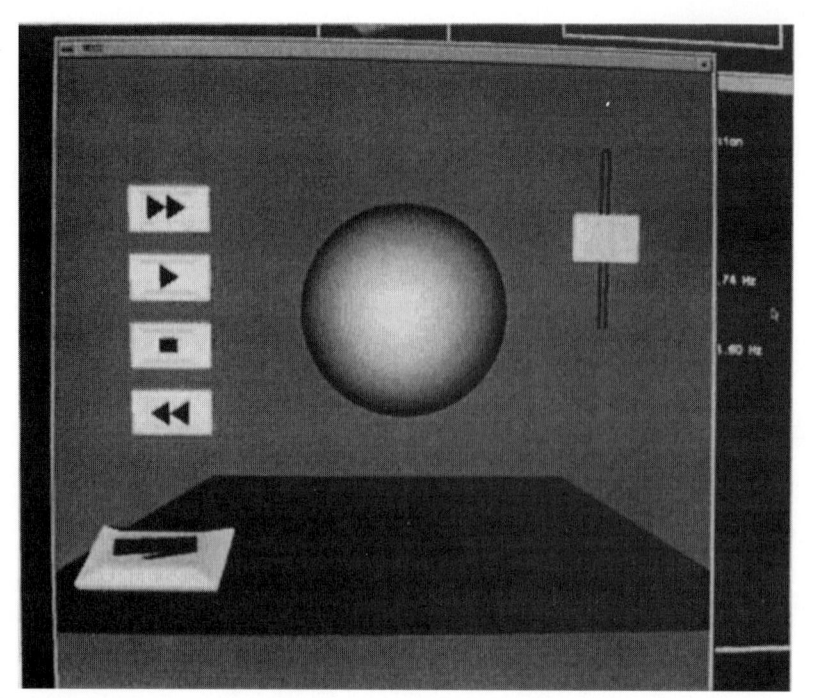

FIGURE 8 User interface of LHX.

Visual information essentially consists of a two-dimensional image. A three-dimensional scene is recognized by binocular parallax cues or motion parallax. Complex 3D objects are often difficult to comprehend because of occlusion. A possible method for visual representation of such objects is semi-transparent graphics. However, multiple objects are overlapped in the image. This drawback leads to difficulty in distinguishing objects.

Visual representation of higher-dimensional and multiparameter data sets is a much harder problem. A typical technique for visualizing those data is iconification. For example, a vector field of fluid dynamics is visualized by streamline. Effectiveness of the technique depends on icon design. Inadequate design of icons leads to a misunderstanding of volume data. Moreover, higher-dimensional values, such as four or five, are difficult to be mapped to icons.

The major objective of our research is representation of volume data by force sensation. Force sensation plays an important role in the recognition of 3D objects. An example of haptic representation of scientific data is found in the work of Brooks *et al.* [1]. A complex molecular docking task is assisted by a force reflective master manipulator. In this work, force display is used for magnifying the length and scale of molecules. We are proposing the haptic mapping of general physical fields.

Force sensation contains six-dimensional information: three-dimensional force and three-dimensional torque. Therefore, higher-dimensional data can be represented by force sensation. The basic idea of volume haptization is mapping voxel data to force and/or torque (Fig. 6). The Haptic Master is used for volume haptization. The force display is combined with real-time visual images of volume data.

B. Methods of Haptization

Volume data consist of scalar, vector, or tensor data found in a three-dimensional space. Data consisting of single scalar values is the simplest case. Often multiple parameters occur at the same voxel, some of which are sets of scalars and vectors. For example, data from computational fluid dynamics may consist of a scalar for density and vectors for velocity. Visualization of such multiparameter data sets is a difficult problem. A combination of visualization techniques can be used, but there is a danger of the image becoming confusing.

We propose representation of volume data by force sensation. Our force display has an ability to apply six-dimensional force and torque at the fingertips. Values at each voxel can be mapped to force and/or torque. Visual information has an advantage of presenting whole images of objects. On the other hand, haptic information has an advantage in presenting complex attributes of local regions. In our system, a visual image of volume data is represented by direct volume rendering using semi-transparent graphics.

Methods of haptization can be classified into the following three categories:

1. Haptic Representation of Scalar Data

There are two possibilities for mapping scalar data to force/torque. One is mapping scalar values to torque vectors:

$$T_z = a[S(x, y, z)], \qquad (1)$$

where $S(x, y, z)$ is a scalar value at each voxel and a is a scaling factor. In this case, the direction of these torque vectors is the same. The user's hand is twisted at each voxel. The other method is mapping gradients of scalar values to three-dimensional force vectors (Fig. 9):

$$F = a[-\text{grad } S(x, y, z)]. \qquad (2)$$

This formula converts the scalar field to a three-dimensional potential field. The user's hand is pulled toward a low-potential area. This method magnifies the

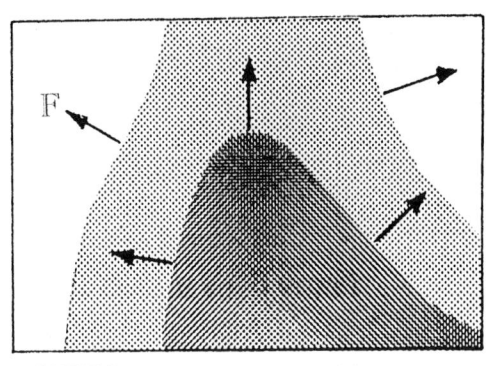

FIGURE 9 Haptic representation of density.

transition area of density data. As for medical imaging such as ultrasound scanning, voxel data are classified according to density. Representation of gradients by force will be effective in such applications.

2. Haptic Representation of Vector/Tensor Data

Vector data have three components, so it can be directly mapped to force:

$$F = aV(x, y, z), \tag{3}$$

where $V(x, y, z)$ are vector data at each voxel. Tensor data is given by a matrix that has nine components. These components cannot be directly mapped to a haptic channel. Some components must be selected according to the user's interest:

$$F \text{ or } T = a(T_{ij}, T_{kl}, T_{mn}), \tag{4}$$

where T_{ij} is a selected component of tensor data at each voxel.

In the case of data from computational fluid dynamics, velocity is mapped to force and one component of vorticity is mapped to torque whose axis has the same direction as the velocity vector (Fig. 10). Velocity and vorticity are simultaneously represented by force display.

3. Haptic Representation of Multiparameter Data Sets

Multiparameter data sets that consist of one or more scalars and vectors can be mapped to force and torque. For example, velocity is mapped to force and density is mapped to one component of torque:

$$F = aV(x, y, z) \tag{5}$$

$$T_z = b[S(x, y, z)]. \tag{6}$$

Representation of multiparameter data sets is rather difficult in the selection of components of a haptic channel. If two different data such as density and

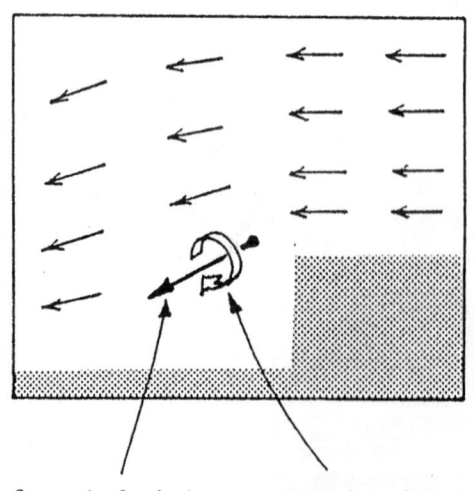

force (velocity)   torque (vorticity)

FIGURE 10 Haptic representation of flow field.

CONSTRUCTION OF VIRTUAL ENVIRONMENTS 561

temperature are mapped to two components of torque, it may confuse the user. In such case, one scalar data may possibly be represented by auditory channel.

C. Volume Haptics Library

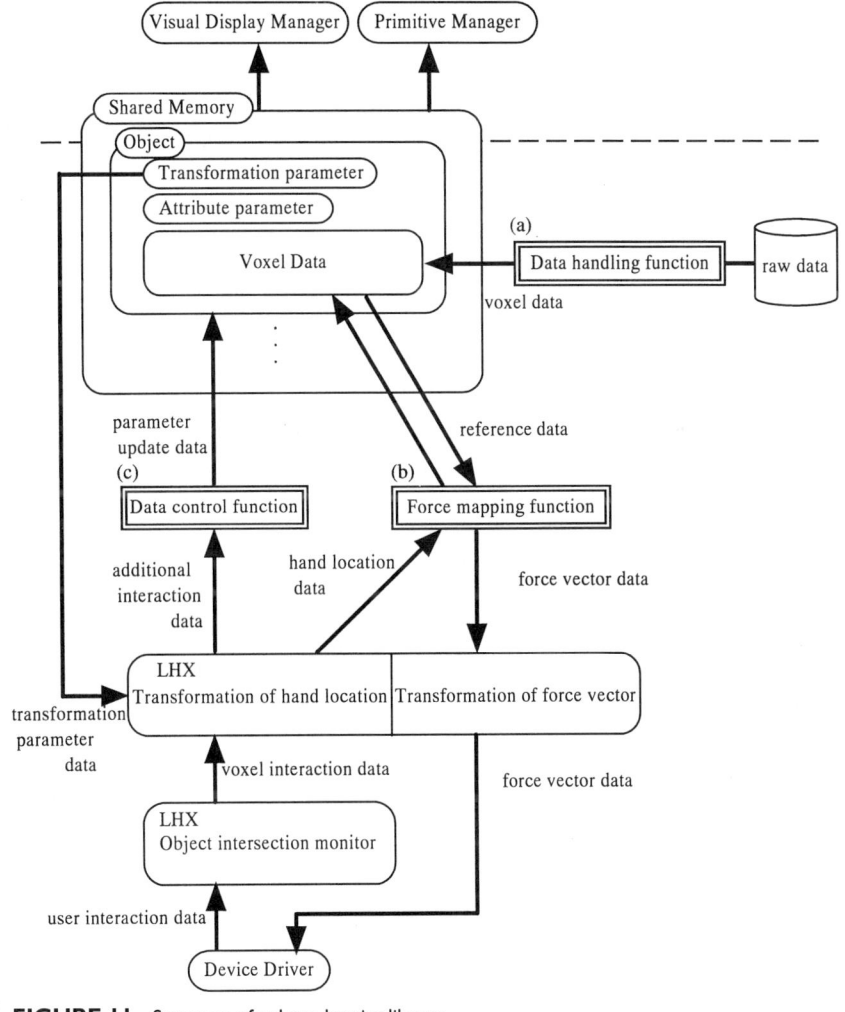

1. Structure of the Volume Haptics Library

LHX includes "volume haptics library." The library supports management of massive volumetric data, and mapping methods of parameters to force. The volume haptics library provides the following three function sets in order to realize environment of volume haptization. Figure 11 shows the structure of these function sets.

FIGURE 11 Structure of volume haptics library.

a. Data Handling Function

Volumetric data should be stored in the memory in order to represent all of the data as visual/haptic at once. To maintain a high update rate in visual/haptic servo loop, the data management function preloads all of the volumetric data into shared memory and reconstructs original data before the servo loop begins. The data management function also serves as a preprocessor of data for compression or extraction.

b. Mapping Method

We should define how to generate haptic feedback from stored volumetric data. We implemented a force/torque mapping method, which is generated from scalar/vector voxel data to the volume render function. Therefore, minimum change of the function makes it possible to exchange another method of haptic representation. In Fig. 11, this function receives hand location data based on a voxel's local coordinates. Then the function refers to shared memory in order to generate the force vector.

c. Data Control Function

In order to treat volumetric data as a primitive, it is necessary to attach the primitive attribute to the volumetric data. The data control function gives such additional primitive parameters so that LHX can utilize various functions such as position transformation or collision detection. As the user moves/rotates the volumetric data, the data control function updates the transformation parameter, and then LHX looks up the parameter to change the coordinate system of the user's hand.

2. Application of Volume Haptics Library

Two applications have been developed by using the three functions mentioned in the previous section. The first one is a multidimensional data browser that presents virtual 4D or higher-dimensional space represented by visual and haptic sensation [16]. In principle force sensation contains six-dimensional information: three-dimensional force and three-dimensional torque. Therefore, six-dimensional data can be represented by force sensation. Our multidimensional space where the data are exposed as volumetric data are geometrically generated by scanning a 3D cube. The user's hand can essentially move in 3D space. We therefore use rotational motion of the hand for scanning a 3D cube in a multidimensional cube. The 3D cube is cutout of the volume of the multidimensional cube, which moves by rotational motion around the roll and the pitch axes of the user's hand. Force display presents the potential field, which indicates the axis of rotation. The user can easily separate rotational motion from transnational motion by a haptic guide.

The second application is a noninvasive surgery support system. This system proposes a method of haptic representation of a noninvasive area to support the system of microsurgery [17]. In case the virtual tool approaches the noninvasive area, force is applied to the operator's hand. Generated force is determined by volume data of the CT image. Figure 12 shows haptic representation of CT data.

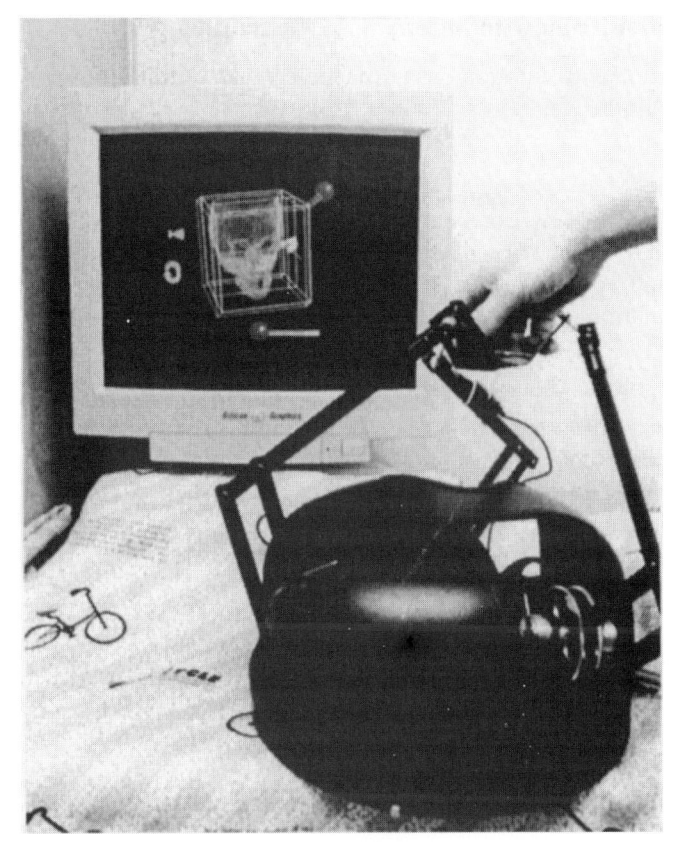

FIGURE 12 Haptic representation of CT data.

IV. APPLICATIONS OF LHX: 3D SHAPE DESIGN USING AUTONOMOUS VIRTUAL OBJECT

A. Shape Design and Artificial Life

The design of 3D shapes is a major application area of virtual reality. Direct manipulation of 3D shapes has been realized in virtual environments. In this case, the shape of the object is originally determined by a human designer. This chapter proposes autonomously growing objects in a virtual environment. Designers are often inspired by the shapes of living creatures.

The creation of living systems by computer software is called artificial life. The major objective of research on artificial life is duplicating the emergent mechanics of biology. We have tried to introduce the emergent mechanics in a virtual environment. The user of our system can interact with artificial life in its morphological process. Parameters of congenital characteristics can be interactively changed. An artificial life shape can be directly manipulated by the user during its growing process. In this way, the autonomous shape and the intentional shape are mixed. Artificial life is implemented as a user application of LHX.

B. Methods for Interaction with Autonomous Virtual Objects

Interaction with autonomous virtual objects can be done through the following three parameters:

1. Time

Our virtual environment has a time clock supervised by the kernel of LHX. Growth or autonomous deformation occurs according to this time clock. The user can freely change the speed of time, and he/she can also reverse it. Direct manipulation of time increases the freedom of the design process.

2. Congenital Characteristics

Autonomous 3D shapes have congenital characteristics, which determine their morphological process. The user can arbitrary change the congenital characteristics. The variation of congenital characteristics results in different shapes. Manipulation of congenital characteristics leads to unexpected forms of virtual objects. In our system, congenital characteristics can be changed in the virtual objects growing process.

3. Acquired Characteristics

Acquired characteristics are obtained by direct manipulation of virtual objects by the user, who can deform autonomous virtual objects at any time.

LHX supports implementation of these parameters.

C. Direct Manipulation of Tree-Like Artificial Life

A tree-like virtual object is selected as artificial life. The principle of growth of the tree is illustrated in Fig. 13. A cylinder in the figure indicates the trunk of the tree. The length and diameter of the cylinder increases according to the time clock of LHX. Ramification occurs in preset frequency. At first, the ramification point h_i is randomly selected from five points as shown in Fig. 13a. Then growth direction L_{jk} is randomly selected from eight point as shown in Fig. 13b. After these selection, a new cylinder appears (Fig. 13c). This principle is applied to the new cylinder. Figure 14 shows an example of the growth of a tree.

The user can directly manipulate the tree-like artificial life by three parameters: time, congenital characteristics, and acquired characteristics. The time of the virtual environment is controlled by four buttons: start, stop, fast forward, and reverse. These buttons are set on the left hand-side of the virtual environment. Operation of the buttons is similar to that of a VCR. Congenital characteristics are determined by the frequency of ramification, which is controlled by a slide bar located on the right-hand side of the virtual environment. Acquired characteristics are determined by chopping off the branches by the user's virtual hand. Branches can be chopped off at any ramification point while the tree is growing. The user can intentionally form the final shape of the tree. This procedure is similar to "bonsai" or dwarf-tree culture.

CONSTRUCTION OF VIRTUAL ENVIRONMENTS 565

(a) SELECT RAMIFICATION POINT h_i

(b) SELECT GROWTH DIRECTION L_{jk}

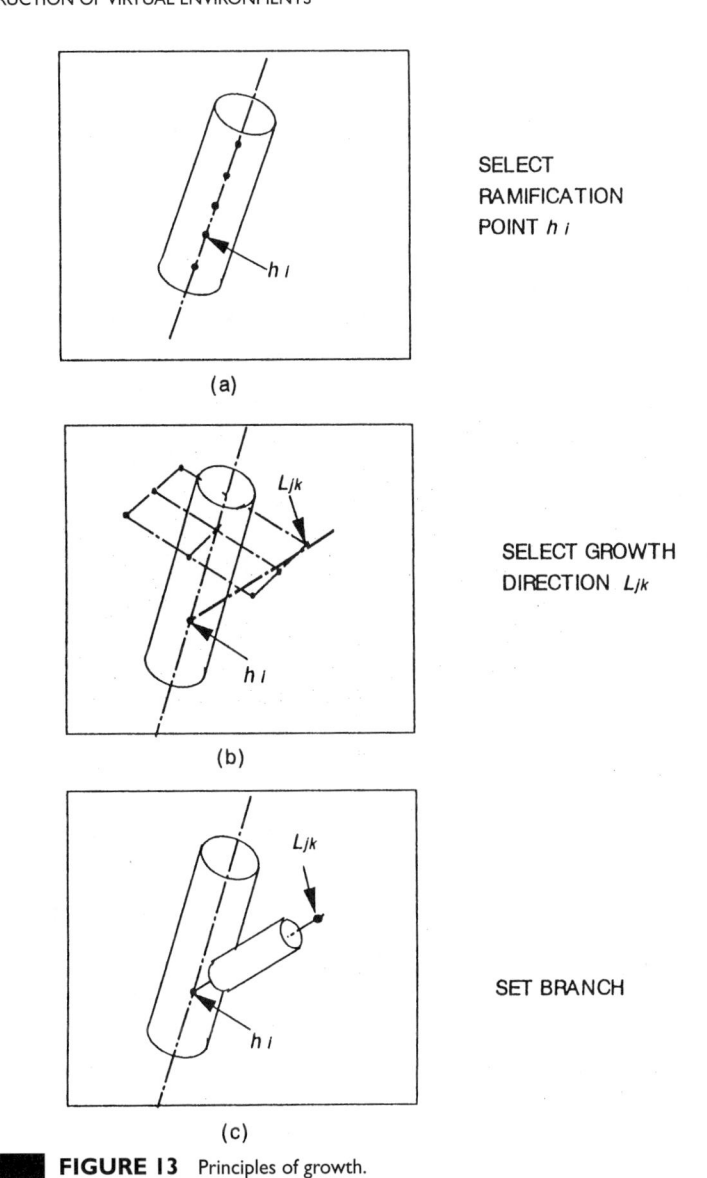

(c) SET BRANCH

FIGURE 13 Principles of growth.

D. Manipulation of Autonomous Free-Form Surface

1. Functions of Autonomous Free-Form Surface

Industrial designers often make a simple mockup using urethane or styrene boards in order to study the theme of the form at the early stage of design development. This process is called form study. We developed an autonomous free-from surface in a virtual environment as a tool for form study [4]. The original shape of the surface is a sphere. The user can freely deform the surface.

FIGURE 14 Virtual tree.

The basic theme of the form is created through deformation of the sphere. We implemented three functions in the autonomous surface:

a. Restoration

Each lattice of the surface is connected by four springs (Fig. 15). These springs generate surface tension. If the surface is pulled or pushed by the user, the surface tension restores the surface to the original sphere (Fig. 16). Unexpected shapes are found during the autonomous deformation process. The user can manipulate the surface while it is autonomously deforming. In

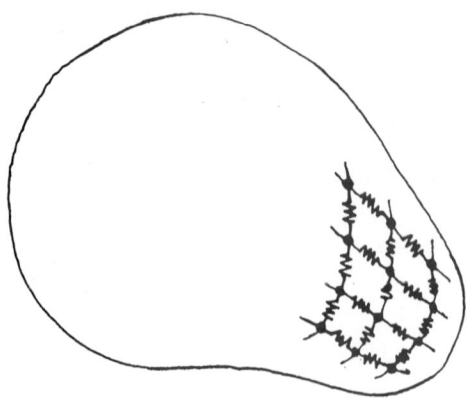

FIGURE 15 Mechanism of surface tension.

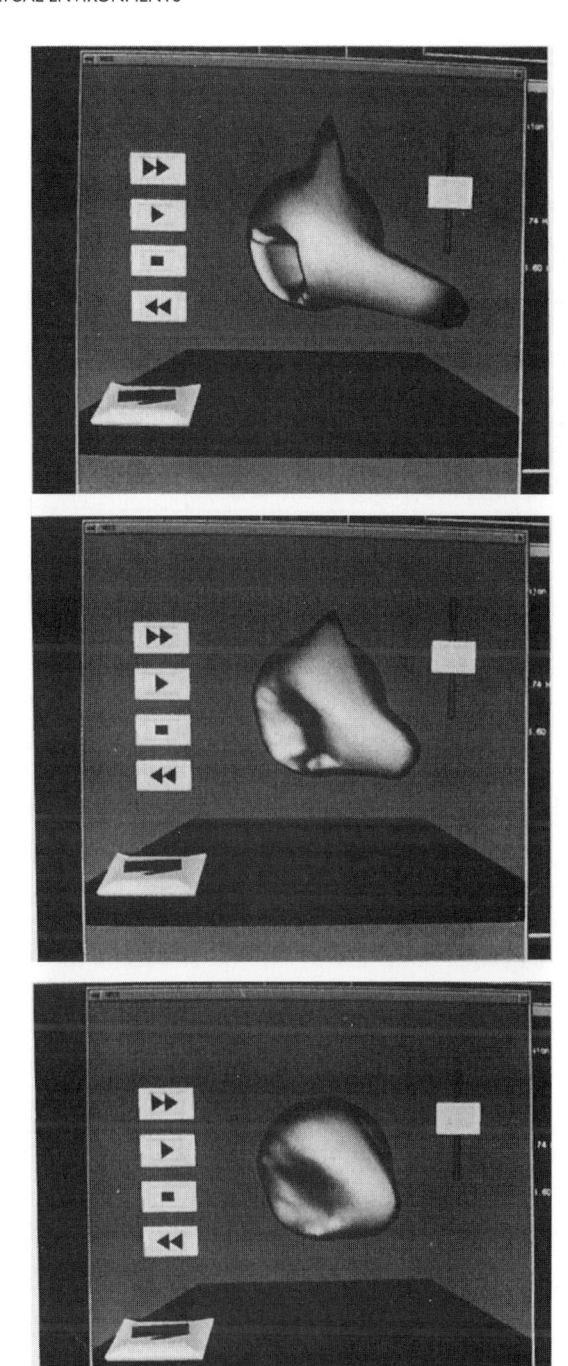

FIGURE 16 An example of restoration.

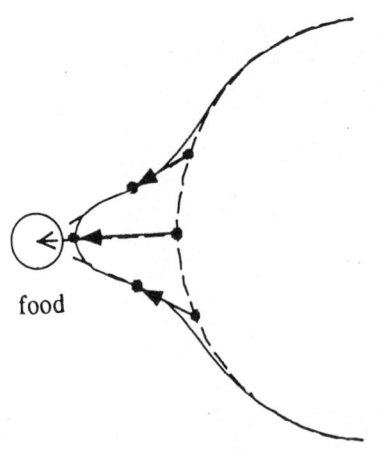

FIGURE 17 Mechanism of reaching action to food.

this case, congenital characteristics are determined by the spring constant of surface tension. The user can change the spring constant by a slide bar. If the spring constant is large, deformation spreads to a wider area.

b. Reaching Action to Food

The user can put out "food" for the surface. If the food comes near, the surface reaches out to it. The motion of each lattice is caused according to the distance between the surface and the food. Transition from the original surface is determined by a negative exponential function (Fig. 17). If the food is large, a large area of the surface deforms.

c. Avoidance from Enemy

The user can put out "enemy" for the surface. If the enemy comes near, the surface avoids it. The motion of each lattice is caused according to the distance between the surface and the enemy. Transition from the original surface is

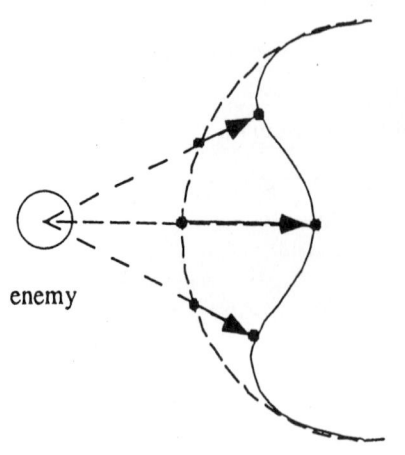

FIGURE 18 Mechanism of avoidance from enemy.

CONSTRUCTION OF VIRTUAL ENVIRONMENTS 569

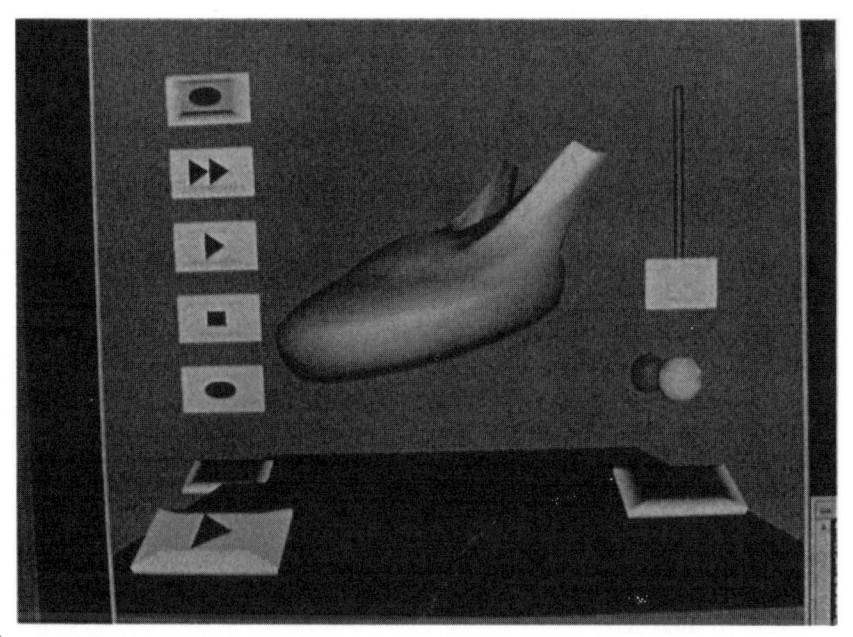

FIGURE 19 An example of a pattern for the form study of car design.

determined by a negative exponential function (Fig. 18). If the enemy is large, a large area of the surface deforms.

2. Usability Study

As a usability tests of the autonomous free-form surface, we examined the modeling task of a complex curved surface. We prepared three patterns, which represent shapes of form study for car design. Figure 19 shows an example of the patterns. Subjects are instructed to make these patterns from a spherical surface.

Two conditions are set for the experiment:

(1) *With function of restoration.* The surface autonomously deforms according to its surface tension.

(2) *Without function of restoration.* In this case, the surface is passive. The subjects make shapes by direct manipulation of the free-form surface. A deformed surface is determined by a sine curve.

We took six volunteer subjects from the students of our university. We examined the accuracy of the modeling task. The deformation distance at each lattice from the original surface was calculated. The total deformation distance was normalized by that of the target pattern. If the error value is 1, the task was perfect. Figure 20 shows the normalized deformation distance of the two conditions. The value of condition (1) is nine times smaller than that of condition (2). The required time for each task was approximately 2 min. for both conditions. Subjects often abandoned making shapes under condition (2). The results show that an autonomous free-form surface improves design tasks.

FIGURE 20 Accuracy of modeling.

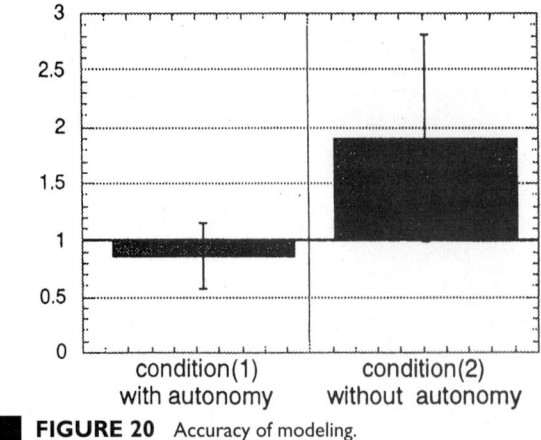

V. OTHER APPLICATIONS OF LHX

A. Surgical Simulator

Laparoscopic surgery requires training in a virtual environment. We are collaborating with Olympus Co. on developing a training simulator for laparoscopy [15]. Two specialized HapticMasters are used for both hands. LHX supports two force displays simultaneously.

Primitives of LHX include autonomous free-form surfaces. The surface has functions similar to that of living creatures. The free-form surface has surface tension, which enables restoration to the original shape. We developed virtual tissue by using an autonomous free-form surface. An operator can feel viscoelasticity of the virtual tissue. The virtual tissue can be cut at any place in realtime.

B. Shared Haptic World

Existing communication media supports only visual and auditory information. We have tried to use haptic information as a tool for communication. We used the network capability of LHX to connect two force displays in the same virtual environment. The two users of our system were able to feel the reaction force simultaneously. They can cooperatively manipulate virtual objects. One user can grasp the other user's virtual hand, and feel the force applied by the other user. This function is beneficial for trainer–trainee interaction.

In the case of using the Internet as a communication line, there is a time delay between the two force displays. We developed visual and haptic aid to assist the work under a time delay. Users of the system were able to feel viscosity while moving the hands. The force realizes natural collaboration under a time delay.

At SIGGRAPH'95, we connected two force displays by Internet. One was located in Los Angels and the other in Tsukuba, Japan. We succeeded in cooperative work between those remote sites [6]. The time delay was constantly 0.4 s.

C. HapticWeb

The "HapticWeb" is a WWW client, which enables a user to feel the rigidity or weight of a virtual object. HapticWeb uses the haptic renderer of LHX. It realizes force feedback from the VRML data set. Users can feel the rigidity or weight of virtual objects stored in a WWW server. The system was demonstrated at SIGGRAPH'96.

We also developed an authoring tool for the HapticWeb. Parameters of the rigidity and weight of virtual objects are presented by 3D icons. The user can change the rigidity or weight of virtual objects by manipulating slide bars.

We observed the behavior of users at SIGGRAPH'96. A total of 647 people experienced our system. Of these, 637 people (98%) could feel force feedback, 446 people (69%) found haptic icons, and 642 people (99%) of them could manipulate the slide bars. The result shows that the design of the haptic icon was successful.

VI. CONCLUSION

This chapter introduced techniques and applications in the development of a database system for a haptic environment. We developed a software infrastructure for a haptic interface named LHX. It achieved the reproductivity of software of virtual environments with force feedback. The software tool has been improved through various applications including haptization of scientific data and 3D shape manipulation. Future work will be the further development of practical software tools such as the volume haptic library.

REFERENCES

1. Brooks, F. P. *et al.* Project GROPE—Haptic displays for scientific visualization. *ACM SIGGRAPH Comput. Graphics* 24(4):177–185, 1990.
2. Iwata, H. Artificial reality with force-feedback: Development of desktop virtual space with compact master manipulator. *ACM SIGGRAPH Comput. Graphics* 24(4):165–170, 1990.
3. Iwata, H., and Yano, H. Artificial life in haptic virtual environment. In *Proceedings of ICAT'93*, pp. 91–96, 1993.
4. Iwata, H., and Yano, H. Interaction with autonomous free-form surface. In *Proceedings of ICAT'94*, pp. 27–32, 1994.
5. Iwata, H. Desktop force display. In *SIGGRAPH'94 Visual Proceedings*, 1994.
6. Yano, H., and Iwata, H. Cooperative work in virtual environment with force feedback. In *Proceedings of ICAT/VRST'95*, pp. 203–210, 1995.
7. *World Tool Kit User's Guide*, SENSE8.
8. dVS, http://www.ptc.com/products/division/index.htm.
9. ViScape, available at http://www.superscape.com.
10. Mark, W. R. *et al.* Adding force feedback to graphics system: Issues and solutions. In *Proceedings of SIGGRAPH'96*, pp. 447–452, 1996.
11. Brochure of SensAble Technologies. GHOST: General Haptics Open Software Toolkit, 1996.
12. Iwata, H., and Hayakawa, K. Force display for grasping virtual object by three fingers. In *Proceedings of the Eleventh Symposium on Human Interface*, pp. 395–400, 1995. [In Japanese.]
13. Iwata, H., and Ichigaya, A. Haptic screen. In *Proceedings of the Virtual Society of Japan Annual Conference*, Vol. 1, pp. 7–10, 1996. [In Japanese.]

14. Iwata, H., and Noma, H. Volume haptization. In *Proceedings of IEEE Symposium on Research Frontiers in Virtual Reality,* pp. 91–96, 1993.
15. Asano, T., Yano, H., and Iwata, H. Basic technology of simulation system for laparoscopic surgery in virtual environment with force display. In *Medicine Meets Virtual Reality,* pp. 207–215, IOS Press.
16. Hashimoto, W., and Iwata, H. Multi-dimensional data browser with haptic sensation. In *Transactions of the Virtual Reality Society of Japan,* Vol. 2, No. 3, pp. 9–16, 1997. [In Japanese.]
17. Hashimoto, W., and Iwata, H. Haptic representation of non-invasive region for surgery based on volumetric Data. In *Transactions of the Virtual Reality Society of Japan,* Vol. 3, No. 4, pp. 197–202, 1998. [In Japanese.]

16

DATA COMPRESSION IN INFORMATION RETRIEVAL SYSTEMS

SHMUEL TOMI KLEIN

Department of Computer Science, Bar-Ilan University, Ramat Gan 52900, Israel

- I. INTRODUCTION 573
- II. TEXT COMPRESSION 579
    - A. Huffman Coding 582
    - B. Huffman Coding without Bit Manipulations 585
    - C. Space-Efficient Decoding of Huffman Codes 595
    - D. Arithmetic Coding 602
    - E. Dictionary-Based Text Compression 604
- III. DICTIONARIES 607
- IV. CONCORDANCES 609
    - A. Using Variable-Length Fields 611
    - B. Model-Based Concordance Compression 618
- V. BITMAPS 622
    - A. Usefulness of Bitmaps in IR 622
    - B. Compression of Bitmaps 624
- VI. FINAL REMARKS 631
    - REFERENCES 631

I. INTRODUCTION

As can be seen from the title, we shall concentrate on techniques that are at the crossroads of two disciplines: *data compression* (DC) and *information retrieval* (IR). Each of these encompass a large body of knowledge that has evolved over the past decades, each with its own philosophy and its own scientific community. Nevertheless, their intersection is particularly interesting, the various files of large full-text IR systems providing a natural testbed for new compression methods, and DC enabling the proliferation of improved retrieval algorithms.

A chapter about data compression in a book published at the beginning of the twenty-first century might at a first glance seem anachronistic. Critics will say that storage space is getting cheaper every day; tomorrow it will be almost given for free, so who needs complicated methods to save a few bytes. What these critics overlook is that for data storage, supply drives demand: our appetite for getting ever-increasing amounts of data into electronic storage grows just as steadily as does the standard size of the hard disk in our current personal computer. Most users know that whatever the size of their disks, they will fill up sooner or later, and generally sooner than they wish.

However, there are also other benefits to be gained from data compression, beyond the reduction of storage space. One of the bottlenecks of our computing systems is still the slow data transfer from external storage devices. Similarly, for communication applications, the problem is not storing the data but rather squeezing it through some channel. However, many users are competing for the same limited bandwidth, effectively reducing the amount of data that can be transferred in a given time span. Here, DC may help reduce the number of I/O operations to and from secondary memory, and for communication it reduces the actual amount of data that must pass through the channel. The additional time spent on compression and decompression is generally largely compensated for by the savings in transfer time.

For these reasons, research in DC is not dying out, but just the opposite is true, as evidenced by the recent spurt of literature in this area. An international Data Compression Conference has convened annually since 1990, and many journals, including even popular ones such as *Byte, Dr. Dobbs, IEEE Spectrum, Datamation, PC Magazine,* and others, have repeatedly published articles on compression recently.

It is true that a large part of the research concentrates on image compression. Indeed, pictorial data are storage voracious so that the expected profit of efficient compression is substantial. The techniques generally applied to images belong to the class of *lossy* compression, because they concentrate on how to throw away part of the data, without too much changing its general appearance. For instance, most humans do not really see any difference between a picture coded with 24 bits per pixel, allowing more than 16 million colors, and the same picture recoded with 12 bits per pixel, giving "only" about 4000 different color shades. Of course, most image compression techniques are much more sophisticated, but we shall not deal with them in the present survey. The interested reader is referred to the large literature on lossy compression, e.g., [1].

Information retrieval is concerned, on the one hand, with procedures for helping a user satisfy his information needs by facilitating his access to large amounts of data, on the other hand, with techniques for evaluating his (dis)satisfaction with whatever data the system provided. We shall concentrate primarily on the algorithmic aspects of IR. A functional full-text retrieval system is constituted of a large variety of files, most of which can and should be compressed. Some of the methods described below are of general applicability, and some are specially designed for an IR environment.

Full-text information retrieval systems may be partitioned according to the level of specificity supported by their queries. For example, in a system operating at the *document* level, queries can be formulated as to the presence of certain keywords in each document of the database, but not as to their exact locations within the document. Similarly, one can define the *paragraph* level and *sentence* level, each of which is a refinement of its predecessor. The highest specificity level is the *word* level, in which the requirement is that the keywords appear within specified distances of each other. With such a specificity level, one could retrieve all the occurrences of A and B such that there are at least two but at most five words between them. In the same way, the paragraph and sentence levels permit also appropriate distance constraints; e.g., at the sentence level one could ask for all the occurrences of A and B in the same or adjacent sentences.

Formally, a typical query consists of an optional level indicator, m keywords, and $m - 1$ distance constraints, as in

$$level : A_1\,(l_1, u_1)\, A_2\,(l_2, u_2) \cdots A_{m-1}(l_{m-1}, u_{m-1})\, A_m. \quad (1)$$

The l_i and u_i are (positive or negative) integers satisfying $l_i \leq u_i$ for $1 \leq i < m$, with the couple (l_i, u_i) imposing lower and upper limits on the distance from A_i to A_{i+1}. Negative distance means that A_{i+1} may appear before A_i in the text. The distance is measured in words, sentences, or paragraphs, as prescribed by the level indicator. In case the latter is omitted, word level is assumed; in this case, constraints of the form $A\,(1, 1)\,B$ (meaning that A should be followed immediately by B) are omitted. Also, if the query is on the document level, then the distances are meaningless and should be omitted (the query degenerates then into a conjunction of the occurrences of all the keywords in the query).

In its simplest form, the keyword A_i is a single word or a (usually very small) set of words given explicitly by the user. In more complex cases a keyword A_i in (1) will represent a set of words $A_i = \bigcup_{j=1}^{n_i} A_{ij}$, all of which are considered synonymous to A_i in the context of the given query. For example, a variable-length-don't-care-character * can be used, which stands for an arbitrary, possibly empty, string. This allows the use of prefix, suffix, and infix truncation in the query. Thus A_i could be comput*, representing, among others, the words computer, computing, computerize, etc., or it could be *mycin, which retrieves a large class of antibiotics; infix truncation also can be useful for spelling foreign names, such as Ba*tyar, where * could be matched by h, k, kh, ch, sh, sch, etc.

Another possibility for getting the variants of a keyword is from the use of a *thesaurus* (month representing January, February, etc.), or from some morphological processing (do representing does, did, done, etc.). Although these grammatical variants can be easily generated in some languages with simple morphology like English, sophisticated linguistic tools are needed for languages such as Hebrew, Arabic, and many others. One of the derivatives of the 2-character word daughter in Hebrew, for example, is a 10-character string meaning and when our daughters, and it shares only *one* common letter with its original stem; a similar phenomenon occurs in French with the verb faire, for example.

For all these cases, the families A_i are constructed in a preprocessing stage. Algorithms for generating the families identified by truncated terms can be found in [2], and for the families of grammatical variants in [3].

This general definition of a query with distance constraints allows great flexibility in the formulation of the query. For example, the query solving (1,3) differential equations will retrieve sentences containing solving differential equations, as well as solving these differential equations and solving the required differential equations, but not solving these systems of differential equations. The query true (−2,2) false can be used to retrieve the phrases true or false and false or true; since these words appear frequently in some mathematical texts, searching for true and false in the same sentence could generate noise. A lower bound greater than 1 in the distance operators is needed, for example, when one wishes to locate phrases in which some words X_1, X_2, ... appear, but the juxtaposition of these words $X_1 X_2$ ... forms an idiomatic expression that we do not wish to retrieve. For example, ...the security of the council members assembled here... should be retrieved by the query security (2,4) council. Note however that (1) implies that one can impose distance constraints only on adjacent keywords. In the query A (1,5) B (2,7) C, the pair (2,7) refers to the distance from B to C. If we wish to impose positive bounds on the distances from A to both B and C, this can be done by using negative distances, C (−7,−2) A (1,5) B, but this procedure cannot be generalized to tying more than two keywords to A.

A well-known problem in retrieval systems is the handling of "negative" keywords, i.e., words, the *absence* of which, in a specified distance from a specified context, is required. A negation operator (represented here by the minus sign −) is particularly useful for excluding known homonyms so as to increase precision. For example, searching for references to the former U.S. President, one could submit the query Reagan (−2,1) −Donald. Another interesting example would be to use the constraints $(l_i, u_i) = (0,0)$ in order to restrict some large families of keywords, as in the example comput∗ (0,0) −computer∗, which would retrieve computing, computation, etc, but not computer or computers. The general definition of a query as given in (1) should therefore include the possibility of negating some—but not all—of the keywords while specifying their appropriate distance constraints.

Queries of type (1) can be of course further combined by the Boolean operators of AND, OR, and NOT, but we shall restrict our attention here to queries of type (1), since they are quite common, on the one hand, and on the other, their efficient processing is anyway a prerequisite to the efficient processing of more complicated ones.

At the end of the search process, the solutions are presented to the user in the form of a list of the identifying numbers or the titles of the documents that contain at least one solution, possibly together with the text of the sentence (or the paragraph) in which this solution occurs. The exact details of the display depend on the specific system, on the target population, and on the human–interface design of the system.

The way to process such queries depends on the size of the database. When the size of the text is small, say up to a few hundred kilobytes, the problem of efficiently accessing the data can generally be solved by some brute-force method that scans the whole text in reasonable time. Such a method is commonly used in text editors. At the other extreme, for very large databases spanning hundreds of megabytes, a complete scan is not feasible. The usual approach in that case is to use so-called *inverted files*.

Every occurrence of every word in the database can be uniquely characterized by a sequence of numbers that give its exact position in the text; typically, in a word-level retrieval system, such a sequence would consist of the document number, the paragraph number (in the document), the sentence number (in the paragraph), and the word number (in the sentence). These are the *coordinates* of the occurrence. For every word W, let $C(W)$ be the ordered list of the coordinates of all its occurrences in the text. The problem of processing a query of type (1) consists then, in its most general form, of finding all the m-tuples $(a_1, \ldots, a_m)$ of coordinates satisfying

$$\forall i \in \{1, \ldots, m\} \quad \exists j \in \{1, \ldots, n_i\} \quad \text{with} \quad a_i \in C(A_{ij})$$

and

$$l_i \leq d(a_i, a_{i+1}) \leq u_i \quad \text{for } 1 \leq i < m,$$

where $d(x, y)$ denotes the distance from x to y on the given level. Every m-tuple satisfying these two equations is called a *solution*.

In the inverted files approach, processing (1) does not involve directly the original text files, but rather the auxiliary *dictionary* and *concordance* files. The concordance contains, for each distinct word W in the database, the ordered list $C(W)$ of all its coordinates in the text; it is accessed via the dictionary that contains for every such word a pointer to the corresponding list in the concordance. For each keyword A_i in (1) and its attached variants A_{ij}, the lists $C(A_{ij})$ are fetched from the concordance and merged to form the combined list $C(A_i)$. Beginning now with A_1 and A_2, the two lists $C(A_1)$ and $C(A_2)$ are compared, and the set of all pairs of coordinates (a_1, a_2) that satisfy the given distance constraints (l_1, u_1) at the appropriate level is constructed. (Note that a unique a_1 can satisfy the requirements with different a_2, and vice versa.) $C(A_2)$ is now purged from the irrelevant coordinates, and the procedure is repeated with A_2 and A_3, resulting in the set $\{(a_1, a_2, a_3)\}$ of partial solutions of (1). Finally, when the last keyword A_m is processed in this way, we have the required set of solutions.

Note that it is not really necessary to always begin the processing with the first given keyword A_1 in (1), going all the way in a left-to-right mode. In some cases, it might be more efficient to begin it with a different keyword A_j, and to proceed with the other keywords in some specified order.

The main drawback of the inverted files approach is its huge overhead: the size of the concordance is comparable to that of the text itself and sometimes larger. For the intermediate range, a popular technique is based on assigning *signatures* to text fragments and to individual words. The signatures are then transformed into a set of bitmaps, on which Boolean operations, induced by the structure of the query, are performed. The idea is first to effectively reduce the size of the database by removing from consideration segments that cannot possibly satisfy the request, then to use pattern-matching techniques to process the query, but only over the—hopefully small—remaining part of the database [4]. For systems supporting retrieval only at the document level, a different approach to query processing might be useful. The idea is to replace the concordance of a system with ℓ documents by a set of *bitmaps* of fixed length ℓ. Given some fixed ordering of the documents, a bitmap $B(W)$ is constructed for every distinct word W of the database, where the ith bit of $B(W)$ is 1 if W occurs in the ith document, and is 0 otherwise. Processing queries then reduces to performing logical OR/AND operations on binary sequences, which is easily done on most machines, instead of merge/collate operations on more general sequences. Davis and Lin [5] were apparently the first to propose the use of bitmaps for secondary key retrieval. It would be wasteful to store the bitmaps in their original form, since they are usually very sparse (the great majority of the words appear in very few documents), and we shall review various methods for the compression of such large sparse bit-vectors. However, the concordance can be dropped only if *all* the information we need is kept in the bitmaps. Hence, if we wish to extend this approach to systems supporting queries also at the paragraph, sentence, or word level, the length of each map must equal the number of paragraphs, sentences, or words respectively, a clearly infeasible scheme for large systems. Moreover, the processing of distance constraints is hard to implement with such a data structure.

In [6], a method in which, basically, the concordance and bitmap approaches are combined is presented. At the cost of marginally expanding the inverted files' structure, compressed bitmaps are *added* to the system; these maps give *partial* information on the location of the different words in the text and their distribution. This approach is described in more detail in Section V.

Most of the techniques below were tested on two real-life full-text information retrieval systems, both using the inverted files approach. The first is the *Trésor de la Langue Française* (TLF) [7], a database of 680 MB of French language texts (112 million words) made up from a variety of complete documents including novels, short stories, poetry, and essays, by many different authors. The bulk of the texts are from the 17th through 20th centuries, although smaller databases include texts from the 16th century and earlier. The other system is the *Responsa Retrieval Project* (RRP) [8], 350 MB of Hebrew and Aramaic texts (60 million words) written over the past ten centuries. For the sake of conciseness, detailed experimental results have been omitted throughout.

Table 1 shows roughly what one can expect from applying compression methods to the various files of a full-text retrieval system. The numbers correspond to TLF. Various smaller auxiliary files are not mentioned here, including grammatical files, and thesauri.

For the given example, the overall size of the system, which was close to 2 Gbytes, could be reduced to fit onto a single CD-Rom.

The organization of this chapter is as follows. The subsequent sections consider, in turn, compression techniques for the file types mentioned above, namely, the text, dictionaries, concordances, and bitmaps. For text compression, we first shortly review some background material. While concentrating on Huffman coding and related techniques, arithmetic coding and dictionary-based text compression are also mentioned. For Huffman coding, we focus in particular on techniques allowing fast decoding, since decoding is more important than encoding in an information retrieval environment. For dictionary and

TABLE I   Files in a Full-Text System

File	Full size (MB)	Compressed size (MB)	Compression (%)
Text	700	245	65
Dictionary	30	18	40
Concordance	400	240	40
Bitmaps	800	40	95
Total		543	

concordance compression the prefix omission method and various variants are suggested. Finally, we describe the usefulness of bitmaps for the enhancement of IR systems and then show how these large structures may in fact be stored quite efficiently.

The choice of the methods to be described is not meant to be exhaustive. It is a blend of techniques that reflect the personal taste of the author rather than some well-established core curriculum in information retrieval and data compression. The interested reader will find pointers to further details in the appended references.

II. TEXT COMPRESSION

We are primarily concerned with information retrieval; therefore this section will be devoted to text compression, as the text is still the heart of any large full-text IR system. We refer to text written in some natural language, using a fixed set of letters called an *alphabet*. It should, however, be noted that the methods below are not restricted to textual data alone, and are in fact applicable to any kind of file. For the ease of discourse, we shall still refer to texts and characters, but these terms should not be understood in their restrictive sense.

Whatever text of other file we wish to store, our computers insist on talking only binary, which forces us to transform the data using some binary *encoding*. The resulting set of elements, called *codewords*, each corresponding to one of the characters of the alphabet, is called a *code*. The most popular and easy to use codes are *fixed-length* codes, for which all the codewords consist of the same number of bits. One of the best-known fixed-length codes is the American Standard Code for Information Interchange (ASCII), for which each codeword is 1 byte (8 bits) long, providing for the encoding of $2^8 = 256$ different elements.

A fixed-length code has many advantages; most obviously, the encoding and decoding processes are straightforward. Encoding is performed by concatenating the codewords corresponding to the characters of the message; decoding is done by breaking the encoded string into blocks of the given size, and then using a decoding table to translate the codewords back into the characters they represent. For example, the ASCII representation of the word Text is

01010100011001010111100001110100,

which can be broken into

01010100 | 01100101 | 01111000 | 01110100.

From the compression point of view, such a code may be wasteful. A first attempt to reduce the space of an ASCII encoding is to note that if the actual character set used is of size n, only $\lceil \log_2 n \rceil$ bits are needed for each codeword. Therefore a text using only the 26 letters of the English alphabet (plus up to six special characters, such as space, period, comma, etc.) could be encoded using just five bits per codeword, saving already 37.5%. However, even for larger alphabets an improvement is possible if the frequency of occurrence of the different characters is taken into account.

As is well known, not all the letters appear with the same probability in natural language texts. For English, E, T, and A are the most frequent, appearing

A	0	A	11	A	11	A	1
B	01	B	110	B	011	B	00
C	110	C	1100	C	0011	C	010
D	1011	D	1101	D	1011	D	0110
		E	11000	E	00011	E	0111
(a)		(b)		(c)		(d)	

FIGURE 1 Examples of codes: (a) Non-UD, (b) UD nonprefix, (c) prefix noncomplete, and (d) complete.

about 12, 10, and 8% respectively, while J, Q, and Z occur each with probability less than 0.1%. Similar phenomena can be noted in other languages. The skewness of the frequency distributions can be exploited if one is ready to abandon the convenience of fixed-length codes, and trade processing ease for better compression by allowing the codewords to have *variable length*. It is then easy to see that one may gain by assigning shorter codewords to the more frequent characters, even at the price of encoding the rare characters by longer strings, as long as the *average* codeword length is reduced. Encoding is just as simple as with fixed-length codes and still consists in concatenating the codeword strings. There are however a few technical problems concerning the decoding that must be dealt with.

A *code* has been defined above as a set of codewords, which are binary strings, but not every set of strings gives a useful code. Consider, for example, the four codewords in column (a) of Fig. 1. If a string of 0's is given, it is easily recognized as a sequence of A's. Similarly, the string 010101 can only be parsed as BBB. However, the string 010110 has two possible interpretations: 0 | 1011 | 0 = ADA or 01 | 0 | 110 = BAC. This situation is intolerable, because it violates our basic premise of reversibility of the encoding process. We shall thus restrict attention to codes for which *every* binary string obtained by concatenating codewords can be parsed only in one way, namely into the original sequence of codewords. Such codes are called *uniquely decipherable* (UD).

At first sight, it seems difficult to decide whether a code is UD, because infinitely many potential concatenations must be checked. Nevertheless, efficient algorithms solving the problem do exist [9]. A necessary, albeit not sufficient, condition for a code to be UD is that its codewords should not be too short. A precise condition has been found by McMillan [10]: any binary UD code with codewords lengths $\{\ell_1, \ldots, \ell_n\}$ satisfies

$$\sum_{i=1}^{n} 2^{-\ell_i} \leq 1. \tag{2}$$

For example, referring to the four codes of Figure 1, the sum is 0.9375, 0.53125, 0.53125, and 1 for codes (a) to (d) respectively. Case (a) is also an example showing that the condition is not sufficient.

However, even if a code is UD, the decoding of certain strings may not be so easy. The code in column (b) of Fig. 1 is UD, but consider the encoded string 11011111110: a first attempt to parse it as 110 | 11 | 11 | 11 | 10 = BAAA10 would fail, because the tail 10 is not a codeword; hence only when trying to decode the fifth codeword do we realize that the first one is not correct, and that the parsing should rather be 1101 | 11 | 11 | 110 = DAAB. In this case, a codeword is not immediately recognized as soon as all its bits are read, but only after a certain *delay*. There are codes for which this delay never exceeds a certain fixed number of bits, but the example above is easily extended to show that the delay for the given code is unbounded.

We would like to be able to recognize a codeword as soon as all its bits are processed, that is, with no delay at all; such codes are called *instantaneous*. A special class of instantaneous codes is known as the class of prefix codes: a code is said to have the *prefix property*, and is hence called a *prefix code*, if none of its codewords is a prefix of any other. It is unfortunate that this definition is misleading (shouldn't such a code be rather called a nonprefix code?), but it is widespread and therefore we shall keep it. For example, the code in Fig. 1(a) is not prefix because the codeword for A (0) is a prefix of the codeword for B (01). Similarly, the code in (b) is not prefix, since all the codewords start with 11, which is the codeword for A. On the other hand, codes (c) and (d) are prefix.

It is easy to see that any prefix code is instantaneous and therefore UD. Suppose that while scanning the encoded string for decoding, a codeword x has been detected. In that case, there is no ambiguity as in the example above for code (b), because if there were another possible interpretation y that can be detected later, it would imply that x is a prefix of y, contradicting the prefix property.

In our search for good codes, we shall henceforth concentrate on prefix codes. In fact, we incur no loss by this restriction, even though the set of prefix codes is a proper subset of the UD codes: it can be shown that given any UD code whose codeword lengths are $\{\ell_1, \ldots, \ell_n\}$, one can construct a prefix code with the same set of codeword lengths [11]. As example, note that the prefix code (c) has the same codeword lengths as code (b). In this special case, (c)'s codewords are obtained from those of code (b) by reversing the strings; now every codeword terminates in 11, and the substring 11 occurs only as suffix of any codeword. Thus no codeword can be the proper prefix of any other. Incidentally, this also shows that code (b), which is not prefix, is nevertheless UD.

There is a natural one-to-one correspondence between binary prefix codes and binary trees. Let us assign labels to the edges and vertices of a binary tree in the following way:

- every edge pointing to a left child is assigned the label 0, and every edge pointing to a right child is assigned the label 1;
- the root of the tree is assigned the empty string Λ;
- every vertex v of the tree below the root is assigned a binary string, which is obtained by concatenating the labels on the edges of the path leading from the root to vertex v.

It follows from the construction that the string associated with vertex v is a prefix of the string associated with vertex w if and only if v is a vertex on the path from the root to w. Thus, the set of strings associated with the *leaves* of any binary tree satisfies the prefix property and may be considered as a prefix code. Conversely, given any prefix code, one can easily construct the corresponding

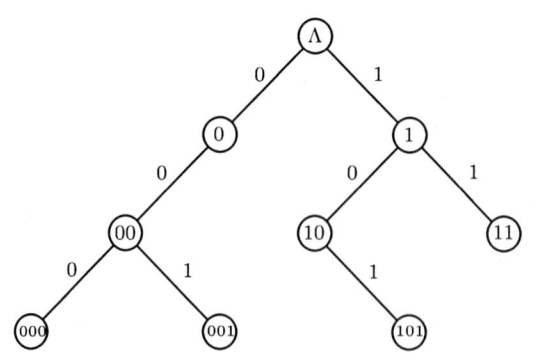

FIGURE 2 Tree corresponding to code {11, 101, 001, 000}.

binary tree. For example, the tree corresponding to the code {11, 101, 001, 000} is depicted in Fig. 2.

The tree corresponding to a code is a convenient tool for decompression. One starts with a pointer to the root and another one to the encoded string, which acts as a guide for the traversal of the tree. While scanning the encoded string from left to right, the tree-pointer is updated to point to the left, respectively right, child of the current node, if the next bit of the encoded string is a 0, respectively a 1. If a leaf of the tree is reached, a codeword has been detected, it is sent to the output, and the tree-pointer is reset to point to the root.

Note that not all the vertices of the tree in Fig. 2 have two children. From the compression point of view, this is a waste, because we could, in that case, replace certain codewords by shorter ones, without violating the prefix property, i.e., build another UD code with a strictly smaller average codeword length. For example, the node labeled 10 has only a right child, so the codeword 101 could be replaced by 10; similarly, the vertex labeled 0 has only a left child, so the codewords 000 and 001 could be replaced by 00 and 01, respectively. A tree for which all internal vertices have two children is called a *complete* tree, and accordingly, the corresponding code is called a complete code. A code is complete if and only if the lengths $\{\ell_i\}$ of its codewords satisfy Eq. (2) with equality, i.e., $\sum_{i=1}^{n} 2^{-\ell_i} = 1$.

A. Huffman Coding

To summarize what we have seen so far, we have restricted the class of codes under consideration in several steps. Starting from general UD codes, we have passed to instantaneous and prefix codes and finally to complete prefix codes, since we are interested in good compression performance. The general problem can thus be stated as follows: we are given a set of n nonnegative weights $\{w_1, \ldots, w_n\}$, which are the frequencies of occurrence of the letters of some alphabet. The problem is to generate a complete binary variable-length prefix code, consisting of codewords with lengths ℓ_i bits, $1 \leq i \leq n$, with optimal compression capabilities, i.e., such that the *total length* of the encoded text

$$\sum_{i=1}^{n} w_i \ell_i \qquad (3)$$

is minimized. It is sometimes convenient to redefine the problem in terms of relative frequencies. Let $W = \sum_{i=1}^{n} w_i$ be the total number of characters in the text; one can then define $p_i = w_i/W$ as the *probability of occurrence* of the ith letter. The problem is then equivalent to minimizing the *average codeword length* (ACL) $\sum_{i=1}^{n} p_i \ell_i$.

Let us for a moment forget about the interpretation of the ℓ_i as codeword lengths, and try to solve the minimization problem analytically without restricting the ℓ_i to be integers, but still keeping the constraint that they must satisfy the McMillan equality $\sum_{i=1}^{n} 2^{-\ell_i} = 1$. To find the set of ℓ_i's minimizing (3), one can use Langrange multipliers. Define a function $L(\ell_1, \ldots, \ell_n)$ of n variables and with a parameter λ by

$$L(\ell_1, \ldots, \ell_n) = \sum_{i=1}^{n} w_i \ell_i - \lambda \left(\sum_{i=1}^{n} 2^{-\ell_i} - 1 \right),$$

and look for local extrema by setting the partial derivatives to 0,

$$\frac{\partial L}{\partial \ell_i} = w_i + \lambda 2^{-\ell_i} \ln 2 = 0,$$

which yields

$$\ell_i = -\log_2 \left(\frac{w_i}{-\lambda \ln 2} \right). \tag{4}$$

To find the constant λ, substitute the values for ℓ_i derived in (4) in the McMillan equality

$$1 = \sum_{i=1}^{n} 2^{-\ell_i} = \frac{1}{-\lambda \ln 2} \sum_{i=1}^{n} w_i = \frac{W}{-\lambda \ln 2},$$

from which one can derive $\lambda = -W/\ln 2$. Plugging this value back into (4), one finally gets

$$\ell_i = -\log_2 \left(\frac{w_i}{W} \right) = -\log_2 p_i.$$

This quantity is known as *the information content* of a symbol with probability p_i, and it represents the minimal number of bits in which the symbol could be coded. Note that this number is not necessarily an integer. Returning to the sum in (3), we may therefore conclude that the lower limit of the total size of the encoded file is given by

$$-\sum_{i=1}^{n} w_i \log_2 p_i = W \left(-\sum_{i=1}^{n} p_i \log_2 p_i \right). \tag{5}$$

The quantity $H = -\sum_{i=1}^{n} p_i \log_2 p_i$ has been defined by Shannon [12] as the *entropy* of the probability distribution $\{p_1, \ldots, p_n\}$, and it gives a lower bound to the weighted average codeword length.

In 1952, Huffman [13] proposed the following algorithm which solves the problem:

1. If $n = 1$, the codeword corresponding to the only weight is the null-string; return.
2. Let w_1 and w_2, without loss of generality, be the two smallest weights.

3. Solve the problem recursively for the $n-1$ weights $w_1 + w_2, w_3, \ldots, w_n$; let α be the codeword assigned to the weight $w_1 + w_2$.
4. The code for the n weights is obtained from the code for $n-1$ weights generated in point 3 by replacing α by the two codewords $\alpha 0$ and $\alpha 1$; return.

In the straightforward implementation, the weights are first sorted and then every weight obtained by combining the two that are currently the smallest is inserted in its proper place in the sequence so as to maintain order. This yields an $O(n^2)$ time complexity. One can reduce the time complexity to $O(n \log n)$ by using two queues, one, Q_1, containing the original elements, the other, Q_2, the newly created combined elements. At each step, the two smallest elements in $Q_1 \cup Q_2$ are combined and the resulting new element is inserted at the end of Q_2, which remains in order [14].

THEOREM. *Huffman's algorithm yields an optimal code.*

Proof. By induction on the number of elements n. For $n = 2$, there is only one complete binary prefix code, which therefore is optimal, namely $\{0,1\}$; this is also a Huffman code, regardless of the weights w_1 and w_2.

Assume the truth of the theorem for $n-1$. Let T_1 be an optimal tree for $\{w_1, \ldots, w_n\}$, with ACL $M_1 = \sum_{i=1}^{n} w_i l_i$.

CLAIM 1. *There are at least two elements on the lowest level of T_1.*

Proof. Suppose there is only one such element and let $\gamma = a_1 \cdots a_m$ be the corresponding binary codeword. Then by replacing γ with $a_1 \cdots a_{m-1}$ (i.e., dropping the last bit) the resulting code would still be prefix, and the ACL would be smaller, in contradiction to T_1's optimality. ∎

CLAIM 2. *The codewords c_1 and c_2 corresponding to the smallest weights w_1 and w_2 have maximal length (the nodes are on the lowest level in T_1).*

Proof. Suppose the element with weight w_2 is on level m, which is not the lowest level ℓ. Then there is an element with weight $w_x > w_2$ at level ℓ. Thus the tree obtained by switching w_x with w_2 has an ACL of
$$M_1 - w_x \ell - w_2 m + w_x m + w_2 \ell < M_1,$$
which is impossible since T_1 is optimal. ∎

CLAIM 3. *Without loss of generality one can assume that the smallest weights w_1 and w_2 correspond to sibling nodes in T_1.*

Proof. Otherwise one could switch elements without changing the ACL. ∎

Consider the tree T_2 obtained from T_1 by replacing the sibling nodes corresponding to w_1 and w_2 by their common parent node α, to which the weight $w_1 + w_2$ is assigned. Thus the ACL for T_2 is $M_2 = M_1 - (w_1 + w_2)$.

CLAIM 4. *T_2 is optimal for the weights $(w_1 + w_2), w_3, \ldots, w_n$.*

Proof. If not, let T_3 be a better tree with $M_3 < M_2$. Let β be the node in T_3 corresponding to $(w_1 + w_2)$. Consider the tree T_4 obtained from T_3 by splitting

β and assigning the weight w_1 to β's left child and w_2 to its right child. Then the ACL for T_4 is

$$M_4 = M_3 + (w_1 + w_2) < M_2 + (w_1 + w_2) = M_1,$$

which is impossible, since T_4 is a tree for n elements with weights $w_1, \ldots, w_n$ and T_1 is optimal among all those trees.

Using the inductive assumption, T_2, which is an optimal tree for $n-1$ elements, has the same ACL as the Huffman tree for these weights. However, the Huffman tree for $w_1, \ldots, w_n$ is obtained from the Huffman tree for $(w_1 + w_2), w_3, \cdots, w_n$ in the same way as T_1 is obtained from T_2. Thus the Huffman tree for the n elements has the same ACL as T_1; hence it is optimal. ∎

B. Huffman Coding without Bit Manipulations

In many applications, compression is by far not as frequent as decompression. In particular, in the context of static IR systems, compression is done only once (when building the database), whereas decompression directly affects the response time for on-line queries. We are thus more concerned with a good *decoding* procedure. Despite their optimality, Huffman codes are not always popular with programmers as they require bit manipulations and are thus not suitable for smooth programming and efficient implementation in most high-level languages.

This section presents decoding routines that directly process only bit blocks of fixed and convenient size (typically, but not necessarily, integral bytes), making it therefore faster and better adapted to high-level languages programming, while still being efficient in terms of space requirements. In principle, byte decoding can be achieved either by using specially built tables to isolate each bit of the input into a corresponding byte or by extracting the required bits while simulating shift operations.

1. Eliminating the Reference to Bits

We are given an alphabet Σ, the elements of which are called *letters*, and a message ($\equiv$ sequence of elements of Σ) to be compressed, using variable-length codes. Let L denote the set of N items to be encoded. Often $L = \Sigma$, but we do not restrict the codewords necessarily to represent single letters of Σ. Indeed, the elements of L can be pairs, triplets, or any n-grams of letters, they can represent words of a natural language, and they can finally form a set of items of completely different nature, provided that there is an unambiguous way to decompose a given file into these items (see, for example, [15]). We call L an *alphabet* and its elements *characters*, where these terms should be understood in a broad sense. We thus include also in our discussion applications where N, the size of the alphabet, can be fairly large.

We begin by compressing L using the variable-length Huffman codewords of its different characters, as computed by the conventional Huffman algorithm. We now partition the resulting bit string into k-bit blocks, where k is chosen so as to make the processing of k-bit blocks, with the particular machine and high-level language at hand, easy and natural. Clearly, the boundaries of these blocks do not necessarily coincide with those of the codewords: a k-bit block may contain several codewords, and a codeword may be split into two (or more) adjacent k-bit blocks. As an example, let $L = \{\texttt{A},\texttt{B},\texttt{C},\texttt{D}\}$, with codewords $\{0,11,100,101\}$ respectively, and choose $k = 3$. Consider the following input string, its coding and the coding's partition into 3-bit blocks:

$$\begin{array}{ccccccccc}
\overbrace{A} & \overbrace{A} & \overbrace{B} & & \overbrace{D} & & \overbrace{B} & & \\
0 & 0 & 1 & 1 & 1 & 0 & 1 & 1 & 1 \\
\underbrace{} & & & \underbrace{} & & & \underbrace{} & & \\
1 & & & 6 & & & 7 & &
\end{array}$$

The last line gives the integer value $0 \leq i < 2^3$ of the block.

The basic idea for all the methods is to use these k-bit blocks, which can be regarded as the binary representation of integers, as *indices* to some tables prepared in advance in the preprocessing stage.

In this section we first describe two straightforward—albeit not very efficient—methods for implementing this idea.

For the first method, we use a table $\mathcal{B}$ of 2^k rows and k columns. In fact, $\mathcal{B}$ will contain only zeros and ones, but as we want to avoid bit manipulations, we shall use one byte for each of the $k2^k$ elements of this matrix. Let $i = I_1 \cdots I_k$ be the binary representation of length k (with leading zeros) of i, for $0 \leq i < 2^k$, then $\mathcal{B}(i, j) = I_j$, for $1 \leq j \leq k$; in other words, the ith line of $\mathcal{B}$ contains the binary representation of i, one bit per byte. The matrix $\mathcal{B}$ will be used to decompose the input string into individual bits, without any bit manipulation. Figure 3(a) depicts the matrix $\mathcal{B}$ for $k = 3$.

The value 0 or 1 extracted from $\mathcal{B}$ is used to decode the input, using the Huffman tree of the given alphabet. The Huffman tree of the alphabet L of our small example is in Fig. 4(a).

A Huffman tree with N leaves (and $N - 1$ internal nodes) can be kept as a table $\mathcal{H}$ with $N - 1$ rows (one for each internal node) and two columns. The internal nodes are numbered from 0 to $N - 2$ in arbitrary order, but for convenience the root will always be numbered zero. For example, in Fig. 4(a),

$\mathcal{B}$	1	2	3
0	0	0	0
1	0	0	1
2	0	1	0
3	0	1	1
4	1	0	0
5	1	0	1
6	1	1	0
7	1	1	1

$\mathcal{S}$	1	2
0	0	0
1	2	0
2	4	0
3	6	0
4	0	1
5	2	1
6	4	1
7	6	1

(a) (b)

FIGURE 3 Tables for Huffman decoding.

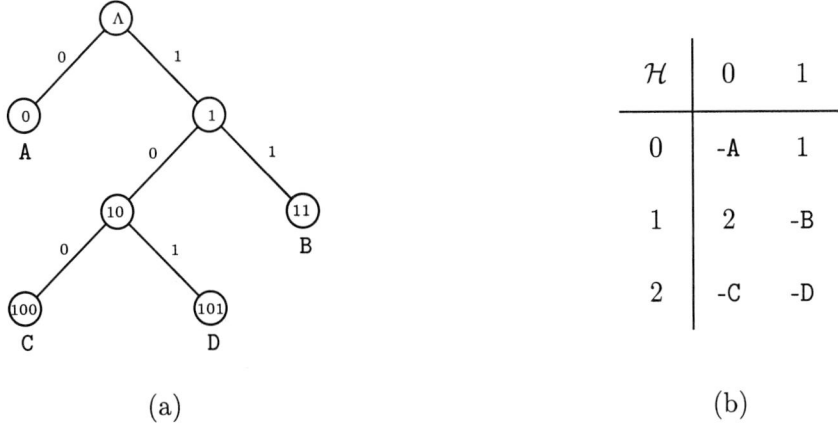

DATA COMPRESSION IN INFORMATION RETRIEVAL SYSTEMS   587

FIGURE 4 Example of Huffman code. (a) Tree form and (b) table form.

the indices of the internal nodes containing Λ, 1, and 10 will be 0, 1 and 2 respectively. The two elements stored in the ith row of Table $\mathcal{H}$ are the left and right children of the internal node indexed i. Each child can be either another internal node, in which case its index is stored, or a leaf, corresponding to one of the characters of the alphabet, in which case this character is stored. We thus need an additional bit per element, indicating whether it is an internal node or a leaf, but generally, one can use the sign bit for that purpose: if the element is positive, it represents the index of an internal node; if it is negative, its absolute value is the representation of a character. Figure 4(b) shows Table $\mathcal{H}$ corresponding to the Huffman tree of Fig. 4(a). The Huffman decoding routine can then be formulated as follows:

Byte Decoding algorithm

```
ind ← 0      [pointer to table H]
repeat
    n ← integer value of next input block
    for j = 1 to k
        newind ← H(ind, B(n, j))    [left or right child of current node]
        if  newind > 0   then   ind ← newind
        else
            output(−newind)
            ind ← 0
    end
until  input is exhausted
```

Another possibility is to replace table $\mathcal{B}$ by the following table $\mathcal{S}$, again with 2^k rows, but only two columns. For $0 \leq i < 2^k$, $S(i, 1)$ will contain $2i \bmod 2^k$, and $S(i, 2)$ will contain the leftmost bit of the k-bit binary representation of i. In the algorithm, the assignment to *newind* must be replaced by

$$newind \leftarrow H(ind, S(n, 2))$$
$$n \leftarrow S(n, 1).$$

The first statement extracts the leftmost bit and the second statement shifts the k-bit block by one bit to the left. Figure 3(b) shows Table S for $k = 3$. Hence we have reduced the space needed for the tables from $k2^k + 2(N-1)$ to $2^{k+1} + 2(N-1)$, but now there are three table accesses for every bit of the input, instead of only two accesses for the first method.

Although there is no reference to bits in these algorithms and their programming is straightforward, the number of table accesses makes their efficiency rather doubtful; their only advantage is that their space requirements are linear in N (k is a constant), while for all other time-efficient variants to be presented below, space is at least $\Omega(N \log N)$. However, for these first two methods, the term 2^k of the space complexity is dominant for small N, so that they can be justified—if at all—only for rather large N.

2. Partial-Decoding Tables

Recall that our goal is to permit a block-per-block processing of the input string for some fixed block-size k. Efficient decoding under these conditions is made possible by using a set of m auxiliary tables, which are prepared in advance for every given Huffman code, whereas Tables B and S above were independent of the character distribution.

The number of entries in each table is 2^k, corresponding to the 2^k possible values of the k-bit patterns. Each entry is of the form (W, j), where W is a sequence of characters and j ($0 \leq j < m$) is the index of the next table to be used. The idea is that entry i, $0 \leq i < 2^k$, of Table 0 contains, first, the longest possible decoded sequence W of characters from the k-bit block representing the integer i (W may be empty when there are codewords of more than k bits). Usually some of the last bits of the block will not be decipherable, being the prefix P of more than one codeword; j will then be the index of the table corresponding to that prefix (if $P = \Lambda$, then $j = 0$). Table j is constructed in a similar way except for the fact that entry i will contain the analysis of the bit pattern formed by the prefixing of P to the binary representation of i. We thus need a table for every possible proper prefix of the given codewords; the number of these prefixes is obviously equal to the number of internal nodes of the appropriate Huffman tree (the root corresponding to the empty string and the leaves corresponding to the codewords), so that $m = N - 1$.

More formally, let P_j, $0 \leq j < N-1$, be an enumeration of all the proper prefixes of the codewords (no special relationship needs to exist between j and P_j, except for the fact that $P_0 = \Lambda$). In Table j corresponding to P_j, the ith entry, $T(j, i)$, is defined as follows: let B be the bit string composed of the juxtaposition of P_j to the left of the k-bit binary representation of i. Let W be the (possibly empty) longest sequence of characters that can be decoded from B, and P_ℓ the remaining undecipherable bits of B; then $T(j, i) = (W, \ell)$.

Referring again to the simple example given above, there are three possible proper prefixes: $\Lambda, 1, 10$, hence three corresponding tables indexed 0,1,2 respectively, and these are given in Fig. 5. The column headed "Pattern" contains for every entry the binary string decoded in Table 0; the binary strings decoded by Tables 1 and 2 are obtained by prefixing "1," respectively "10," to the strings in "Pattern."

| | Pattern | Table 0 | | Table 1 | | Table 2 | |
Entry	for Table 0	W	ℓ	W	ℓ	W	ℓ
0	000	AAA	0	CA	0	CAA	0
1	001	AA	1	C	1	CA	1
2	010	A	2	DA	0	C	2
3	011	AB	0	D	1	CB	0
4	100	C	0	BAA	0	DAA	0
5	101	D	0	BA	1	DA	1
6	110	BA	0	B	2	D	2
7	111	B	1	BB	0	DB	0

FIGURE 5 Partial-decoding tables.

For the input example given above, we first access Table 0 at entry 1, which yields the output string AA, Table 1 is then used with entry 6, giving the output B, and finally Table 2 at entry 7 gives output DB.

The utterly simple decoding subroutine (for the general case) is as follows ($M(i)$ denotes the ith block of the input stream, j is the index of the table currently being used, and $T(j, \ell)$ is the ℓth entry of table j):

Basic Decoding Algorithm

$$j \leftarrow 0$$
for $i \leftarrow 1$ **to** length of input **do**
  $(\text{output}, j) \leftarrow T(j, M(i))$
end

As mentioned before, the choice of k is largely governed by the machine-word structure and the high-level language architecture. A natural choice in most cases would be $k = 8$, corresponding to a byte context, but $k = 4$ (half-byte) or $k = 16$ (half-word) are also conceivable. The larger k is, the greater the number of characters that can be decoded in a single iteration, thus transferring a substantial part of the decoding time to the preprocessing stage. The size of the tables, however, grows exponentially with k, and with every entry occupying (for $N \leq 256$ and $k = 8$) 1 to 8 bytes, each table may require between 1 and 2 Kbytes of internal memory. For $N > 256$, we need more than one byte for the representation of a character, so that the size of a table will be even larger, and for larger alphabets these storage requirements may become prohibitive. We now develop an approach that can help reduce the number of required tables and their size.

3. Reducing the Number of Tables: Binary Forests

The storage space needed by the partial-decoding tables can be reduced by relaxing somewhat the approach of the previous section, and using the conventional Huffman decoding algorithm no more than once for every block, while still processing only k-bit blocks. This is done by redefining the tables and adding some new data structures.

Let us suppose, just for a moment, that after deciphering a given block B of the input that contains a "remainder" P (which is a prefix of a certain codeword), we are somehow able to determine the correct complement of P and its length ℓ, and accordingly its corresponding encoded character. More precisely, since a codeword can extend into more than two blocks, ℓ will be the length of the complement of P in the next k-bit block which contains also other codewords; hence $0 \leq \ell < k$. In the next iteration (decoding of the next k-bit block not yet entirely deciphered), table number ℓ will be used, which is similar to Table 0, but *ignores* the first ℓ bits of the corresponding entry, instead of *prefixing* P to this entry as in the previous section.

Therefore the number of tables reduces from $N-1$ (about 30 in a typical single-letter natural-language case, or 700–900 if we use letter pairs) to only k (8 or 16 in a typical byte or half-word context), where entry i in Table ℓ, $0 \leq \ell < k$, contains the decoding of the $k-\ell$ rightmost bits of the binary representation of i. It is clear, however, that Table 1 contains two exactly equal halves, and in general table ℓ ($0 \leq \ell < k$) consists of 2^ℓ identical parts. Retaining then in each table only the first $2^{k-\ell}$ entries, we are able to compress the needed k tables into the size of only two tables. The entries of the tables are again of the form (W, j); note however that j is not an index to the next table, but an identifier of the remainder P. It is only after finding the correct complement of P and its length ℓ we can access the right table ℓ.

For the same example as before one obtains the tables of Fig. 6, where table t decodes the bit strings given in "Pattern," but ignoring the t leftmost bits, $t = 0$, 1, 2, and $l = 0, 1, 2$ corresponds respectively to the proper prefixes Λ, 1, 10.

The algorithm will be completed if we can find a method for identifying the codeword corresponding to the remainder of a given input block, using of course the following input block(s). We introduce the method through an example.

Entry	Pattern for Table 0	Table 0 W	ℓ	Table 1 W	ℓ	Table 2 W	ℓ
0	000	AAA	0	AA	0	A	0
1	001	AA	1	A	1	–	1
2	010	A	2	–	2		
3	011	AB	0	B	0		
4	100	C	0				
5	101	D	0				
6	110	BA	0				
7	111	B	1				

FIGURE 6 Substring Translate Tables.

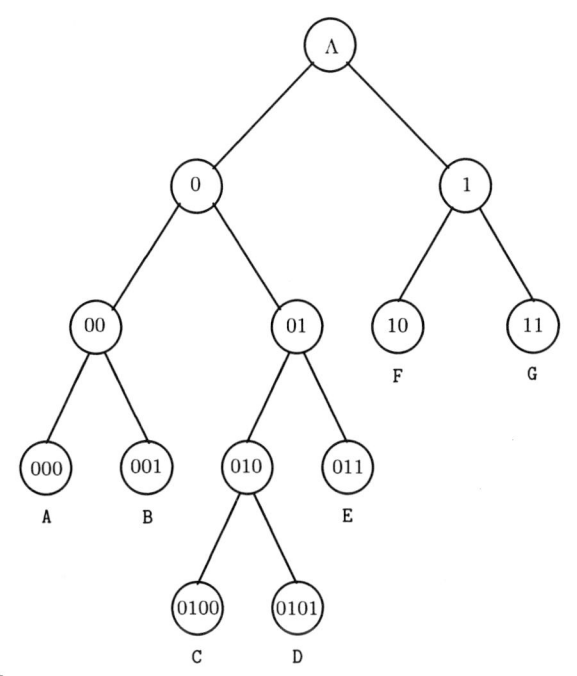

DATA COMPRESSION IN INFORMATION RETRIEVAL SYSTEMS   591

FIGURE 7 The Huffman tree H.

Figure 7 shows a typical Huffman tree H for an alphabet L of $N = 7$ characters. Assume now $k = 8$ and consider the following adjacent blocks of input: 00101101 00101101. The first block is decoded into the string BE and the remainder $P = 01$. Starting at the internal node containing 01 and following the first bits of the following block, we get the codeword C, and length $l = 2$ for the complement of P, so that Table 2 will be used when decoding the next block; ignoring the first 2 bits, this table translates the binary string 101101.

For the general case, let us for simplicity first assume that the depth of H, which is the length of the longest codeword, is bounded by k. Given the nonempty remainder P of the current input block, we must access the internal node corresponding to P, and proceed downwards turning left (0) or right (1) as indicated by the first few bits of the next k-bit block, until we reach a leaf. This leaf contains the next character of the output. The number of edges traversed is the index of the table to be used in the next iteration.

Our goal is to simulate this procedure without having to follow a "bit-traversal" of the tree. The algorithm below uses a binary forest instead of the original Huffman tree H. For the sake of clarity, the construction of the forest is described in two steps.

First, replace H by $N - 2$ smaller trees H_i, which are induced by the proper subtrees rooted at the internal nodes of H, corresponding to all nonempty proper prefixes of the codewords. The nodes of the trees of the forest contain binary strings: Λ for the roots, and for each other node v, a string obtained by concatenating the labels of the edges on the path from the root to v, as in the Huffman tree, but padded at the right by zeroes so as to fill a k-bit block. In addition, each leaf contains also the corresponding decoded character. The

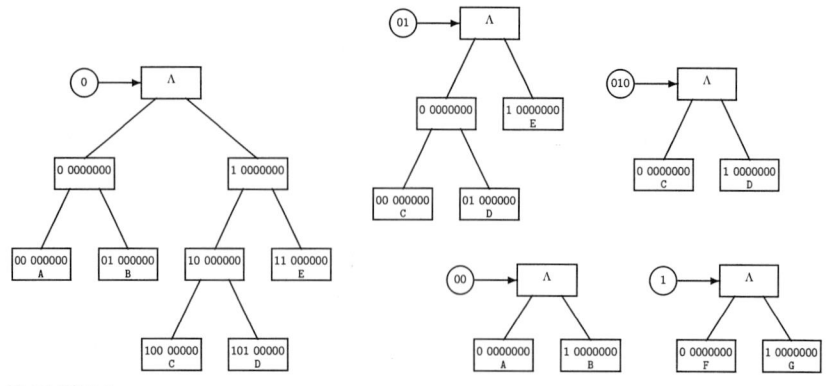

FIGURE 8 Forest of proper prefixes.

string in node v is denoted by VAL(v). Figure 8 depicts the forest obtained from the tree of our example, where the pointer to each tree is symbolized by the corresponding proper prefix. The idea is that the identifier of the remainder in an entry of the tables described above is in fact a pointer to the corresponding tree. The traversal of this tree is guided by the bits of the next k-bit block of the input, which can directly be compared with the contents of the nodes of the tree, as will be described below.

Consider now also the possibility of long codewords, which extend over several blocks. They correspond to long paths so that the depth of some trees in the forest may exceed k. During the traversal of a tree, passing from one level to the next lowest one is equivalent to advancing one bit in the input string. Hence when the depth exceeds k, all the bits of the current k-bit block were used, and we pass to the next block. Therefore the above definition of VAL(v) applies only to nodes on levels up to k; this definition is generalized to any node by the following: VAL(v) for a node v on level j, with $ik < j \leq (i+1)k, i \geq 0$, is the concatenation of the labels on the edges on the path from level ik to v.

In the second step, we compress the forest as could have been done with any Huffman tree. In such trees, every node has degree 0 or 2; i.e., they appear in pairs of siblings (except the root). For a pair of sibling nodes (a, b), VAL(a) and VAL(b) differ only in the jth bit, where j is the level of the pair (here and in what follows, the level of the root of a tree is 0), or more precisely, $j =$ (level $-$ 1) mod $k + 1$. In the compressed tree, every pair is represented by a unique node containing the VAL of the right node of the pair, the new root is the node obtained from the only pair in level 1, and the tree structure is induced by the noncompressed tree. Thus a tree of ℓ nodes shrinks now to $(\ell - 1)/2$ nodes. Another way to look at this "compression" method is to take the tree of internal nodes, and store it in the form of a table as described in the previous section. We use here a tree-oriented vocabulary, but each tree can equivalently be implemented as a table. Figure 9 is the compressed form of the forest of Fig. 8.

We can now compare directly the values VAL stored in the nodes of the trees with the k-bit blocks of the Huffman encoded string. The VAL values have the following property: let v be a node on level j of one of the trees in the compressed forest, with $ik < j \leq (i+1)k, i \geq 0$ as above, and let $I(B)$ be the

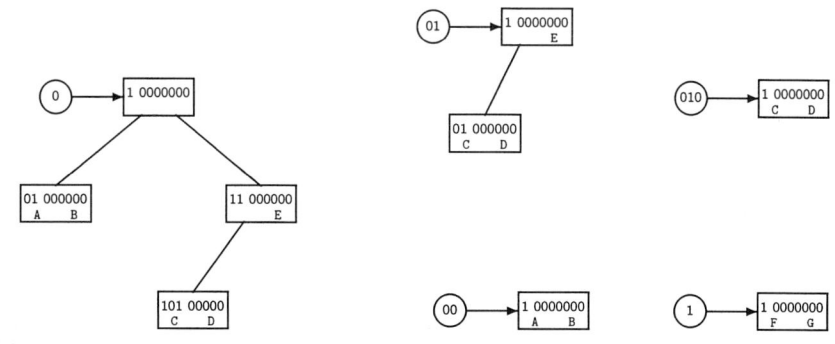

FIGURE 9 Compressed forest.

integer value of the next k-bit block B. Then

$$I(B) < \text{VAL}(v) \quad \text{if and only if} \quad \text{bit}(1 + j \bmod k) \text{ of } B \text{ is } 0.$$

Thus after accessing one of the trees, the VAL of its root is compared with the next k-bit block B. If B, interpreted as a binary integer, is smaller, it must start with 0 and we turn left; if B is greater or equal, it must start with 1 and we turn right. These comparisons are repeated at the next levels, simulating the search for an element in a binary search tree [16, Section 6.2.2]. This leads to the modified algorithm below. Notations are like before, where ROOT(t) points to the tth tree of the forest, and every node has three fields: VAL, a k-bit value, and LEFT and RIGHT, each of which is either a pointer to the next level or contains a character of the alphabet. When accessing Table j, the index is taken modulo the size of the table, which is 2^{k-j}.

Revised Decoding Algorithm

$i \leftarrow 1$
$j \leftarrow 0$
repeat
  (output, tree-nbr) $\leftarrow T(j, S(i) \bmod 2^{k-j})$
  $i \leftarrow i + 1$
  $j \leftarrow 0$
  if tree-nbr $\neq 0$ **then** TRAVERSE (ROOT(tree-nbr))
until input is exhausted

where the procedure TRAVERSE is defined by

TRAVERSE (node)
  repeat
    if $S(i) <$ VAL(node) **then**
       node $\leftarrow$ LEFT(node)
    else node $\leftarrow$ RIGHT(node)
    if node is a character C **then** output C
    $j \leftarrow j + 1$ [j is the number of bits in $S(i)$ which are 'used up']
    if $j = k$ **then**
       $j \leftarrow 0$
       $i \leftarrow i + 1$ [advance to next k-bit block]
  until a character was output
end

Any node v of the original (compressed) Huffman tree H' generates several nodes in the forest, the number of which is equal to the level of v in H'. Hence the total number of nodes in the forest is exactly the *internal path length* of the original (uncompressed) Huffman tree H, as defined by Knuth [17]. This quantity is between $O(N \log N)$ (for a full binary tree) and $O(N^2)$ (for a degenerate tree), and at the average, with all possible shapes of Huffman trees equally likely, proportional to $N\sqrt{N}$.

Therefore even in the worst case, the space requirements are reasonable in most practical applications with small N. If, for large N and certain probability distributions, $O(N^2)$ is prohibitive, it is possible to keep the space of the forest bounded by $O(N \log N)$, if one agrees to abandon the optimality of the Huffman tree. This can be done by imposing a maximal length of $K = O(\log N)$ to the codewords. If K does not exceed the block-size k, the decoding algorithm can even be slightly simplified, since in the procedure TRAVERSE there is no need to check whether the end of the block was reached. Another advantage of bounding the depth of the Huffman tree is that this tends to lengthen the shortest codeword. Since the number of characters stored at each entry in the partial-decoding tables is up to $1 + \lceil (k-1)/s \rceil$, where s is the length of the shortest codeword, this can reduce the space required to store each table. An algorithm for the construction of an optimal tree with bounded depth in time and space $O(KN)$ can be found in [18]. Nevertheless, it might often not seem worthwhile to spend so much efforts obtaining an *optimal* code of bounded length. As an alternative one can use a procedure proposed in [19], which gives a suboptimal average codeword length, but uses less space and is much faster. Moreover, the codes constructed by this method are often very near to optimal.

4. Huffman Codes with Radix $r > 2$

The number of tables can also be reduced by the following simple variants which, similar to the variants with bounded codeword length, yield compression factors slightly lower than those of the methods described above. Let us apply the Huffman algorithm with radix r, $r > 2$, the details of which can be found in Huffman's original paper [13]. In such a variant, one combines at each step, except perhaps the first, the r smallest weights (rather than only the smallest two in the binary algorithm) and replaces them with their sum. The number of weights combined in the first step is chosen so that the number h of weights remaining after this step verifies $h \equiv 1 \pmod{r-1}$. In the corresponding r-ary tree, every internal node has r sons, except perhaps one on the next-to-lowest level of the tree, which has between 2 and r sons. If we choose $r = 2^\ell$, we can encode the alphabet in a first stage using r different symbols; then every symbol is replaced by a binary code of ℓ bits. If in addition ℓ divides k, the "borders" of the k-bit blocks never split any ℓ-bit code. Hence in the partial-decoding tables, the possible remainders are sequences of one or more r-ary symbols. There is therefore again a correspondence between the possible remainders and the internal nodes of the r-ary Huffman tree, only that their number now decreased to $\lceil (n-1)/(r-1) \rceil$. Moreover, there may be some savings in the space needed for a specific table. As we saw before, the space for each table depends on the length s of the shortest codeword, so this can be k with the binary algorithm when $s = 1$, but at most $\lceil k/2 \rceil$ in the 4-ary case.

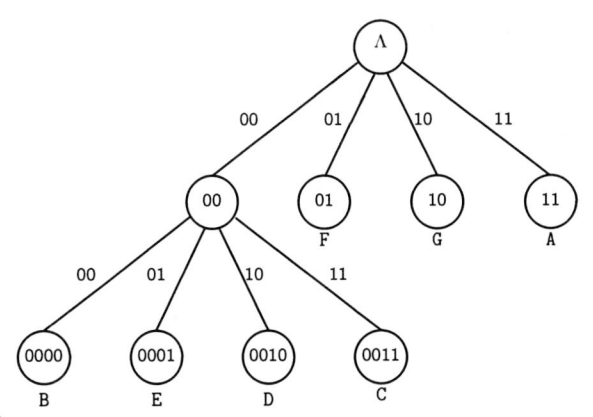

FIGURE 10 Quaternary Huffman tree.

Due to the restrictions on the choice of r, there are only few possible values. For example, for $k = 8$, one could use a quaternary code ($r = 2^2$), where every codeword has an even number of bits and the number of tables is reduced by a factor of 3, or a hexadecimal code ($r = 2^4$), where the codeword length is a multiple of 4 and the number of tables is divided by 15. Note that for alphabets with $N \leq 31$, the hexadecimal code can be viewed as the classical method using "restricted variability" (see, for example, [20]): assign 4-bit encodings to the 15 most frequent characters and use the last 4-bit pattern as "escape character" to indicate that the actual character is encoded in the next 4 bits. Thus up to 16 least frequent characters have 8-bit encodings, all of which have their first 4 bits equal to the escape character.

Referring to the Huffman tree given in Fig. 7, suppose that a character corresponding to a leaf on level ℓ appears with probability $2^{-\ell}$, then the corresponding 2^2-ary tree is given in Fig. 10. Note that the only proper prefixes of even length are Λ and 00, so that the number of tables dropped from 6 to 2.

However, with increasing r, compression will get worse, so that the right tradeoff must be chosen according to the desired application.

C. Space-Efficient Decoding of Huffman Codes

The data structures needed for the decoding of a Huffman encoded file (a Huffman tree or lookup table) are generally considered negligible overhead relative to large texts. However, not all texts are large, and if Huffman coding is applied in connection with a Markov model [21], the required Huffman forest may become itself a storage problem. Moreover, the "alphabet" to be encoded is not necessarily small, and may, e.g., consist of all the different words in the text, so that Huffman trees with thousands and even millions of nodes are not uncommon [22]. We try here to reduce the necessary internal memory space by devising efficient ways of encoding these trees. In addition, the suggested data structure also allows a speed-up of the decompression process, by reducing the number of necessary bit comparisons.

1. Canonical Huffman Codes

For a given probability distribution, there might be quite a large number of different Huffman trees, since interchanging the left and right subtrees of any internal node will result in a different tree whenever the two subtrees are different in structure, but the weighted average path length is not affected by such an interchange. There are often also other optimal trees, which cannot be obtained via Huffman's algorithm. One may thus choose one of the trees that has some additional properties. The preferred choice for many applications is the *canonical* tree, defined by Schwartz and Kallick [23], and recommended by many others (see, e.g., [24,25]).

Denote by $(p_1, \ldots, p_n)$ the given probability distribution, where we assume that $p_1 \geq p_2 \geq \cdots \geq p_n$, and let ℓ_i be the length in bits of the codeword assigned by Huffman's procedure to the element with probability p_i; i.e., ℓ_i is the depth of the leaf corresponding to p_i in the Huffman tree. A tree is called canonical if, when scanning its leaves from left to right, they appear in nondecreasing order of their depth (or equivalently, in nonincreasing order, as in [26]). The idea is that Huffman's algorithm is only used to generate the lengths $\{\ell_i\}$ of the codewords, rather than the codewords themselves; the latter are easily obtained as follows: the ith codeword consists of the first ℓ_i bits immediately to the right of the "binary point" in the infinite binary expansion of $\sum_{j=1}^{i-1} 2^{-\ell_j}$, for $i = 1, \ldots, n$ [27]. Many properties of canonical codes are mentioned in [24,28].

The following will be used as a running example in this section. Consider the probability distribution implied by Zipf's law, defined by the weights $p_i = 1/(i H_n)$, for $1 \leq i \leq n$, where $H_n = \sum_{j=1}^{n}(1/j)$ is the nth harmonic number. This law is believed to govern the distribution of the most common words in a large natural language text [29]. A canonical code can be represented by the string $\langle n_1, n_2, \ldots, n_k \rangle$, called a *source*, where k denotes, here and below, the length of the longest codeword (the depth of the tree), and n_i is the number of codewords of length i, $i = 1, \ldots, k$. The source corresponding to Zipf's distribution for $n = 200$ is $\langle 0, 0, 1, 3, 4, 8, 15, 32, 63, 74 \rangle$. The code is depicted in Fig. 11.

We shall assume, for the ease of description in the current section, that the source has no "holes"; i.e., there are no three integers $i < j < \ell$ such that $n_i \neq 0$, $n_\ell \neq 0$, but $n_j = 0$. This is true for many, but not all, real-life distributions.

One of the properties of canonical codes is that the codewords having the same length are the binary representations of consecutive integers. For example, in our case, the codewords of length 9 bits are the binary integers in the range from 110011100 to 111011010. This fact can be exploited to enable efficient decoding with relatively small overhead: once a codeword of ℓ bits is detected, one can get its relative index within the sequence of codewords of length ℓ by simple subtraction.

The following information is thus needed: let $m = \min\{i \mid n_i > 0\}$ be the length of the shortest codeword, and let $base(i)$ be the integer value of the first codeword of length i. We then have

$$base(m) = 0$$
$$base(i) = 2(base(i-1) + n_{i-1}) \qquad \text{for } m < i \leq k.$$

DATA COMPRESSION IN INFORMATION RETRIEVAL SYSTEMS **597**

```
  0  000
  1  0010
  2  0011
  3  0100
  4  01010
  5  01011
  6  01100
  7  01101
  8  011100
  9  011101
 10  011110
 11  011111
 12  100000
 13  100001
 14  100010
 15  100011
 16  1001000
 17  1001001
 18  1001010
 19  1001011
...   ...
 29  1010101
 30  1010110
 31  10101110
 32  10101111
 33  10110000
...   ...
 61  11001100
 62  11001101
 63  110011100
 64  110011101
...   ...
124  111011001
125  111011010
126  1110110110
127  1110110111
...   ...
198  1111111110
199  1111111111
```

FIGURE 11 Canonical Huffman code for Zipf-200.

Let $B_s(k)$ denote the standard s-bit binary representation of the integer k (with leading zeros, if necessary). Then the jth codeword of length i, for $j = 0, 1, \ldots, n_i - 1$, is $B_i(base(i) + j)$. Let $seq(i)$ be the sequential index of the first codeword of length i:

$$seq(m) = 0$$
$$seq(i) = seq(i-1) + n_{i-1} \quad \text{for } m < i \leq k.$$

Suppose now that we have detected a codeword w of length ℓ. If $I(w)$ is the integer value of the binary string w (i.e., $w = B_\ell(I(w))$), then $I(w) - base(\ell)$ is the relative index of w within the block of codewords of length ℓ. Thus $seq(\ell) + I(w) - base(\ell)$ is the relative index of w within the full list of codewords. This can be rewritten as $I(w) - diff(\ell)$, for $diff(\ell) = base(\ell) - seq(\ell)$. Thus all one needs is the list of integers $diff(\ell)$. Table 2 gives the values of n_i, $base(i)$, $seq(i)$, and $diff(i)$ for our example.

TABLE 2 Decode Values for Canonical Huffman Code for Zipf-200

i	n_i	base(i)	seq(i)	diff(i)
3	1	0	0	0
4	3	2	1	1
5	4	10	4	6
6	8	28	8	20
7	15	72	16	56
8	32	174	31	143
9	63	412	63	349
10	74	950	126	824

We suggest in the next section a new representation of canonical Huffman codes, which not only is space-efficient, but may also speed up the decoding process, by permitting, at times, the decoding of more than a single bit in one iteration. Similar ideas, based on tables rather than on trees, were recently suggested in [26].

2. Skeleton Trees for Fast Decoding

The following small example, using the data above, shows how such savings are possible. Suppose that while decoding, we detect that the next codeword starts with 1101. This information should be enough to decide that the following codeword ought to be of length 9 bits. We should thus be able, after having detected the first 4 bits of this codeword, to read the following 5 bits as a block, without having to check after each bit if the end of a codeword has been reached. Our goal is to construct an efficient data structure that permits similar decisions as soon as they are possible. The fourth bit was the earliest possible in the above example, since there are also codewords of length 8 starting with 110.

Decoding with sk-trees

The suggested solution is a binary tree, called below an *sk-tree* (for skeleton tree), the structure of which is induced by the underlying Huffman tree, but which has generally significantly fewer nodes. The tree will be traversed like a regular Huffman tree. That is, we start with a pointer to the root of the tree, and another pointer to the first bit of the encoded binary sequence. This sequence is scanned, and after having read a zero (respectively, a 1), we proceed to the left (respectively, right) child of the current node. In a regular Huffman tree, the leaves correspond to full codewords that have been scanned, so the decoding algorithm just outputs the corresponding item, resets the tree pointer to the root and proceeds with scanning the binary string. In our case, however, we visit the tree only up to the depth necessary to identify the length of the current codeword. The leaves of the sk-tree then contain the lengths of the corresponding codewords.

The formal decoding process using an sk-tree is depicted in Fig. 12. The variable *start* points to the index of the bit at the beginning of the current

DATA COMPRESSION IN INFORMATION RETRIEVAL SYSTEMS

```
{
    tree_pointer ⟵ root
    i ⟵ 1
    start ⟵ 1
    while i < length_of_string
    {
        if string[i] = 0        tree_pointer ⟵ left(tree_pointer)
        else                    tree_pointer ⟵ right(tree_pointer)
        if value(tree_pointer) > 0
        {
            codeword ⟵ string[start ⋯ (start + value(tree_pointer) −1)]
            output   ⟵ table[ I(codeword)−diff[ value(tree_pointer)] ]
            tree_pointer ⟵ root
            start    ⟵ start + value(tree_pointer)
            i        ⟵ start
        }
        else                    i ⟵ i + 1
    }
}
```

FIGURE 12 Decoding procedure using sk-tree.

codeword in the encoded string, which is stored in the vector *string*[]. Each node of the sk-tree consists of three fields: a *left* and a *right* pointer, which are not null if the node is not a leaf, and a *value* field, which is zero for internal nodes, but contains the length in bits of the current codeword, if the node is a leaf. In an actual implementation, we can use the fact that any internal node has either zero or two sons, and store the *value*-field and the *right*-field in the same space, with *left* = *null* serving as flag for the use of the *right* pointer. The procedure also uses two tables: $table[j]$, $0 \leq j < n$, giving the jth element (in nonincreasing order of frequency) of the encoded alphabet; and $diff[i]$ defined above, for i varying from m to k, that is, from the length of the shortest to the length of the longest codeword.

The procedure passes from one level in the tree to the one below according to the bits of the encoded string. Once a leaf is reached, the next *codeword* can be read in one operation. Note that not all the bits of the input vector are individually scanned, which yields possible time savings.

Figure 13 shows the sk-tree corresponding to Zipf's distribution for $n = 200$. The tree is tilted by 45°, so that left (right) children are indicated by arrows pointing down (to the right). The framed leaves correspond to the last codewords of the indicated length. The sk-tree of our example consists of only 49 nodes, as opposed to 399 nodes of the original Huffman tree.

Construction of sk-trees

While traversing a standard canonical Huffman tree to decode a given codeword, one may stop as soon as one gets to the root of any full subtree of depth h, for $h \geq 1$, i.e., a subtree of depth h that has 2^h leaves, since at this stage it is known that exactly h more bits are needed to complete the codeword. One way to look at sk-trees is therefore as standard Huffman trees from which all

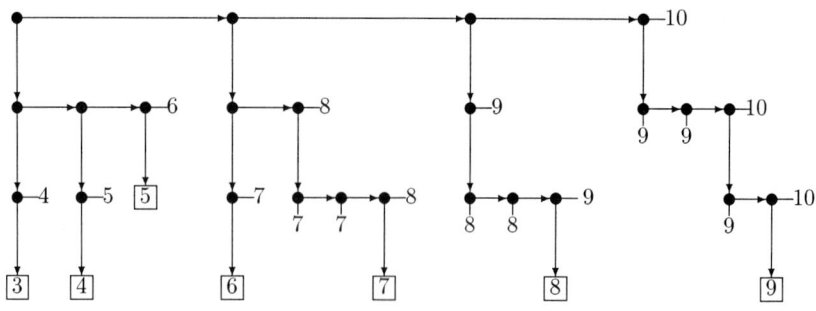

FIGURE 13 Sk-tree for Zipf-200 distribution.

full subtrees of depth $h \geq 1$ have been pruned. A more direct and much more efficient construction is as follows.

The one-to-one correspondence between the codewords and the paths from the root to the leaves in a Huffman tree can be extended to define, for any binary string $S = s_1 \cdots s_e$, the path $P(S)$ induced by it in a tree with given root r_0. This path will consist of $e + 1$ nodes r_i, $0 \leq i \leq e$, where for $i > 0$, r_i is the left (respectively, right) child of r_{i-1}, if $s_i = 0$ (respectively, if $s_i = 1$). For example, in Fig. 13, $P(111)$ consists of the four nodes represented as bullets in the top line. The skeleton of the sk-tree will consist of the paths corresponding to the last codeword of every length. Let these codewords be denoted by L_i, $m \leq i \leq k$; they are, for our example, 000, 0100, 01101, 100011, etc. The idea is that $P(L_i)$ serves as "demarcation line": any node to the left (respectively, right) of $P(L_i)$, i.e., a left (respectively, right) child of one of the nodes in $P(L_i)$, corresponds to a prefix of a codeword with length $\leq i$ (respectively, $> i$).

As a first approximation, the construction procedure thus takes the tree obtained by $\bigcup_{i=m}^{k-1} P(L_i)$ (there is clearly no need to include the longest codeword L_k, which is always a string of k 1's); and adjoins the missing children to turn it into a complete tree in which each internal node has both a left and a right child. The label on such a new leaf is set equal to the label of the closest leaf following it in an in-order traversal. In other words, when creating the path for L_i, one first follows a few nodes in the already existing tree, then one branches off creating new nodes; as to the labeling, the missing right child of any node in the path will be labeled $i + 1$ (basing ourselves on the assumption that there are no holes), but only the missing left children of any *new* node in the path will be labeled i.

A closer look then implies the following refinement. Suppose a codeword L_i has a zero in its rightmost position, i.e., $L_i = \alpha 0$ for some string α of length $i - 1$. Then the first codeword of length $i + 1$ is $\alpha 10$. It follows that only when getting to the ith bit can one decide if the length of the current codeword is i or $i + 1$. However, if L_i terminates in a string of 1's, $L_i = \beta 01^a$, with $a > 0$ and $|\beta| + a = i - 1$, then the first codeword of length $i + 1$ is $\beta 10^{a+1}$, so the length of the codeword can be deduced already after having read the bit following β. It follows that one does not always need the full string L_i in the sk-tree, but only its prefix up to and not including the rightmost zero. Let $L_i^* = \beta$ denote this prefix. The revised version of the above procedure starts with the tree obtained by $\bigcup_{i=m}^{k-1} P(L_i^*)$. The nodes of this tree are depicted as bullets in Fig. 13. For each path $P(L_i^*)$ there is a leaf in the tree, and the left child of this leaf is the new terminal node, represented in Fig. 13 by a box containing the number i. The additional leaves are then filled in as explained above.

Space Complexity

To evaluate the size of the sk-tree, we count the number of nodes added by path $P(L_i^*)$, for $m \leq i < k$. Since the codewords in a canonical code, when ordered by their corresponding frequencies, are also alphabetically sorted, it suffices to compare L_i to L_{i-1}. Let $\gamma(m) = 0$, and for $i > m$, let $\gamma(i)$ be the longest common prefix of L_i and L_{i-1}, e.g., $\gamma(7)$ is the string 10 in our example. Then the number of nodes in the sk-tree is given by

$$size = 2 \left(\sum_{i=m}^{k-1} \max(0, |L_i^*| - |\gamma(i)|) \right) - 1,$$

since the summation alone is the number of internal nodes (the bullets in Fig. 13).

The maximum function comes to prevent an extreme case in which the difference might be negative. For example, if $L_6 = 010001$ and $L_7 = 0101111$, the longest common prefix is $\gamma(7) = 010$, but since we consider only the bits up to and not including the rightmost zero, we have $L_7^* = 01$. In this case, indeed, no new nodes are added for $P(L_7^*)$.

An immediate bound on the number of nodes in the sk-tree is $O(\min(n, k^2))$, since on the one hand, there are up to $k - 1$ paths $P(L_i^*)$ of lengths $\leq k - 2$, but on the other hand, it cannot exceed the number of nodes in the underlying Huffman tree, which is $2n - 1$. To get a tighter bound, consider the nodes in the upper levels of the sk-tree belonging to the full binary tree F with $k - 1$ leaves and having the same root as the sk-tree. The depth of F is $d = \lceil \log_2(k-1) \rceil$, and all its leaves are at level d or $d - 1$. The tree F is the part of the sk-tree where some of the paths $P(L_i^*)$ must be overlapping, so we account for the nodes in F and for those below separately. There are at most $2k - 1$ nodes in F; there are at most $k - 1$ disjoint paths below it, with path $P(L_i^*)$ extending at most $i - 2 - \lfloor \log_2(k-1) \rfloor$ nodes below F, for $\log_2(k-1) < i \leq k$. This yields as bound for the number of nodes in the sk-tree

$$2k + 2 \left(\sum_{i=1}^{k-2-\lfloor \log_2(k-1) \rfloor} i \right) = 2k + (k - 2 - \lfloor \log_2(k-1) \rfloor)(k - 1 - \lfloor \log_2(k-1) \rfloor).$$

There are no savings in the worst case, e.g., when there is only one codeword of each length (except for the longest, for which there are always at least two). More generally, if the depth of the Huffman tree is $\Omega(n)$, the savings might not be significant, but such trees are optimal only for some very skewed distributions. In many applications, like for most distributions of characters or character pairs or words in most natural languages, the depth of the Huffman tree is $O(\log n)$, and for large n, even the constant c, if the depth is $c \log_2 n$, must be quite small. For suppose the Huffman tree has a leaf on depth d. Then by [30, Theorem 1], the probability of the element corresponding to this leaf is $p < 1/F_{d+1}$, where F_j is the jth Fibonacci number, and we get from [17, Exercise 1.2.1–4] that $p < (1/\phi)^{d-1}$, where $\phi = (1 + \sqrt{5})/2$ is the golden ratio. Thus if $d > c \log_2 n$, we have

$$p < \left(\frac{1}{\phi}\right)^{c\log_2 n} = n^{-c\log_2(1/\phi)} = n^{-0.693c}.$$

To give a numeric example, a Huffman tree corresponding to the different words in English, as extracted from 500 MB (87 million words) of the *Wall Street Journal* [31], had $n = 289,101$ leaves. The probability for a tree of this size to have a leaf at level $3\log_2 n$ is less than 4.4×10^{-12}, which means that even if the word with this probability appears only once, the text must be at least 4400 billion words long, enough to fill about 35,000 CD-Roms! However, even if the original Huffman tree would be deeper, it is sometimes convenient to impose an upper limit of $B = O(\log n)$ on the depth, which often implies only a negligible loss in compression efficiency [19]. In any case, given a logarithmic bound on the depth, the size of the sk-tree is about

$$\log n\,(\log n - \log\log n).$$

D. Arithmetic Coding

We have dealt so far only with Huffman coding, and even shown that they are optimal under certain constraints. However, this optimality has often been overemphasized in the past, and it is not always mentioned that Huffman codes have been shown to be optimal only for *block codes*: codes in which each new character is encoded by a fixed bit pattern made up of an integral number of bits.

The constraint of the integral number of bits had probably been considered as obvious, since the possibility of coding elements in fractional bits is quite surprising. *Arithmetic codes* overcome the limitations of block codes. In fact, arithmetic codes have had a long history [32,33], but became especially popular after Witten *et al.*'s paper [34] in 1987.

The approach taken by arithmetic coding is quite different from that of Huffman coding. Instead of using the probabilities of the different characters to generate codewords, it defines a *process* in the course of which a binary number is generated. Each new character of the text to be encoded allows a more precise determination of the number. When the last character is processed, the number is stored or transmitted.

The encoding process starts with the interval [0,1), which will be narrowed repeatedly. We assign to each character a subinterval, the size of which is proportional to the probability of occurrence of the character. Processing a certain character x is then performed by replacing the current interval by the subinterval corresponding to x. Refer to the example in Fig. 14. We assume our alphabet consists of the four characters {A, B, C, D}, appearing with probabilities 0.4, 0.3, 0.1, and 0.2, respectively. We arbitrarily choose a corresponding partition of the interval [0, 1), for example, [0, 0.1) for C, [0.1, 0.4) for B, [0.4, 0.8) for A, and finally [0.8, 1) for D. This partition is depicted as the leftmost bar in Fig. 14.

Suppose now that the text we wish to encode is BDAAC. The first character is B, so the new interval after the encoding of B is [0.1,0.4). This interval is now partitioned similarly to the original one; i.e., the first 10% are assigned to C, the

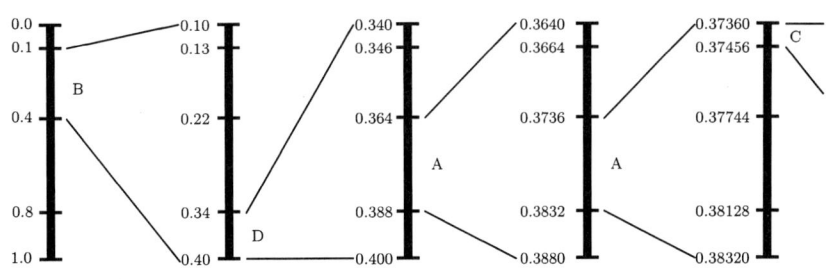

FIGURE 14 Example of arithmetic coding.

next 30% to B, etc. The new subdivision can be seen next to the second bar from the left. The second character to be encoded is D, so the corresponding interval is [0.34, 0.40). Repeating now the process, we see that the next character, A, narrows the chosen subinterval further to [0.364, 0.388), and the next A to [0.3736, 0.3832), and finally the last C to [0.37360, 0.37456).

To allow unambiguous decoding, it is this last interval that should be transmitted. This would, however, be rather wasteful: as more characters are encoded, the interval will get narrower, and many of the leftmost digits of its upper limit will overlap with those of its lower limit. In our example, both limits start with 0.37. One can overcome this inefficiency and transmit only a single number if some additional information is given. For instance, if the number of characters is also given to the decoder or, as is customary, a special end-of-file character is added at the end of the message, it suffices to transmit any single number within the final interval. In our case, the best choice would be $y = 0.3740234375$, because its binary representation 0.0101111111 is the shortest among the numbers of the interval.

Decoding is then just the inverse of the above process. Since y is between 0.1 and 0.4, we know that the first character must be B. If so, the interval has been narrowed to [0.1, 0.4). We thus seek the next subinterval that contains y, and find it to be [0.34, 0.40), which corresponds to D, etc. Once we get to [0.37360, 0.37456), the process must be stopped by some external condition; otherwise we could continue this decoding process indefinitely, for example, by noting that y belongs to [0.373984, 0.374368), which could be interpreted as if the following character were A.

As has been mentioned, the longer the input string, the more digits or bits are needed to specify a number encoding the string. Compression is achieved by the fact that a frequently occurring character only slightly narrows the current interval. The number of bits needed to represent a number depends on the required precision. The smaller the given interval, the higher the precision necessary to specify a number in it; if the interval size is p, $\lceil -\log_2 p \rceil$ bits might be needed.

To evaluate the number of bits necessary by arithmetic coding, we recall the notation used in Section II. A. The text consists of characters $x_1 x_2 \cdots x_W$, each of which belongs to an alphabet $\{a_1, \ldots, a_n\}$. Let w_i be the number of occurrences of letter a_i, so that $W = \sum_{i=1}^{n} w_i$ is the total length of the text, and let $p_i = w_i/W$ be the probability of occurrence of letter a_i, $1 \leq i \leq n$. Denote by p_{x_j} the probability associated with the jth character of the text.

After having processed the first character, x_1, the interval has been narrowed to size p_{x_1}; after the second character, the interval size is $p_{x_1} p_{x_2}$; etc. We get that the size of the final interval after the whole text has been processed is $p_{x_1} p_{x_2} \cdots p_{x_W}$. Therefore the number of bits needed to encode the full text is

$$-\log_2 \left(\prod_{j=1}^{W} p_{x_j} \right) = -\sum_{j=1}^{W} \log_2 p_{x_j} = -\sum_{i=1}^{n} w_i \log_2 p_i$$

$$= W \left(-\sum_{i=1}^{n} p_i \log_2 p_i \right) = W H,$$

where we get the second equality by summing over the letters of the alphabet with their frequency instead of summing over the characters of the text, and where H is the entropy of the given probability distribution. Amortizing this per character, we get that the average number of bits needed to encode a single character is just H, which has been shown in Eq. (5) to be the information theoretic lower bound.

We conclude that from the point of view of compression, arithmetic coding has an optimal performance. However, our presentation and the analysis are oversimplified: they do not take into account the overhead incurred by the end_of_file character nor the fractions of bits lost by alignment for each block to be encoded. It can be shown [28] that although these additions are often negligible relative to the average size of a codeword, they might be significant relative to the *difference* between the codeword lengths for Huffman and arithmetic codes. There are also other technical problems, such as the limited precision of our computers, which does not allow the computation of a single number for a long text; there is thus a need for incremental transmission, which further complicates the algorithms, see [34].

Despite the optimality of arithmetic codes, Huffman codes may still be the preferred choice in many applications: they are much faster for encoding and especially decoding, they are less error prone, and after all, the loss in compression efficiency, if any, is generally very small.

E. Dictionary-Based Text Compression

The text compression methods we have seen so far are called *statistical* methods, as they exploit the skewness of the distribution of occurrence of the characters. Another family of compression methods is based on *dictionaries,* which replace variable-length substrings of the text by (shorter) pointers to a dictionary in which a collection of such substrings has been stored. Depending on the application and the implementation details, each method can outperform the other.

Given a fixed amount of RAM that we would allocate for the storage of a dictionary, the selection of an optimal set of strings to be stored in the dictionary turns out to be a difficult task, because the potential strings are overlapping. A similar problem is shown to be NP-complete in [35], but more restricted versions of this problem of optimal dictionary construction are tractable [36].

For IR applications, the dictionary ought to be fixed, since the compressed text needs to be accessed randomly. For the sake of completeness, however, we mention also *adaptive* techniques, which are the basis of most popular compression methods. Many of these are based on two algorithms designed by Ziv and Lempel [37,38].

In one of the variants of the first algorithm [37], often referred to as LZ77, the dictionary is in fact the previously scanned text, and pointers to it are of the form (d, ℓ), where d is an offset (the number of characters from the current location to the previous occurrence of a substring matching the one that starts at the current location), and ℓ is the length of the matching string. There is therefore no need to store an explicit dictionary. In the second algorithm [38], the dictionary is dynamically expanded by adjoining substrings of the text that could not be parsed. For more details on LZ methods and their variants, the reader is referred to [25].

Even once the dictionary is given, the compression scheme is not yet well defined, as one must decide how to *parse* the text into a sequence of dictionary elements. Generally, the parsing is done by a *greedy* method; i.e., at any stage, the longest matching element from the dictionary is sought. A greedy approach is fast, but not necessarily optimal. Because the elements of the dictionary are often overlapping, and particularly for LZ77 variants, where the dictionary is the text itself, a different way of parsing might yield better compression. For example, assume the dictionary consists of the strings $D = \{$abc, ab, cdef, d, de, ef, f$\}$ and that the text is $S = $ abcdef; assume further that the elements of D are encoded by some fixed-length code, which means that $\lceil \log_2(|D|) \rceil$ bits are used to refer to any of the elements of D. Then parsing S by a greedy method, trying to match always the longest available string, would yield abc-de-f, requiring three codewords, whereas a better partition would be ab-cdef, requiring only two.

The various dictionary compression methods differ also by the way they encode the elements. This is most simply done by a fixed length code, as in the above example. Obviously, different encoding methods might yield different optimal parsings. Returning to the above example, if the elements abc, d, de, ef, f, ab, cdef of D are encoded respectively by 1, 2, 3, 4, 5, 6, and 6 bits, then the parsing abc-de-f would need 9 bits for its encoding, and for the encoding of the parsing ab-cdef, 12 bits would be needed. The best parsing, however, for the given codeword lengths, is abc-d-ef, which neither is a greedy parsing nor does it minimize the number of codewords, and requires only seven bits.

The way to search for the optimal parsing is by reduction to a well-known graph theoretical problem. Consider a text string S consisting of a sequence of n characters $S_1 S_2 \cdots S_n$, each character S_i belonging to a fixed alphabet Σ. Substrings of S are referenced by their limiting indices; i.e., $S_i \cdots S_j$ is the substring starting at the ith character in S, up to and including the jth character. We wish to compress S by means of a dictionary D, which is a set of character strings $\{\sigma_1, \sigma_2, \ldots\}$, with $\sigma_i \in \Sigma^+$. The dictionary may be explicitly given and finite, as in the example above, or it may be potentially infinite, e.g., for the Lempel–Ziv variants, where any previously occurring string can be referenced.

The compression process consists of two independent phases: parsing and encoding. In the *parsing* phase, the string S is broken into a sequence of consecutive substrings, each belonging to the dictionary D, i.e., an increasing sequence of indices $i_0 = 0, i_1, i_2, \ldots$ is found, such that

$$S = S_1 S_2 \cdots S_n = S_1 \cdots S_{i_1} S_{i_1+1} \cdots S_{i_2} \cdots,$$

with $S_{i_j+1} \cdots S_{i_{j+1}} \in D$ for $j = 0, 1, \ldots$. One way to assure that at least one such parsing exists is to force the dictionary D to include each of the individual characters of Σ. The second phase is based on an *encoding* function $\lambda: D \longrightarrow \{0,1\}^*$, which assigns to each element of the dictionary a binary string, called its encoding. The assumption on λ is that it produces a code that is UD. This is most easily obtained by a fixed length code, but as has been seen earlier, a sufficient condition for a code being UD is to choose it as a prefix code.

The problem is the following: given the dictionary D and the encoding function λ, we are looking for the optimal partition of the text string S, i.e., the sequence of indices $i_1, i_2, \ldots$ is sought, that minimizes $\sum_{j \geq 0} |\lambda(S_{i_j+1} \cdots S_{i_{j+1}})|$.

To solve the problem, a directed, labeled graph $G = (V, E)$ is defined for the given text S. The set of vertices is $V = \{1, 2, \ldots, n, n+1\}$, with vertex i corresponding to the character S_i for $i \leq n$, and $n+1$ corresponding to the end of the text; E is the set of directed edges: an ordered pair (i, j), with $i < j$, belongs to E if and only if the corresponding substring of the text, that is, the sequence of characters $S_i \cdots S_{j-1}$, can be encoded as a single unit. In other words, the sequence $S_i \cdots S_{j-1}$ must be a member of the dictionary, or more specifically for LZ77, if $j > i + 1$, the string $S_i \cdots S_{j-1}$ must have appeared earlier in the text. The label L_{ij} is defined for every edge $(i, j) \in E$ as $|\lambda(S_i \cdots S_{j-1})|$, the number of bits necessary to encode the corresponding member of the dictionary, for the given encoding scheme at hand. The problem of finding the optimal parsing of the text, relative to the given dictionary and the given encoding scheme, therefore reduces to the well-known problem of finding the shortest path in G from vertex 1 to vertex $n + 1$. In our case, there is no need to use Dijkstra's algorithm, since the directed graph contains no cycles, all edges being of the form (i, j) with $i < j$. Thus by a simple dynamic programming method, the shortest path can be found in time $O(|E|)$.

Figure 15 displays a small example of a graph, corresponding to the text abbaabbabab and assuming that LZ77 is used. The edges connecting vertices i to $i + 1$, for $i = 1, \ldots, n$, are labeled by the character S_i.

As an example of an encoding scheme, we refer to the on-the-fly compression routine recently included in a popular operating system. It is based on [39], a variant of LZ77, using hashing on character pairs to locate (the beginning of)

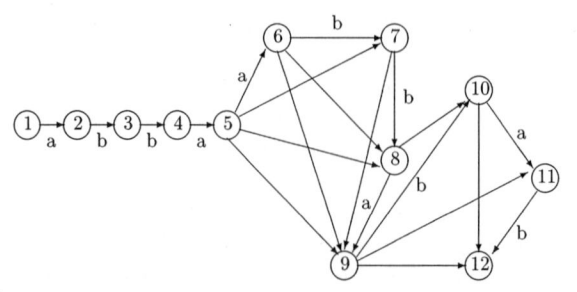

FIGURE 15 Graph corresponding to text abbaabbabab.

recurrent strings. The output of the compression process is thus a sequence of elements, each being either a single (uncompressed) character or an offset-length pair (d, ℓ). The elements are identified by a flag bit, so that a single character is encoded by a zero, followed by the 8-bit ASCII representation of the character, and the encoding of each (d, ℓ) pair starts with a 1. The sets of possible offsets and lengths are split into classes as follows: let $B_m(n)$ denote the standard m-bit binary representation of n (with leading zeros if necessary), then, denoting the encoding scheme by λ_M,

$$\lambda_M(\text{offset } d) = \begin{cases} 1\,B_6(d-1) & \text{if } 1 \leq d \leq 64 \\ 01\,B_8(d-65) & \text{if } 64 < d \leq 320 \\ 11\,B_{12}(d-321) & \text{if } 320 < d \leq 4416 \end{cases}$$

$$\lambda_M(\text{length } \ell) = \begin{cases} 0 & \text{if } \ell = 2 \\ 1^{j+1}\,0\,B_j(\ell - 2 - 2^j) & \text{if } 2^j \leq \ell - 2 < 2^{j+1}, \\ & \text{for } j = 0, 1, 2, \ldots. \end{cases}$$

For example, the first few length encodings are 0, 10, 1100, 1101, 111000, 111001, 111010, 111011, 11110000, etc. Offsets are thus encoded by 8, 11, or 15 bits, and the number of bits used to encode the lengths ℓ is 1 for $\ell = 2$ and $2\lceil \log_2(\ell - 1) \rceil$ for $\ell > 2$.

III. DICTIONARIES

All large full-text retrieval systems make extensive use of dictionaries of all kinds. They are needed to quickly access the concordance, they may be used for compressing the text itself, and they generally provide some useful additional information that can guide the user in the choice of his keywords.

Dictionaries can of course be compressed as if they were regular text, but taking their special structure into account may lead to improved methods [40]. A simple, yet efficient, technique is the *prefix omission method* (POM), a formal definition of which can be found in [2], where it is called *front-end compression*.

The method is based on the observation that consecutive entries in a dictionary mostly share some leading letters. Let x and y be consecutive dictionary entries and let m be the length (number of letters) of their longest common prefix. Then it suffices to store this common prefix only once (with x) and to omit it from the following entry, where instead the length m will be kept. This is easily generalized to a longer list of dictionary entries, as in the example in Fig. 16.

Note that the value given for the prefix length does not refer to the string that was actually stored, but rather to the corresponding full-length dictionary entry. The compression and decompression algorithms are immediate.

If the dictionary entries are coded in standard format, with one byte per character, one could use the first byte of each entry in the compressed dictionary to store the value of m. There will mostly be a considerable gain, since the average length of common prefixes of consecutive entries in large dictionaries is generally much larger than 1. Even when the entries are already compressed,

dictionary entry	prefix length	stored suffix
FORM	0	FORM
FORMALLY	4	ALLY
FORMAT	5	T
FORMATION	6	ION
FORMULATE	4	ULATE
FORMULATING	8	ING
FORTY	3	TY
FORTHWITH	4	HWITH

FIGURE 16 Example of the prefix omission method.

for example, by a character-by-character Huffman code, one would still achieve some savings. For convenience, one could choose a fixed integer parameter k and reserve the first k bits of every entry to represent values of m for $0 \leq m < 2^k$, where k is not necessarily large enough to accommodate the longest omitted prefix. In the above example, k could for example be chosen as 3, and the entry corresponding to FORMULATING would then be (7, TING).

A standard dictionary does, however, not provide the flexibility required by sophisticated systems. For instance, a prominent feature would be the possibility of processing truncated terms of several kinds by means of a variable-length don't-care character ∗. Examples of the use of ∗ for prefix, suffix, and infix truncation have been given in Section I.

Suffix truncation can be handled by the regular dictionary. To enable prefix truncation, the problem is that the relevant terms are scattered throughout the file and therefore hard to locate. A possible solution is to adjoin an *inverse* dictionary to the system: for each term, form its reversed string, then sort the reversed strings lexicographically. To search, e.g., for ∗ache, we would access the inverse dictionary with the string ehca, retrieve the entries prefixed by it (they form a contiguous block), e.g., ehcadaeh and ehcahtoot, and reverse these strings again to get our terms, e.g., headache and toothache. The solution of the inverse dictionary cannot be extended to deal with prefix and suffix truncation simultaneously.

An elegant method allowing the processing of any kind of truncation is the *permuted dictionary* suggested in [2]. Given a dictionary, the corresponding permuted dictionary is obtained by the following sequence of steps:

1. append to each term a character / which does not appear in any term;
2. for a term x of length n characters, form $n + 1$ new terms by cyclically shifting the string $x/$ by k characters, $0 \leq k \leq n$;
3. sort the resulting list alphabetically.

Figure 17 shows these steps for the dictionary consisting of the strings JACM, JASIS, and IPM. The first column lists the terms with the appended /. In the second column, the permuted terms generated by the same original term appear consecutively, and the third column is sorted. The last column shows how the permuted dictionary can be compressed by POM.

DATA COMPRESSION IN INFORMATION RETRIEVAL SYSTEMS 609

original	permuted	sorted	compressed m	suffix
JACM	JACM/	/IPM	0	/IPM
JASIS	ACM/J	/JACM	1	JACM
IPM	CM/JA	/JASIS	3	SIS
	M/JAC	ACM/J	0	ACM/J
	/JACM	ASIS/J	1	SIS/J
	JASIS/	CM/JA	0	CM/JA
	ASIS/J	IPM/	0	IPM/
	SIS/JA	IS/JAS	1	S/JAS
	IS/JAS	JACM/	0	JACM/
	S/JASI	JASIS/	2	SIS/
	/JASIS	M/IP	0	M/IP
	IPM/	M/JAC	2	JAC
	PM/I	PM/I	0	PM/I
	M/IP	S/JASI	0	S/JASI
	/IPM	SIS/JA	1	IS/JA

FIGURE 17 Example of the permuted dictionary.

The key for using the permuted dictionary efficiently is a function get(x), which accesses the file and retrieves all the strings having x as prefix. These strings are easily located since they appear consecutively, and the corresponding original terms are recovered by a simple cyclic shift. To process truncated terms, all one needs is to call get() with the appropriate parameter. Figure 18 shows in its leftmost columns how to deal with suffix, prefix, infix, and simultaneous prefix and suffix truncations. The other columns then bring an example for each of these categories: first the query itself, then the corresponding call to get(), the retrieved entries from the permuted dictionary, and the corresponding reconstructed terms.

IV. CONCORDANCES

Every occurrence of every word in the database can be uniquely characterized by a sequence of numbers that give its exact position in the text. Typically, such a sequence would consist of the document number d, the paragraph number p (in the document), the sentence number s (in the paragraph), and the word number w (in the sentence). The quadruple (d, p, s, w) is the *coordinate* of the occurrence, and the corresponding fields will be called for short d-field, p-field,

X*	get(/X)	JA*	get(/JA)	/JACM, /JASIS	JACM, JASIS
*X	get(X/)	*M	get(M/)	M/IP, M/JAC	IPM, JACM
X*Y	get(Y/X)	J*S	get(S/J)	S/JASI	JASIS
X	get(X)	*A*	get(A)	ACM/J, ASIS/J	JACM, JASIS

FIGURE 18 Processing truncated terms with permuted dictionary.

s-field, and w-field. In the following, we assume for the ease of discussion that coordinates of every retrieval system are of this form; however, all the methods can also be applied to systems with a different coordinate structure, such as book–page–line–word, etc. The concordance contains, for every word of the dictionary, the lexicographically ordered list of all its coordinates in the text; it is accessed via the dictionary that contains for every word a pointer to the corresponding list in the concordance. The concordance is kept in compressed form on secondary storage, and parts of it are fetched when needed and decompressed. The compressed file is partitioned into equi-sized blocks such that one block can be read by a single I/O operation.

Since the list of coordinates of any given word is ordered, adjacent coordinates will often have the same d-field, or even the same d- and p-fields, and sometimes, especially for high-frequency words, identical d-, p-, and s-fields. Thus POM can be adapted to the compression of concordances, where to each coordinate a *header* is adjoined, giving the *number of fields* that can be copied from the preceding coordinate; these fields are then omitted. For instance in our model with coordinates (d, p, s, w), it would suffice to keep a header of 2 bits. The four possibilities are don't copy any field from the previous coordinate, copy the d-field, copy the d- and p-fields, and copy the d-, p-, and s-fields. Obviously, different coordinates cannot have all four fields identical.

For convenient computer manipulation, one generally chooses a fixed length for each field, which therefore must be large enough to represent the maximal possible values. However, most stored values are small; thus there is usually much wasted space in each coordinate. In some situations, some space can be saved at the expense of a longer processing time, as in the following example.

At RRP, the maximal length of a sentence is 676 words! Such long sentences can be explained by the fact that in the Responsa literature punctuation marks are often omitted or used very scarcely. At TLF, there is even a "sentence" of more than 2000 words (a modern poem). Since on the other hand most sentences are short and it was preferred to use only field-sizes that are multiples of half-bytes, the following method is used: the size of the w-field is chosen to be one byte (8 bits); any sentence of length $\ell > 256$ words, such that $\ell = 80k + r (0 \le r < 80)$, is split into k units of 80 words, followed (if $r > 0$) by a sentence of r words. These sentences form only a negligible percentage of the database. While resolving the storage problem, the insertion of such "virtual points" in the middle of a sentence creates some problems for the retrieval process. When in a query one asks to retrieve occurrences of keywords A and B such that A and B are adjacent or that no more than some small number of words appear between them, one usually does not allow A and B to appear in different sentences. This is justified, since "adjacency" and "near vicinity" operators are generally used to retrieve expressions, and not the coincidental juxtaposition of A at the end of a sentence with B at the beginning of the following one. However in the presence of virtual points, the search should be extended also into neighboring "sentences," if necessary, since the virtual points are only artificial boundaries that might have split some interesting expression. Hence this solution further complicates the retrieval algorithms.

The methods presented in the next section not only yield improved compression, but also get rid of the virtual points.

A. Using Variable-Length Fields

The basic idea of all the new methods is to allow the p-, s-, and w-fields to have variable length. As in POM, each compressed coordinate will be prefixed by a header that will encode the information necessary to decompress the coordinate. The methods differ in their interpretation of the header. The choice of the length of every field is based on statistics gathered from the entire database on the distribution of the values in each field. Thus for dynamically changing databases, the compression method would need frequent updates, so that the methods are more suitable for retrieval systems with static databases. However, if the text changes only slowly, say, it is a large corpus to which from time to time some documents that have characteristics similar to the documents already in the corpus are adjoined, then the methods will still perform well, though not optimally.

The codes in the header can have various interpretations: they can stand for a length ℓ, indicating that the corresponding field is encoded in ℓ bits; they can stand for a certain value v, indicating that the corresponding field contains that value; and finally they can indicate that no value for the corresponding field is stored and that the value of the preceding coordinate should be used. This is more general than the prefix-omission technique, since one can decide for every field individually whether to omit it, while in POM, the p-field is only omitted if the d-field is, etc.

The d-field is treated somewhat differently. Since this is the highest level of the hierarchy in our model, this field may contain also very large numbers (there are rarely 500 words in a sentence or 500 sentences in a paragraph, but a corpus may contain tens of thousands of documents). Moreover, the d-fields of most coordinates will contain values, in the representation of which one can save at most one or two bits, if at all. On the other hand, the d-field is the one where the greatest savings are achieved by POM. Thus we shall assume in the sequel that for the d-field, we just keep one bit in the header, indicating whether the value of the preceding coordinate should be copied; if not, the d-field will appear in its entire length.

We now describe the specific methods in detail.

A. The simple method. The header contains codes for the size (in bits) of every field.

(i) Allocate two bits for each of the p-, s-, and w-fields, giving four possible choices for each.

We consider the following variations:

a. One of the possible codes indicates the omission of the field; thus we are left with only three possible choices for the length of each field.
b. The four choices are used to encode field lengths, thus not allowing the use of the preceding coordinate.
c. Use a for the p- and s-fields, and b for the w-field.

Method A(i)c is justified by the fact that consecutive coordinates having the same value in their w-field are rare (3.5% of the concordance at RRP). The reason is that this corresponds to a certain word appearing in the same relative location in different sentences, which is mostly a pure coincidence; on the other hand, consecutive coordinates having the same value in one of their other fields correspond to a certain word appearing more than once in the same sentence, paragraph, or document, and this occurs frequently. For instance, at RRP, 23.4% of the coordinates have the same s-field as their predecessors, 41.7% have the same p-field, and 51.6% have the same d-field.

Note that the header does not contain the binary encoding of the lengths, since this would require a larger number of bits. By storing a *code* for the lengths the header is kept smaller, but at the expense of increasing decompression time, since a table that translates the codes into actual lengths is needed. This remark applies also to the subsequent methods.

> (ii) Allocate three bits in the header for each of the p-, s-, and w-fields, giving 8 possible choices for each.

The idea of (ii) is that by increasing the number of possibilities (and hence the overhead for each coordinate), the range of possible values can be partitioned more efficiently, which should lead to savings in the remaining part of the coordinate. Again three methods corresponding to a, b, and c of (i) were checked.

> B. Using some fields to encode frequent values.

For some very frequent values, the code in the header will be interpreted directly as one of the values, and not as the length of the field in which they are stored. Thus, the corresponding field can be omitted in all these cases. However, the savings for the frequent values come at the expense of reducing the number of possible choices for the lengths of the fields for the less frequent values. For instance, at RRP, the value 1 appears in the s-field of more than 9 million coordinates (about 24% of the concordance); thus, all these coordinates will have no s-field in their compressed form, and the code in the part of the header corresponding to the s-field, will be interpreted as "value 1 in the s-field."

> (i) Allocate 2 bits in the header for each of the p-, s-, and w-fields; one of the codes points to the most frequent value.
> (ii) Allocate 3 bits in the header for each of the p-, s-, and w-fields; three of the codes point to the three most frequent values.

There is no subdivision into methods a, b, and c as in A (in fact the method used corresponds to a), because we concluded from our experiments that it is worth keeping the possibility of using the previous coordinate in case of equal values in some field. Hence, one code was allocated for this purpose, which left only two codes to encode the field lengths in (i) and four codes in (ii). For (ii) we experimented also with allowing two or four of the eight possible choices to encode the two or four most frequent values; however, on our data, the optimum was always obtained for three. There is some redundancy in the case of consecutive coordinates having both the same value in some field, and this value being the most frequent one. There are then two possibilities to encode the second coordinate using the same number of bits. In such a case, the code for the frequent value should be preferred over that pointing to the previous coordinate, as decoding of the former is usually faster.

> C. Combining methods A and B.

Choose individually for each of the p-, s-, and w-fields the best of the previous methods.

D. Encoding length combinations.

If we want to push the idea of A further, we should have a code for *every* possible length of a field, but the maxima of the values can be large. For example, at RRP, one needs 10 bits for the maximal value of the w-field, 9 bits for the s-field, and 10 bits for the p-field. This would imply a header length of 4 bits for each of these fields, which cannot be justified by the negligible improvement over method A(ii).

The size of the header can be reduced by replacing the three codes for the sizes of the p-, s-, and w-fields by a single code in the following way. Denote by $l_p, l_s,$ and l_w the lengths of the p-, s-, and w-fields respectively, i.e., the sizes (in bits) of the binary representations without leading zeros of the values stored in them. In our model $1 \le l_p, l_s, l_w \le 10$, so there are up to 10^3 possible triplets (l_p, l_s, l_w). However, most of these length combinations occur only rarely, if at all. At RRP, the 255 most frequent (l_p, l_s, l_w) triplets account already for 98.05% of the concordance. Therefore:

(i) Allocate 9 bits as header, of which 1 bit is used for the d-field; 255 of the possible codes in the remaining 8 bits point to the 255 most frequent (l_p, l_s, l_w) triplets; the last code is used to indicate that the coordinate corresponds to a "rare" triplet, in which case the p-, s-, and w-fields appear already in their decompressed form.

Although the "compressed" form of the rare coordinates, including a 9-bit header, may in fact need more space than the original coordinate, we still save on the average.

Two refinements are now superimposed. We first note that one does not need to represent the integer 0 in any field. Therefore one can use a representation of the integer $n-1$ in order to encode the value n, so that only $\lfloor \log_2(n-1) \rfloor + 1$ bits are needed instead of $\lfloor \log_2 n \rfloor + 1$. This may seem negligible, because only one bit is saved and only when n is a power of 2, thus for very few values of n. However, the first few of these values, 1, 2, and 4, appear very frequently, so that in fact this yields a significant improvement. At RRP, the total size of the compressed p-, s-, and w-fields (using method D) was further reduced by 7.4%, just by shifting the stored values from n to $n-1$.

The second refinement is based on the observation that since we know from the header the exact length of each field, we know the position of the left-most 1 in it, so that this 1 is also redundant. The possible values in the fields are partitioned into classes C_i defined by $C_0 = \{0\}, C_i = \{\ell : 2^{i-1} \le \ell < 2^i\}$, and the header gives for the values in each of the p-, s-, and w-fields the indices i of the corresponding classes. Therefore if $i \le 1$, there is no need to store any additional information because C_0 and C_1 are singletons, and for $\ell \in C_i$ for $i > 1$, only the $i-1$ bits representing the number $\ell - 2^{i-1}$ are kept. For example, suppose the values in the p-, s-, and w-fields are 3, 1, and 28. Then the encoded values are 2, 0, and 27, which belong to $C_2, C_0,$ and C_5 respectively. The header thus points to the triplet (2, 0, 5) (assuming that this is one of the 255 frequent ones), and the rest of the coordinate consists of the five bits 01011, which are parsed from left to right as 1 bit for the p-field, 0 bits for the s-field, and 4 bits for the w-field. A similar idea was used in [15] for encoding run lengths in the compression of sparse bit vectors.

(ii) Allocate 8 bits as header, of which 1 bit is used for the d-field; the remaining 7 bits are used to encode the 127 most frequent (l_p, l_s, l_w) triplets.

The 127 most frequent triplets still correspond to 85.19% of the concordance at RRP. This is therefore an attempt to save one bit in the header of each coordinate at the expense of having more noncompressed coordinates.

Another possibility is to extend method D also to the d-field. Let b be a Boolean variable corresponding to the two possibilities for the d-field, namely T = the value is identical to that of the preceding coordinate; thus omit it, or F = different value, keep it. We therefore have up to 2000 quadruples (b, l_p, l_s, l_w), which are again sorted by decreasing frequency.

(iii) Allocate 8 bits as header; 255 of the codes point to the 255 most frequent quadruples.

At RRP, these 255 most frequent quadruples cover 87.08% of the concordance. For the last two methods, one could try to get better results by compressing also some of the coordinates with the nonfrequent length combinations, instead of storing them in their decompressed form. We did not, however, pursue this possibility.

1. Encoding

After choosing the appropriate compression method, the concordance is scanned sequentially and each coordinate is compressed with or without using the preceding one. For each of the above methods, the length of the header is constant; thus, the set of compressed coordinates forms a prefix code. Therefore, the compressed coordinates, which have variable lengths, can simply be concatenated. The compressed concordance consists of the resulting very long bit string. This string is partitioned into blocks of equal size, the size corresponding to the buffer size of a read/write operation. If the last coordinate in a block does not fit there in its entirety, it is moved to the beginning of the next block. The first coordinate of each block is considered as having no predecessor, so that if in the original encoding process a coordinate that is the first in a block referred to the previous coordinate, this needs to be corrected. This makes it possible now to access each block individually, while adding only a negligible number of bits to each block.

2. Decoding

Note that for a static information retrieval system, encoding is done only once (when building the database), whereas decoding directly affects the response time for on-line queries. In order to increase the decoding speed, we use a small precomputed table T that is stored in internal memory. For a method with header length k bits, this table has 2^k entries. In entry i of T, $0 \leq i < 2^k$, we store the relevant information for the header consisting of the k-bit binary representation of the integer i.

For the methods in **A**, the relevant information simply consists of the lengths, P, S, and W, of the p-, s-, and w-fields (recall that we assume that only one bit is kept in the header for the d-field, so either the d-field appears in its entire length D, which is constant, or it is omitted), and of the sum of all these lengths (including D), which is the length of the remaining part of the coordinate. We shall use the following notations: for a given internal structure of a decompressed coordinate, let h_d, h_p, h_s, and h_w be the indices of the leftmost bit of the d-, p-, s-, and w-fields respectively, the index of the rightmost bit of a coordinate being 0. For example with a 4-byte coordinate and one byte for each field we would have $h_d = 31$, $h_p = 23$, $h_s = 15$, and $h_w = 7$; these values are constant for the entire database. COOR and LAST are both addresses of a contiguous space in memory in which a single decompressed coordinate can fit (hence of length $h_d + 1$ bits). The procedure SHIFT(X, y, z) shifts the substring of X, which is obtained by ignoring its y rightmost bits, by z bits to the left. Then the following loop could be used for the decoding of a coordinate:

1. **loop** while there is more input or until a certain coordinate is found
2. $H \leftarrow$ next k bits   // read header
3.   (TOT, P, S, W) $\leftarrow \mathcal{T}(H)$ // decode header using table
4.   COOR $\leftarrow$ next TOT bits   // right justified suffix of coordinate
5.   SHIFT(COOR, W, $h_w - W$)   // move d-, p-, and s-fields
6.   SHIFT(COOR, $h_w + S$, $h_s - S$)   // move d- and p-fields
7.   SHIFT(COOR, $h_s + P$, $h_p - P$)   // move d-field
8.   **if** TOT $= P + S + W$ **then** copy d-field from LAST
9.   **if** $P = 0$ **then** copy p-field from LAST
10.   **if** $S = 0$ **then** copy s-field from LAST
11.   **if** $W = 0$ **then** copy w-field from LAST
12.   LAST $\leftarrow$ COOR
13. **end** of loop

There is no need to initialize LAST, since the first coordinate of a block never refers to the preceding coordinate.

For the methods in **B** and **C**, we store sometimes actual values, and not just the lengths of the fields. This can be implemented by using negative values in the table $\mathcal{T}$. For example, if $P = -2$, this could be interpreted as "value 2 in the p-field." Note that when the value stored in a field is given by the header, this field has length 0 in the remaining part of the coordinate. Thus we need the following updates to the above algorithm: line 3 is replaced by

$$(\text{TOT}, P1, S1, W1) \leftarrow \mathcal{T}(H)$$
$$\text{if } P1 < 0 \text{ then } P \leftarrow 0 \text{ else } P \leftarrow P1$$

and statements similar to the latter for the s- and w-fields. After statement 11 we should insert

$$\text{if } P1 < 0 \text{ then put} -P1 \text{ in p-field of COOR}$$

and similar statements for the s- and w-fields.

The decoding of the methods in **D** is equivalent to that of **A**. The only difference is in the preparation of the table $\mathcal{T}$ (which is done only once). While for **A** to each field correspond certain fixed bits of the header that determine the length of that field, for **D** the header is nondivisible and represents the lengths

TABLE 3 Distribution of Values Stored in p-, s-, and w-Fields

Value		1	2	3	4	5	79	83	87	93	119	120
Ignoring	p-field	14.1	35.2	46.5	54.2	60.2		99				
Preceding	s-field	24.2	40.2	51.1	58.8	64.5	99					
Coordinate	w-field	3.0	5.8	8.6	11.4	14.0					99	
Using	p-field	9.6	25.2	36.5	45.0	51.7				99		
Preceding	s-field	17.9	33.0	44.3	52.6	58.9			99			
Coordinate	w-field	1.9	4.4	7.1	9.7	12.4						99

of all the fields together. This does not affect the decoding process, since in both methods a table-lookup is used to interpret the header. An example of the encoding and decoding processes appears in the next section.

3. Parameter Setting

All the methods of the previous section were compared on the concordance of RRP. Each coordinate had a (d, p, s, w) structure and was of length 6 bytes (48 bits). Using POM, the average length of a compressed coordinate was 4.196 bytes, i.e., a compression gain of 30%.

Table 3 gives the frequencies of the first few values in each of the p-, s-, and w-fields, both with and without taking into account the previous coordinate. The frequencies are given in cumulative percentages; e.g., the row entitled s-field contains in the column headed i the percentage of coordinates having a value $\leq i$ in their s-field. We have also added the values for which the cumulative percentage first exceeds 99%.

As one can see, the first four values in the p- and s-fields account already for half of the concordance. This means that most of the paragraphs consist of only a few sentences and most of the documents consist of only a few paragraphs. The figures for the w-field are different, because short sentences are not preponderant. While the (noncumulative) frequency of the values i in the s-field is a clearly decreasing function of i, it is interesting to note the peek at value 2 for the p-field. This can be explained by the specific nature of the Responsa literature, in which most of the documents have a question–answer structure. Therefore the first paragraph of a document usually contains just a short question, whereas the answer, starting from the second paragraph, may be much longer.

When all the coordinates are considered (upper half of Table 3), the percentages are higher than the corresponding percentages for the case where identical fields in adjacent coordinates are omitted (lower half of Table 3). This means that the idea of copying certain fields from the preceding coordinate yields to savings, which are, for the small values, larger than could have been expected from knowing their distribution in the noncompressed concordance.

Using the information collected from the concordance, all the possible variants for each of the methods in A and B have been checked. Table 4 lists for each of the methods the variant for which maximal compression was achieved. The numbers in boldface are the frequent values used in methods B and C; the other numbers refer to the lengths of the fields. The value 0 indicates that the field of the preceding coordinate should be copied.

DATA COMPRESSION IN INFORMATION RETRIEVAL SYSTEMS

TABLE 4 Optimal Variants of the Methods

Method	p-field	s-field	w-field
A(i)a	0 2 5 10	0 2 5 9	0 4 6 10
A(i)b	1 3 5 10	1 3 5 9	3 5 6 10
A(ii)a	0 1 2 3 4 5 6 10	0 1 2 3 4 5 6 9	0 1 3 4 5 6 7 10
A(ii)b	1 2 3 4 5 6 7 10	1 2 3 4 5 6 7 9	1 2 3 4 5 6 7 10
B(i)	0 2 4 10	0 1 4 9	0 4 6 10
B(ii)	0 1 2 3 3 4 5 10	0 1 2 3 3 4 5 9	0 3 4 5 3 5 6 10
C	0 2 5 10	0 1 2 3 3 4 5 9	3 5 6 10

The optimal variants for the methods A(ii) are not surprising: since most of the stored values are small, one could expect the optimal partition to give priority to small field lengths. For method C, each field is compressed by the best of the other methods, which are A(i)a for the p-field, B(ii) for the s-field, and A(i)b for the w-field, thus requiring a header of $1 + 2 + 3 + 2 = 8$ bits (including one bit for the d-field).

The entries of Table 4 were computed using the first refinement mentioned in the description of method D, namely storing $n - 1$ instead of n. The second refinement (dropping the leftmost 1) could not be applied, because it is not true that the leftmost bit in every field is a 1. Thus for all the calculations with methods A and B, an integer n was supposed to require $\lfloor \log_2(n - 1) \rfloor + 1$ bits for $n > 1$ and one bit for $n = 1$.

As an example for the encoding and decoding processes, consider method C, and a coordinate structure with $(h_d, h_p, h_s, h_w) = (8, 8, 8, 8)$, i.e., one byte for each field. The coordinate we wish to process is (159, 2, 2, 35). Suppose further that only the value in the d-field is the same as in the previous coordinate. Then the length D of the d-field is 0; in the p-field the value 1 is stored, using two bits; nothing is stored in the s-field, because 2 is one of the frequent values and directly referenced by the header; and in the w-field the value 34 is stored, using 6 bits. The possible options for the header are numbered from left to right as they appear in Table 4; hence the header of this coordinate is 0-10-011-11, where dashes separating the parts corresponding to different fields have been added for clarity; the remaining part of the coordinate is 01-100010. Table T has $2^8 = 256$ entries; at entry 79 (= 01001111 in binary) the values stored are $(TOT, P1, S1, W1) = (8, 2, -2, 6)$. When decoding the compressed coordinate 0100111101100010, the leftmost 8 bits are considered as header and converted to the integer 79. Table T is then accessed with that index, retrieving the 4-tuple $(8, 2, -2, 6)$, which yields the values $(P, S, W) = (2, 0, 6)$. The next TOT = 8 bits are therefore loaded into COOR of size 4 bytes, and after the three shifts we get

$$\text{COOR} = 00000000 - 00000010 - 00000000 - 00100010.$$

Since TOT = $P + S + W$ the value of the d-field is copied from the last coordinate. Since $P1 < 0$, the value $-S1 = 2$ is put into the s-field.

On our data, the best method was D(i) with an average coordinate length of 3.082 bytes, corresponding to 49% compression relative to the full 6-byte coordinate, and giving a 27% improvement over POM. The next best method was C with 3.14 bytes. Nevertheless, the results depend heavily on the statistics of the specific system at hand, so that for another database, other methods could be preferable.

The main target of the efforts was to try to eliminate or at least reduce the unused space in the coordinates. Note that this can easily be achieved by considering the entire database as a single long run of words, which we could index sequentially from 1 to N, N being the total number of words in the text. Thus $\lfloor \log_2 N \rfloor + 1$ bits would be necessary per coordinate. However, the hierarchical structure is lost, so that, for example, queries asking for the cooccurrence of several words in the same sentence or paragraph are much harder to process. Moreover, when a coordinate is represented by a single, usually large, number, we lose also the possibility of omitting certain fields that could be copied from preceding coordinates. A hierarchical structure of a coordinate is therefore preferable for the retrieval algorithms. Some of the new compression methods even outperform the simple method of sequentially numbering the words, since the latter would imply at the RRP database a coordinate length of 26 bits = 3.25 bytes.

B. Model-Based Concordance Compression

For our model of a textual database, we assume that the text is divided into documents and the documents are made up of words. We thus use only a two-level hierarchy to identify the location of a word, which makes the exposition here easier. The methods can, however, be readily adapted to more complex concordance structures, like the 4-level hierarchy mentioned above. In our present model, the conceptual concordance consists, for each word, of a series of (d, w) pairs, d standing for a document number, and w for the index, or offset, of a word within the given document:

$$\text{word}_1 : (d_1, w_1)(d_1, w_2) \cdots (d_1, w_{m_1})$$
$$(d_2, w_1)(d_2, w_2) \cdots (d_2, w_{m_2})$$
$$\cdots$$
$$(d_N, w_1) \cdots (d_N, w_{m_N})$$
$$\text{word}_2 : \cdots$$

For a discussion of the problems of relating this conceptual location to a physical location on the disc, see [7].

It is sometimes convenient to translate our 4-level hierarchy to an equivalent one, in which we indicate the index of the next document containing the word, the number of times the word occurs in the document, followed by the list of word indices of the various occurrences:

$$\text{word}_1 : (d_1, m_1; w_1, w_2, \ldots, w_{m_1})$$
$$(d_2, m_2; w_1, \ldots, w_{m_2})$$
$$\cdots$$
$$(d_N, m_N; w_1, \ldots, w_{m_N})$$
$$\text{word}_2 : \cdots$$

Our task is to model each of the components of the latter representation, and use standard compression methods to compress each entity. Below we assume that we know (from the dictionary) the total number of times a word occurs in the database, the number of different documents in which it occurs, and (from a separate table) the number of words in each document. The compression algorithm is then based on predicting the probability distribution of the various values in the coordinates, devising a code based on the predicted distributions, and using the codeword corresponding to the actual value given.

We thus need to generate a large number of codes. If so, the Shannon–Fano method (as defined in [41]) seems the most appropriate if we are concerned with processing speed. Thus an element, which according to the model at hand appears with probability p, will be encoded by $\lceil -\log_2 p \rceil$ bits. Once the length of the codeword is determined, the actual codeword is easily generated. However, Shannon–Fano codes are not optimal and might in fact be quite wasteful, especially for the very low probabilities.

While Shannon–Fano coding is fast, when high precision is required Huffman codes are a good alternative. Under the constraint that each codeword consists of an integral number of bits, they are optimal; however, their computation is much more involved than that of Shannon–Fano codes, because every codeword depends on the whole set of probabilities. Thus more processing time is needed, but compression is improved. On the other hand, Huffman codes are not effective in the presence of very high probabilities. Elements occurring with high probability have low information content; yet their Huffman codeword cannot be shorter than one bit. If this is a prominent feature, arithmetic coding must be considered.

Arithmetic coding more directly uses the probabilities derived from the model, and overcomes the problem of high-probability elements by encoding entire messages, not just codewords. Effectively, an element with probability p is encoded by exactly $-\log_2 p$ bits, which is the information theoretic minimum. While in many contexts arithmetic codes might not improve much on Huffman codes, their superiority here might be substantial, because the model may generate many high probabilities. There is of course a time/space tradeoff, as the computation of arithmetic codes is generally more expensive than that of Huffman codes.

Initially we are at the beginning of the document list and are trying to determine the probability that the next (when we start, this is the first) document containing a term is d documents away from our current location. We know the number of documents that contain the term, say N, and the number of documents, say D, from which these are chosen. (More generally, after we have located a number of documents that contain the term, D and N will respectively represent the total number of remaining documents and, of these, the number that contain the term. Our reasoning will then continue in parallel to that of the first occurrence.)

Our first question, then, is what is the probability distribution of the first/next document containing the term? Assuming that the events involved are independent and equally distributed, this is equivalent to asking, if N different objects are selected at random from an ordered set of D objects, what is the probability that d is the index of the object with minimum index?

Because of the uniformity assumption, each of the $\binom{D}{N}$ ways of picking N out of D objects have same probability, viz, $1/\binom{D}{N}$, but of these, only $\binom{D-d}{N-1}$ satisfy the condition that d is the minimum index. That is, certainly one document must be the dth one, so we only have freedom to choose $N-1$ additional documents. Since all of these must have index greater than d, we have only $D-d$ options for these $N-1$ selections. Thus the probability that the next document has (relative) position d is $\Pr(d) = \binom{D-d}{N-1}/\binom{D}{N}$.

We first note this is a true probability

$$\sum_d \Pr(d) = \sum_{d=1}^{D-N+1} \frac{\binom{D-d}{N-1}}{\binom{D}{N}} = \sum_{k=N-1}^{D-1} \frac{\binom{k}{N-1}}{\binom{D}{N}} = \frac{\binom{D}{N}}{\binom{D}{N}} = 1,$$

where the last equality uses the well-known combinatoric identity that permits summation over the upper value in the binomial coefficient [11]. Second, we note that we can rewrite the probability as

$$\left(\frac{N}{D-N+1}\right) \times \left(1 - \frac{d}{D}\right) \times \left(1 - \frac{d}{D-1}\right) \times \cdots \times \left(1 - \frac{d}{D-N+2}\right).$$

If $d \ll D$, this is approximately $(N/D) \times (1 - d/D)^{N-1}$, which is in turn approximately proportional to $e^{-d(N-1)/D}$ or γ^d, for $\gamma = e^{-(N-1)/D}$. This last form is that of the geometric distribution recommended by Witten et al. [42].

The encoding process is then as follows. We wish to encode the d-field of the next coordinates $(d, m; w_1, \ldots, w_m)$. Assuming that the probability distribution of d is given by $\Pr(d)$, we construct a code based on $\{\Pr(d)\}_{d=1}^{D-N+1}$. This assigns codewords to all the possible values of d, from which we use the codeword corresponding to the actual value d in our coordinate. If the estimate is good, the actual value d will be assigned a high probability by the model, and therefore be encoded with a small number of bits.

Next we encode the number of occurrences of the term in this document. Let us suppose that we have T occurrences of the term remaining (initially, this will be the total number of occurrences of the term in the database). The T occurrences are to be distributed into the N remaining documents the word occurs in. Thus we know that each document being considered must have at least a single term, that is, $m = 1 + x$, where $x \geq 0$. If $T = N$, then clearly $x = 0$ ($m = 1$), and we need output no code—m conveys no information in this case. If $T > N$, then we must distribute the $T - N$ terms not accounted for over the remaining N documents that contain the term. We assume, for simplicity, that the additional amount, x, going to the currently considered document is Poisson distributed, with mean $\lambda = (T - N)/N$. The Poisson distribution is given by $\Pr(x) = e^{-\lambda} \frac{\lambda^x}{x!}$. This allows us to compute the probability of x for all possible values ($x = 0, 1, \ldots, T - N$) and to then encode x using one of the encodings above.

We must finally encode all the m offsets, but this problem is formally identical to that of encoding the next document. The current document has W words, so the distribution of w, the first occurrence of the word, is given by the probabilities $\binom{W-w}{m-1}/\binom{W}{m}$. Once this is encoded, we have a problem identical to the initial one in form, except that we now have $m-1$ positions left to encode and $W-w$ locations. This continues until the last term, which is uniformly distributed over the remaining word locations.

DATA COMPRESSION IN INFORMATION RETRIEVAL SYSTEMS

Then we encode the next document, but this is again a problem identical in form to the initial problem—only we now have one fewer document ($N-1$) having the term, and d fewer target documents ($D-d$) to consider.

The formal encoding algorithm is given in Fig. 19. We begin with a conceptual concordance, represented for the purpose of this algorithm as a list of

```
{
    for s ← 1 to S        /* for each word in concordance */
    {
        D   ←   total number of documents
        T   ←   total number of occurrences of word s
        N   ←   total number of documents in which word s occurs
        d₀  ←   0
        for i ← 1 to N        /* for each document containing word s */
        {
            /* process document i */
            output d_code(dᵢ − dᵢ₋₁, N − i, D)
            if T > N
                output m_code(mᵢ − 1, (T − N)/N, T − N)
            /* process occurrences of word s in document i */
            W   ←   total number of words in document i
            w₀  ←   0
            for j ← 1 to mᵢ
            {
                output w_code(wⱼ − wⱼ₋₁, mᵢ − j, W)
                W   ←   W − (wⱼ − wⱼ₋₁)
            }
            /* update parameters and continue */
            D   ←   D − (dᵢ − dᵢ₋₁)
            T   ←   T − mᵢ
        }
    }
}
d_code(d, N, D)
{
    construct a code 𝒞₁ based on probabilities that d = k: $\left\{ \binom{D-k}{N} / \binom{D}{N+1} \right\}_{k=1}^{D-i+1}$
    return 𝒞₁(d)
}
m_code(x, λ, max)
{
    F   ←   $\sum_{k=0}^{max} e^{-\lambda} \frac{\lambda^k}{k!}$        /* correction factor for truncated Poisson distribution */
    construct a code 𝒞₂ based on probabilities that x = k: $\left\{ \frac{1}{F} e^{-\lambda} \frac{\lambda^k}{k!} \right\}_{k=0}^{max}$
    return 𝒞₂(x)
}
w_code(w, m, W)
{
    construct a code 𝒞₃ based on probabilities that w = k: $\left\{ \binom{W-k}{m} / \binom{W}{m+1} \right\}_{k=1}^{W-i+1}$
    return 𝒞₃(w)
}
```

FIGURE 19 Concordance Compression Algorithm.

entries. Our concordance controls S different words. For each word, there is an entry for each document it occurs in, of the form $(d_i, m_i; w_1, \ldots, w_{m_i})$, where d_i, m_i, and w_j are given similarly to the second representation defined above.

Note that we do not encode the absolute values d_i and w_j, but the relative increases $d_i - d_{i-1}$ and $w_j - w_{j-1}$; this is necessary, because we redefine, in each iteration, the sizes D, W, and T to be the *remaining* number of documents, the number of words in the current document, and the number of occurrences of the current word, respectively.

In fact, one should also deal with the possibility where the independence assumptions of the previous section are not necessarily true. In particular, we consider the case where terms cluster not only within a document, but even at the between document level. Details of this model can be found in [43].

V. BITMAPS

For every distinct word W of the database, a bitmap $B(W)$ is constructed, which acts as an "occurrence" map at the document level. The length (in bits) of each map is the number of documents in the system. Thus, in the RRP for example, the length of each map is about 6K bytes. These maps are stored in compressed form on a secondary storage device. At RRP, the compression algorithm was taken from [44], reducing the size of a map to 350 bytes on the average. This compression method was used for only about 10% of the words, those which appear at least 70 times; for the remaining words, the *list* of document numbers is kept and transformed into bitmap form at processing time. The space needed for the bitmap file in its entirety is 33.5 MB, expanding the overall space requirement of the entire retrieval system by about 5%.

At the beginning of the process dealing with a query of the type given in Eq. (1), the maps $B(A_{ij})$ are retrieved, for $i = 1, \ldots, m$ and $j = 1, \ldots, n_i$. They are decompressed and a new map ANDVEC is constructed:

$$\text{ANDVEC} = \bigwedge_{i=1}^{m} \left(\bigvee_{j=1}^{n_i} B(A_{ij}) \right).$$

The bitmap ANDVEC serves as a "filter," for only documents corresponding to 1 bits in ANDVEC can possibly contain a solution. Note that no more than three full-length maps are simultaneously needed for its construction.

For certain queries, in particular when keywords with a small number of occurrences in the text are used, ANDVEC will consist only of zeros, which indicates that nothing should be retrieved. In such cases the user gets the correct if somewhat meager results, without a single merge or collate action having been executed. However, even if ANDVEC is not null, it will usually be much sparser than its components. These maps can improve the performance of the retrieval process in many ways to be now described.

A. Usefulness of Bitmaps in IR

First, bitmaps can be helpful in reducing the number of I/O operations involved in the query-processing phase. Indeed, since the concordance file is usually too large to be stored in the internal memory, it is kept in compressed form in secondary storage, and parts of it are fetched when needed and decompressed. The compressed concordance file is partitioned into equisized blocks such that one block can be read by a single I/O operation; it is accessed via the dictionary, which contains for each word a pointer to the corresponding (first) block. A block can contain coordinates of many "small" words (i.e., words with low frequency in the database), but on the other hand, the coordinate list of a single "large" (high-frequency) word may extend over several consecutive blocks. In the RRP, for example, about half of the words appear only once, but on the other hand there are some words that occur hundreds of thousands of times! It is for the large words that the bitmap ANDVEC may lead to significant savings in the number of I/O operations. Rather than reading *all* the blocks to collect the list of coordinates that will later be merged and/or collated, we access only blocks which contain coordinates in the documents specified by the 1 bits of ANDVEC. Hence if the map is sparse enough, only a small *subset* of the blocks need to be fetched and decompressed. To implement this idea, we need, in addition to the bitmap, also a small list $L(W)$ for each large word W, $L(W) = \{(f_j, \ell_j)\}$, where f_j and ℓ_j are respectively the document numbers of the first and last coordinate of W in block number j, and j runs over the indices of blocks that contain coordinates of W. The list $L(W)$ is scanned together with the bitmap, and if there is no 1 bit in ANDVEC in the bit range $[f_j, \ell_j]$, the block j is simply skipped.

There are, however, savings beyond I/O operations. Once a concordance block containing some coordinates that might be relevant is read, it is scanned in parallel with ANDVEC. Coordinates with document numbers corresponding to 0 bits are skipped. For the axis, which is the first keyword A_i to be handled, this means that only parts of the lists $C(A_{ij})$ will be transferred to a working area, where they are merged. In order to save internal memory space during the query processing, the lists of the keywords A_{kj}, for $k \neq i$, are not merged like the lists of the axis, but are directly collated with the axis. Such collations can be involved operations, as the distance constraints may cause each coordinate of the axis to be checked against several coordinates of every variant of other keywords, and conversely each such coordinate might collate with several coordinates of the axis. Therefore the use of ANDVEC may save time by reducing the number of collations. Moreover, after all the variants of the second keyword have been collated with the axis, the coordinates of the axis not matched can be rejected, so that the axis may shrink considerably. Now ANDVEC can be updated by deleting some of its 1 bits, which again tends to reduce the number of read operations and collations when handling the following keywords. The updates of the axis and ANDVEC are repeated after the processing of each keyword A_j of the query (1).

For conventional query-processing algorithms, the consequence of increasing the number m of keywords is an increased processing time, whereas the set of solutions can only shrink. When m is increased with the bitmap approach, however, the time needed to retrieve the maps and to perform some additional logical operations is usually largely compensated for by the savings in I/O operations caused by a sparser ANDVEC. The new approach seems thus to be particularly attractive for a large number of keywords. Users are therefore encouraged to change their policy and to submit more complex queries!

Another possible application of the bitmaps is for getting a selective display of the results. A user is often not interested in finding *all* the occurrences of a certain phrase in the database, as specified by the query, but only in a small subset corresponding to a certain author or a certain period. The usual way to process such special requests consists in executing first the search ignoring the restrictions, and then filtering out the solutions not needed. This can be very wasteful and time-consuming, particularly if the required subrange (period or author(s)) is small. The bitmaps allow the problem to be dealt with in a natural way, requiring only minor changes to adapt the search program to this application. All we need is to prepare a small repertoire $\mathcal{R}$ of fixed bitmaps, say one for each author, where the 1 bits indicate the documents written by this author, and a map for the documents of each year or period, etc. The restrictions can now be formulated at the same time the query is submitted. In the construction algorithm, ANDVEC will not be initialized by a string containing only 1's, but by a logical combination of elements of $\mathcal{R}$, as induced by the additional restrictions. Thus user-imposed restrictions on required ranges to which solutions should belong on one hand, and query-imposed restrictions on the co-occurrence of keywords on the other, are processed in exactly the same way, resulting in a bit vector, the sparsity of which depends directly on the severity of the restrictions. As was pointed out earlier, this may lead to savings in processing time and I/O operations.

Finally, bitmaps can be also helpful in handling negative keywords. If a query including some negative keywords $\underline{D_i}$ is submitted at the document-level, one can use the binary complements $\overline{B(D_i)}$ of the maps, since only documents with no occurrence of D_i (indicated by the 0 bits) can be relevant. However, for other levels, the processing is not so simple. In fact, if the query is not on the document level, the bitmaps of the negative keywords are useless, and ANDVEC is formed only by the maps of the positive keywords. This difference in the treatment of negative and positive keywords is due to the fact that a 0 bit in the bit vector of a positive keyword means that the corresponding document cannot possibly be relevant, whereas a 1 bit in the bit vector of a negative keyword D_j only implies that D_j appears in the corresponding document; however, this document can still be retrieved, if D_j is not in the specified neighborhood of the other keywords. Nevertheless, even though the negative keywords do not contribute in rendering ANDVEC sparser, ANDVEC will still be useful also for the negative words: only coordinates in the relevant documents must be checked *not* to fall in the vicinity of the axis, as imposed by the (l_i, u_i).

B. Compression of Bitmaps

It would be wasteful to store the bitmaps in their original form, since they are usually very sparse (the great majority of the words occur in very few documents). Schuegraf [45] proposes to use *run-length coding* for the compression of sparse bit vectors, in which a string of consecutive 0's terminated by a

1 (called a *run*) is replaced by the length of the run. A sophisticated run-length coding technique can be found in Teuhola [46]. Jakobsson [47] suggests to partition each vector into k-bit blocks, and to apply Huffman coding on the 2^k possible bit patterns. This method is referred to below as the method NORUN.

1. Hierarchical Compression

In this section we concentrate on *hierarchical bit-vector compression*: let us partition the original bit vector v_0 of length l_0 bits into k_0 equal blocks of r_0 bits, $r_0 \cdot k_0 = l_0$, and drop the blocks consisting only of 0's. The resulting sequence of nonzero blocks does not allow the reconstruction of v_0, unless we add a list of the indices of these blocks in the original vector. This list of up to k_0 indices is kept as a binary vector v_1 of $l_1 = k_0$ bits, where there is a 1 in position i if and only if the ith block of v_0 is not all zero. Now v_1 can further be compressed by the same method.

In other words, a sequence of bit vectors v_j is constructed, each bit in v_j being the result of ORing the bits in the corresponding block in v_{j-1}. The procedure is repeated recursively until a level t is reached where the vector length reduces to a few bytes, which will form a single block. The compressed form of v_0 is then obtained by concatenating all the nonzero blocks of the various v_i, while retaining the block-level information. Decompression is obtained simply by reversing these operations and their order. We start at level t, and pass from one level to the next by inserting blocks of zeros into level $j - 1$ for every 0 bit in level j.

Figure 20 depicts an example of a small vector v_0 of 27 bits and its derived levels v_1 and v_2, with $r_i = 3$ for $i = 0, 1, 2$ and $t = 2$. The sizes r_j of the blocks are parameters and can change from level to level for a given vector, and even from one word of the database to another, although the latter is not practical

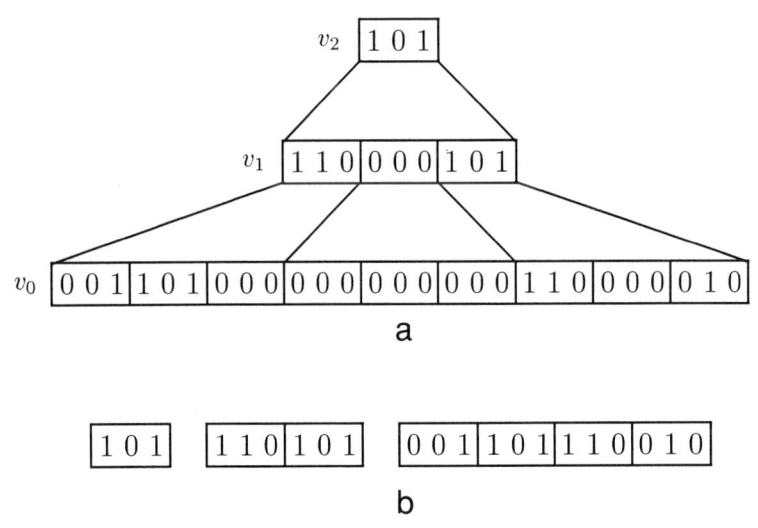

FIGURE 20 Hierarchical bit-vector compression. (a) Original vector and two derived levels and (b) compressed vector.

for our applications. Because of the structure of the compressed vector, we call this the TREE method, and shall use in our discussion the usual tree vocabulary: the *root* of the tree is the single block on the top level, and for a block x in v_{j+1}, which is obtained by ORing the blocks $y_1, \ldots, y_{r_j}$ of v_j, we say that x is the *parent* of the nonzero blocks among the y_i.

The TREE method was proposed by Wedekind and Härder [48]. It appears also in Vallarino [49], who used it for two-dimensional bitmaps, but only with one level of compression. In [50], the parameters (block size and height of the tree) are chosen assuming that the bit vectors are generated by a memoryless information source; i.e., each bit in v_0 has a constant probability p_0 for being 1, independently from each other. However, for bitmaps in information retrieval systems, this assumption is not very realistic a priori, as adjacent bits often represent documents written by the same author; there is a positive correlation for a word to appear in consecutive documents, because of the specific style of the author or simply because such documents often treat the same or related subjects.

We first remark that the hierarchical method does not always yield real compression. Consider, for example, a vector v_0 for which the indices of the 1 bits are of the form ir_0 for $i \le l_0/r_0$. Then there are no zero-blocks (of size r_0) in v_0; moreover all the bits of v_i for $i > 0$ will be 1, so that the whole tree must be kept. Therefore the method should be used only for sparse vectors.

In the other extreme case, when v_0 is very sparse, the TREE method may again be wasteful: let $d = \lceil \log_2 l_0 \rceil$, so that a d-bit number suffices to identify any bit position in v_0. If the vector is extremely sparse, we could simply list the positions of all the 1 bits, using d bits for each. This is in fact the inverse of the transformation performed by the bit vectors: basically, for every different word W of the database, there is one entry in the inverted file containing the list of references of W, and this list is transformed into a bitmap; here we change the bitmap back into its original form of a list.

A small example will illustrate how the bijection of the previous paragraph between lists and bitmaps can be used to improve method TREE. Suppose that among the $r_0 \cdot r_1 \cdot r_2$ first bits of v_0 only position j contains a 1. The first bit in level 3, which corresponds to the ORing of these bits, will thus be set to 1 and will point to a subtree consisting of three blocks, one on each of the lower levels. Hence in this case a single 1 bit caused the addition of at least $r_0 + r_1 + r_2$ bits to the compressed map, since if it were zero, the whole subtree would have been omitted. We conclude that if $r_0 + r_1 + r_2 \ge d$, it is preferable to consider position j as containing zero, thus omitting the bits of the subtree, and to add the number j to an appended list L, using only d bits. This example is readily generalized so as to obtain an optimal partition between tree and list for every given vector, as will now be shown.

We define l_j and k_j respectively as the number of bits and the number of blocks in v_j, for $0 \le j \le t$. Note that $r_j \cdot k_j = l_j$. Denote by $T(i, j)$ the subtree rooted at the ith block of v_j, with $0 \le j \le t$ and $1 \le i \le k_j$. Let $S(i, j)$ be the size in bits of the compressed form of the subtree $T(i, j)$, i.e., the total number of bits in all the nonzero blocks in $T(i, j)$, and let $N(i, j)$ be the number of 1 bits in the part of the original vector v_0, which belongs to $T(i, j)$.

During the bottom-up construction of the tree these quantities are recursively evaluated for $0 \leq j \leq t$ and $1 \leq i \leq k_j$ by

$$N(i, j) = \begin{cases} \text{number of 1 bits in block } i \text{ of } v_0 & \text{if } j = 0, \\ \sum_{h=1}^{r_j} N((i-1)r_j + h, j-1) & \text{if } j > 0; \end{cases}$$

$$S(i, j) = \begin{cases} 0 & \text{if } j = 0 \text{ and } T(i, 0) \text{ contains only zeros,} \\ r_0 & \text{if } j = 0 \text{ and } T(i, 0) \text{ contains a 1 bit,} \\ r_j + \sum_{h=1}^{r_j} S((i-1)r_j + h, j-1) & \text{if } j > 0. \end{cases}$$

At each step, we check the condition

$$d \cdot N(i, j) \leq S(i, j). \tag{6}$$

If it holds, we prune the tree at the root of $T(i, j)$, adding the indices of the $N(i, j)$ 1 bits to the list L, and setting then $N(i, j)$ and $S(i, j)$ to 0. Hence the algorithm partitions the set of 1 bits into two disjoint subsets: those compressed by the TREE-method and those kept as a list. In particular, if the pruning action takes place at the only block of the top level, there will be no tree at all.

Note that by definition of $S(i, j)$, the line corresponding to the case $j > 0$ should in fact be slightly different: r_j should be added to the sum $X = \sum_{h=1}^{r_j} S((i-1)r_j + h, j-1)$ only if $X \neq 0$. However, no error will result from letting the definition in its present form. Indeed, if $X = 0$, then also $N(i, j) = 0$ so that the inequality in (6) is satisfied in this case, thus $S(i, j)$ will anyway be set to 0. Note also that in case of equality in (6), we execute a pruning action although a priori there is no gain. However, since the number of 1 bits in v_j is thereby reduced, this may enable further prunings in higher levels, which otherwise might not have been done.

We now further compress the list L (of indices of 1 bits which were "pruned" from the tree) using POM, which can be adapted to the compression of a list of d-bit numbers: we choose an integer $c < d - 1$ as parameter, and form a bitmap v of $k = \lceil l_0/2^c \rceil$ bits, where bit i, for $0 \leq i < k$, is set to 1 if and only if the integer i occurs in the $d - c$ leftmost bits of at least one number in L. Thus a 1 bit in position i of v indicates that there are one or more numbers in L in the range $[i2^c, (i+1)2^c - 1]$. For each 1 bit in v, the numbers of the corresponding range can now be stored as relative indices in that range, using only c bits for each, and an additional bit per index serving as flag, which identifies the last index of each range. Further compression of the list L is thus worthwhile only if

$$d \cdot |L| > k + (c+1)|L|. \tag{7}$$

The left-hand side of (7) corresponds to the number of bits needed to keep the list L uncompressed. Therefore this secondary compression is justified only when the number of elements in L exceeds $k/(d - c - 1)$.

For example, for $l_0 = 128$ and $c = 5$, there are 4 blocks of 2^5 bits each; suppose the numbers in L are 36, 50, 62, 105, and 116 (at least five elements are necessary to justify further compression). Then there are three elements in the second block, with relative indices 4, 18, and 30, and there are two elements in the fourth block, with relative indices 9 and 20, the two other blocks being empty. This is shown in Fig. 21.

```
                    ┌─────────┐
                v   │ 0 1 0 1 │
                    └─────────┘
```

┌────────┐ ┌────────┐ ┌────────┐   ┌────────┐ ┌────────┐
│0-00100 │ │0-10010 │ │1-11110 │   │0-01001 │ │1-10100 │
└────────┘ └────────┘ └────────┘   └────────┘ └────────┘

indicates the end of the sequence

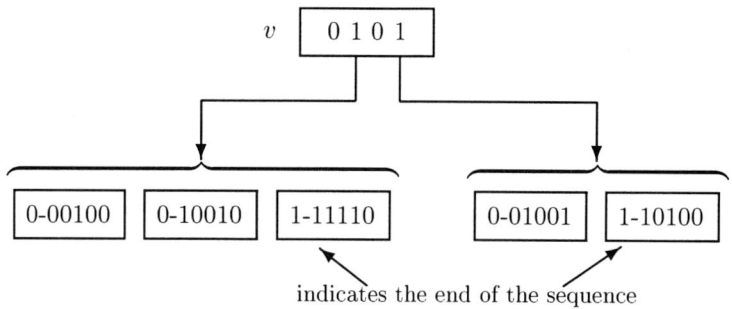

FIGURE 21 Further compression of index list.

Finally we get even better compression by adapting the cutoff condition (6) dynamically to the number of elements in L. During the construction of the tree, we keep track of this number and as soon as it exceeds $k/(d-c-1)$, i.e., it is worthwhile to further compress the list, we can relax the condition in (6) to

$$(c+1) \cdot N(i,j) \leq S(i,j), \tag{8}$$

since any index that will be added to L will use only $c+1$ bits for its encoding.

In fact, after recognizing that L will be compressed, we should check again the blocks already handled, since a subtree $T(i,j)$ may satisfy (8) without satisfying (6). Nevertheless, we have preferred to keep the simplicity of the algorithm and not to check again previously handled blocks, even at the price of losing some of the compression efficiency. Often, there will be no such loss, since if we are at the top level when $|L|$ becomes large enough to satisfy (7), this means that the vector v_0 will be kept in its entirety as a list. If we are not at the top level, say at the root of $T(i,j)$ for $j < t$, then all the previously handled trees will be reconsidered as part of larger trees, which are rooted on the next higher level. Hence it is possible that the subtree $T(i,j)$, which satisfies (8) but not (6) (and thus was not pruned at level j), will be removed as part of a larger subtree rooted at level $j+1$.

2. Combining Huffman and Run-Length Coding

As we are interested in sparse bit strings, we can assume that the probability p of a block of k consecutive bits being zero is high. If $p \geq 0.5$, method NORUN assigns to this 0 block a codeword of length one bit, so we can never expect a better compression factor than k. On the other hand, k cannot be too large since we must generate codewords for 2^k different blocks.

In order to get a better compression, we extend the idea of method NORUN in the following way: there will be codewords for the $2^k - 1$ nonzero blocks of length k, plus some additional codewords representing runs of zero-blocks of different lengths. In the sequel, we use the term "run" to designate a run of zero-blocks of k bits each.

The length (number of k-bit blocks) of a run can take any value up to l_0/k, so it is impractical to generate a codeword for each: as was just pointed out, k

cannot be very large, but l_0 is large for applications of practical importance. On the other hand, using a fixed-length code for the run length would be wasteful since this code must suffice for the maximal length, while most of the runs are short. The following methods attempt to overcome these difficulties.

Starting with a fixed-length code for the run lengths, we like to get rid of the leading zeros in the binary representation $B(\ell)$ of run length ℓ, but we clearly cannot simply omit them, since this would lead to ambiguities. We *can* omit the leading zeros if we have additional information such as the position of the leftmost 1 in $B(\ell)$. Hence, partition the possible lengths into classes C_i, containing run lengths ℓ that satisfy $2^{i-1} \leq \ell < 2^i, i = 1, \ldots, \lfloor log_2(l_0/k) \rfloor$. The $2^k - 1$ nonzero block-patterns and the classes C_i are assigned Huffman codewords corresponding to the frequency of their occurrence in the file; a run of length ℓ belonging to class C_i is encoded by the codeword for C_i, followed by $i - 1$ bits representing the number $\ell - 2^{i-1}$. For example, a run of 77 0-blocks is assigned the codeword for C_7 followed by the 6 bits 001101. Note that a run consisting of a single 0-block is encoded by the codeword for C_1, without being followed by any supplementary bits.

The Huffman decoding procedure must be modified in the following way: The table contains for every codeword the corresponding class C_i as well as $i - 1$. Then, when the codeword that corresponds to class C_i is identified, the next $i - 1$ bits are considered as the binary representation of an integer m. The codeword for C_i followed by those $i - 1$ bits represent together a run of length $m + 2^{i-1}$; the decoding according to Huffman's procedure resumes at the ith bit following the codeword for C_i. Summarizing, we in fact encode the length of the binary representation of the length of a run, and the method is henceforth called LLRUN.

Method LLRUN seems to be efficient since the number of bits in the binary representation of integers is reduced to a minimum, and the lengths of the codewords are optimized by Huffman's algorithm. However, encoding and decoding are admittedly complicated and thus time consuming. We therefore propose other methods for which the encoded file will consist only of codewords, each representing a certain string of bits. Even if their compression factor is lower than LLRUN's, these methods are justified by their simpler processing.

To the $2^k - 1$ codewords for nonzero blocks, a set S of t codewords is adjoined representing $h_0, h_1, \ldots, h_{t-1}$ consecutive 0 blocks. Any run of zero-blocks will now be encoded by a suitable linear combination of some of these codes. The number t depends on the numeration system according to which we choose the h_i's and on the maximal run length M, but should be low compared to 2^k. Thus in comparison with method NORUN, the table used for compressing and decoding should only slightly increase in size, but long runs are handled more efficiently. The encoding algorithm now becomes:

Step 1. Collect statistics on the distribution of run lengths and on the set NZ of the $2^k - 1$ possible nonzero blocks. The total number of occurrences of these blocks is denoted by N_0 and is fixed for a given set of bitmaps.

Step 2. Decompose the integers representing the run lengths in the numeration system with set S of "basis" elements; denote by TNO(S) the total number of occurrences of the elements of S.

Step 3. Evaluate the relative frequency of the appearance of the $2^k - 1 + t$ elements of NZ $\cup$ S and assign a Huffman code accordingly.

For any $x \in$ (NZ $\cup$ S), let $p(x)$ be the probability of the occurrence of x and $\ell(x)$ the length (in bits) of the codeword assigned to x by the Huffman algorithm. The weighted average length of a codeword is then given by AL(S) = $\sum_{x \in (NZ \cup S)} p(x)\ell(x)$ and the size of the compressed file is

$$AL(S) \times (N_0 + TNO(S)).$$

After fixing k so as to allow easy processing of k-bit blocks, the only parameter in the algorithm is the set S. In what follows, we propose several possible choices for the set $S = \{1 = h_0 < h_1 < \ldots < h_{t-1}\}$. To overcome coding problems, the h_i and the bounds on the associated digits a_i should be so that there is a unique representation of the form $L = \sum_i a_i h_i$ for every natural number L.

Given such a set S, the representation of an integer L is obtained by the simple procedure

$$\begin{aligned}&\text{for } i \leftarrow t - 1 \text{ to } 0 \text{ by } -1 \\ &\quad a_i \leftarrow \lfloor L/h_i \rfloor \\ &\quad L \leftarrow L - a_i \times h_i \\ &\text{end}\end{aligned}$$

The digit a_i is the number of times the codeword for h_i is repeated. This algorithm produces a representation $L = \sum_{i=0}^{t-1} a_i h_i$, which satisfies

$$\sum_{i=0}^{j} a_i h_i < h_{j+1} \qquad \text{for } j = 0, \ldots, t-1. \tag{9}$$

Condition (9) guarantees uniqueness of representation (see [51]).

A natural choice for S is the standard binary system (method POW2), $h_i = 2^i, i \geq 0$, or higher base numeration systems such as $h_i = m^i, i \geq 0$ for some $m > 2$. If the run length is L, it will be expressed as $L = \sum_i a_i m^i$, with $0 \leq a_i < m$ and if $a_i > 0$, the codeword for m^i will be repeated a_i times. Higher base systems can be motivated by the following reason.

If p is the probability that a k-bit block consists only of zeros, then the probability of a run of r blocks is roughly $p^r(1-p)$; i.e., the run lengths have approximately geometric distribution. The distribution is not exactly geometric since the involved events (some adjacent blocks contain only zeros; i.e., a certain word does not appear in some consecutive documents) are not independent. Nevertheless the experiments showed that the number of runs of a given length is an exponentially decreasing function of run length. Hence with increasing base of the numeration systems, the relative weight of the h_i for small i will rise, which yields a less uniform distribution for the elements of NZ $\cup$ S calculated in Step 3. This has a tendency to improve the compression obtained by the Huffman codes. Therefore passing to higher-order numeration systems will reduce the value of AL(S).

On the other hand, when numeration systems to base m are used, TNO(S) is an increasing function of m. Define r by $m^r \leq M < m^{r+1}$ so that at most r m-ary digits are required to express a run length. If the lengths are uniformly distributed, the average number of basis elements needed (counting multiplicities) is proportional to $(m-1)r = (m-1)\log_m M$, which is increasing for $m > 1$, and this was also the case for our nearly geometric distribution. Thus from this point of view, lower base numeration systems are preferable.

As an attempt to reduce TNO(S), we pass to numeration systems with special properties, such as systems based on Fibonacci numbers

$$F_0 = 0, \quad F_1 = 1, \quad F_i = F_{i-1} + F_{i-2} \quad \text{for } i \geq 2.$$

(a) The binary Fibonacci numeration system (method FIB2): $h_i = F_{i+2}$. Any integer L can be expressed as $L = \sum_{i \geq 0} b_i F_{i+2}$ with $b_i = 0$ or 1, such that this binary representation of L consisting of the string of b_i's contains no adjacent 1's. This fact for a binary Fibonacci system is equivalent to condition (9), and reduces the number of codewords we need to represent a specific run length, even though the number of added codewords is larger than for POW2 (instead of $t(\text{POW2}) = \lfloor \log_2 M \rfloor$ we have $t(\text{FIB2}) = \lfloor \log_\phi(\sqrt{5}M) \rfloor - 1$, where $\phi = (1 + \sqrt{5})/2$ is the golden ratio). For example, when all the run lengths are equally probable, the average number of codewords per run is asymptotically (as $k \to \infty$) $\frac{1}{2}(1 - 1/\sqrt{5})t(\text{FIB2})$ instead of $\frac{1}{2}t(\text{POW2})$.

(b) A ternary Fibonacci numeration system: $h_i = F_{2(i+1)}$, i.e., we use only Fibonacci numbers with even indices. This system has the property that there is at least one 0 between any two 2's. This fact for a ternary Fibonacci system is again equivalent to (9).

VI. FINAL REMARKS

Modern information retrieval systems are generally based on inverted files and require large amounts of storage space and powerful machines for the processing of sophisticated queries. Data compression techniques that are specifically adapted to the various files in an IR environment can improve the performance, both by reducing the space needed to store the numerous auxiliary files and by reducing the necessary data transfer and thereby achieving a speedup.

We have presented a selected choice of techniques pertaining to the different files involved in a full-text IR system; some are given with considerable detail, others are only roughly described. We hope that, nevertheless, the reader will get a useful overall picture, which can be completed by means of the appended literature.

Our main focus has been on IR systems using inverted files. With the development of ever more powerful computers, it may well be that brute force methods, like searching large files using some pattern matching techniques (see, e.g., [52]) or probabilistic approaches using signature files (see, e.g., [53]), will again be considered a feasible alternative, even for very large files.

REFERENCES

1. Pennebaker, W. B., and Mitchell, J. L. *JPEG: Still Image Data Compression Standard*. Van Nostrand Reinhold, New York, 1993.
2. Bratley, P., and Choueka, Y. *Inform. Process. Manage.* 18:257–266, 1982.

3. Attar, R., Choueka, Y., Dershowitz, N., and Fraenkel, A. S. *J. Assoc. Comput. Mach.* **25**: 52–66, 1978.
4. Bookstein, A., and Klein, S. T. *Inform. Process. Manage.* **26**:525–533, 1990.
5. Davis, D. R., and Lin, A. D. *Commun. ACM* **8**:243–246, 1965.
6. Choueka, Y., Fraenkel, A. S., Klein, S. T., and Segal, E. In *Proc. 10th ACM-SIGIR Conf.*, New Orleans, pp. 306–315, 1987.
7. Bookstein, A., Klein, S. T., and Ziff, D. A. *Inform. Process. Manage.* **28**:795–806, 1992.
8. Fraenkel, A. S. *Jurimetrics J.* **16**:149–156, 1976.
9. Even, S. *IEEE Trans. Inform. Theory* **9**:109–112, 1963.
10. McMillan, B. *IRE Trans. Inform. Theory* **2**:115–116, 1956.
11. Even, S. *Graph Algorithms.* Comput. Sci. Press, New York, 1979.
12. Shannon, C. E. *Bell System Tech. J.* **27**:379–423, 623–656, 1948.
13. Huffman, D. *Proc. of the IRE* **40**:1098–1101, 1952.
14. Van Leeuwen, J. In *Proc. 3rd ICALP Conference*, pp. 382–410. Edinburgh Univ. Press, Edinburgh, 1976.
15. Fraenkel, A. S., and Klein, S. T. *Combinatorial Algorithms on Words*, NATO ASI Series Vol. F12, pp. 169–183. Springer-Verlag, Berlin, 1985.
16. Knuth, D. E. *The Art of Computer Programming*, Vol. III, *Sorting and Searching*, Addison-Wesley, Reading, MA, 1973.
17. Knuth, D. E. *The Art of Computer Programming*, Vol. I, *Fundamental Algorithms*, Addison-Wesley, Reading, MA, 1973.
18. Larmore, L. L., and Hirschberg, D. S. *J. Assoc. Comput. Mach.* **37**:464–473, 1990.
19. Fraenkel, A. S., and Klein, S. T. *Computer J.* **36**:668–678, 1993.
20. Reghbati, H. K. *Computer* **14**(4):71–76, 1981.
21. Bookstein, A., and Klein, S. T. *ACM Trans. Inform. Systems* **8**:27–49, 1990.
22. Moffat, A., Turpin, A., and Katajainen, J. *Proc. Data Compression Conference DCC-95*, Snowbird, UT, pp. 192–201, 1995.
23. Schwartz, E. S., and Kallick, B. *Commun. ACM* **7**:166–169, 1964.
24. Hirschberg, D. S., and Lelewer, D. A. *Commun. ACM* **33**:449–459, 1990.
25. Witten, I. H., Moffat, A., and Bell, T. C. *Managing Gigabytes: Compressing and Indexing Documents and Images.* Van Nostrand Reinhold, New York, 1994.
26. Moffat, A., Turpin, A. In *Proc. Data Compression Conference DCC-96*, Snowbird, UT, pp. 182–191, 1996.
27. Gilbert, E. N., and Moore, E. F. *Bell System Tech. J.* **38**:933–968, 1959.
28. Bookstein, A., and Klein, S. T. *Computing* **50**:279–296, 1993.
29. Zipf, G. K. *The Psycho-Biology of Language.* Houghton, Boston, 1935.
30. Katona, G. H. O., and Nemetz, T. O. H. *IEEE Trans. Inform. Theory* **11**:284–292, 1965.
31. Moffat, A., Zobel, J., and Sharman, N. *IEEE Trans. Knowledge Data Engrg.* **9**:302–313, 1997.
32. Rissanen, J. *IBM J. Res. Dev.* **20**:198–203, 1976.
33. Rissanen, J., and Langdon, G. G. *IBM J. Res. Dev.* **23**:149–162, 1979.
34. Witten, I. H., Neal, R. M., and Cleary, J. G. *Commun. ACM* **30**:520–540, 1987.
35. Fraenkel, A. S., Mor, M., Perl, Y. *Acta Inform.* **20**:371–389, 1983.
36. Fraenkel, A. S., Mor, M., and Perl, Y. In *Proc. 19th Allerton Conf. on Communication, Control and Computing*, pp. 762–768, 1981.
37. Ziv, J., and Lempel, A. *IEEE Trans. Inform. Theory* **23**:337–343, 1977.
38. Ziv, J., and Lempel, A. *IEEE Trans. Inform. Theory* **24**:530–536, 1978.
39. Whiting, D. L., George, G. A., and Ivey, G. E. U. S. Patent 5,126,739 (1992).
40. Fraenkel, A. S., and Mor, M. *Computer J.* **26**:336–343, 1983.
41. Hamming, R. W. *Coding and Information Theory.* Prentice-Hall, Englewood Cliffs, NJ, 1980.
42. Witten, I. H., Bell, T. C., and Nevill, C. G. In *Proc. Data Compression Conference*, Snowbird, UT, pp. 23–32, 1991.
43. Bookstein, A., Klein, S. T., and Raita, T. *ACM Trans. Inform. Systems* **15**:254–290, 1997.
44. Choueka, Y., Fraenkel, A. S., Klein, S. T., and Segal, E. In *Proc. 9th ACM-SIGIR Conf.*, Pisa, pp. 88–96. ACM, Baltimore, MD, 1986.
45. Schuegraf, E. J. *Inform. Process. Manage.* **12**:377–384, 1976.
46. Teuhola, J. *Inform. Process. Lett.* **7**:308–311, 1978.
47. Jakobsson, M. *Inform. Process. Lett.* **7**:304–307, 1978.

48. Wedekind, H., and Härder, T. *Datenbanksysteme II*. Wissenschaftsverlag, Mannheim, 1976.
49. Vallarino, O. Special Issue, *SIGPLAN Notices,* **2**:108–114, 1976.
50. Jakobsson, M. *Inform. Process. Lett.* **14**:147–149, 1982.
51. Fraenkel, A. S. *Amer. Math. Monthly* **92**:105–114, 1985.
52. Boyer, R. S., and Moore, J. S. *Commun. ACM* **20**:762–772, 1977.
53. Faloutsos, C., and Christodulakis, S. *ACM Trans. Office Inform. Systems* **2**:267–288, 1984.